SPIRIT TECH

SPIRIT TECH

The Brave New World of Consciousness Hacking and Enlightenment Engineering

Wesley J. Wildman, PhD
& Kate J. Stockly, PhD

ST. MARTIN'S PRESS
NEW YORK

First published in the United States by
St. Martin's Press, an imprint of St. Martin's Publishing Group

www.stmartins.com

Designed by Michelle McMillian

Library of Congress Cataloging-in-Publication Data

Names: Wildman, Wesley J., 1961– author. | Stockly, Kate J., author.
Title: Spirit tech : the brave new world of consciousness hacking and
enlightenment engineering / Wesley J. Wildman & Kate J. Stockly.
Description: First edition. | New York : St. Martin's Press, 2021. |
Includes bibliographical references and index.
Identifiers: LCCN 2020053529 | ISBN 9781250274939 (hardcover) |
ISBN 9781250274946 (ebook)
Subjects: LCSH: Technology—Religious aspects. | Hallucinogenic
drugs and religious experience. | Spirituality.
Classification: LCC BL265.T4 W55 2021 | DDC 204—dc23
LC record available at https://lccn.loc.gov/2020053529

Our books may be purchased in bulk for promotional,
educational, or business use. Please contact your local bookseller or
the Macmillan Corporate and Premium Sales Department at
1-800-221-7945, extension 5442, or by email at
MacmillanSpecialMarkets@macmillan.com.

First Edition: 2021

10 9 8 7 6 5 4 3 2 1

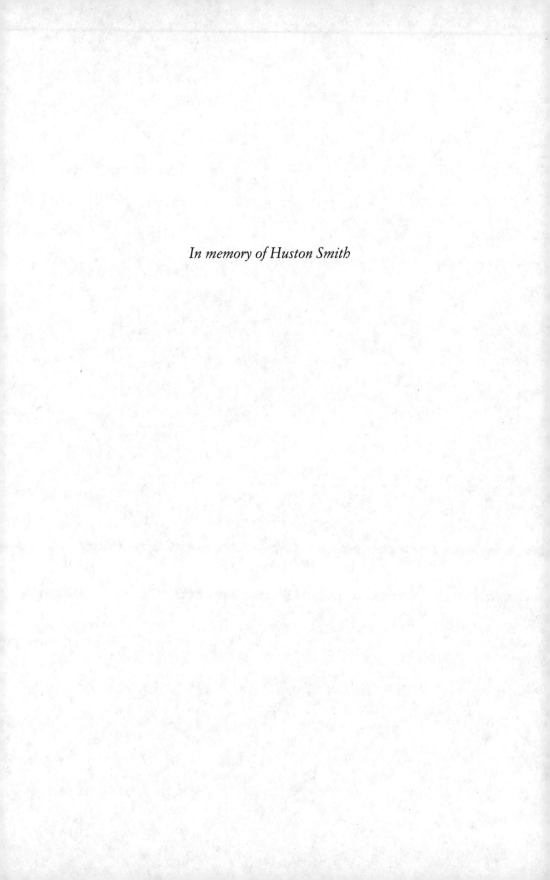

In memory of Huston Smith

Contents

Foreword by Mikey Siegel   ix

Preface   xiii

1. The Scattered Supermarket of Special Spiritual Services   1

2. Stimulating the Brain   13

3. Neurofeedback-Guided Meditation   44

4. Engineering Togetherness   76

5. Virtual Sacred Reality   101

6. Cleansing the Doors of Perception   133

7. Spirit Plants and Their High-Tech Replacements   165

8. A New Horizon in Spiritual Direction   193

9. Is Spirit Tech Authentic?   216

10. Is Spirit Tech Healthy?   234

11. Spirit Tech and the Future of Spirituality   251

Afterword: What's Going to Happen Next?   259

Acknowledgments   263

Appendix 1. How Did We Get Here?   265

Appendix 2. How Do We Know What We Know?   275

Appendix 3. Suggestions for Further Reading   311

Notes   *321*

Illustration Credits   *361*

Index   *363*

Foreword

Technology and spirituality are two of the strongest forces shaping the landscape of human culture and consciousness; yet we rarely speak of them in the same breath. Over the coming decade, that may radically change as we witness a revolution in the way we practice and access spirituality. Already, millions of people use meditation apps, department stores sell brain-training wearables that help us quiet our minds, virtual reality can take us on a psychedelic—or *technodelic*—journey, and advanced brain stimulation is on the cusp of facilitating states which usually require thousands of hours of meditation.

This brave new world of Spirit Tech naturally brings up a host of questions, concerns, and profound possibilities. Are these new advances shortcuts? Are they missing some vital part of the spiritual or religious journey we'd typically traverse with traditional methods? Is there something fundamentally different between a traditional method, such as meditating on a cushion, and using an app or wearable? Are the spiritual experiences attained through something like brain stimulation authentic? What are the implications of a profound mystical experience being as easily accessible as our cell phones?

These are just a small sampling of the questions and issues at this emerging intersection—with implications that reach into the very depths of what it means to be human and the future of humanity. Yet, remarkably, *Spirit Tech* is the first significant text devoted to discussing them, and I can't overemphasize its importance. Wesley and Kate have dedicated their academic careers to exploring spirituality and religion as it intersects with modern culture. In *Spirit Tech*, they have beautifully written about this cross-disciplinary topic, touching neuroscience, engineering, consciousness, religion, and ethics, in a style that is both rigorous and accessible to the nonacademic.

This text will help us to navigate these new, wild, and hopefully wonderful tools in a way that maximizes the benefit to ourselves and humanity. This is important as the increasing power of technology combined with the fundamental nature of spirituality opens the door for both existential dangers and profound possibilities. It was these possibilities that captured my imagination ten years ago when I began my own journey to bridge these seemingly separate worlds. Inspired by the first line of the United Nations' UNESCO Constitution, "That since wars begin in the minds of men, it is in the minds of men that the defenses of peace must be constructed," I applied my engineering skills to change the world from the inside out by creating modern tools to heal and awaken the minds and hearts of humanity.

When I began that journey, it was quite lonely. In academia, meditation had already become a popular research topic, but the idea of applying that scientific understanding toward the development of meditation technologies was mostly unheard of. The companies focused in this area were often fringe and plagued by pseudoscientific or new-age beliefs. Not content with the existing landscape, I started a global community and nonprofit called Consciousness Hacking. Later I developed and taught three courses at Stanford University, cofounded conferences such as the Transformative Technology Conference* and Awakened

---

* Cofounded and now completely run by Jeffery A. Martin and Nichol Bradford,

Futures Summit, and developed a tech platform for human connection (which you can read about in chapter 4, Engineering Togetherness).

I'd like to share a few of my observations and learnings accumulated over the years, which I hope will add useful perspective as you read this book.

People often feel that technology is somehow fundamentally different from, or at odds with, spirituality. This is a well-founded concern, and I'll be the first to acknowledge that our *modern* tech landscape feels anything but spiritual. However, for millennia the spiritual landscape has produced its own technologies. Though not silicon-based, the history of spiritual practice and religion is defined by invention and innovation. Meditation techniques, temples, prayer, ritual—these are all tools and methods designed to more reliably access our spiritual nature. If we take the definition of technology to be "the skills, methods, and processes used to achieve goals," then are these not technologies? We might even say that the creation of spiritual technologies is one of the defining qualities of modern humans.

Yet, many of us are still uncomfortable with the idea of modern technology playing a part in our spiritual lives. We feel that something is dissonant about our devices—we enjoy their usefulness, but at a cost. What is that dissonance?

After traveling the world and speaking with thousands of people about their experience, while simultaneously diving deeply into my own journey toward creating tools for connection, I've boiled it down to a simple observation: Modern technology is out of harmony with life's natural rhythms because we, as modern humans, are out of harmony. We are disconnected from our planet, stripping it for its resources so we can create and consume more. We are disconnected from each other, practically enslaving ourselves both as workers building the gadgets we love, and as consumers saving up for the latest upgrade. Most significantly, we are disconnected from ourselves, hungry for distraction

who are also featured in this book.

from the anxiety and emptiness buried within. In essence, we are disconnected from our spiritual nature, and our resistance to modern tech as a spiritual tool is because in it we sense the spiritual disconnect embedded in its design.

But technology can be anything, limited only by imagination and the laws of physics; it is the amplification of its driving intention. If we overlook the possibility that technology can be skillful, can actually meet us where we're at, can be kind, gentle, and loving, then we are missing out on one of the most important capacities that humanity has. Namely, our ability to innovate on the means of spiritual growth. What happens if we stifle our *human* development while our technological power grows at an exponential rate? What happens when you give the power of the universe to a child who is selfish, heartless, and afraid?

We could also ask the opposite question: What happens when you give the power of the universe to a mind that is clear, a heart that is open, and a soul that is wise? In the words of Alan Watts, "Technology is destructive only in the hands of people who do not realize that they are one and the same process as the universe."

The incredible power of technology has been irrevocably unleashed. The question now is, What do we do with it? If its valence is indeed an extension of the intention wielding it, then there is an incredible opportunity. My hope is that we build our future from a place of wisdom, love, and the desire to uplift humanity, and thus create the spiritual technologies that will push humanity toward its greatest potential. I'm grateful to this book and its authors for opening our minds, posing the questions, and inspiring the sense of possibility that will guide us in that direction.

—Mikey Siegel, January 2021

Preface

This book is about the intensifying interaction between technology and spirituality—specifically, brain-based technologies designed to trigger, enhance, accelerate, modify, or measure spiritual experience. Some people find this territory wonderfully exciting, while for others it is alarming. It's certainly a brave new world out there, and having accurate information can help navigate it successfully. That's our overall aim in this book: we'll explain how the various technologies work; share information from the experts, innovators, and pioneers of each technology; and relate our conversations with the people who are already using these technologies. Along the way we'll address the big philosophical, psychological, and ethical questions that spirit tech elicits—questions of authenticity, meaning, safety, and social responsibility.

But first, we want to tell you about how we each became interested in studying spiritual experiences. It seems only fair that our readers have an opportunity to assess our motivation. After all, motivations make a difference in intellectual work, as in every other sphere of human life.

WESLEY

In August 1987, my partner, Suzanne, and I left Australia, flew from Sydney to San Francisco, and took up residence in Berkeley. I was pursuing a PhD in philosophy of religion at the Graduate Theological Union, located on Holy Hill, along the north side of the University of California, Berkeley. We started out living in a beautiful apartment at Pacific School of Religion, nestled among the branches of ancient trees. It was like living in a tree house, with squirrels staring at me through the windows while I tried to work. When I wasn't being eyeballed by squirrels, I was taking courses with John Searle and Hubert Dreyfus in UC Berkeley's philosophy department and studying modern Western religious thought with my adviser, Claude Welch, who had just retired as president and dean of the Graduate Theological Union.

It was an amazing place and time: the weather was perfect, the intellectual environment was endlessly fascinating, and our living situation was fabulous. Even the earthquakes and fires were awe-inspiring. What better way for newly landed immigrants to figure out America?

Though it took me a while to realize that Berkeley is a slightly misleading introduction to the United States, the town surely was a blast. It boasted affordable restaurants of every kind, people from every place, bookstores galore, and every variety of cultural activity. The view of San Francisco Bay from Holy Hill was breathtaking, a daily reminder of our great good fortune to be living there.

Early in my second year at Berkeley, my friend and fellow student Kate McCarthy (now a professor and dean of undergraduate education at Chico State University in northern California) recruited me to work as a teaching assistant in a world religions class for undergraduates on the UC Berkeley campus. I had three years of coursework in religious studies from an earlier degree in Australia, so I felt ready. And here's the kicker: the course was to be taught by none other than the world-famous Huston Smith. Guru to countless people and bestselling author of *The World's Religions*, Huston was the mainstay of the

Figure 1. Huston Smith communicating energetically, as usual.

UC Berkeley religious studies teaching program, which he taught as an adjunct professor because the university had no religious studies department. I was eager to take on the challenge, so Kate soon introduced me to the grand old man.

Thus began a beautiful, and beautifully complex, relationship. I functioned as a teaching assistant three times for Huston, twice in the World Religions introduction and once in a class on mysticism and the so-called perennial philosophy, which was essentially about his spiritual worldview. Regardless of the class, Huston would be swept away as he described the wondrous worldview of the perennial philosophy, the great chain of being with its layers of meaning and intensity, stretching from inanimate matter, through plants and animals, through human beings with their souls, upward to realms of supernatural beings including angels and demons and ghosts and jinns, and still further to God, and finally to the God Beyond God, about which we can know and say nothing. I would behold Huston with rapt attention. He was a true believer.

In parallel with those teaching adventures, and for some time after they ended, Huston met weekly through the academic year with Kate McCarthy and me, along with one other mutual friend, to discuss anything and everything. I was in and out of his (and wife Kendra's) home, constantly talking, intensely debating, grappling with big ideas, and beholding Huston's extraordinary mind. We'd debate what is really real, with Huston eloquently articulating the perennial philosophy's picture that things higher up on the great chain of being are more real than things lower down, and me arguing that more complexity and importance doesn't necessarily mean more intensity of being. We'd discuss the fate of the contemporary university, with Huston arguing that it was selling out to science and me saying that the humanities were losing influence because they weren't making a good case for their value in the minds of scientists and ordinary citizens. We'd discuss the legalization of mescaline-rich peyote cactus–button brew for the Native American Church, which was an issue at the time. We'd roam over the world's religions, picking up resonances and dissonances, trying to come to grips with the near universal cultural phenomenon of religion, with its spiritual quests and supernatural worldviews. My goodness, what an education he gave me.

The exciting weekly conversations within our little group went on for three years. I think Huston kept it up because he was fascinated with our intransigence: we just wouldn't be persuaded by his (or any other) version of the so-called perennial philosophy, which suggests that the central beliefs of all religions are literally true (Jesus really did rise from the dead! Gautama really did attain enlightenment under a bodhi tree! Reincarnation is real!) and their mutual contradictions reconciled within the great chain of being. According to Huston, every religion, every religious belief, and every religious practice takes shape within this multilayered worldview, and mystical experience allows us to see it for ourselves.

He wanted us to see the beautiful world he saw. We thought we could see his world just fine, but it struck us as too neat to be anything but an abstract fantasy version of the real thing. There might be a presence in most religious traditions of mystical philosophers who affirm some version of the perennial philosophy's great chain of being, but that's an elite viewpoint. The religious worldviews of most regular religious people don't look like that, and they are wildly diverse. Moreover, from cognitive psychology we learn about built-in human tendencies to believe in supernatural beings, stabilized in the long evolutionary process. The discovery of that cognitive bias toward supernatural worldviews in our species predicts that people will believe in invisible beings who act in the world even though they appear to be unnecessary for explaining everyday life and the workings of nature. Huston's perennial philosophy seemed totally nonresponsive to that profound challenge to supernatural religion arising from the scientific study of evolved human minds.

While we thought Huston was insensitive to these sorts of problems with the perennial philosophy, he thought we were casually casting aside the one true metaphysical viewpoint that could save the world from the insane future toward which it was careening. Yet he was the one with all the life history, including deep immersion experiences in many of the world's religions, so we listened to him with great seriousness and pondered every word. In fact, I doubt that he ever had a more attentive audience. Despite our conflict over his perennial philosophy, we found Huston irresistible. We loved getting to know him, loved fighting with him, loved teaching with him, and loved learning from him—we loved him.

I would often meet with Huston for a few minutes before class in his office. There we would talk about teaching matters while he charged up with the energy he needed to teach. Though quite healthy, he was already elderly at the time and was suffering from serious hearing loss, so every class was a challenge for him. Based on experience, he believed he could increase his energy to the required level by slowly consuming a very particular bar of chocolate, which he did while we chatted. Then we would meander to the lecture hall. That chocolate became a running joke between us, and I would hand him a bar of it most times I saw him in the years that followed after I left Berkeley for Boston.

The UC Berkeley campus we walked through on our way to class was packed with concrete and asphalt, so the cluster of struggling trees above a patch of grizzly grass just outside our lecture hall stood out. It stood out to Huston anyway; most people streamed by without even noticing it. We would always walk underneath the trees and, momentarily pausing, he would take a deep breath. Sometimes he would declare, "Ah, my little Daoist dell." Then he would enter the vast lecture hall, packed with eager learners, and *teach*, helping his students grasp the inner logic and profound insights of each of the world's great religious traditions.

As a lecturer, Huston was clear, succinct, well organized, and moving. A couple of times he stood on his head, performing the inverted lotus position. One of those times his legs wouldn't hold, and he apologized to the class, wryly blaming the slippery material of his trousers. If a student had a question, Huston would have to walk all the way to where the student was sitting and lean over to hear it. The students quickly realized that there was little point in asking questions unless they were seated along one of the aisles. I watched every little movement, savored every carefully chosen word, and took it all in. I learned a lot—about religion, about teaching, about connecting with students, about mentoring teaching assistants. Mostly I savored each moment with him.

It is in those classrooms and discussions with Huston that I became especially interested in religious and spiritual experiences. This was in large part because he was fascinated by those experiences himself. Unlike me, however, he was a true adventurer. He knew all about how certain substances allowed spiritual realities to show forth within our experience. He not only successfully advocated for the Native Americans who were fighting to keep their peyote rituals alive and legal, but he also traveled to those communities and tried out the cactus-button brew for himself. He introduced me to members of a Christian church that uses LSD for its sacrament instead of bread and wine. He was fascinated with every type of entheogen—materials that could bring about powerful spiritual experiences. He told us about his adventures in Sufism, in Zen training, and in a wide variety of meditation techniques, all of which put mind and body in extraordinary situations designed to create some longed-for insight or change. He was hands-on, all the way.

For Huston, spiritual experiences have a purpose: they disclose the ultimate reality that lies hidden beneath the surface of our conventional reality. He thought that we human beings are built for those experiences and that we need them, for otherwise we would remain ignorant of the most important truths about the human condition and about the wider reality we inhabit. For him, cultivating expertise in various forms of spiritual experience—from enteogenic mystical states to postural meditation, from individual to corporate, from Buddhist to Christian to nothing in particular—allows us to *cleanse the doors of perception* (his favorite phrase from William Blake) and thereby to see beyond conventional reality to the captivating, intoxicating, and spiritually all-important ultimate reality.

For me, spiritual experiences were a puzzle. By comparison with Huston's serene confidence in their revelatory function, I was a resolute skeptic, even in relation to my own comparatively modest collection of spiritual experiences. Nevertheless, I learned from him about their transformative power, and I developed an abiding respect both for them and for the people who sought them. People were authentically engaged with something in many of those experiences. That engagement drew them further into the depths of their own existence while conferring upon them the flexibility and power needed to craft authentic lives. Yet what was seen when the doors of perception were allegedly cleansed did not form anything remotely like a coherent picture of ultimate reality. I became personally convinced that spiritual experiences could be simultaneously existentially authentic, morally efficacious, and potentially *cognitively unreliable*.

This disagreement with Huston played out repeatedly in our conversations as we explored its many angles, presuppositions, and implications. Huston could see what I saw, obviously. He knew that what people say about reality based on their spiritual experiences varies greatly. He knew that people can be irrationally attached to the cognitive content of such experiences, leading to painfully implausible and sometimes dangerous beliefs, often matched by correspondingly disturbing or destructive behaviors. He saw all this but did not infer from it what I did, namely that the surface cognitive content of spiritual experiences is not to be trusted. Rather, he thought that most of the beliefs inspired by spiritual experiences could be reconciled in a grand synthesis of perspectives, with the perennial philosophy's great chain of being as the kaleidoscope lens that lets you see how everything fits together. We both saw the practical problem, and we agreed that it had to be addressed (in part) within religious communities by means of discernment practices, education, and rules capable of inhibiting bad behavior. We both saw the theoretical problem of reconciling conflicting beliefs as well, and he thought he had the answer. So did I, but our answers dramatically diverged.

All artists need mentors to engage, to criticize, so that their styles can form in ways that mean something distinctive in the history of art. It is like that in intellectual life as well. In the domain of spiritual experiences, Huston was the master artist whose style inspired my own. I might not agree with his perennial philosophy reading of human spirituality, but there is no question that it has deeply affected me, just as he has. And I know that he would be absolutely fascinated with brain-based technologies of spiritual enhancement and would love nothing more than to try them all out as heartily and open-mindedly as possible. It is as much his endless fascination with spiritual experiences as his influence on my life that inspired my coauthor, Kate, and me to dedicate this book to him.

KATE

This project represents an exciting erasure of the already blurry line between my academic research interests and my personal interests. Such an experience is not unheard of among scholars of religion, but it is always relished.

When I chose a major in religion as an undergraduate, it was a hobby. I was also majoring in psychology, which I believed was my path to a successful career. But I saw religion as the most interesting thing humans do and the best way to get to the heart of the human experience—the ways that religious beliefs, behaviors, and groups form and are enacted seemed to me to express humanity's deepest and most profound impulses, intuitions, and desires. I studied psychology to learn how human minds worked, but I felt that studying religion actually dug closer to the meat of that question. I was also lucky that at Pacific Lutheran University, where I was an undergraduate, my professors encouraged me to use whatever approaches and methods I felt were necessary to answer the questions I had about religion. I savored the courses that used traditional religious studies methods like textual analysis, philosophy, and history; I especially relished learning to read ancient Greek. But I also loved applying theories and data from other fields like anthropology, psychology, sociology, biology, and cognitive science. This flexibility and openness to interdisciplinary thinking felt liberating. However, studying religion was never just an intellectual curio. It was in many ways an extension and maturation of my religious upbringing. It was a self-examination, an engagement with my own humanity, a meditation on humans' place within the history of biological evolution, and an expression of my fascination with the ways that we relate to the physical universe. Studying religion is now my career, but a certain expression of that engaged self-examination remains my hobby—exploring the ways that I and other humans are spiritual and religious beings.

I find various forms of traditional religion, ancient wisdom, and alternative spiritual routes both deeply intellectually fascinating and personally enchanting. For example, for my thirty-first birthday I gifted myself a training course to become a certified practitioner of Reiki—Reiki is a form of Japanese energy healing brought to the United States in the 1940s. The fact that the class was taught by a no-nonsense, straight-talkin', middle-aged Jewish woman with a PhD in anthropology delighted me and made me feel right at home. Like me, she was skeptical of the hype and the new age spin that some Westerners bring to energy healing, but I loved her respect and reverence for the tradition and the way she created an educational space for our lessons and a sacred space for our initiation (called *attunement*). I found both her and the healing practices to be full of wisdom and love. Another example is my yoga practice. I intersperse yoga throughout long hours of researching and writing, and it helps keep me balanced and present. It has become an integral part of my life. Because I am a former collegiate athlete, this kind of embodied practice makes intuitive sense to me. At times I focus on the physiological aspects of my yoga workout, the positive effects of which have been proven by Western biomedicine. Other times I bracket those thoughts, close my eyes, suspend any disbelief, and attempt to access ancient Buddhist and Hindu wisdom through the asanas.

As we've seen with the scientific study of yoga and Transcendental Meditation (translated into a Western biomedical context and redubbed the relaxation response), I've always felt strongly that, as we learn about the human body and brain, scientific knowledge will slowly catch up to many forms of age-old wisdom. I suspect Reiki might join these ranks one day, too—in fact, I know of hospital nurses who use Reiki on their patients (with the hospitals' and patients' permission). It's at once amusing and exciting when eager science writers declare that science has *discovered* the physiological and psychological benefits of meditation, contemplative practices, or participating in authentic communion with others. How does one "discover" insights that have been known and taught for millennia? Yet that doesn't detract from how thrilling it is to add a new layer and type of evidence—a new way of knowing—to some of the most meaningful aspects of human existence.

Pursuing this conviction—that scientific knowledge is catching up to ancient wisdom—in my research has often meant investigating the biological and neurocognitive aspects of religious rituals—asking what happens in the brain and body during different types of rituals that generate a feeling of righteousness and peacefulness, a commitment to building community, and a desire to repeat the ritual. I've always tended to eschew easy answers and simplified paradigms, because the complexity of these effects involves so many different biopsychosocial systems. Simplifications feel cheap. So there was, perhaps, a time when I would also have eschewed many forms of spirit tech, which appear to reduce the vast complexity of traditional modes of spiritual practice and growth to its least common denominator and then claim to fast-track you to the benefits, skipping over all the richness and dynamics that I so dearly loved to study.

But what I began to see when I started interviewing experts and writing about their goals is that many spirit tech innovators have a deep and abiding appreciation for the spiritual traditions that inspired them. Rather than trying to reduce or simplify ancient traditions, their goal is *translation*: to bring these wise teachings into the contemporary scientific language of our time and to take advantage of our new ways of knowing in order to expand and transform accessibility. They simply wanted to *do* something to increase spiritual wellness with the same types of findings and insights that have motivated my studies. Whether or not I always agree that they are going about this in the right way—and even though occasionally money, fame, or impatience might sometimes take a toll—I've been moved by their sense of mission and am so excited to share their stories.

Each tech has its own community of researchers, innovators, and users, so while submerging myself in each one, I often felt as though I could write a whole book solely on that particular spirit tech application (and then the next one and the next one). But even better than producing eight different books was the task of tying the technologies together and seeing them as a set—a wave, a movement, an emergent collaboration finally between science and religion. Although scholars of Western religion have been aware of the "spiritual but not religious" crowd for quite some time, they have almost entirely overlooked a whole realm of spiritual (and sometimes religious) expression surrounding contemporary spirit tech. The breadth and depth of expertise, monumental effort, and ceaseless creativity of these communities is almost as shocking as the lack of formal writing about their relevance to the future of religion and spirituality. As a scholar interested in how postsecular spirituality is practiced in our contemporary world, this was incredibly exciting for me. After becoming aware of the diverse and vibrant communities emerging around spirit tech, it was clear that the time had come for a book like *Spirit Tech*.

Many of the groups and organizations you'll meet in this book—

such as the Transformative Technology Lab, Consciousness Hacking and their associated Awakened Futures Summit, and the Multidisciplinary Association for Psychedelic Study—have the resources and energy to scale spirit tech to the masses. Moreover, spirit tech innovators tap into the aesthetic of the exponentially expanding contemporary health and wellness movement to emphasize spiritual wellness and maturity as much as they can. This is a powerful combination.

For me, asking the question *What does this mean?* in relation to spirit tech's inevitable rise is both exciting and terrifying. In our world today, technology, social media, and artificial intelligence are often seen as *threats* to psychological and spiritual wellness, as *unnatural* invasions, and as distractions (at best) from what matters most. The sheer power and unstoppable force behind our light-speed escalation of technological innovation will undoubtedly cause great harm. This is a given. But it is also a given that technology will facilitate new paths toward human flourishing. This book explores technology's potential in the spiritual realm: Will spirit tech innovators be successful in their goal of harnessing STEM for goodness, peace, and kindness? I think this book is a conversation starter. I hope this honest and thorough exploration demonstrates how it is possible to talk about the implications of spirit tech while balancing openness with caution and excitement with wisdom. We need such conversations to navigate this brave new world. I hope *Spirit Tech* will provide knowledge, evidence, and counsel sufficient to assuage some fears about spirit tech while also reining in reckless or naive ambitions.

Writing this book has been one of the most rewarding experiences of my life. Taking a deep dive into each mode of spirit tech—learning the science supporting each technology, building a map of the network of experts involved, and analyzing each tech's risks and benefits—was a daunting task. But it was always 100 percent worth it. Meeting each of these spirit tech pioneers, who so graciously shared their perspectives, dreams, and knowledge with me, left deep impressions on me as a scholar and as a person. Hearing, writing, and being trusted to share their stories has been a great honor.

[1]

The Scattered Supermarket of Special Spiritual Services

There is a depth to the potential of these technologies that is rarely addressed. Because this isn't just about reducing stress. This is about a really mind-boggling possibility: What if the deepest aspects of human experience, which are often only accessible through twenty thousand hours meditating in a cave . . . , are all of a sudden accessible at the push of a button?

—Mikey Siegel[1]

hether we welcome it or fear it, the era in which we can use technology to induce, intensify, and even control spiritual experience has arrived. Religious groups and spiritual seekers have always used whatever means were available to attain their spiritual goals, from mantras to icons to relics to rituals; and today we are no different. What *is* different, and radically so, is the use of technological aids that are engineered to facilitate and enhance spiritual experience. Already, we routinely rely on technology to manage our health, sleep, moods, relationships, calendars, travel, and finances, so it's really no surprise that we're turning to high-tech aids for the spiritual journey. As these innovations are rapidly proliferating and becoming ever more sophisticated, we are on the brink of the next and potentially most transformative revolution in the practice of religion: an era in which technological advancement merges with spiritual seeking.

Welcome to the fascinating world of spirit tech, which is swiftly changing the way we practice our faith; the way we connect with religious communities and other spiritual seekers; and even how we experience the Sacred, find True Meaning, reach enlightenment, or whatever we name the ultimate goal of our spiritual quests.

In the fast-tracked pace of the spirit tech era, it's already commonplace to worship remotely through livestreamed services and rituals (even before pandemics forced experimentation upon us), meet with religious leaders or spiritual mentors through Zoom or FaceTime, submit prayer requests online, and meditate or pray with the aid of an app. A quick survey of the App Store reveals thousands of apps that help you pray the rosary, sit zazen, harness the power of crystals, cast a spell, attend a live virtual darshan, monitor your chakras, or read any number of sacred texts, including the Torah, Bible, Quran, Bhagavad Gita, or Guru Granth Sahib—and the options are steadily multiplying. Just as our smartphones and watches remind us to exercise, attend a meeting, or run an errand, they can now remind us to perform the sacred duties of our faith traditions. Naturally, those ubiquitous dings and beeps we've all grown accustomed to can be customized to virtually any sacred sound: an *adhan* (the Muslim call to prayer); the tone of a bell, gong, or Tibetan singing bowl; the thump of a tabla; a snippet of Gregorian (or Vedic or Buddhist) chant.

As amazing as all these developments are, what's happening with smartphones and apps and web interfaces is really just the tip of a much larger and more complex spirit tech iceberg. Because of remarkable advances in technology, neuroscience, and psychology, we are increasingly able to measure spiritual experiences, describe them, and distinguish between them. We can evaluate their social functions, behavioral consequences, and health effects. We are also more and more able to trigger spiritual experiences, stop them, alter them, and even exert control over the way people interpret them. This is what we'll be exploring in this book—the *brain-based technologies of spirituality* that carry the potential to be game changers for the way we practice religion in the twenty-first century and beyond.

Before we get into the specific types of spirit tech on the horizon, let us be clear about what this book is *not*. This is not a book about technology supposedly used to detect or monitor the activity of so-called spirits. If you picked up this book expecting ectoplasm detectors, let us save you some time and disappointment.

What we are discussing is the *technology of spiritual experiences*. Through the course of our research we've come to refer to this eclectic corner of spiritual exploration and practices as the Scattered Supermarket of Special Spiritual Services. Yes, this is a scholarly attempt at humor, but look a bit closer and you'll see that the name gets at something unique about spirit tech. Pop into this very specialized market and you'll find that it's already well stocked with novel technologies people are using with the intention of enhancing spirituality—and the options are continually diversifying. People using one type of technology are often unaware of what's on the shelves a couple of aisles over—that's what makes the supermarket *scattered*. Nonetheless, spirit tech options represent a rapidly growing niche in modern economies, so it most definitely is a *market*. In fact, we predict that spirit tech will follow a trend similar to the massive wellness movement, which means it will soon be quite the economic juggernaut. And as spirit tech becomes more refined, it will move from a scattered supermarket of special spiritual services to a *focused* market with products tested and optimized for regular use and customized according to each person's spiritual preferences and goals.

That's a point worth lingering on: in the spirit tech era, not only are we more aware than ever of the astonishing diversity of religions and spiritual practices around the world, we are freer than ever to explore them and to incorporate what we like into our own faith journeys and practices. There are obvious exceptions, of course, but in cultures that enjoy a pluralistic attitude toward religious diversity, we are free to participate in a religion (or not), and free to mix and match from different faith traditions and practices. It is now no longer uncommon for a person to be a member of a Jewish synagogue as well as a Buddhist sangha, for example. Or for a mainline Christian to seek guidance from Jesus as well as from a psychic or tarot card reader. And this freedom to explore and customize applies doubly to spirit tech. Returning to our supermarket metaphor, we can shop from any aisle and there's nobody telling us we can't.

Psychotherapist and bestselling author Jonathan Robinson captures the sentiment of the spirit tech age: "I like playing mad scientist," he says about his spiritual life. "You try one thing and see what effect it has on you. . . . Now everybody gets to play mad scientist. . . . You have to find what works for you. Because it's not a one-size-fits-all world anymore. You know, we have personalized medicine, and now we need personalized meditation and personalized spiritual technologies that will get us to the next place. So it's a really exciting time for people who are willing to experiment."[2]

For decades now, risk-taking cybernauts and tech-savvy spiritual seekers have been doing just that: experimenting, innovating, disrupting, iterating, optimizing. Some were motivated by a quest to find a fast-track path to spiritual growth: Why spend twenty thousand hours meditating when you can reach deep states of awareness much more efficiently with an electrode-delivered intervention? Others were looking to control spiritual experiences in some way, such as triggering an encounter with the divine or enhancing a mystical experience. Still others sought to facilitate and deepen spiritual connection between spiritual seekers.

We'll explore all of this in *Spirit Tech*. We'll take you on a guided tour of the scattered supermarket of special spiritual services, showcasing the most exciting items on the shelves, and we'll introduce you to the people who are building spirit tech applications and the people who are using them. We hope to do so in such a way that you can empathize with those who employ these special spiritual services. To that end, we present an array of perspectives from people who have embraced one or another form of spirit tech as part of their spiritual practice. We tell their stories with appreciation and curiosity rather than evaluation.

We're sensitive to these concerns because we're well aware that there are those who would dismiss spirit tech outright. Some are well-meaning religious people inherently suspicious of spirit tech. Why do I need a "God gadget," the thinking goes, if I already have direct access to God? Others worry that these newfangled modalities will lead them astray from their spiritual path, or that they're outright evil. Still others may protest that any spiritual experience that's generated by an external source—whether that's a spirit tech modality, a hallucinogenic drug, or a traumatic brain injury or illness—is not an authentic spiritual experience. Another group objects to spirit tech on intellectual or philosophical grounds. We know this group well because we've repeatedly come across it among scholars of religion who, for some unexplained reason and in advance of thorough investigation, feel sure that they can trust their first thought about spirit tech. The problem of bias in this corner of the world of religion and spirituality studies is very real.

The same goes for nonexperts of course, so we'd like to address this concern up front. Personally, we have found that trusting our first instincts when it comes to the brave new world of spirit tech does not work well, and we suspect it doesn't work well for anyone. We need to let the data unfold first, and then invest in analyzing it carefully before coming to definite conclusions.

Here's one example of an insight that studying spirit tech has brought to us. We'll return to this later, but we want to show, right at the outset of this journey, how an understanding of spirit tech might challenge common assumptions about human spirituality.

Many people labor under the mistaken impression that spiritual experiences lie beyond human control and understanding—they have special meaning and importance partly because they hit us from out of the blue spontaneously. These people may be inclined to think this because they believe spiritual experiences have supernatural origins— origins that can't be located within the causal web of nature. This assumption about spontaneity makes sense on the surface: the absence of any discernible causes at the onset of a spiritual experience really might be a marker of supernatural origins.

As it happens, we've come to think that the idea of nonnatural supernatural origins doesn't make sense: any this-worldly effect always arises within a complex web of this-worldly causes. For the sake of argument, however, let's take nonnatural supernatural origins seriously for a moment. The thinking goes like this: spiritual experiences with supernatural origins will be authentic precisely because of those supernatural origins, at least when they are angelic or godly rather than demonic, and the main marker is their spontaneity. Meanwhile, spiritual experiences with natural origins, lacking spontaneity, caused by machines, will be inauthentic fabrications. Thus, on the surface, spontaneity seems like a first-rate way to decide on authenticity.

However, this is a misconstrual of how conscious experience arises. As Mikey Siegel, one of the leaders in the spirit tech community and the author of our foreword says, "The perceived difference between 'spontaneous' or 'natural' experiences and 'externally caused' experiences is illusory. All experience arises within consciousness within a context."[3] Indeed, truly understanding the high degree of control people have always exerted over spiritual experiences challenges this connection between spontaneity and authenticity. The history of religions is full of examples of people using all sorts of materials, exercises, and artistic expression (for example, in architecture, song, or patterned movements) to prepare their hearts and minds and to set the stage for spiritual experiences.

Contemporary scientific advancements provide an evidence-based way to understand the complexity of causality—as Siegel says, "There is no distinction between internal and external, or natural and unnatural that stands up to investigation."[4] First, with sophisticated new

measurement techniques, we now have a concrete grasp of the physiological correlates of many types of spiritual experiences, and the spontaneity factor seems unimportant as a predictor of what happens in
brains. Second, by listening to hundreds of people's experiences and
reflections—many of which are featured in this book—we've gathered
a nuanced understanding of the existential meaning that technologically enhanced spiritual experiences hold for people who have them.
As far as we have been able to tell, these nonspontaneous spiritual
experiences are every bit as spiritually authentic and behaviorally potent as the supposedly spontaneous experiences that arise in nontech-
nological, traditional settings. We think both sorts of experience—tech
assisted and traditional—also yield virtuous qualities in individuals
to about the same degree, and behavioral or emotional changes for
good and for bad with about the same frequency.

We are reporting our personal impressions based on an unusually
broad exposure to a wide variety of people and experiences, through
our scholarly research activity as well as our personal affiliations, rather
than on a scientifically established measurement. We'd love to study
this issue more concretely. But it has been forceful enough as an impression to induce us to surrender any linkage between spontaneity
and authenticity.

The insistence on spontaneity for authenticity may be an instance
of a blind spot, dancing around the fact that humans have bodies that
express all these experiences. Our bodies express even the experiences
that some people say have no natural causes or conditions. But the
more we conceive the experiences as bodily, the less plausible the claim
of their unconditioned spontaneity becomes. It is not that we can prove
spontaneity wrong. It is that we lose interest in defending the idea after
a while. What difference does it make? Whether spontaneous or not, we
eventually prefer to evaluate the authenticity of our spiritual experiences
on other grounds—say, based on their effects in people's lives. Empha-
sizing spontaneity also ignores the plethora of traditional methods that
religious traditions have encouraged to consciously help bring about

spiritual connections and experiences—fasting, trance states, prayer beads, and chanting, for example.

Sometimes the prizing of spontaneity is inspired by allegiance to traditional religious worldviews. For example, Christians and some other religious people say that the spirit moves where it will and can never be predicted or controlled. However, even this view can be conceptualized as a way of guiding one's experience—it helps people cultivate the skillful means to better align themselves to the will of God. But spirit tech poses an additional sharp challenge to this perspective. When a spiritual experience triggered and shaped by spirit tech feels the same or even more meaningful and transformative than one unaided by spirit tech, and when both have the same types of benefits, the claim that it is impossible to predict or control spiritual experiences becomes tenuous. Most people with the relevant experience eventually just give up on that altogether and start believing the opposite: that to some extent, we actually do have some agency and co-creative role in authentic spiritual experiences.

Then there are the extreme views that go beyond spontaneity to a *particular type* of spontaneity: to be authentic and good, spiritual experiences must be caused by good supernatural beings rather than by evil supernatural beings. Those evil supernatural beings—demons or jinns, perhaps—are capable of faking spiritual experiences and thereby seducing people into taking the wrong spiritual path. This way of thinking lends itself to demonizing spirit tech with a flourish of rhetoric, playing on people's fears in the absence of any useful information. In response, we are inclined to affirm the commonsense (not to mention biblical) approach to evaluating authenticity: by their fruits you shall know them.

We grow concerned when people who lack the relevant exposure and knowledge dismiss spirit tech prematurely, before they learn about it or properly consider what it means for people. It is not just traditional religious people who are inclined to sweeping judgments of this kind. Allergies to traditional religious interpretations of spiritual experiences can lead to equally strong conclusions about the authenticity and value of spirit tech. It is common for religious skeptics to reject spiritual experiences as nonsense, for example, or to frame them merely as side effects of a complex brain's cognitive-emotional system with no more meaning or value than steam from a kettle. Naturally, spirit tech gets dismissed in the very same flood of annoyed but typically uninformed condemnation of spiritual experiences generally. Here again, we are worried about a blind spot, dismissing such experiences too quickly, too easily.

But to dismiss spirit tech prior to understanding it would be folly. As we've indicated, it's already here, and it's rapidly growing, both in terms of its reach and its sophistication. If there's one thing that's been proven time and time again, it's that the manner and speed with which technological advancements will change our world is often beyond our wildest imaginations.

In the 1960s, sociologists studying religion began to predict the decline of religion once and for all, a position that would become known as the secularization thesis.[5] These scholars were convinced that religious belief systems were being gradually replaced by knowledge gleaned from biology, physics, chemistry, neuroscience, psychology, sociology, and economics. This was not only the result of rapid advancements in science, which were progressively closing the gaps in knowledge that were previously filled by supernatural agencies—such as God, paranormal energy, ghosts, or spirits—but also of the accumulation of awareness and tolerance of other worldviews, religions, and cultures. People started to question the inevitability of their belief systems when they began to accept that other perfectly reasonable and even enlightened people held drastically different religious views. After all, they thought, how could it make sense to claim that throughout time and across the whole world, *their* specific tradition was the *only* one that interpreted the world and spiritual reality correctly?

And yet, those secularization thesis scholars missed the mark. Sociologists and scholars of religion have been surprised to find that, despite these logical and practical challenges, religious and spiritual belief and practice has, in fact, not declined in the way they predicted. Religion is on the rise in Asia and most of the global south. Even in secularizing cultures it has persisted, though it has also *changed*—with many traditional religious groups losing members rapidly, a few traditional groups growing at surprising rates, and a lot of nontraditional forms of spirituality springing up like unruly vines around decaying ruins. Overall, religion and spirituality continue to play a powerful role in many people's lives, and religious institutions and rhetoric remain pervasive and hugely influential throughout most of the world. In fact, the scholar most famously known for developing the secularization thesis, sociologist Peter L. Berger, later retracted his theory and declared that religion is here to stay.[6] Berger realized that secularization describes only a global, hypereducated elite and fails to describe the religious and spiritual lives of regular people.

By contrast with the molasses-like rate of change that characterizes ancient religious institutions, such as the Catholic Church, contemporary people rapidly adapt their spiritual beliefs and practices to changing times. Religions and spiritual expressions have always shifted and changed, being shaped by their cultural contexts just as much as they contribute to the construction of those same contexts. So this flexibility of spiritual and religious ideas and practices is by no means a distinctly modern phenomenon. However, the *specific* ways in which spirituality and religion have shifted in our information age is truly spectacular. Not only are we surrounded in person and through media by a rich diversity of religious heritages and spiritual traditions that are dramatically different from our own, but the technological revolution has also transformed the way we do nearly *everything*, and that includes spirituality and religion. The reality of remote religion in the era of the coronavirus pandemic drives that home. And these adaptive transformations in spirituality are not slowing down.

Our technological control over spiritual experiences may be coarse at this point, but it is rapidly becoming more refined. Soon we will know a great deal more about the functional and anatomical neurology of many aspects of spiritual experiences, thereby exposing the relevant brain functions and structures to selective inhibition and enhancement. If our current pace of technological change continues, capacities for control that today come to us only in dreams and nightmares, in science fiction and fantasy, will in short order be familiar aspects of life.

Some spiritual and religious leaders bemoan this revolution, as we will see later. Others advise careful and cautious openness to change. The rapid pace of technological change is here to stay, but we have agency and power to join the conversation without fear, empowered by knowledge. We can even help shape the way our societies harness the growing force of spirit tech. As these technologies become better known and more widely accessible, their applications to spirituality will become even more important to understand.

Beyond understanding a basic taxonomy of spirit tech—what types of spirit tech are in use, what's under development, what they purport to do, how to access them—we must also grapple with a host of ethical quandaries of enormous weight. What does the level of control afforded by spirit tech say about the authenticity of spiritual experiences? Can we trust the ideas they inspire us to believe? Will they help or hurt our religious communities? Does our ability to cultivate moral virtues effectively using spirit tech, perhaps in some cases more effectively than by traditional methods, *oblige* us to use it? Does our responsibility to protect vulnerable people, especially children, oblige us to *resist* it?

Evaluating these questions is the task of the final chapters. It is difficult to draw any sound evaluative conclusions, however, without first deeply understanding tech-assisted spiritual experiences from the perspective of those who undergo them: what they feel like, what they accomplish, why people turn to them in the first place. It is at this meaningful level of personal lives and practical decisions where moral quandaries and value questions are often felt most sharply. Thus, it is by means of the personal stories from real people throughout the book that we can best raise the vital questions about meaning, value, reliability, and safety.

The future of spirit tech is still being written. But it is clear that technology is rapidly changing the way we operate in the world and the way we experience reality—including sacred reality. Like many technological advancements that once seemed the stuff of science fiction, spirit tech is unfurling in spectacular ways and will soon be a regular part of life for ordinary people. It's here, and it's here to stay. We best be ready.

2

Stimulating the Brain

The world of rigorous science and the world of deep meditation are beginning a mating dance that could rapidly alter human history for the better.

—*Shinzen Young[1]*

SHINZEN'S HAPPIEST THOUGHT

In 1907, Albert Einstein had what he later called "the happiest thought of my life": the idea that gravitational fields have only a relative existence. This thought formed the basis for his theory of general relativity, which would usher in one of the most dramatic paradigm shifts in the history of science.[2]

Some hundred years later, world-renowned meditation teacher, author, and contemplative neuroscience pioneer Shinzen Young had his own "happiest thought," a thought he believes has the potential to usher in a paradigm shift in humanity's relationship to our own consciousness and "fundamentally change [our] perspective on the nature of spiritual reality."[3] Shinzen's happiest thought was this: "*Most likely, there are things that are true and important about enlightenment that neither the Buddha nor any of the great masters of the past knew, because to know them requires an understanding of modern science.*"[4]

Shinzen's epiphany wasn't a flash of spiritual insight, nor was it a mystical vision: it was the realization that science provides a unique perspective for studying the mechanisms of consciousness from the *outside*, while meditation studies consciousness from the *inside*. If these two approaches were combined, they could unlock tools and methods for reaching enlightenment the likes of which have never been imagined.

Shinzen Young is now at the forefront of the scientific research and development that we predict will likely lead to the manifestation and fruition of his happiest thought. Let's take a short step back to see how this dream came to be.

In the late 1960s, Shinzen was a PhD student in Buddhist studies at the University of Wisconsin. He had extensively studied the languages, texts, and doctrines of Buddhism but was advised to go *see* the topic of his research in living color. So, to conduct research for his dissertation on a form of Japanese Buddhism called Shingon, he traveled to a mountaintop Buddhist community called Mount Kōya (or Kōyasan) in the Wakayama Prefecture of Japan. Mount Kōya is like the Vatican for Shingon—it is home to hundreds of temples and remains an important destination for pilgrims and students of Buddhism. Once settled in Mount Kōya, however, Shinzen learned that gaining access to the experts and material he needed for his research wasn't just a matter of waltzing in and asking—he would need to prove himself worthy. In Mount Kōya, that wouldn't happen through a display of his erudition but through spiritual practice—but Shinzen was not a Buddhist and didn't even have a regular meditation practice. Shingon, he was told, was "not an intellectual curio," and if he actually wanted to learn what the master had to offer, he would need to devote himself to transformation.[5] As a self-identified "agitated, impatient, and wimpy sort of guy," Shinzen was terrified.[6] But he was also determined and ended up living in the Shinno-in Temple for three years, going through several phases of initiation, and ultimately was ordained as a Shingon monk. The entire experience was a personal, spiritual, and intellectual crucible that transformed Shinzen's life.

A serendipitous meeting at a Zen retreat in Kyoto would spark a transformation in his career. There Shinzen met Father William (Bill) Johnston, a Jesuit priest who had practiced Zen for decades. The two hit it off right away and eventually became good friends. During one particularly exciting conversation shortly before Shinzen returned to the United States, Father Bill told Shinzen about the budding scientific study of contemplative and mystical experiences. Researchers, he said, had begun to identify and provide objective physiological evidence to confirm the effects of meditation—they were seeing how the brain looks during, and as a result of, meditation. Shinzen was floored. "Then and there," he says in the book he later wrote about the experience, *The Science of Enlightenment*, "I decided what was next for me. I knew I would be spending the rest of my life in the practice and teaching of meditation. In parallel with that, I resolved I would study science so that perhaps, at some future time, when my Buddhist practice had deepened, I would be able to intelligently dialogue and collaborate with scientists, helping them to understand meditative states and perhaps even how enlightenment comes about. That meeting with Father Bill changed the course of my life."[7]

Sure enough, Shinzen began reading and learning everything he could about the neuroscientific study of brain states, and over the decades he has remained true to this vocation. He has now played important roles in neuroscientific research on meditation at several top research universities in the United States, including Harvard Medical School, Carnegie Mellon University, and the University of Vermont. Although there is still much to learn, Shinzen remains convinced that the pairing of our ever-increasing knowledge about the brain with extraordinary technological innovations has the potential to greatly expand access to enlightenment and nirvana. Not only is contemporary science identifying physiological correlates for contemplative practices, but it has also discovered *new* insights about enlightenment, especially with regard to how people can access it. Once we understand what enlightenment *looks like in the brain*, there are ways to lead, stimulate, and manipulate the brain into that state. Thus, brain stimulation may hold a key, or at least a powerful set of training wheels, to enlightenment for those of us who don't want to wait decades to get a taste.

JAY'S HAPPY THOUGHT

Meanwhile, an eager undergraduate neuroscience student at the University of North Carolina at Wilmington named Jay Sanguinetti had his own happy thought. In an audience of thirty thousand brain scientists at the 2005 national conference for the Society for Neuroscience in Washington, DC, Jay heard something that would change the course of his life.[8] His Holiness the Dalai Lama (whose mere invitation to speak at the conference had already caused a controversy) was giving a keynote presentation when someone in the audience asked what he thought about the possibility of scientific interventions leading to spiritual awakenings.[9] The Dalai Lama said, "If it was possible to become free of negative emotions by a riskless implementation of an electrode—without impairing intelligence and the critical mind—I would be the first patient."[10]

After the talk, Jay and a group of undergraduate students got the honor of meeting the Dalai Lama. The students filed through one by one, each anxiously waiting for their turn to approach the Dalai Lama, who asked each student, "What do you want to do with your life?" When it was Jay's turn, he answered, "I want to make your thing—help people meditate." The Dalai Lama replied, "Well, first you have to learn what meditation is." And so, when Jay got back to Wilmington, he began learning meditation—exploring the workings of his mind from the inside.

This new North Star came as a very welcome relief. Jay had been working in a neurosurgery lab—actually drilling into rats' heads—and it had become incredibly taxing for him. On the one hand, he was fascinated by how successful and clear his experimental results were—if you change the brain, you change behavior. And yet, on the other hand, he said, "I was feeling really horrible about it because I got attached to my rats, which you're not supposed to do as a neuroscientist. . . . I was having nightmares. I became vegan. I couldn't touch meat. I just felt really bad for the rats."[11] So even though he could tell that the work was fruitful and important for advancing the field, he could not continue. Instead, he began looking for techniques for brain change that wouldn't require drilling into anyone's brains and research that wouldn't require killing rats, which led him to noninvasive brain stimulation.

Jay began experimenting on his own time and built his own direct-current electrical brain stimulation system while he was still an undergraduate. He was his own guinea pig, firing up the device and stimulating his retinas. Sure enough, Jay's device caused him to see phosphenes—very obvious rings of light in his visual field. "I freaked out!" he said. "I thought I had burned my retina. I was only eighteen or nineteen years old, so I thought, 'Yeah, I'm going to put this down until I understand what I'm doing.'" But the freak-out was paired with exhilaration. He was encouraged and determined.[12]

The wisdom inherent in the Dalai Lama's directions—that Jay must learn the contours of his own mind through meditation before he'd be able to work toward a device to help others meditate—stuck with Jay. He knew he had to do some deep, ethical, and defining work before he could really approach this particular research question. "My whole path," he said, "was learning how to be a good scientist, learning to experience the effects of meditation, and then learning the brain stimulation stuff and what I can ethically do with it, before I could bring it all together."[13] This process of accumulating and building the tools he needed to approach his life's goal led him to begin an MA/PhD program in cognition and neural systems and psychology at the University of Arizona in 2009.

There, Jay worked in Dr. John Allen's lab investigating the use of ultrasound stimulation for the treatment of depression. Jay began considering: Could ultrasound stimulation provide the type of technological intervention the Dalai Lama described? Ultrasound beams reach more deeply and more precisely than any other type of noninvasive (nonsurgical) technique, so perhaps this was the key that Jay had been searching for. If we could deeply stimulate parts of the brain that we know are involved in meditation, he thought, perhaps we could induce deep meditative states in people.

One weekend, his roommate, Tucker Peck, a PhD student in clinical psychology, was teaching a meditation retreat with the Arizona Meditation Research Interest Group (AMRIG). Jay and Tucker had bonded over their efforts in meditation, and Tucker was determined to make meditation a central part of his future clinical therapy practice. That retreat's special guest teacher was none other than Shinzen Young, now a famous meditation master who was teaching all around the country. Jay and Tucker were both excited to meet Shinzen; Jay, especially, was eager to share his ideas about the potential of ultrasound stimulation. However, when Jay told Shinzen his idea, Shinzen seemed to brush it off, expressing minimal interest.

Jay laughed as he recalled that initial meeting with Shinzen, who was singularly unimpressed with the ramblings of a random PhD student. "I was still a student," he said. "I had just started and didn't have any way to back up my idea." However, in 2016, after Jay had graduated, he became a research assistant professor at the University of New Mexico and began working as a postdoctoral fellow with the Army Research Laboratory to design mindfulness training for support personnel. He reached out to Shinzen again. This time, Shinzen was intrigued. "Two years into my postdoc, I had some actual evidence," Jay said. "Shinzen didn't want to work with me until I had evidence. So that made me like him even more. He wasn't interested in the hype—he was like, I want you to show me the money."[14] And, of course, money in this case isn't at all about dollar bills—it's hard evidence, statistically significant results from well-designed scientific studies. Still, Shinzen needed convincing. He told Jay, "I'll give you one day a month—we can talk for an hour and I'll collaborate with you."

Their monthly conversations were mutually enriching and got more and more interesting. Shinzen was already curious about the potential for focused ultrasound stimulation, and gradually came to see that, although he and Jay had taken different paths to get there, they shared a vision. They were both dedicated to the goal of using neuromodulation to enhance and democratize the benefits of meditation. By the beginning of 2017, Shinzen decided to come to Albuquerque and spend a couple of months working with Jay.

Their personalities clicked, giving rise not only to an incredibly fruitful meeting of minds but also to a lovely friendship. In fact, as Jay was relaying their story over the phone, he laughed and told me he was in the car on his way to drop something off at Shinzen's house. "He lives a mile down the road from me," Jay said. "He's my teacher, my friend, my colleague. It's just been a really great relationship. I feel insanely lucky. I wouldn't have had the courage to pivot my life to meditation research without him. He's really been the rock who's guided me."[15]

A TECHNOBOOST FOR MEDITATION

Shinzen brought to their working relationship a particular orientation that would prove to be a game changer: Rather than conceptualize enlightenment as something that a brain builds toward, he told Jay, they should think of enlightenment as the brain's most natural starting point. The task then is to *remove* the roadblocks built up over the course of a lifetime in order to access enlightenment.

Shinzen also told Jay about a rare neurological disorder called athymhormia that could hold a key to their ongoing research. Much brain stimulation research has been achieved by studying the effects of brain injuries or illnesses, as scientists are able to see what happens when certain areas or functions of the brain are inhibited. In the case of athymhormia, damage to the basal ganglia causes a loss of internal motivation to do anything. Sufferers have no apparent needs, will, or desires, but their ability to be motivated by outside suggestion remains fully intact. So, despite the fact that they're capable of many intellectual and cognitive functions, their conscious thought and sense of self seems completely vacant. For example, one patient with athymhormia suffered massive sunburns while lying on the beach. Once in the sun, she experienced a complete lack of concern or desire to move into the shade. She reported being completely aware of the burning and pain, but the awareness caused her no sense of suffering or distress. In other words, she was immersed in the present moment without being affected by its reality.[16]

If you're even casually aware of the literature on meditation, bells are already ringing. This unfortunate woman found herself in the state for which so many meditators yearn—full immersion in the present moment and full equanimity, despite her present circumstances. Moreover, she got there effortlessly. Now, as Shinzen and others would rightly point out, we would describe her state as a kind of pseudo enlightenment, as it was the unintended by-product of compromised brain function, not something she desired or sought out. But her experience provides rare insight for researchers seeking to access true enlightenment by way of brain stimulation: in a twisted way, athymhormia appears to have removed one of the roadblocks to enlightenment. It thrust this woman into a state of full, present-moment awareness, in which she lost all sense of self and any experience of suffering.

Another patient, a sixty-year-old professor who had previously been energetic, motivated, and highly invested in his professional and personal interests and achievements, suddenly lost all enthusiasm and reported a complete lack of thought unless someone or something directly engaged him. He could perform tasks but only out of duty and routine. A brain MRI revealed several small lacunar infarctions, or strokes involving small blood vessels, within the basal ganglia. He showed no signs of depression and had no complaints about his condition even as his friends and family became very concerned.[17] Shinzen succinctly explains this lack of distress: "No self, no problem."[18]

Again, Shinzen recognized these symptoms as a form of pseudo

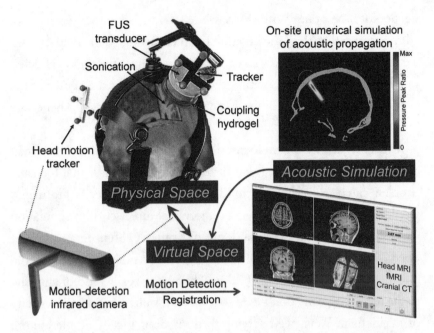

Figure 2. A tFUS transducer. Notice the head motion tracker on the person's forehead along with the tracker on the transducer. tFUS is extremely precise.

no-self, a tragic caricature of the goal of meditation. To be able to quiet the mind's chatter, become fully immersed in the present moment, achieve nonattachment, and eliminate suffering may sound great, but in folks with athymhormia, it happens to a pathological degree.

Nonetheless, the area of the brain affected by athymhormia was of special interest to Shinzen and Jay. They wondered if targeting that area in the brains of healthy people and downregulating it (rather than eliminating its function altogether, as in the case of athymhormia) could stimulate a state of mindfulness. A type of therapy called transcranial focused ultrasound stimulation (tFUS) had already been studied extensively for benefits such as mood alteration and the treatment of chronic pain, so they were confident that it should be safe physiologically, but applying it to mindfulness meditation was brand new.

Shinzen and Jay's hunch was that tFUS could be the best modality of brain stimulation for meditation enhancement because it has a far superior ability to target very specific brain areas and to penetrate much deeper into the brain. With tFUS, we're talking a very focused *beam* of stimulation rather than the creation of an electromagnetic field or even a current. This ability is key since the basal ganglia—the region affected in athymhormia—is deep within the limbic system at the center of the brain, so there is a lot of brain tissue the tFUS beam needs to penetrate in order to affect it.

Currently, as tFUS is *so* focused, it requires an MRI to create a map of the brain and guide the focus of the stimulation, but if that focusing problem can be solved, tFUS could easily be put into a headset form and would be about as affordable as a transcranial direct-current simulation (tDCS) headset. That being said, out of principle, Shinzen and Jay are open. "We feel like focused ultrasound is the most likely tool to get the effect we're looking for," Jay told us, "but we're really kind of agnostic to the tech. We really don't care so much if it's ultrasound or electricity or magnetism. What we're trying to do is dramatically accelerate the effects of meditation and mindfulness."[19]

The first step, of course, is experimentation. Give it a try and see what happens. Given his level of experience with very deep meditation states, Shinzen volunteered as the guinea pig. Jay and Shinzen knew they were taking a chance, so Jay built an entire set of equipment and set up a lab at his house to avoid placing liability on the university or the army were Shinzen to get hurt. Jay and Shinzen were quiet, but not secretive, about their extracurricular consciousness hacking (to use Mikey Siegel's term), which felt exciting and pioneering. "It was fun," Jay said. "I was like, this is why I got into science."

However, the potential for danger was real. "I worried a lot about killing Shinzen," Jay said with a laugh. Even though they knew the ultrasound stimulation should be safe for brains, Jay had to trust Shinzen that he could handle the psychological impact of whatever happened. In their makeshift lab, Shinzen sat while Jay fired up the neuronavigation software. Loaded with an MRI image of Shinzen's brain and a camera to locate Shinzen's head in space and account for any movements he made, the software mapped the brain and guided Jay in

Figure 3. Jay Sanguinetti applying tFUS to Shinzen Young.

finding their target and stimulating it with precision. Jay fired up the ultrasound transducer—a plastic wand—and located Shinzen's basal ganglia. Shinzen began meditating and Jay administered the pulse.

To their great relief, nothing dramatic happened. But *something* happened. "Shinzen basically felt like it was a deep, interesting experience, but nothing big," Jay said. So they ran the protocol again. This time, Shinzen was genuinely shocked to find that the ultrasound stimulation made him go even deeper, triggering a profound meditative experience. After this, Jay decided they'd better wait a week before doing it again to let Shinzen's brain rest and integrate the experience.

Shinzen received tFUS twice a week, getting small doses of focused ultrasound stimulation throughout his ninety-minute meditation sessions. "This is it," Shinzen said after a couple of weeks. This is what they were looking for. He was experiencing less resistance to entering a state of equanimity, less grasping of the ego, and more fluidity of thought and emotion. As Jay reported in his TEDxBigSky talk in January 2019,

Shinzen said that the third week of stimulation gave him "one of the most significant effects he's ever had with meditation"—and he's been meditating for fifty years![20]

As Shinzen summarized it, that experience felt like a deep remembering of what he really was, his true self, and what meditation, mindfulness, and the Buddhist path are all about. In meditation, by quieting the ego-self and working toward a sense of no-self, what is revealed is the *true self*, which some might call *Buddha nature*. So, Jay explained to us, we can think of this goal state as having two dimensions: a quieting of self-referential thinking and a deep sense of equanimity. These two dimensions are profoundly intertwined, interdependent, and coemerging. The idea is that at the core of each person is a *true* self, a Buddha self. This self is characterized by equanimity—awareness, mindfulness, and profound presence with no judgment or desire. However, on a species scale, eons of evolution, and on a person scale, years of life experiences, have encouraged the building up of incredibly strong psychological structures and cognitive processes that are helpful for survival but cloud the true self. These psychological and cognitive aspects of our existence create what we often think of as our selves—the ego-self. The self that has a narrative history, a dynamic personality, a truckful of memories and wounds, and countless practiced emotional investments and reactions to the people and world around us. This ego-self that is deeply concerned about its life is far from useless and cannot be done away with completely. However, habitual foci and demand for attention can begin to override our ability to perceive and be aware—it can override our access to the wisdom of the true self. Therefore, meditation does not *build* a sense of equanimity and presence but rather *quiets* the ego-self so that we can access the true self with more clarity, concentration, and fluidity. In short (while acknowledging that such things are difficult to describe "in short"), the profound experience of the true self is a deep and abiding equanimity.

The question, then, is *how* does shooting ultrasound beams into someone's brain make this more likely? We'll consider this question on a couple of different levels, but first, let's look at brain structures and functions. The two primary brain structures that Jay and Shinzen have been targeting are the posterior cingulate cortex (PCC) and the basal ganglia. Both of these structures play a role in self-referential thinking—the creation of the ego-self. For example, the PCC is activated when someone asks you to describe yourself or when you're processing or remembering an event that makes you feel great about yourself or makes you feel ashamed or self-conscious. Judson Brewer and his colleagues at Yale University and MIT explain that PCC activity is associated with getting caught up in things like self-related and social processing, processing meaningful memories, or daydreaming about the future.[21] The basal ganglia, on the other hand, is associated with motivation, reward, and the habit formation system. It helps build and maintain patterns of thought and behavior—both beneficial and not so beneficial. It is easy to imagine how a painful cycle of rumination—habitual self-referential thinking—may involve both the PCC and the basal ganglia. Hitting these areas of the brain with ultrasound can downregulate these systems so that the automatic self-referential thinking and habits and patterns of reacting to the world are loosened and begin to clear away—making space for equanimity to breathe.

Another important brain system is called the default mode network.

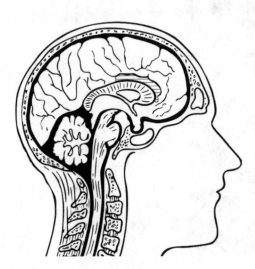

Figure 4. Midline section of a human brain showing the basal ganglia *(with radial hatching)* and posterior cingulate cortex *(with horizontal hatching)*.

This is the system that kicks in when the brain isn't paying attention to the outside world, when a person is simply allowing their mind to wander. In many ways, meditation is an effort to *resist* the wandering mind. Often, recorded guided meditations will soothingly remind us: "If your mind begins to wander, simply draw it back to the present moment." Typically, the posterior cingulate cortex is a core functional hub of the default mode network. But, Jay told us, "if you look at long-term meditators, their PCC is now connected to the attention network instead of the default mode network at rest. . . . When you put Shinzen in the scanner and tell him to rest, it looks like there's just the attention center watching his default mode."[22] It's a very clear difference between typical brains and the brains of master meditators. "That's one of the core markers of long-term practice," Jay said. "Their default mode is to be in the world instead of in their head." Without longitudinal studies, we can't say for sure that this is an *effect* of long-term meditation—perhaps people with that kind of brain simply find meditation easier to master— but it is certainly a marker that we see in long-term meditators.

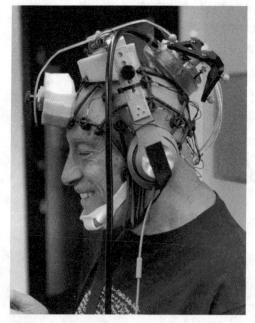

Figure 5. Shinzen Young wearing the headset prototype.

Philosophically, equanimity is at your core, true self and is revealed when the ego-self is recognized as an illusion; physiologically, equanimity is the experience revealed when the self-referential brain areas are downregulated. The wisdom and freedom of equanimity is not a prize to acquire but rather a reality to be discovered. In this way, the tech does not "zap you with enlightenment," Shinzen explains in his book. "Rather, if anything got zapped, it would be what *gets in the way* of the enlightenment that's already there."[23]

After so much success with their initial experiment, Shinzen and Jay later replicated it with twelve advanced meditation practitioners, who had, on average, thirty years of meditation experience each. In this study, the participants received only four days of intervention. But by the fourth day, *all* of them reported similar effects—less resistance to centering the mind and the ability to dive deeper and more quickly into the meditation practice, and then more fluidity and ease in their experience of equanimity. Indeed, Jay said that participants in the tFUS meditation sessions reported receiving the types of insights experts get only after meditating for a long time and that they'd really only expect to gain during an intensive meditation retreat.[24]

Jay and Shinzen were both shocked and delighted by the success of their experiments. Though they are both very careful to emphasize how much work and clarification is needed before we'll know if, how, and when a retreat-use or home-use device is ready to implement, these preliminary demonstrations make it clear that an ultrasound device for meditation enhancement has the potential to be dramatically effective, and is a very real possibility in the near future.

SILICON VALLEY PSYCHONAUTS

When I (Kate), first met Jay and Shinzen in 2018, they were living in a mansion high in the hills of Palo Alto. I had just presented at a science and spirituality conference in San Jose and had been informed that Jay was *the* guy I needed to talk to about brain stimulation and spirituality. Jay by then was a research assistant professor at the University of New Mexico, director of UNM's Non-Invasive Cognitive Enhancement Lab, and associate director of the University of Arizona Center for Consciousness Studies. He had quickly become one of the world's leading experts on ultrasound brain stimulation for meditation. Shinzen and Jay had both recently moved to the Palo Alto mansion, which housed a research lab and a group of Silicon Valley spirit tech innovators, as researchers in residence. Given that grant funding from the National Institutes of Health or the National Science Foundation isn't always readily awarded to researchers whose stated goals are to enlighten people, Jay and Shinzen were eager to be among like-minded, well-funded folks interested in supporting the burgeoning science of meditation and enlightenment.

The Transformative Technology Lab (TTL) is an extraordinary team of researchers, clinicians, entrepreneurs, and meditation experts centered around technological innovation, scientific collaboration, and spiritual wellness. Their mission is to develop spirit tech applications to make well-being, spiritual insight, and enlightenment available to the public on a massive scale. Their goal is no less than to harness the world's most advanced technologies, transform the human experience, and usher in the next phase of human evolution.

Along with Jay and Shinzen, several other spirit tech pioneers were present the night I visited: Dr. Sanjay Manchanda, a psychotherapist and meditation teacher for more than twenty-five years and the leading expert on magnetic brain stimulation for meditation; Dr. Jeffery A. Martin, bestselling author, research professor, serial entrepreneur, and cofounder of TTL; and Nichol Bradford, executive director and cofounder of TTL and founder and CEO of the Willow Group, a company devoted to sparking personal transformation and enhancing well-being. TTL currently has multiple research projects underway. With their motivation to bring spiritual transformation to the masses combined with their funding streams, we are convinced that they are set to change the future not just of spirit tech but of human spirituality. The very existence of TTL hints at what is to come.

Along with being a site for dreaming, planning, and sharing a vision, the mansion housed a small lab where Shinzen and Jay conducted tFUS experiments. As word of their exciting research spread, psychonauts, fellow spirit tech innovators, meditators, and curious visitors and friends came to the house with high hopes of taking their turn with this brand-new tech. But as the power and potency of tFUS became increasingly clear to Jay and Shinzen, they grew concerned about two things: safety and operationalization.

MAKING IT WORK SAFELY

They knew that, physically, ultrasound stimulation should be safe. The current FDA limits for clinical ultrasound imaging in humans is 720 milliwatts per centimeter squared.[25] So as long as the brain stimulation remained below that level, there should be no damage. That being said, the dangerous part isn't the stimulation itself, it's the *effects* of the stimulation. A technology powerful enough to thrust a person into a fairly deep state of mindfulness might be jarring, especially for a beginner. "As a practitioner myself, having experienced some negative things on retreats," Jay told us, "I was thinking, 'Wow, the public is not ready for that.' And we're not ready as scientists and clinicians; we don't have any context for that yet. So just to create a device this powerful and sell it at Walmart or on the Internet, that would be insanely dangerous."[26] The mind-altering power of ultrasound stimulation might not be quite as powerful as, say, taking a psychedelic, but the profundity of the experience approaches that level and can, therefore, have life-changing, transformative effects. Being careful to establish protocols for preparation, guidance, intentions, and integration for this kind of intervention is a must.

Second, simply *understanding* exactly what it means and how it is possible to externally trigger these profound types of consciousness is not as simple as it seems. From a scientist's point of view, operationalizing enlightenment in order to measure it and gauge the effectiveness of an enlightenment intervention is a complicated task to say the least. Jay and Shinzen believe that it is, in theory, possible to see and understand the positive effects of meditation as they manifest physically in the brain. And so, theoretically, manipulating the brain into that physical state could potentially produce the corresponding mental state that is achieved by meditation. This is a fairly simple conceptual cause-and-effect model. And yet, the jump from complex Buddhist philosophical and phenomenological concepts such as *enlightenment* or *no-self* or *equanimity* to a specific activation of neuronal networks requires some very careful thought.

"We're taking Buddhist ideas and kind of an ethical framework of Buddhism and we're talking about how to use those tools to make a person fundamentally change in terms of happiness and well-being and a sense of self," Jay explained. "There's this very biophysical piece, which is the brain/body change. And then there's this human piece: How do we make sure that we're changing the human in a positive direction? And then there's a psychosocial piece: what does that mean? If you're a father and you have two children, what does it mean to change you [with brain stimulation]? Because you still need to be able to take care of your children and be motivated to do that. So we don't want to make you happy detached, we want to make you happy embodied and a happy, better human being in your society and the specific sociocultural context that you're in."[27] The multifaceted nature of this question is one of the most difficult, intriguing, and meaningful parts of the project for Jay. "The more I dig into it," he said, "the more I think this is exactly what I want to be working on *and* this may be an impossible problem."[28]

Eventually, Jay and Shinzen decided that they needed to return to a more traditionally scientific, less entrepreneurial approach with tFUS before it would be ready to scale in the way that Silicon Valley developers are excited for. Silicon Valley is interested in rapid innovation, but "science is slow and boring and it costs a lot of money and takes a lot of time," Jay pointed out. "It's kind of the opposite of exponential."[29] Pressure within Silicon Valley to find "an enlightenment button" and to promise effectiveness is exciting and hopeful, but there are still so many scientific questions that need to be answered before such products and promises will be possible with tFUS. "The push in Silicon Valley was to make a general-purpose device that everybody can use," Jay said. "And that was the step I wasn't ready to take, as a scientist and as a practitioner myself."[30]

So Jay and Shinzen left the Bay Area in December 2018 and moved back to Tucson to start their own lab—the Sonication Enhanced Mindful Awareness (SEMA) Lab at the University of Arizona. Jay is the principal investigator and codirector of the lab, while Shinzen is codirector and in charge of protocol development. The SEMA Lab has a uniquely joint structure, involving experts from the College of Science, the College of Social and Behavioral Sciences, and the College of Medicine. Not only does this collaborative approach allow them to explore more difficult multidimensional questions than any one discipline could alone, it also means that the lab must comply with multiple sets of ethical guidelines and constraints. For Jay, these constraints aren't a nuisance but rather a huge benefit, supplying the accountability their research requires. For example, the Neuroscience Department maintains a laser-sharp focus on the basic biophysics and safety concerns when dealing with human brains; the Clinical Psychology Department helps the team keep track of concerns about psychological health; the College of Social and Behavioral Sciences asks big-picture questions about the impact the technology might have on society and social communities; and the College of Medicine always has a plan for how to avoid and handle medical emergencies. The team as a whole allows the project to maintain an integrated multidimensional understanding of the human subject: "And really keeping the human at the center is an interesting scientific clinical question," Jay said, "because at the foundation a lot of what we're talking about is changing the human."[31]

The SEMA lab has three interlocking research trajectories. First, they are validating, through careful and replicable experimentation using neuroimaging techniques and behavioral monitoring, that tFUS does indeed enhance mindfulness training. Second, they are applying mindfulness-based interventions to clinical populations such as those with addiction and chronic pain. These populations have been found to benefit from mindfulness-based stress reduction, so the question for SEMA is: Does adding neuromodulation increase the effectiveness even further? Third, the ultimate goal for the lab is to invent a personal-use device that creates a closed-loop stimulation system with neurofeedback. This means that in addition to receiving ultrasound stimulation, you would also be wearing an EEG cap while you're meditating to track what is happening in your brain in response to the stimulation paired with meditation. A representation of your brain's activity is displayed as feedback for you as you meditate. Essentially, you're learning what it feels like when your ego drive or self-referential thinking is turned off—what it feels like to simply experience the sensory world free of ego. Jay said, "And you may think, 'Oh my God, that feels so good.' And while you have that 'oh my God' moment, you *see* which brain areas are downregulating on the screen, so your brain is getting a little extra feedback about what you already know subjectively."[32] With this two-pronged approach of stimulation and neurofeedback, Jay explained, "you're starting to learn—you *subjectively*—but also your brain is unconsciously learning how to get into the state. So it's about the state, but really underneath, it's about the brain learning how to get into the state."[33]

The idea is that eventually a person would no longer need the technoboost, at least not every time, because their brain will have learned how to enter a mindful state—it will be practiced and proficient in targeting the neural networks and activating them with meditation. So after identifying and figuring out how to apply tFUS effectively, the researchers are left with the question: "What does it actually mean, not just to be in a mindful state but actually to have those skills learned in the system and how does the network change?" Jay pondered, "That's the fundamental science of the lab that I feel has to be done before you make a technology that you can take to the public."[34]

Another burning research question for the SEMA Lab and other ultrasound researchers continues to be *how* exactly beams of ultrasound vibrations stimulate neurons in such a way as to produce something as profound as a state of mindfulness that yields wise insights and healing effects. It's hard to say whether it's more incredible that stimulating the brain can lead to mindfulness or that humans can and do often reach these states without stimulation. Both incredible realities are testaments to an extraordinarily complex system of mind and matter. When we asked Jay what exactly tFUS does to the neuronal networks, he smiled and said, "That's a million-dollar question. Maybe a billion-dollar question!"[35]

Of the four common modalities of brain stimulation—electric, magnetic, light, and ultrasound—we know least about the underlying mechanism of ultrasound. But all four stimulation mechanisms are poorly understood. Electricity and magnetism *seem* straightforward: scientists hypothesize that sufficiently strong electromagnetic fields directly affect the movement of ions that carry electrical signals through neurons. Certain FDA-approved treatments for depression rely on transcranial magnetic stimulation and are approved on the basis of this hypothesis about how they work; but there could be other mechanisms in play as well, so it's a murky situation. In the meditation context, the causal mechanisms of electromagnetism are even murkier. Most spirituality-related electrical and magnetic stimulation protocols involve such low levels of current that it's unclear that they'd even penetrate the skull, let alone significantly influence ion movement. Yet strong claims are made about the efficacy of those protocols, as we'll see later. We are in the same place with ultrasound neurostimulation: we have good reasons to believe that it works, but we haven't yet figured out precisely how.

For ultrasound, moreover, there is an additional layer of mystery. Here's why. *Excitability* refers to the likelihood that a neuron will fire, and a neuron firing is understood as an electrical event. This is why we use *electrodes* for an *electro*encephalogram (EEG) to measure the *electromagnetic* waves brain activity causes. Now, the electromagnetic spectrum encompasses a huge range of frequencies—X-rays, ultraviolet radiation, visible light (the rainbow spectrum), microwaves, and radio waves. What we think of as visible light is just one kind of electromagnetic radiation. Since the brain emits electromagnetic waves, whether you're primarily creating a magnetic field, an electrical current, or flashes of near-infrared light (photobiomodulation), it makes sense that these might affect brain function by somehow interfering with the electromagnetic properties of brain function. However, *ultrasound* is high-frequency *sound* waves, which are a completely different type of wave with a different spectrum of variations, unrelated to electromagnetism. Just as humans can see only a small portion of the electromagnetic spectrum with our eyes (perceived as color), humans can hear only a small portion of the acoustic spectrum with our ears. Ultrasound is a much higher frequency than humans can perceive. Since the current understanding of brain activity, generally speaking, is that the brain runs on electrochemical circuitry, trying to make sense of how *acoustic* vibrations could influence brain activity requires a different approach and an additional set of hypotheses. Even with research going back to the 1920s showing that ultrasound influences neurons and nerves, scientists are still working with several hypotheses to answer the *how* question.

For example, it's possible that the ultrasound vibrations are pushing and pulling on neurons' potassium ion channels, affecting the speed and voltage of the electrical current when the neurons fire.[36] Or it is possible that ultrasound vibrations cause oscillations in the two layers of the cell walls, increasing tension to induce temporary pores or lesions in the wall as the layers are stretched and pulled apart.[37] Or one lab hypothesizes that the different rates of expansion and contraction of very particular regions of the cell membrane may cause the cell to displace some of its accumulating charge, thereby slowing its rise to the firing threshold.[38] Either way, the ultrasound is affecting the electromagnetic properties of the cell, which are then affecting the neuronal firing. "My intuition as a scientist," Jay said, "is that ultrasound is probably acting on all of these levels at once. And that makes the mechanism hard to understand because these things are probably nonlinearly interacting."[39] Just as we don't *fully* understand how many pharmaceuticals, including some popular antidepressants, work, we also don't *fully* understand how the exact mechanisms behind brain-based medical interventions work, and that is par for the course; it does not detract from their effectiveness and safety. Clearly, there is still much to learn about tFUS, the brain, and consciousness.

Given the rapid advances and incredible achievements that have occurred just in the last decades, it may be a surprise to learn that the inspiration to directly stimulate the brain in an effort to trigger and control altered states of consciousness is actually far from new. In fact, it's worth backing up and taking a look at the dramatic history behind brain stimulation and spiritual experiences.

BRAIN ZAPPING THROUGHOUT HISTORY

At the end of the nineteenth century, scientists were feverishly exploring the ways they could manipulate electromagnetism for medical, communication, and entertainment purposes. More than a half century earlier, the brilliant self-taught son of a poor blacksmith, Michael Faraday, had helped scientists understand that electricity and magnetism, which had formerly been thought to be distinct physical phenomena, interacted and were in fact inextricably intertwined—two sides of the same coin. With this discovery, the technological possibilities seemed limitless. Ever more efficient dynamos, electromagnets, and electric motors were on the way and becoming commercially viable. James Clerk Maxwell, possessed of a mind comparable only to that of Sir Isaac Newton and Albert Einstein, had clarified all phenomena related to electricity and magnetism in a glorious set of equations that seemed to imply that light *was* electromagnetic radiation. Not long after that, Heinrich Hertz figured out how to transmit electromagnetic waves through the air, and soon the technique was being refined in early radio. The industrial revolution was about to get a major boost, and the communications revolution was just beginning.[40]

It was in this heady era of high-tech creativity that an English Quaker named Silvanius P. Thompson rose to prominence as a physicist and electrical engineer, most notably through his textbooks on electromagnetic machinery. Thompson was especially intrigued by the late-nineteenth-century discovery of electrical signals in the brain based on animal studies. He was an inventor and had the bright idea of trying to stimulate or modify the electrical activity in the human brain using magnetism. Quite charitably, he parked his own head in a strong magnetic field to see what would happen, but reported that all he sensed were flecks in his visual field.[41]

Thompson was close to a breakthrough, though. Maxwell's equations tell us that there are two ways to get interactions between electricity and magnetism and Thompson fell short on both. On the one hand, a magnetic field can produce an electrical current, though it is not the strength of the field that matters but the rate that the magnetic field changes. Think of an old bicycle dynamo: you pedal to turn the wheels, which spins a magnet inside the dynamo, which changes the magnetic field rapidly, which produces an electric current, which powers a bulb to light your way at night; the faster you pedal, the brighter the light (these days people tend to use bike lights powered by batteries). Changing magnetic fields quickly enough to induce biologically relevant electrical currents was not easy in Thompson's time. On the other hand, a static magnetic field can influence charged particles so long as they are moving across the field; then, instead of moving in straight lines, they spin in circles. In neurons that are channeling charged particles (ions), a magnetic field could disrupt normal function, depending on angles and directions. This effect is responsible for the flecks in Thompson's vision, as he disrupted electrical activity associated with visual processing. But to do anything interesting, those static magnetic fields have to be focused in a useful direction, which is something scientists didn't know how to do in Thompson's era.[42]

In 1985 a group at Sheffield University led by Anthony Barker, a biomedical engineer, was able to produce muscle twitches using transcranial magnetic stimulation (TMS), a noninvasive technique similar to Thompson's using the second technique just described: it sends an electrical current through a large coil to generate magnetic fields strong enough to modify electrical activity in the brain.[43] "Transcranial" means that the magnetic fields are applied from outside the head, which is a big bonus because nobody likes brain surgery unless it's absolutely necessary. Barker's research paved the way for medically relevant applications of repetitive TMS (rTMS), which rapidly grew more refined as growing understanding of neuroanatomy facilitated useful targeting. One of the most promising applications has been as a treatment for chronic depression. At the present time, it is usually reserved for people who are nonresponsive to standard antidepressant medications, but rTMS has proven effective for many people.

rTMS has also been used to treat as well as study the brains of people with autism spectrum disorder (ASD). Though its use as a treatment modality is still considered experimental, it seems to be effective, as it is for depression, for many people. John Elder Robison, who was diagnosed with Asperger's syndrome at the age of forty, volunteered for a research study on using rTMS to treat ASD and got much more than he bargained for. As he describes in his memoir *Switched On: A Memoir of Brain Change and Emotional Awakening*, his experience with the experimental treatment was nothing less than spiritually transformative.[44]

It completely reframed his interpersonal relationships—in fact, in some cases, it *cost* him important relationships, including his marriage, some friends, and a few clients—as he struggled to negotiate his renewed perspective. It seems that the treatment had dramatically switched on an aspect of Robison's social cognition that had until then lain dormant—it opened his eyes to other people's emotions. If human emotions were colors, it was as if he had lived his entire life in black and white. Now, overnight, he was seeing in color. He described it as simultaneously a gift and absolutely devastating because what he *thought* he was missing was joy, love, and passion; and although he did see some of that, what he was completely overwhelmed by was the sense of other people's anxiety, fear, sadness, and even contempt. He still welcomed the incredibly powerful experience, however, because it propelled him into a more enlightened and compassionate existence.

The effects of the experimental treatment protocol have by now largely faded, and the protocol is not something yet available for repeated treatments, but the awakening and the insights Robison gained stay with him every day. When some of his friends asked him if he feels cheated that the colors are fading, that he only got a taste of this awareness without achieving permanent effects, he reported that he "just smiled," without a hint of disappointment. "I'm not a churchgoing person, but for me the experience felt miraculous, like a religious vision," he said. "For a brief time, I felt a deeper reality, and even as it was happening I knew my memory of the experience would never leave me."[45]

rTMS technology and treatment will almost certainly continue to grow in prevalence, and as the technology becomes more refined, more and more practitioners are willing to expand the applications of rTMS from a means to treat maladies to a tool that can enhance performance, self-development, and even spiritual growth.

There are several other types of brain stimulation that have already been adopted and implemented for explicitly spiritual uses. First, there is the weak-electric-field NeuroField stimulation, which we'll encounter later. NeuroField therapy uses pulsed electromagnetic field (pEMF) technology, which emits bursts of very low-frequency electromagnetic waves believed to improve the function of intricately structured neuron cell membranes, thereby facilitating the smooth movement of calcium, sodium, and potassium ions across cell membranes, which is critical for their healthy functioning. NeuroField was developed for relaxation and stress release, and is often paired with or used as a prelude to other forms of neurotherapy like neurofeedback and brain stimulation.

Second, E-meditation headsets use medical-grade transcranial direct-current stimulation to enhance meditation practice, both reducing the learning curve involved in meditation and enhancing its positive mood, attentional, and stress-reduction effects—or, as *New Scientist* magazine put it, they "supercharge your zen."[46] One example is the Zendo headset created by Bodhi Neurotech. It works by sending a current between two patches—one over the left eyebrow and one on the right temple—and is purported to be "2.5 times more powerful than conventional meditation training."[47] Generally, users have found that it leaves them feeling calmer, less physically and mentally restless, and more focused. tDCS sends a constant (rather than pulsed) low electrical current through the skull and into the brain, and is believed to cause either a depolarization or hyperpolarization of neurons, which affects neuronal excitability—either increasing or inhibiting how often and how easily the neurons fire. (By contrast, NeuroField stimulation is not strong enough to affect polarization.) tDCS is commonly used in medical settings to treat depression, addiction, epilepsy, chronic pain, motor problems, and attentional disorders. In one study, a single session of

Figure 6. The Zendo headset in use.

tDCS was shown to reduce stress levels by 75 percent.[48] To date, no serious adverse effects have been associated with tDCS, so it appears to be a safe, low-risk intervention.[49]

In November 2018, Shinzen Young taught at the world's first ever weeklong public mindfulness meditation retreat using Zendo devices. Shinzen was initially skeptical about their effectiveness but was happy to support his colleagues in the field of neuromodulation for meditation enhancement, Dr. Bashar Badran and Dr. Edward Baron Short, the founders of Zendo E-meditation. And sure enough, the headsets seemed to work! Jay relayed to us that most of the people who used them felt that the Zendo sped up their ability to access deep meditative states and overall had a decidedly positive impact on their retreat experience. Up until spring 2020, Badran and Baron Short had been conducting application-only test sessions with the Zendo headsets. After more than nine hundred such sessions, they hit the market for the public in late 2020.[50]

In an interesting twist, demonstrating just how dynamic and exploratory our understanding of the brain and its functions really is, the mechanism behind tDCS—the way that it actually exerts influence over the brain—has recently been called into question. When a research group led by György Buzsáki at New York University tried to determine exactly what conditions were required to affect neurons and brain circuits with electrical stimulation, they found that at least 75 percent and up to 90 percent of the electric currents were redirected or blocked by the scalp and skull.[51] In other words, less than 25 percent of the electric pulse made its way into the brain. This means that dramatic effects on neurons are very unlikely. Buzsáki says you'd need at least twice the amount of electricity usually used in tDCS to affect the firing of neurons.[52] He isn't alone in his skepticism. Another set of researchers reviewed the results of twenty different studies and found that, overall, there were *no* reliable effects of tDCS related to cognition.[53] The results of such studies don't necessarily mean that tDCS isn't working at all—but it appears that it's not working in the way we think it is. At the very least, we need to accept that the *mechanism* by which it affects the brain remains unknown for now.

A third type of brain stimulation is low-intensity magnetic fields with intricate rhythmic variations. The original research was conducted by Canadian neuroscientist Michael A. Persinger and the technology involved in powering his God helmet is the most infamous of the older forms of brain stimulation within the spirit tech domain. Experts still haven't figured out how such magnetic fields affect the brain, or even if they do. What's more, there's a colorful academic controversy about research in this area, making it a first-rate case study on how we arrive at confident knowledge in the domain of spirit tech. This controversy arose because a Danish team of researchers tried and failed to replicate key results from Persinger's lab. We'll recount the details in Appendix 2.

HACKING THE SPIRITUAL BRAIN

Unlike Persinger's weak magnetic fields, all the other stimulation methods we've looked at here—tFUS, rTMS, tDCS, and pEMF—have been approved for clinical use to treat a variety of conditions. For these technologies to be plausible options for spirit tech within the consciousness-hacking and enlightenment-engineering (a term first introduced by MIT-trained engineer and mysticism researcher Jeff Lieberman) communities, however, they need to accelerate the benefits of meditation quickly and without any negative effects. Without studies of long-term use, this is something we simply can't know yet. Sure, expert meditators can handle electromagnetic and ultrasound stimulation, but what about beginners and nonexperts? What are the short-term effects of being thrust into a deeper meditative state than you've ever imagined? And what are the long-term effects of receiving (and with take-home spirit tech, *self-administering*) brain stimulation continually?

There are potential physical effects related to brain health. There are psychological and mental health risks. There are even some social risks as the technologies have the potential to subvert ancient traditions, either mimicking or legitimately fast-tracking people toward levels of deeply altered states of consciousness that were previously only attainable through years and years of committed practice. We even think it's reasonable to consider the possibility that the function of something like brain stimulation for enhanced meditation could turn into a crutch for the brain—potentially an addictive crutch. But sustained study will resolve these questions and show us how to mitigate any risks of these kinds.

Let's review and take stock. The production of an altered state of consciousness using neuromodulation stimulation continues to be controversial. Shinzen and Jay are certainly hopeful and confidently pursuing their research, but they are insistent that the science of consciousness and consciousness hacking is a long game—there is still so much to learn and so many careful studies to be completed before we can expect a home-use device.

That being said, E-meditation headsets (using electrical stimulation, tDCS) are on the market and spreading rapidly. Although we deeply respect Jay and Shinzen's cautious timeline, it's exciting to imagine what a home-use transcranial focused ultrasound headset might look like. Whether or not we see this soon, we are confident that the research surrounding ultrasound will continue to produce valuable and unprecedented insights for spirit tech development.

What remains unresolved—and it is one of the most important questions in spiritual-experience research—is the extent to which altered-state experiences can be reliably produced in a diverse range of human brains. Many people openly report powerful spiritual experiences using this type of technology. But we fully understand neither the reasons for these special effects nor the characteristics of individuals that render them responsive versus nonresponsive to this type of technology.

Presumably brain-stimulation technologies will gradually be more deeply understood and could eventually become precise, powerful, and predictable. In a later chapter, we will learn about a practitioner at the Brain Wellness Center in Bronxville, New York, who, through years of very careful transcranial magnetic stimulation clinical practice and observation, appears well on his way to understanding these precise parameters. While some states of consciousness may remain immune to any amount of transcranial stimulation, a few might prove to be reliably affected—hopefully without the side effects associated with electroconvulsive therapy for persistent severe depression, and without the controversy surrounding Persinger's work.

For example, we may discover how to use transcranial magnetic stimulation to induce in many people basic emotional states such as fear or happiness, suspicion or trust. This would amount to the brain writing half of the technology needed to realize elementary mind-to-mind communication of emotions without the aid of language, facial reading, or any other sensory meditation. This would be nothing like mind-to-mind transferral of fully formed ideas, but it would be technology-mediated, mind-to-mind communication of emotions. The brain reading half of this technology is detecting those emotions in someone's mind via EEG, which we will discuss in the next chapter.

Stimulating the brain from outside the cranium represents a brave new world of technology, going far beyond the scalp massages and clubs to the head that have defined the state of the art in transcranial influence on brain states for millennia. However we evaluate it, its potential to revolutionize spirituality seems beyond doubt. Shinzen closes *The Science of Enlightenment* with a quote emulating the predictions of H. G. Wells: "It is not *unreasonable* that in contact with *modern* science, and inspired by the spirit of history, the original *discoveries* of Gautama, *rigorized* and *extended*, *will* play a large part in the direction of human destiny."[54]

3

Neurofeedback-Guided Meditation

Each person has a self, and that self often experiences suffering. When people come into my office in crisis, they begin a journey of self-healing through exploration of the self. . . . What is this *self* that is so often the source of so much pain and confusion? Isn't it interesting that psychology and religion both focus on the issue so much?

—*Richard Soutar*

HEIDI MICHELLE'S TRANSFORMATIVE DISCOVERY

I s this okay? Is it going to hurt me? Is it harmful? My brain is healthy— what am I doing?"

These were the thoughts yoga instructor and retreat leader Heidi Michelle expressed to neurotherapists Sarah and James Roy as they prepared her for her first session.[1] Heidi Michelle was about to partake in one of the most explicitly spiritual applications of neurofeedback technology on the market: an intense series of twelve neurofeedback sessions offered by London-based clinic Brainworks through one of their innovative Transformational Retreats. Aimed at "spiritual practitioners who wish to take a step forward in their path,"[2] these intensive, week-long retreats were limited to six people and took place in one of two picturesque locations: the Ariège Pyrenees National Park in Tourné, France, or the Baru rain forest in Costa Rica.[3] Heidi Michelle attended a retreat in Costa Rica, where she already lived and managed a yoga retreat center. Her experience also included three sessions of bodywork or massage, a group shamanic trauma-release ritual, daily yoga and mindfulness training, and three private yoga classes or life-coaching sessions, all structured around, as she put it, "absolutely outlandishly amazing meals."

In the neurotherapy suite she closed her eyes and breathed deeply as James squirted oily, gooey conductive gel onto her scalp, and then positioned nineteen electrodes that would conduct her brain's electrical signals to an electroencephalogram (EEG) machine. Feeding the EEG data into a computer and running it through complex analysis software would produce a map of the electrical activity in her brain, which would identify specific areas of concern to be targeted in her subsequent neurotherapy sessions.

Before we go further into Heidi Michelle's session, however, let us first locate this particular type of brain-based spirit tech within the

Figure 7. One variety of neurofeedback therapy in action. In this case, Jeff Tarrant from the NeuroMeditation Institute (*left*) is watching a screen and supplying feedback to the patient on the basis of quantitative information about brain states, which are measured using just a few electrodes attached to the scalp.

wider field of neurotherapy. In simplest terms, neurofeedback is a form of biofeedback for the brain. While biofeedback measures bodily activity such as heart rate and muscle tension and teaches you how to regulate them, neurofeedback aims to help a person regulate their own brain waves—patterns of electrical activity associated with different mental states and psychological conditions—so as to produce more brain waves of certain desirable frequencies in particular brain locations and fewer brain waves of less desirable types in other locations.

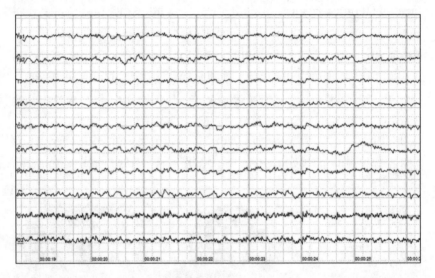

Figure 8. An electroencephalogram readout, graphing electrical activity near the surface of the brain. Each squiggly line corresponds to a single electrode affixed to the scalp; the electrodes affixed to the forehead, measuring executive function, are in the top four rows in the diagram. This EEG is from an average brain, but an expert reader of EEGs could examine those four lines to determine the presence of attentional challenges, such as those associated with ADHD.

Neurofeedback works through the use of an EEG machine, which detects the different voltage changes associated with different brain states in real time through electrodes affixed to the scalp and provides the clinician with a visual display of the brain wave activity, usually in the form of squiggly lines on paper or a computer screen, one line for each electrode.

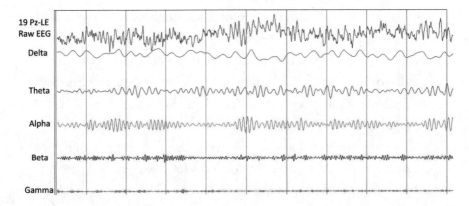

Figure 9. Illustration of brain waves of different frequencies as measured by an electro-encephalogram.

An EEG readout thus gives us a real-time glimpse of the brain's electrical activity in the midst of various mental states, such as confusion, alertness, calm, focus, anxiety, or relaxation. Once we know what those states look like in terms of brain wave patterns, the *feedback* of neurofeedback comes into play. Quantitative analysis software makes sense of the EEG signals and produces visual or auditory positive feedback for the subject—moving images or sounds that the brain finds rewarding—and coaxes the brain to produce more of the desired brain waves and thus to move from an undesirable state to a more desirable state. This brain-training process requires no special effort from the person receiving neurofeedback except to relax, sit quietly, and watch and listen to the feedback—the brain does all the work!

So what exactly is a brain wave and what does it tell us about brain activity? Brain waves are rhythmic patterns in the electrical activity of the brain's neurons. Brain wave frequencies are generally classified into five broad categories, ranging from low to high frequency and quantified by hertz (Hz), which indicate cycles per second, where one cycle is the distance between peaks on an EEG line.

- Delta waves (1 to 4 Hz) are the slowest. They're associated with dreamless sleep, unconsciousness, and unawareness.

- Theta waves (4 to 8 Hz) are also associated with sleep, but these tend to appear while dreaming, or when awake but in a state of deep relaxation or deep meditation. Theta waves can also be associated with depression, anxiety, and distractibility.
- Alpha waves are sometimes divided into low alpha (8 to 10 Hz) and high alpha (10 to 12 Hz). They're indicative of the brain in a resting but alert state, such as when one is in deep thought.
- Beta waves may also be subdivided—low beta (12 to 15 Hz), beta (15 to 20 Hz), and high beta (20 to 30 Hz)—but generally this is the most common type of brain wave that occurs during normal, waking hours. Beta waves appear when we're alert and attentive and focused on a task or problem. High beta waves have been associated with hyperalertness and anxiety.
- Gamma waves (above 30 Hz) are the fastest, and are associated with peak concentration and performance, high levels of cognitive processing, and mental acuity.

Once you have a basic grasp of brain waves, it's easy to see why some wave types are more desirable than others for each activity and goal, and at what times. If you're trying to fall asleep, for example, you wouldn't want to be filled with distracting beta wave activity. On the other hand, if you're a concert pianist about to give a performance, those beta waves are going to come in pretty handy. *Synchrony*—when brain waves are synchronized in one or more areas of the brain—is also a common goal, especially for certain meditative states. In fact, according to Les Fehmi, director of the Princeton Biofeedback Centre and a founding member of the Biofeedback Research Society (now the Association for Applied Psychophysiology and Biofeedback), synchronization of alpha waves between the right, left, anterior (forward), and posterior (rear) areas of the brain is key for meditation since it "reduces stress and allows fluid communication among different regions of the brain, improving mental function effortlessly and naturally."[4]

The electrical activity of the brain is layered and complex, so expert neurofeedback clinicians will attend to lots of different wave features and patterns, including amplitude, frequency, synchrony, and coherence. Brainworks cofounder and neurotherapist James Roy likes to compare brain waves to an orchestra seeking harmony.[5] Each frequency—delta, theta, alpha, beta, and gamma—can be conceptualized as a different instrument potentially in need of tuning as well as volume and timing regulation. Like a symphony, he explains, life is full of moments that encourage or require crescendos, diminuendos, and expressive rhythmic freedom. Neurofeedback tunes the frequencies and revitalizes the brain's natural ability to be flexible, present, and responsive to environmental and cognitive stimuli while maintaining an overall balance and resiliency.

This theoretical background becomes immediately relevant when we take a look at neurofeedback's clinical applications. Neurofeedback training has been used to treat a wide array of diseases and disorders, including anxiety, autism spectrum disorder, depression, epilepsy, insomnia and other sleep disorders, learning disabilities, and memory problems. It has also become popular for use in healthy people seeking to reach higher levels of concentration, athletic ability, artistic creativity, or other forms of peak performance.[6] And in combination with *bio*feedback, which targets things like heart rate and skin conductance (sweat), neurofeedback technology has been used with increasing effectiveness in stress management, lie detection, and pain management,[7] as well as ADHD, anxiety disorders, and depression.

Let's take a look at one of the most well-researched areas of neurofeedback therapy to explain how it actually works. This is the treatment of attention deficit hyperactivity disorder, or ADHD.[8] The majority of children with ADHD who receive brain maps show high levels of theta waves and low levels of beta waves in the front part of the brain, where executive functions are handled. This is a bit like being asleep in those areas—obviously not good for concentration.[9] Ritalin (and other brand-name medications based on the stimulant methylphenidate) works by decreasing theta and increasing beta, effectively waking up the brain—an effect that is easy to see in the EEG data.[10]

One viable nonmedication option for a person with ADHD is to use neurofeedback to create the same effect of waking up the front part of the brain. With a few EEG electrodes placed on the patient's forehead, a neurofeedback clinician can see the frequency of brain waves produced in the front of the brain in real time. For example, if the person closes their eyes and focuses on a thought, the clinician may see a jump in alpha waves; or if the person becomes distracted by a loud, threatening noise, the clinician may observe a spike in beta waves. Once a goal state is determined—in this case the desired non-ADHD wave patterns—the parameters can be entered into the neurofeedback software, which will compare the brain's actual brain states to the target states. The software then produces rewarding sounds, such as soft chimes, or visually rewarding moving and morphing images on a computer screen, such as a blooming flower or perhaps an animation of a basketball player trying to sink shots from a long distance. Through positive feedback, these sounds and images draw the brain toward the desired state—the brain likes to hear certain sounds and wants to see the flower unfurl or the player make the shot. The closer the subject gets to the target brain state, the closer the basketball gets to the net, enticing more and more of those types of waves. By trying to get the basketball through the net, the subject's brain subconsciously learns how to produce the target mental state, and the subject consciously learns the feel of both the target mental state's presence as well as its absence. A therapist can even watch a real-time display of the subject's brain data and provide encouraging vocal feedback.[11] No special effort is required from the subject beyond remaining attentive to the feedback. But the closer the brain gets to the desired state, the more rewarding the feedback becomes.

Experienced EEG practitioners can detect which of the various frequencies is dominant just by reviewing raw EEG readouts. Some neurofeedback clinicians prefer to interpret these squiggles, or EEG traces, directly, but the interpretation process can be more like an art than a science and for clinical use tends to be somewhat subjective and inconsistent.

There's another way, though. Software to analyze this raw information about brain waves quantitatively (that's the *q* in qEEG) is a game changer. Quantitative analysis of the EEG traces shows the strength of every frequency grouping simultaneously for each moment in time (or an average over a period of time) and at each location being measured. No human reader of EEG traces is capable of that, no matter how expert they are, so qEEG has become the standard.

qEEG technology has led us to a high-tech yet coarse form of mind reading, and experts have found ways to make it useful for therapeutic applications. This begins by creating digital representations of the most relevant information about the brain's electrical activity in a clinically powerful visualization: a brain map. Brain maps are a popular form of qEEG analysis, involving a series of images of the brain, one for each frequency cluster, with different colors indicating activity levels. The brain map shows how prominent each main frequency of waves is in the various parts of the brain under the electrodes, offering powerful support for an experienced clinician's interpretation of EEG data.[12] For example, figure 14 (in the color insert) shows a qEEG brain map of a person with ADHD. Figure 15 (in the color insert) shows how a brain map can be used to visualize the effect of a brain intervention—in this case, microdosing psilocybin. Figures 16a and 16b (in the color insert) are from the same study, using brain maps to show the effects of a certain form of breathwork meditation on brain function.

The qEEG analyses can also detect whether brain waves in particular brain regions are synchronized and a variety of other clinically relevant issues. These qEEG brain maps capture characteristic neurological signals for particular mental or behavioral health conditions, which helps clinicians make diagnoses.[13] Ultimately this defines therapeutic treatment goals that target specific mental states in neurotherapy.[14]

qEEG brain maps are the technological basis for a fabulously rich and clinically potent database. With enough qEEG data analyses—along with surveys, neuropsychological tests, and the interpretative findings of clinicians—it is possible to generate typical profiles for different types of people (for example, men versus women, young versus old) and different states of mind (for example, anxiety, distraction, meditation). The qEEG data profiles for anxiety, obsessive thinking, relaxation, sleep, dreaming, various meditation states, and dozens of other states of mind have been identified and appear to be similar across individuals. EEGs suitable for qEEG analysis can be tricky and require expertise to administer properly. But clinicians can perform such an EEG, submit the data for quantitative analysis, and obtain a report that compares their patient's qEEG brain map landscape data with existing qEEG norms, thereby getting a sense for what clinically relevant conditions to expect.

So let's now return to Heidi Michelle. Her initial qEEG brain map revealed that her fight-or-flight response was overactive and her higher thinking and logical functioning areas were underactive. In terms of brain waves, this might be indicated by an overabundance of high beta waves in her right frontal area and posterior lobes and too much slow wave activity in her left frontal lobes.[15] The results "felt right on," she said. "I have extreme trauma in my very early childhood, and at [the time of the retreat], I was going through high pressure and stress in a contracted job. I had some family issues that were affecting my entire family, and I had just ended a very troublesome relationship. So all of these factors, I have to believe, contributed [to the results], which weren't surprising to me. I was actually quite excited to learn this and to learn that there was something I could do about it."

Heidi Michelle speculated that her dedication to a regular yoga and meditation practice had probably kept some of the more severe symptoms of stress and anxiety at bay, at least temporarily. In fact, she actually asked James Roy about the efficacy of simply continuing with her current path.

"'So why am I doing all this?' I said to James. 'Why can't I just do yoga and meditate and transform that way?' He said, 'Well, yes, you can—and it would likely take you about ten years to do the work that we're doing here.'"

And right here is one of the key purported benefits of neurofeedback-guided meditation: it offers a fast track toward wellness. Such shortcuts make some people uneasy. Heidi Michelle was among them: she worried that using neurofeedback would amount to cheating. But in the end, her desire for health and wholeness won out. "As an advocate for peace, and one who just wants people to feel healthy," she said, "I feel that anything that we can do, *anything* that we can do, to increase mental and physical and emotional health—*Yes*. Let's do it."

Heidi Michelle's brain had settled into deeply entrenched patterns to compensate for her hyperactive fight-or-flight system, trauma responses, and mild depression. To help pull her brain out of those ruts, James began her therapy with NeuroField pulsed electromagnetic field stimulation (pEMF) before beginning neurofeedback. This is the slight exception to the no-stimulation, neurofeedback focus of Brainworks's neurotherapy. James described the NeuroField stimulation to Heidi Michelle as a way to interrupt or "break up the conditioned patterns of the neuronal networks."[16] It involves placing an additional cap over the nineteen-electrode EEG cap used for neurofeedback. The second cap stimulates specific brain regions with a very subtle electric field for ten to fifteen minutes. The electric field is twenty million times weaker than medical brain stimulation and supposedly works by disrupting brain waves instead of using strong electrical force on the neurons, but the mechanism is not understood, if indeed there is an effect.[17] By mimicking brain wave activity, the subtle magnetic pulses are supposed to loosen up the brain's preestablished patterns and ruts, allowing "the brain to be more dynamic, and more responsive to neurofeedback."[18] James and Sarah do not use NeuroField stimulation with all clients, but they say it can be helpful for people with certain long-standing or stubborn issues.

Heidi Michelle likened the effects of NeuroField stimulation to being blindfolded and spun around until you lose track of your surroundings, then stopping and trying to find your balance and internal compass again. Of course, with NeuroField stimulation, which Heidi Michelle referred to as "brain scrambling," a person doesn't literally become disoriented or dizzy; she said it's more like a subtle emotional shaking out. Reflecting on her first session, she wrote in her journal: "I had a meltdown today. . . . After the first treatment, the 'volume' turned down in my mind. The places my mind had been going to that were causing me stress weren't an option. With so much space, I just felt so sad, spacey, and tired. Not in my power. Could be from so much travel, my body's hormone changes, a new environment. Why do I feel threatened even when I am perfectly safe?"[19]

Ideally, after the initial NeuroField session, the subsequent neurofeedback treatments assist the brain in navigating the space created by the NeuroField therapy by coaxing the scrambled brain waves into new healthy patterns—helping them find their way again. And luckily, by the time she had finished her second session of neurofeedback, Heidi Michelle felt more alert, lively, grounded, and solid than she had in a long time.

To her relief, the neurofeedback sessions themselves were completely noninvasive and caused no pain or distress. Neurofeedback does not require conscious effort and does not produce any physical sensations. And yet, after each session it was clear to Heidi Michelle that her brain had been exercised, stretched, and encouraged into new modes. "It's intense!" she said. "And it was quite exhausting, really. I would leave the sessions feeling tired. The therapy does not hurt, it's not painful in any way, but your brain is actually being exercised in new ways in order to reprogram, in order to create the patterns that are most beneficial to us to function in a healthy emotional state."[20]

All of the other aspects of the retreat—the yoga, guided meditations, shamanic release ritual, massage, and whole foods meals—are carefully designed to nurture, support, and rejuvenate the participants during the transformational process that begins in the neurotherapy suite. Even though she's had years of both yoga training and retreat facilitation, Heidi Michelle considered the Transformational Retreat, with its focus on brain health and function, as the most well-rounded retreat she had ever been a part of.

"I can't really quantify how much the therapy supported me," she said. "I can say, just from a very personal perspective, I probably wouldn't have made it through that season without the therapy."[21] And the effects were lasting. In the months and years following her neurofeedback sessions, she has experienced an increased clarity, focus, and ability to adopt a balanced and wise perspective on her stressors and emotional challenges. "I have had an incredible growth rate," she said. "I've been able to make some extremely tough life decisions. I've felt more confident. I've felt much more in control of my choices—in control of my life."[22] She notes that when such multidimensional improvements take place, it can be hard to point to direct causes. And yet, she is confident that the neurotherapy played a significant role in her personal and spiritual development.

"What I'm noticing is an ease in my being and a realization that, prior to the retreat, I was depressed," she said. "It's one of those things that you don't see when you're in the middle of it. Kind of like emerging into bright sunshine after being in a thick cloud of fog. I didn't know I was so depleted until my body and mind felt better."[23]

Heidi Michelle had certainly been aware of her heightened stress levels and increasing anxiety, but the neurofeedback seems to have simultaneously revealed and relieved a deeper level of pain and struggle. Her perceptions, moods, and problem-solving ability were polished, balanced, and clarified as a result of what she describes as the adjustment and harmonization of her brain wave patterns.

A SHORTCUT TO ENLIGHTENMENT

While the benefits of neurofeedback for treating disorders like ADHD and achieving greater emotional balance are clear, what relevance does all this have for spirituality? Let's take a closer look at some of the science that's being harnessed to trigger meditative and spiritually meaningful states and to achieve long-term goals of spiritual growth.

It's not an exaggeration to say that we are in the midst of a meditation craze. The salubrious effects of meditation are well documented and represent a laundry list of positive mental and physical health outcomes: lower levels of stress, blood pressure, and anxiety; improved mental acuity, memory, self-awareness, attention, and sleep; faster recovery from illness and injury. Meditation classes, at least of the mindfulness type, can now easily be found in corporate settings, hospitals, fitness centers, libraries, community centers, and, yes, many religious spaces. And, of course, meditation as an explicitly spiritual practice has been an integral part of many religions and belief systems for millennia.

But as anyone who gets past the dabbling stage of meditation will discover, meditation is hard work. Whether one is pursuing it alone or with the aid of an app, a teacher, or a group, it takes years of practice to become proficient at meditation, and even advanced practitioners can struggle with restlessness, a wandering mind, intrusive thoughts, or hindrances as pedestrian as an aching back or boredom. It is not uncommon to feel confusion, disorientation, disillusionment, futility, or a sense of failure due to the fact that the hoped-for states of mind often do not materialize or do not last for long if they do. Meditation teachers would be quick to emphasize that this is all part of the process—and in fact, learning to just sit through these very common experiences and not become disturbed by or overly attached to them is a necessary step in every meditator's evolution. Nevertheless, these are just the types of experiences that discourage novice meditators and cause many to give up. Further, especially in Western, results-driven culture, many people become frustrated because meditation doesn't appear to be accomplishing or producing *anything*, much less a highly desired change or outcome, whether that's equanimity, enlightenment, laser focus, or happiness.

Many who give it a try, thinking some peace and quiet sounds nice, find that doing "nothing" is in fact extremely difficult. "We get misled by the ads in magazines," said Buddhist nun and renowned meditation teacher Pema Chödrön, "where people are looking blissful in their matching outfits, which also match their meditation cushions. We can get to thinking that meditation and the spiritual path is about transcending the difficulties of your life and finding this just-swell place."[24] But, she said, "if meditation was just about feeling good (and I think all of us secretly hope that is what it's about), we would often feel like we must be doing it wrong. . . . A very common experience of the meditator, in a typical day or on a typical retreat, is the experience of boredom, restlessness, a hurting back, pain in the knees—even the mind might be hurting—so many 'not feeling good' experiences."[25] Many people find that sitting alone with their thoughts, lost in the forests of the mind with none of the usual distractions, can be anything from boring to disconcerting to frightening—especially if one is experiencing emotional problems or struggles with mental illness. For an entire host of reasons, then, reaching advanced meditative states is extremely difficult, and the majority of meditators find themselves stuck in the domain of low-level changes of consciousness. Only a few lucky students manage to get very far.

Renowned meditation teacher Shinzen Young, whom we met in the previous chapter, actually describes the brain he was born with as "antimeditative." He admits that, for months, his meditation practice—during which his Zen teacher insisted he sit in the full lotus position—was hugely painful. "But after a few months, I started to notice something interesting toward the end of my sit," he said. "My breath would slow down spontaneously, my body would relax despite the pain, and—miracle of miracles—the voice in my head would stop frantically screaming. It was still there, but more like an undercurrent, a whisper."[26] Shinzen had studied Sanskrit, Pali, and Tibetan, had become fluent in Japanese, and had finished his PhD coursework in Buddhist Studies before ever reaching the first stages of *zammai* (in Japanese) or samadhi (from Sanskrit), which both mean "concentration."

With neurofeedback, however, reaching samadhi doesn't have to be limited to those who are able to devote ten thousand hours to it.

By joining neurofeedback with advancing knowledge of the physiology of meditation, we can use externally generated information about the state of our embodied minds, information that cannot be produced internally, to guide—and, yes, speed up—our meditation practice. Recall James Roy's words to Heidi Michelle: with neurofeedback, she could accomplish in a week what would take ten years on her own. While we're not sure that's literally true, the available evidence suggests he does have a point.

The analytical and diagnostic power of qEEG data can also be used to identify targets for states of mind achieved in meditation, as long as the qEEG profile for the particular meditation state of interest has previously been determined so that clinicians know what to aim for. The current neurofeedback technology has developed to the point that it can lead meditators into the basic entry-level meditative state (samadhi); as meditators move into deeper levels of meditation, they must rely on traditional techniques without the aid of neurofeedback—for now. That being said, even as a front gate to deeper states of meditation, samadhi *is* an altered state, qualitatively different from anything that resembles normal waking consciousness. Entry-level samadhi is an incredible achievement for meditators, usually taking many years of regular practice to reach.[27] "The alpha pattern that emerges during meditation is different from other states we usually pass through," explained Dr. Richard Soutar, one of the leading neurofeedback clinicians in the country today. "Meditation is a special state reflecting an extraordinary balance of activity in the brain."[28] Connecting a person to an EEG setup that produces quantitative analyses on the fly is the key to making this type of technology useful for both neurofeedback in general and neurofeedback-guided meditation specifically.

This effort to utilize neurofeedback as an aid for meditation and spiritual growth began with research on altered states of consciousness reached by spiritual masters such as Buddhist monks, Hindu yogis, and healers who enter trance states.[29] Such research has demonstrated specific patterns of brain activity, or neurological signatures, for a variety of meditative techniques and levels of consciousness, which we'll cover in a moment.[30] In 1979, physicist and Zen master Maxwell Cade identified a unique brain wave distribution that was common among all meditators and healers, with slight variations—he called it "the awakened mind."[31] He used a special EEG device he designed called the Mind Mirror that maps activity in many regions of the brain and generates an immediate spectral display. He found he could predict differences in distributions among successful meditators based on their years of experience and levels of proficiency.[32] The most experienced meditators display brain wave shifts that reflect greater coherence and synchrony in brain function, corresponding to the subjective experience of greater depth and profundity of consciousness.

In 1981, Anna Wise, a student of Cade's who continued his work after his death, operationalized Cade's Mind Mirror for use in therapeutic and meditation settings. Wise was particularly interested in the process of developing and training the awakened mind. She explained, "I worked with both the state and the content of consciousness and how they interrelate, using content to develop and train the brain wave state, and using the state to access and transform content."[33] In other words, Wise targeted the dynamic interplay between a person's conscious thoughts, feelings, and emotions (the content of the mind) and their brain wave patterns (reflecting the state of the mind). With each person hooked up to a Mind Mirror device, Wise led visualization and sensualization exercises in which she asked meditators to imagine and attempt to embody both visual and physiological feelings evoked by her guided meditation. She could then monitor each participant's brain wave pattern and conduct customized guided meditations based on the profiles of the brains in real time.[34]

Wise taught guided meditation and brain wave training in both individual and group settings for three decades all over the world, including California's Esalen Institute in Big Sur. Recalling a workshop he cofacilitated with Wise, Soutar said, "It was really an amazing thing to watch—really innovative and really stunning. I don't know if she ever got the credit she deserved for pioneering that, and I think there's a real future in it."[35] Between 2001 and 2009, just before her death, Wise trained and certified the next generation of Awakened Mind practitioners, who continue to hold similar meditation and brain wave training workshops around the world.[36]

Contemporary neurofeedback takes a slightly different approach from Wise's. She used the Mind Mirror to monitor her participants, and she provided feedback to them only through shifts in her spoken words as she guided the meditators—changing what she said based on the live feedback she saw from the meditators' brains. But the newer technology and equipment provides direct visual feedback to clients on a computer screen. During eyes-open meditation sessions, neurofeedback technology allows practitioners to monitor their own progress toward samadhi while an expert provides additional verbal feedback and guidance based on the more technical information related to brain wave coherence, phase, symmetry, and magnitude visible only on the expert's monitoring screen.

FROM THE CLINIC TO ENLIGHTENMENT

Dr. Richard Soutar founded the New Mind Center for neurofeedback therapy in Roswell, Georgia, as well as the New Mind Academy, which trains clinicians on how to use neurofeedback. His approach unites Western medical and cybernetic technological innovation with ancient Eastern and South Asian philosophy and practice. For more than twenty-five years, he has been at the forefront of advocating for neurofeedback's ability to enhance meditation and spiritual well-being. When we asked about his unique range of expertise, he explained that the philosophy and theory of meditation and spiritual growth has always been an integral aspect of his life's work. In fact, his interest in meditation is what led him to the field of neurofeedback in the first place.

Soutar began meditating and studying the human mind years before ever encountering neurofeedback technology. His meditation practice began after one particularly poignant, slightly disturbing, mostly inspiring experience in his teens: "I was just putting on my shoes one day when they came to me."[37] What had arrived were all the dreams Soutar had ever had during sleep. Suddenly, "in the wink of an eye," they flooded his mind. "I was astounded and confused for months afterward," he said. "I wanted to say to myself, 'This didn't happen,' because if it had actually happened, I would be forced to fundamentally reconsider my very definition of reality. But it did happen, and I can't avoid that experience."[38] At the age of eighteen, Soutar fully devoted himself to exploring not only his own mind but also the notions of transcendence and transformation and the possibility of reducing human suffering. "I stopped reading fiction and anything that was not directly related to the task of understanding the human riddle."[39] He started meditating and immersed himself in wisdom literature from the world's religious traditions. But it wasn't until the early 1970s, when he was in college—"or when I got tired of college, let me put it that way," he said—"that I encountered a book on the psychology of meditation by a psychologist who had begun, for the first time, to look at brain waves and relate them to meditation."[40] This was Soutar's first taste of the potential for a scientific, empirical take on meditation, and he was hooked. "I read that book and I just fell in love with it. I thought, I have to pursue this. I have to do this."[41] He went on to receive a PhD in psychology from Oklahoma State University and hasn't looked back.

Now Soutar is both a respected pioneer in the field of mainstream clinical neurofeedback for treating mental disorders *and* the leading clinician of the movement to harness neurofeedback as a spiritual technology. His New Mind Center is dedicated to clients seeking healing as well as those seeking to learn or enhance their meditation practices (or often both), while his New Mind Academy offers clinicians courses, workshops, and certifications, including the first accredited online training course for neurofeedback. He has also developed a comprehensive system called the New Mind qEEG Analysis and Client Management System that is now used by clinicians all across the United States. It not only provides a customizable interface for patient-doctor interaction, it also does the work of brain map analysis and assessment, offers suggested brain training protocols, monitors sessions, and tracks progress. Soutar travels widely throughout Europe and the United States to give workshops on neurofeedback and on using neurofeedback to learn meditation more quickly and easily, and he has consulted on grants and research projects at Emory University, the University of Central Florida, the University of North Carolina, and the University of Malaysia, as well as for the US military.

Soutar explained to us that many clinicians, in the process of leading people to recovery, find themselves encountering patients who are seeking not only physical and mental health but also spiritual insight and transcendence. Such clinicians often regard this simultaneously as a great honor and an intimidating prospect. This leads to a second problem: most clinicians feel underprepared and underqualified because they haven't been trained in these matters or in how to navigate the different religious perspectives that their diverse clients may present. In fact, he points out, this has always been a challenge for all sorts of psychologists and therapists. Soutar himself has spent his whole life studying spiritual philosophies and the world's religious traditions, so he has developed an ecumenical approach and welcomes the opportunity to engage neurofeedback clients on the spiritual level. But, he said, "not [all clinicians] do extensive meditation, prayer, or retreat. Some of them do—that small group that does love this, they dive into it, and they *are* using it. But it's a very tiny group."[42] However, Soutar is convinced that as the field expands, training, knowledge, and comfort among clinicians about the spiritually transformative potential of this technology will also expand, assuaging some of these concerns.

There may also be some skepticism from traditional expert meditators who fear that the technology is treading on sacred territory in an unsavory fashion. "And I can appreciate why," Soutar said. "[They might wonder] have we got it right, really? Are we misleading people? Are we going to start ranking people with the technology? Will we try to devalue somebody else's belief or method because it doesn't match up with the benchmark?"[43] For these reasons, some expert meditators resist the measurement and quantification of religious experiences.

Nonetheless, many leaders, such as the Dalai Lama, support and encourage this use of technology to enhance practice. Indeed, Soutar likens neurofeedback to ancient spiritual technologies such as prayer wheels, or mantras and yantras, which are tools meant to aid in the meditative journey by directing attention and perception. He also notes the plethora of Tibetan literature detailing the features and process of meditation: "There are thousands of pages written on just where you are and what it looks like—how to deal with space and void, and thought, mood, and morale," he said. "It's a very detailed and almost scientific body of literature on how to achieve the state."[44] In that sense, utilizing EEG data and neurofeedback is a very natural extension of the tradition. Soutar explained, "It seems evident at this point that those of us who live in modern Western culture have difficulty accessing the more ancient methods of transformation and transcendence and that we will need to rely on our technology to do the same job that those older methods once did."[45] He sees no reason that access to transformative states of consciousness should be limited to expert meditators.

Many people use neurofeedback regularly in conjunction with traditional, unassisted meditation and other spiritual practices. This is the story of Dr. Soutar's patient Bill.[46] In 2007, Bill had recently retired from twenty-two years in the army and his life was crumbling around him—his marriage was ending; he was having financial difficulties; and due to childhood epilepsy and a history of rugby-induced concussions, his brain had fallen into unhealthy ruts in an attempt to compensate for unaddressed issues and injuries. On top of this, he was suffering from intensely disruptive post-traumatic stress disorder (PTSD) and dealing with disturbing issues of moral injury. *Moral injury* is the way psychologists refer to the ramifications of violating one's own deeply held moral code, and Bill's experiences in the military had caused overwhelming shame, alienation, and moral disorientation. The grief and often spiritual distress induced when someone violates their own moral conscience and ethical boundaries can severely compound the symptoms of PTSD. In addition, Bill was struggling to navigate the dynamics of his undiagnosed bipolar disorder. All these preconditions and disordered brain function snowballed until the symptoms became unbearable. Frequent night terrors sometimes made it unsafe for his wife to sleep beside him. It was a perfect storm, to say the least, and it had become painfully clear to Bill that his brain, mind, and spirit needed some serious assistance. After having been misdiagnosed with depression years before, he finally received a correct diagnosis of bipolar disorder, and when his psychiatrist mentioned neurofeedback, Bill figured he'd give it a try without quite knowing what to expect. He had nothing to lose.

At the time, Bill was living in Puerto Rico and the only neurofeedback practitioner in the area focused on opioid addiction. So he looked a little further and found Dr. Soutar in Georgia, and knew immediately he wanted to work with him. The Chinese and Japanese philosophy courses Bill had taken in college had had a powerful influence on his life, and he had already developed a consistent meditation practice. So Soutar's philosophical grounding and his approach of integrating the biophysical, humanistic, and spiritual sides of psychology felt like the right fit.

To his great disappointment, Bill didn't feel anything at first. In fact, after six weeks of twice-weekly sessions, he wasn't convinced that the neurofeedback was doing anything. "I'm a man of faith," he said, "but I'm also a profound skeptic, so I require proof at some point in time."[47] But Dr. Soutar encouraged him to be patient and allow his brain to do the hard work of healing and retraining. Bill liked Dr. Soutar's calm and wise approach, and was willing to try just about anything that might bring relief, so he continued coming in twice a week. Sure enough, about two months into his treatments, Bill began to experience a subtle shift.

"Something fell into place that was out of place," he said. "That is the closest way I can describe it. It gave me hope . . . that, in fact, I can heal."[48] Eventually, he was sold completely. Not only did the neurofeedback treatment help address his bipolar and PTSD symptoms, it also enhanced his meditation practice and played an integral role in what he calls his spiritual awakening. "While I was trying to rebuild myself and rebuild my life," Bill said, "I realized that I was not only rebuilding my ethical, moral integrity, which had been shattered . . . I can tell you that my own spirituality began to simultaneously grow deeper and clearer at the same time. Not only have I rewired my ethical integrity, I rewired my mind, my heart, and my gut. As these things have taken place, they have coincided with the deepening of my spirit and . . . the synchronization between my heart and my brain and my gut and the whole rest of my being."[49]

Neurofeedback has continued to be a vital part of Bill's spiritual and self-care regimen; after going twice a week on and off for years, Bill is now down to once a week. He is quick to note, however, that even though neurofeedback remains a cornerstone for his health and spiritual wellness, it is far from a panacea. "You still have to do the work," he said. "Neurofeedback isn't going to soothe the savage beast and undo the trauma, but it's going to prepare your mind for the possibilities of healing to occur."[50] Bill also practices yoga, meditates regularly, and pays close attention to his diet and exercise to maintain balance and wellness. And yet, he said, "in a given week, if I have time for only one healthy practice, and I have to choose among all the different things I do, I'll be damned, I'm going to try to make it to neurofeedback."[51]

TODAY'S MARKET FOR NEUROFEEDBACK-GUIDED MEDITATION

Reviewing the historical development and theoretical basis of brain wave training, it seems that Soutar is part of a long line of spiritually minded neurofeedback researchers and practitioners. Meditative philosophy is already embedded in the field of neurofeedback. "And part of the reason," Soutar said, "is because *I'm* embedding it in our field. But I'm not alone."[52]

At the NeuroMeditation Institute in Eugene, Oregon, Dr. Jeff Tarrant uses technology that Dr. Soutar developed to lead people in meditation practice. The NeuroMeditation Institute invites those interested in spiritual growth to think of regularly incorporating neuromeditation into their lives in the same way they'd think of going to the gym. Both are about health and fitness. And Tarrant has a full staff of personal trainers ready to craft a customized brain workout just for you. He trains people in four different types of meditation—focus, mindfulness, open heart, and quiet mind—each with quite distinctive brain wave patterns, requiring different brain regions to be activated and quieted.[53] So, a visit to the NeuroMeditation Institute would begin with the NeuroMeditation Style Inventory, which can be completed online before ever stepping foot in the studio. This quiz helps identify which style of meditation, and therefore which neurofeedback protocol, is the most appropriate for your specific life goals. You might also be paired with a coach who can walk you through the meditation options and appraise your mental and emotional fitness and your preparedness for undertaking this new practice, possibly suggesting some basic preliminary exercises or treatment protocols before diving into more intense altered states of consciousness and relaxation. After all, these states can present dangers for certain types of vulnerable people, such as those with traumatic brain injury, ADHD, or unipolar depression.[54] Expert instructors are on hand to help you make this vital decision and to customize your NeuroMeditation experience.

Once you and your NeuroMeditation guide have chosen the meditation style that is right for you, you would be situated in a comfortable room where noninvasive equipment is used to produce the relevant neurofeedback signals, either as attractive sounds or images displayed on a screen. Your task would then be, simply, to meditate. The neurofeedback signals function as training wheels, but you still must push the pedals. So you would have to work hard, maintaining the same level of focus and attention that every student of meditation does—after all, this *is* meditation. But you would no longer be guessing about what works, constantly overwhelmed with frustration. At last you would have the tools to make the most of your brain's ability to produce transformative states of consciousness—all thanks to neurofeedback-enhanced meditation technology.

For example, *focused-attention meditation* works toward increasing fast high beta and gamma activity in the frontal lobe by focusing very intensely on one thing—perhaps a mandala or a sacred object—which wakes up and brightens the mind. High beta and gamma waves are fast and indicate careful cortical processing. On the other hand, some people may want to *calm* their overactive cortical processing—when beta waves appear with higher amplitudes, this indicates anxiety. In this case, *open-monitoring mindfulness meditation* might be the way to go. Open-monitoring mindfulness is characterized by nonjudgmental awareness of the present moment. The meditator strives to shift their mind into an accepting role, observing everything from the thoughts in their own mind to the people walking by with calm nonattachment. Open-monitoring mindfulness meditation seeks to increase slow theta waves in the frontal midline area of the brain, which are associated with daydreaming and drowsiness—the exact opposite state from an anxiety response. Next is *automatic self-transcendence meditation*, or *quiet mind meditation*, which has the goal of expanding consciousness and transcending the ego, similar to Zen or Transcendental Meditation. This targets the default mode network in the brain, which is associated with thoughts about yourself and your life, like planning for the future or processing an important conversation. Automatic self-transcendence meditation works to increase slow alpha waves and achieve alpha synchrony throughout multiple areas of the brain. And lastly, *open heart*, or *loving-kindness and compassion meditation*, has the goal of activating, engaging with, and sending positive emotions like love, gratitude, and forgiveness. Open heart meditation tends to shift frontal lobe activation to the left side of the lobe and increase fast gamma waves. This can help facilitate things like cultivating empathy, overcoming anger, or positively processing grief.

The NeuroMeditation Institute maintains a welcoming studio, and in addition to neurofeedback-guided meditation, it offers several other healing spiritual modalities, including NeuroMeditation yoga (four styles of yoga that each affect your nervous system in unique ways that correspond with the four types of meditation), virtual reality Neuro-Meditation (four different story-based experiences in virtual reality settings—"the world's first VR platform fueled by your mind"), and two sound-based options that harness vibrations either from singing bowls and gongs to alter brain wave patterns or through earphones to deliver vibro-acoustic therapy that has been compared to a float tank experience.[55]

Clearly Soutar isn't alone in his commitment to integrating ancient wisdom into clinical practice, and clinicians like Tarrant are fully embracing the market demands of the wellness culture, developing their own systems and meditational offerings. Yet there is still some debate within the field of neurofeedback about how exactly to integrate the science and philosophy. Some of Soutar's peer clinicians are anxious to define the boundaries of the field in ways that suit the perspectives of Western biomedicine and project legitimacy within the medical and therapeutic communities. They may hesitate to incorporate meditation training into their practice for fear of being perceived as too new age or veering too far from the scientific norms of biomedicine. For other clinicians, advertising their businesses in a way that appears to challenge the dominant biomedical model by incorporating spiritual or philosophical language and theory may be counterproductive or even self-sabotaging. These clinicians want to make their practices appear as approachable, comfortable, and trustworthy to the average Westerner as possible. Soutar is fully aware of the skepticism with which his efforts to integrate biomedicine and South Asian philosophy are often met: "A mysterious waste of time to the technical people in the field," he said.[56] Nonetheless, he maintains a lighthearted and good-natured approach to the divergent, and sometimes competing, interests, motivations, and priorities of neurofeedback researchers and clinicians. "It's still the Wild West with this new developing technology," he said. "The concept of cybernetic interface is still in its infancy."[57]

Given these various levels of resistance from both the technical side of neurofeedback and the spiritual, meditative side, how plausible is a productive future for neurofeedback-guided meditation?

THE FUTURE OF NEUROFEEDBACK-GUIDED MEDITATION

Dr. Soutar clearly has high hopes for the spiritual and transformational potential of neurofeedback-guided meditation. But he also remains realistic about both the limits of the technology and the profound challenge of achieving even the entry-level meditative state, whether assisted by technology or not. "It's not a magic bullet," he said. "People who are really interested in a sustained long-term effort to achieve something that's unique and of deep value [constitute only] a small percentage of the population—most of the planet is looking for excitement."[58] Meditation and spiritual transformation are life-long journeys with levels of success that ebb and flow over time for any practitioner. "It is clearly not the type of achievement that one attains with a few meditation lessons, a short workshop, or even a few years of dabbling," he observed.[59] Meditation is, plain and simple, hard work. Neurofeedback can help, and it does speed up the learning process, but it is far from a quick-fix solution.

Let's take stock. What do we know about neurofeedback-guided meditation right now?

First, neurofeedback-guided meditation shortens the meditation learning curve. It also transforms meditation learning by introducing the possibility of clear-cut, goal-directed behavior to help tame the unruly meditating mind.[60]

Second, neurofeedback-guided meditation produces what seems to be the same quality of experience as traditional meditation. This conclusion is based on subjective reports about states of mind as well as objective measurements of brain states of both experts and beginners, all in the context of a specific type of meditation practice. This is controversial, of course, because some people refuse to accept that technology can produce authentic meditation states.[61] But the claim of similarity is less problematic when we notice that both neurofeedback-guided meditation and traditional meditation require great effort. Meditation is going on in both cases, and the technology assists merely by defining goals and furnishing a method for achieving them more efficiently.

Third, neurofeedback-guided meditation mitigates a series of challenges that meditators, especially beginners, face. The dirty secret of many meditators is that they often focus on the enjoyable parts of their meditation practice in discussions with others, politely shrouding their disappointment. The complexity and frustration of meditation practice is just as real as the positive aspects, but it tends to come out only in discussions with trusted companions on a shared spiritual path. Neurofeedback can't make someone *want* to meditate, but it can help someone who wants to meditate learn to do so with less frustration, producing faster results and achieving concrete goals by deploying the human capacity to focus attention.[62] Just like James told Heidi Michelle, she *could* achieve her goals of mental strength and peace of mind through a traditional practice of meditation and yoga, but it would likely take her years to do the same amount of work that she could achieve far more quickly through a neurofeedback practice.

Fourth, the personal benefits of any sustained meditation practice seem to kick in regardless of whether neurofeedback or traditional meditation techniques are employed.[63] For instance, numerous studies have shown that beginners in mindfulness meditation can expect increased impulse control, self-acceptance, relaxation, ability to focus attention, self-awareness, and spiritual awe.[64] Beginners in neurofeedback-guided meditation who choose goals appropriate to mindfulness meditation can expect the same effects (though presumably more quickly). Other, harder-to-achieve effects—increasing pain control, being present in the moment, sustaining positive emotion, overcoming addiction, heightening empathy, and attaining profound spiritual insight,[65] for example—will take longer for *both* types of meditation (though, again, presumably not as long for neurofeedback-guided meditation). There is no magic bullet here: neurofeedback-guided meditation adds goal-orientation and guidance to meditation, but meditation is still required, and the changes that occur are a result of the meditation, not the technology alone.

Fifth, neurofeedback-guided meditation produces potent spiritual experiences that yield a rich sense of spiritual orientation in people who are practicing it with that intention.[66] That is, it enhances spiritual growth by opening up the deep realms of meaning in ordinary life, which in turn changes our relationships to ourselves, to the people around us, to the wider environment, to all other beings, and to ultimate reality itself, however we conceive of that strangest of concepts. This is what traditional meditation practices do also, of course. It's just that neurofeedback-guided meditation speeds it up. That makes neurofeedback-guided meditation of great importance to anyone interested in enhancing and deepening human spirituality.

Sixth, neurofeedback-guided meditation currently functions at a basic level. Neuroimaging data and qEEG brain maps for several types of meditation states already exist and the research is growing.[67] But there are many less common types of meditation and most of them have not yet been studied. Moreover, we don't yet know much about how meditation states might vary in the way they manifest in the brain from individual to individual. Some traditional meditation practitioners report mental pathways to desired states of consciousness, which are something like trail markers that hikers expect to encounter along the way to a desired end point. In fact, there is probably more than one pathway for any given state. So far, neurofeedback-guided meditation has focused on getting people to the front gate, or entry-level meditation state, which remains an individually customized process led by the clinician. The qEEG characteristics of the more complex and advanced states of meditation have not yet been explored. There is no reason neurofeedback-guided meditation can't get to that point, but so far it has not happened.

Seventh, the dangers of neurofeedback in general and of neurofeedback-guided meditation in particular appear to be minimal. The person using this technology is meditating, after all; the EEG is merely recording what the brain does, and the stimulation is entirely noninvasive. That said, neurofeedback can be a powerful tool and practitioners would do well to receive guidance from a trained professional. The potential risks associated with neurofeedback—for example if a protocol isn't right for a person—could exacerbate symptoms or lead the brain into an anxious or hyperaroused state. But those risks seem small and manageable. The more dangerous risks, therefore, are about the same as for meditation itself. There are real dangers associated with some types of meditation, particularly for people with psychiatric vulnerabilities, and it is reasonable to expect that those dangers would apply to neurofeedback-guided meditation as well.

Eighth, these summary claims about neurofeedback-guided meditation require further study. It may well turn out, upon close examination, that the qualities of neurofeedback-guided meditation states differ from the qualities of traditional meditation states in significant and detectable ways. Similarly, neurofeedback-guided meditation may turn out to be better for managing impulse control but not as effective as traditional meditation techniques for producing spiritual insight, or perhaps some other differences might emerge. Only further research can settle such fine-grained questions. For now, though, we can say that neurofeedback-guided meditation delivers what it promises, subject both to the limitations of extant technology and to knowledge about target goal states for meditation practice.

We predict that defenders of traditional meditation and prayer practices will have their hands full arguing against the validity or advisability of this kind of spirit tech. For most people, the proof lies in the experience: Does it produce the promised effects of meditation or not? If tech-assisted meditation does produce the desired experiential, behavioral, and spiritual consequences, then why should it matter whether technology helped people get there?

Eventually even the most ardent protesters against neurofeedback-guided meditation will likely calm down and focus their concern in other directions, such as making sure a healthy social context, wise counsel, and reliable sources of wisdom are available to help people make sense of their neurofeedback-guided meditation experiences.

At present, organizations such as the Brainworks Transformational Retreats, the NewMind Neurofeedback Center in Roswell, Georgia, and the NeuroMeditation Institute in Eugene, Oregon, are among only a few clinics in the English-speaking world offering meditational services. However, we believe they are certain to increase in presence and popularity within the next few years as the word spreads and as technology stabilizes enough to make it easier to implement in a reliable, affordable way. We also have every reason to think that the technology will rapidly improve in sophistication in the near future. EEG equipment has already become more precise, and quantitative interpretation of EEG time-series data has become faster and cheaper. But it is important to grasp that *people are already using this technology every day.* The NewMind Neurofeedback Center and the NeuroMeditation Institute both hold workshops for clinicians and teach people how to do neurofeedback-guided meditation using their equipment.[68]

Furthermore, there is an emerging market of affordable wearable devices. The Muse brain-sensing headband—a new neurofeedback headset designed to improve meditation practice—is one of the most popular at-home forms of spirit tech. It has seven EEG sensors on a band that runs across the forehead, an accelerometer to track body movement, a gyroscope to track breathing, and an oximeter to track heart rate; it pairs wirelessly with a smartphone app that provides guided meditations, feedback soundscapes, and tracks your goals and progress. It is significantly

Figure 10. The Muse 2 and associated smart-phone app in action. Seven EEG electrodes are built into the device: two rest on the forehead, two sit over the ears, and three are reference sensors.

less sophisticated and customizable than working with a clinician, but at about $250, it is affordable and seems to work well. Muse cofounder and CEO Ariel Garten is also a fashion designer, psychotherapist, and entrepreneur; she is one of the most vibrant and in-demand speakers and influencers within the transformative technology community. The bold phrase "Meditation Made Easy" is one of Muse's taglines.

In short, as the scientific understanding of the nature, function, and mechanisms of meditative states expands, so, too, is neurofeedback-guided meditation sure to expand. We will likely see this technology taken up by both new age and Silicon Valley spiritual entrepreneurs and as a natural outgrowth of already established neurofeedback clinics currently focused primarily on treating disorders such as ADHD. This is the hope of dedicated proponents such as Dr. Soutar, who believe that it "has the potential to transform the social order in a manner that we have only dreamed of in the past."[69]

We'll have to wait and see about a transformation of the social order. What seems apparent right now is that neurofeedback-assisted transformation of individuals and families is well within reach, and is in fact already happening. Protesting these developments can be likened to a refusal to fly across oceans in airplanes in favor of the traditional method of sailing. It is meditation either way; one just produces results faster than the other and for a wider range of people.

4

Engineering Togetherness

There is so much of me in all of you. You are a way for me
to know myself.

—*Kamand Kojouri, Iranian poet*

In 1902, psychologist William James famously said that religion is
about "the feelings, acts, and experiences of individual men in their
solitude."[1] And, sure, religious people do often pray and meditate in
private. But what about the communal worship experiences that take
place at temples, tribal meetings, retreats, drum circles, and cathe-
drals? Don't these places tell us something important about religion,
too? What about singing, kneeling, bowing, dancing, spinning, or other
forms of moving in precise ritual synchronization with other people? It
would seem that James missed something.

So far we've focused primarily on the ways that *individuals* use technology for spiritual practices and experiences, but many of the most
important aspects of spirituality take shape in social spaces. Relationships, community, and bonding within and through spiritual practice
are central not only to religious institutions but also to individual spiritual well-being. Many people are discovering that the modern promise
of strength through individuality, autonomy, and going it alone turns
out to have its limits. Most of us need and sometimes even crave the
company of other people. We know the empowerment and joy that

accompanies being surrounded by our best friends, and we've experienced the contagious nature of a loved one's laugh.

In the spring of 2020, the SARS-CoV-2 pandemic sent people all around the world into social distance and quarantine. Technology came to the rescue with electronically mediated togetherness, though everything still felt a bit weird, and the mental health toll is daunting. It is a reminder of how much we want and need to connect with others. And that's the driving motivation behind another whole aisle in the scattered supermarket of special spiritual services.

CONNECTION AND SPIRITUAL WELLNESS

"My basic understanding," said Mikey Siegel, an MIT-trained roboticist who coined the term *consciousness hacking*, founded an international community by the same name, and now regularly teaches courses at Stanford University about technology and wellness, "is that not only do we as humans have a *capacity* for a really deep, vulnerable, open, honest connection, but it is actually a basic human need. With a lack of quality connection in our lives, we're lonely—we're literally dying of loneliness."[2] However, loneliness is not simply reflective of social isolation.[3] Many people find themselves constantly around others, yet they still crave spiritually meaningful and authentic connections and relationships. Fulfilling relationships, and a fulfilling life, include having space to express the deepest parts of oneself and to explore the deepest mysteries of the universe. For Siegel, a successful career in robotics engineering, which earned him prestige, financial stability, and ample intellectual stimulation, still left him with a subtle sense of emptiness and dissatisfaction. For his own well-being, he turned toward studying and exploring consciousness, and soon enough he decided to devote his entire career to innovating technologies for facilitating spiritual depth and growth. This was a way to honor not only the deepest parts of himself but also to draw out and encourage others' spiritual journeys.

After years of working, teaching, and advocating for the types of spirit tech we've looked at so far—life-changing techniques for hacking consciousness and engineering enlightenment on the individual level—Siegel felt the need to shift his attention toward enhancing connection, community, and mutual spiritual growth. Solitary pursuits and adventures into one's own consciousness are valuable and important, but he is now committed to developing technology that would facilitate *group* consciousness, *communal* spiritual connection, and interpersonal intimacy. He wants tech that is "a permissioning tool that gives people an excuse or a pathway to open up more and become less defended, so that they can be more real and more vulnerable with themselves and with one another," he said.[4] Siegel now regularly hosts ritualized spiritual gatherings that involve the use of electrodes, wires, flashing lights, and electronic sounds—all with the goal of enhancing deeply honest, transformative, life-giving spiritual connection among participants.

But before we get into Siegel's revolutionary technology, let's explore the fundamental human capacity he's working with: What really happens when humans come together in groups? And more specifically, what happens when groups of people invoke religious and spiritual ideas or engage in religious or spiritual acts, such as singing, chanting, worshipping at shrines, dancing, or corporate prayer?

Over a hundred years ago, sociologist Émile Durkheim declared that what was *really* happening during communal religious rituals was the production of what he called *collective effervescence*, the feeling of shared energy, excitement, and emotion among group members. This is such a powerful experience, he argued, that ritual participants believed it *must* come from God—only God's presence could be so powerful and so unifying.[5] For the past century, Durkheim's theory of religion has been tremendously influential. Even those who refuse to reduce God to a mere natural sociological force, insisting instead on supernatural powers, cannot deny the incredibly compelling experience of participating in a crowd of people with a common goal or focus. If you've ever been swept up in the energy of a concert, a club, a political rally, a sporting event, a self-improvement workshop, or even a religious ritual or gathering, you have some notion of collective effervescence.

Something is happening when human bodies are together. Can modern technology measure, enhance, stimulate, or simulate this potent feeling? Scientists are slowly but surely beginning to take seriously the profound physiological and psychological effects that bodies can have on each other. After reviewing the literature on synchronized body movement in infants, pairs, and groups, Rollin McCraty, a researcher at the HeartMath Institute in Boulder Creek, California, explained that "feelings of cooperation, trust, compassion and increased prosocial behaviors depend largely on the establishment of a spontaneous synchronization of various physiological rhythms between individuals."[6] In other words, our bodies have a remarkable biological ability to sense other people's bodies and to respond with a subconscious effort to synchronize heart rate and breathing rhythms. This ability seems to be at least part of what makes us able to empathize, trust, cooperate, and form healthy attachments with others.

If this is the case for people who are simply *near* each other, you can imagine how effective military marching drills are for establishing a tightly bonded, loyal, and cohesive army. Or how effective synchronized swaying and clapping are for entraining emotions and establishing a committed, faithful, and trusting congregation—the *ummah*, or "community," for Muslims; the body of Christ for Christians; the sangha for Mahayana Buddhists.

Scientific efforts to get to the bottom of this amazing human capacity for connection and cohesion have focused both on large-group interactions and one-on-one contacts. For example, psychologists at the University of California found that if two people who are in an intimate relationship sit next to each other, even without any physical contact, their heart rates sync.[7] But it turns out you don't even have to be in a relationship to achieve this deep synchrony. In 2017, a team of researchers from University College London found that the heartbeats of audience members at live theater performances begin to synchronize throughout the show, regardless of whether or not the audience members know each other. Interestingly, during the intermission the synchrony of the entire group broke temporarily, but pairs and small groups of people who spent the intermission chatting about the show maintained synchrony among themselves. "This clearly demonstrates that the physiological synchrony observed during the performance was strong enough to overcome social group differences and engage the audience as a whole," said Dr. Joe Devlin, one of the lead researchers.[8]

When he first read about the research on physiological synchrony, Mikey Siegel felt he had stumbled across something fundamental to the human experience, something that was missing from his own life: deep, communal human connection. He wondered: Could spirit tech bring an entire group of people into a synchronized physiological and emotional state?

His first attempt to do so was with an invention called HeartSync, a feedback system that connects six people (see figure 17 in the color insert).[9] Participants sit in a half circle around what's called the Heart-Sync box, an electronic box about the size of a brick with a wood veneer. Six wires with sensors extend from the box, and everyone clips one sensor to an earlobe and faces a large computer screen that displays a visual representation of each person's heart rate in a different color. The colors pulse and overlap, creating a soothing image that constantly morphs in real time. The system also produces calming synthesized meditative sounds, the intensity and volume of which rise and fall to reflect the data picked up by the sensors—and, in a key mechanism that encourages group connection, the sounds become more "rewarding" as the group approaches synchronization. Lastly, the screen gives visual cues directing the group when to inhale and when to exhale, bringing the participants' breathing into a steady rhythm. Eventually, sparkling white dots appear in the middle of the collective heart rate image to indicate successful synchronization.[10] "So if you want to think of it as a game," Siegel said, "it's a game where the only way to win is for the entire group to completely surrender."[11]

Siegel's vision for ritualized flow and synchronization is constantly expanding. HeartSync has now evolved into what he calls GroupFlow (see figure 18 in the color insert). GroupFlow is a customizable setup that allows for larger groups of participants and several different procedures of ritual engagement. After working within the field of spirit tech in various capacities for many years, Siegel has now almost completely devoted himself to the mission of fostering real and authentic human connection through GroupFlow rituals.

"There's no other technology in the transformative technology space that I feel as connected to or as excited about as GroupFlow," he said. "No other technology that I know of is focused on supporting an unconditionally accepting and loving, present-moment, embodied experience of ourselves and of the other, interpersonally."[12] In other words, technologies that stimulate your brain with electrical currents or ultrasound, or that use neurofeedback to help you dive into deeply altered states of consciousness, are incredibly helpful and transformative for your *individual* quality of life and engagement with reality, but they do not address the spiritual hunger for authentic human connection. That's exactly where GroupFlow comes in.

We spoke with Mark and Lynne, a couple from Florida who had flown all the way to the Esalen Institute in Big Sur, California, to participate in a weekend of enlightenment-engineering workshops featuring GroupFlow rituals.[13] Lynne, a hypnotherapist and regular meditator, was curious to see how the workshop would marry contemplative practice and technology—perhaps even in ways that she could incorporate into her hypnotherapy practice. Mark, a shoulder and elbow surgeon, was interested in exploring new ways of fostering connection and meaning because he is keenly aware of the problem of professional burnout within the medical community and those in caring fields and is hopeful that finding more healthy ways of engaging with technology can help. They arrived with excitement at Esalen, a nonprofit retreat center that emerged with the Human Potential Movement in the early 1960s as the symbolic headquarters of countercultural transformation; it is sometimes called the "Cape Canaveral of inner space."[14] It's the perfect place to experiment with new spiritual modes, methods, and technologies. Ironically, Esalen is the type of space that encourages attendees to *unplug* from electronics and devices, whereas GroupFlow has people plug *in*, albeit in a new way.

Lynne and Mark were unsure of what to expect, but they were pleasantly surprised by the GroupFlow setup. The ritual was to take place inside a large yurt on the Esalen campus, but before they could enter, Siegel had participants line up, cultivate a contemplative silence, and receive a cleansing sage smudging from one of the workshop facilitators. Within the yurt, Mark and Lynne found meditation pillows positioned around a beach ball–sized, softly glowing sphere made of LED lights. Wires ran out from the sphere to smaller orbs in mason jars placed in front of each meditation pillow. Siegel acknowledged that the presence of so many wires and electronic devices can conjure anxiety, distraction, and alienation. But, he said, "this is technology with a very different kind of intention and a very different kind of design, a technology that we're going to treat differently in the hopes that it treats us differently. And in the hopes that we get something very different from it."[15] To that end, he takes special care to create a ritual space and cultivate a reflective and contemplative mood among the participants. "Every part of it is treated as a sacred ritual," he said. "It's a way of shifting people's expectations. It's a way of opening the mind in a certain direction. It's a way of making the mind and body comfortable and receptive to real connection."[16]

After removing their shoes, Lynne and Mark and the rest of the group settled onto their meditation pillows. A teacher led them in a guided meditation to set an intention of openness and connection. While participants maintained a reverent silence, group facilitators carefully made their way around the room to initiate each person into the ritual space. The *initiation*—a term chosen intentionally to evoke the sense of sacred ritual—involves methodically sticking ECG (electrocardiography) electrodes on each participant's torso to measure the electrical activity of their heart. Robin Arnott, a long-time friend and colleague of Siegel's who develops forms of spirit tech using virtual reality (we'll meet him in the next chapter), took on the priestly role of anointing the participants with the ECG electrodes during Mark and Lynne's session.[17] Each person's mason jar orb then flashed in time with their heart. Lynne was genuinely moved by having her heartbeat visually displayed by the little mason jar orb, which she could hold. "Actually seeing my heartbeat was really profound," she said. "It felt like I was literally holding my heart in my hands."

Participants wear high-quality headphones during the GroupFlow ritual, which allows them to hear their own heartbeats as they watch the colored orb pulse. They can also trade orbs with a partner and listen to someone else's heartbeat. That's one of the exercises Mark and Lynne experienced.[18]

The goal for this type of ritual, Siegel explained, is radical acceptance and love of oneself and the other. To get there, Siegel directs the participants in a slow and sacred process that recognizes the humanness of the other and encourages partners to meditate on the possible heartaches, joys, and love that their partner's heart has been through. The way participants are directed to interact with their orb encourages a sense of reverence and connection. "There's a whole ritual in how we pick up our heart lights," Siegel said. "We go through a guided process of imbuing this object with a deep sense of sacredness and meaning. So when we finally get to picking it up, you see people delicately cradling it as if they're holding their own heart. Yes of course, it's just a glass jar, but ceremony and intention make it so much more, which in turn supports a deeper experience."[19]

For Siegel, one of the best parts of the GroupFlow technology and setup is its flexibility and its openness to experimentation and creativity. He described another ceremony format in which two people are sitting face-to-face and gazing at each other in silence. Initially, the mason jars orb lights sit between them, but turned off. Only when one person picks up their "heart" does the light turn on, and then the partner can hear that person's heartbeat through their headphones. "And then you hand them your heart," Siegel said. "They listen to it as long as they want, they hold it, they look at you, and people cry often. It's a very special thing. When they're done, they hand the person's heart back, and they can go back and forth as many times as they want."[20]

Other GroupFlow rituals are designed to focus more on creating synchronization and unity among the group—usually by syncing breath rates—rather than intimate connection with a partner. Usually, intentional respiratory synchronization involves some sort of leader or metronome to guide the participants' pace of inhalations and exhalations—or when technology is involved, the most common intervention seems to be a feedback mechanism that indicates when you are in or out of sync. But Siegel's GroupFlow technology introduces novel ways to achieve synchrony. Rather than telling the group how and when to breathe, he explained, he wants to facilitate and enhance the synchrony that emerges *organically* from a focused gathering of people. "So I asked, how do you design a system that supports an emergent synchrony of breathing without any external idea of what that breath rhythm should be?"[21]

To facilitate this unbiased and nonjudgmental feedback toward synchrony, Siegel uses the large sphere consisting of three hundred LED lights sitting in the middle of the circle of participants. The sphere represents the *average* of breathing rates in the room. If there were only one person connected to the sphere, the glowing sphere would become brighter and brighter as the person inhaled, and then dim to darkness as the person fully exhaled. With twenty-four people wired into the system, the random distribution of breaths means that the sphere will fluctuate around an undulating medium brightness. If everyone inhaled at exactly the same time, the sphere would be at maximum brightness; and if everyone exhaled at exactly the same time, the sphere would be totally dark. Participants gaze at the sphere like a crystal ball, a visual representation of the group's collective experience, and allow themselves to tune into that collectivity.

"In the beginning there's nothing really to follow," Siegel said, since the sphere maintains a fairly steady average glow. But as people watch the sphere, they begin to pick up on any slight changes and they begin to breathe with it. "When ten people do that, it amplifies it," Siegel said. "And when that gets amplified, that means another five people will begin to notice, and pretty soon the whole group catches this breath wave."[22]

Wordlessly, the group collectively decides how long each breath is, how deep that breath is, when that breath starts and finishes. Even though there's no facilitator guiding the inhalations and exhalations, the group naturally finds synchrony. The glowing sphere does provide feedback, but it is anonymous and subtle—no individual data is represented.

For many participants, the experience of natural group synchrony leads to spiritual experience—or is a spiritual experience in and of itself. "For me," said one GroupFlow participant, "connecting with everyone gave me a perspective of the power of connection and the unity of humanity. Of just *all* of our beings . . . I often feel isolated from everyone, and then connecting to the sound . . . and just how powerful that sound is . . . and then imagining the sound of all the heartbeats of all humans in the world, of all beings, it just gives me chills to realize the power we possess when we are one. Such a profound and beautiful experience."[23] GroupFlow demonstrates the profundity of even very simple interactions when framed by and focused on spiritual connection.

Siegel stresses that the power of the GroupFlow experience isn't limited to the fact that everyone is meditating on their heartbeat or breath rate at the same time in the same space. Rather, the intention of the session is to appreciate the sanctity of each person in the room and the effervescence that is created when they are united. Another GroupFlow participant said, "I found that getting to hear the actual heartbeats of us all together . . . was a tremendous sound. I didn't realize how incredible it would be. It just sounded so thunderous! And it felt like there were beat frequencies that were happening as they were overlaying. It would have been really interesting if we could just experience that for an hour, just that. Just meditate for an hour and listen to how the beats change over time—that would be really powerful."[24]

At one point, Siegel invited participants to share their own creative ideas for using the GroupFlow technology. Another participant encouraged Lynne to experiment with group hypnosis. "So I led the whole group," Lynne told us, "through a hypnosis where they're tuned into their own heart. And then once they feel that they're in a flow state, I had them repeat the phrase 'I am becoming one now' over and over like a mantra." Then, she said, "the tech guy who was watching and in charge of all the technology said, 'Wow, I don't know if this is confirmation bias but it appeared on the monitor that everybody's heart rate actually did start to sync up!' So that was pretty cool."

One of the most compelling moments during Mark and Lynne's weekend workshop was another experimental exercise led by a participant named Mike. "I'm going to do something different," Mike said. "I'm going to try to agitate you."[25] He invited his fellow participants to imagine that they were driving to an important meeting. Traffic looks clear at first, but all of a sudden brake lights come into view and you're forced to slow down. At this point the sound and light technician turned some of the heartbeat orbs red, symbolizing brake lights. Then Mike raised the stakes: "Soon it becomes clear that you're going to be late to your meeting, and you start to panic." Lynne and Mark found that their heart rates began to rise, and it seemed as though the whole room was becoming somewhat agitated, all too easily able to imagine the frustration of terrible traffic at just the wrong time. "Now," Mike said, "imagine that each of the red brake lights in front of you [is] someone's beating heart. Instead of being car brakes, they're people, fellow humans, and they're right there with you. And you don't need to be anywhere, anywhere except where you are right now."[26] Immediately the energy in the room shifted. Anger was replaced by compassion and connection. Lynne and Mark were both deeply moved and struck by the profound shift caused by such a small shift in perception. They've found themselves pondering that exercise many times after leaving Esalen.

GroupFlow "can really be a profound experience for people," Siegel said. "I've had people who were in suicidal depression who say they've come out of it from this experience—by connecting with their own heart."[27] While hearing their heartbeat may not be an unusual experience for many people—doctors hear heartbeats all the time, and athletes check their pulses frequently to assess performance—it's the spiritual and ritual setting of GroupFlow that imbues these biological facts with spiritual meaning. "I can frame the sound [of my heart] in a new and meaningful way," one participant said. "In such a way that something mundane is suddenly remembered as being extraordinary. I had heard my own heartbeat before, but as soon as I heard [it at GroupFlow], I burst into tears. I had this sense of connection."[28]

Gratitude for the consistency, perseverance, and profound existence of one's own heart and body often floods participants with an unexpected intensity. Others describe the experience of holding another person's heart—whether that person is their intimate partner or a complete stranger—as deeply moving and spiritual. Some people find the vulnerable moment of handing over their own heart to the other person to be the most profound part of the experience. One woman explained: "I didn't really 'get' my own heart—I had trouble connecting with it. But then when my partner was seeing me and hearing my heart, somehow having that witness really helped me connect with it more."[29] This participant was partnered with her husband, which certainly contributed to their connection, but even strangers find that sharing their heartbeats in this way can foster a deep sense of connection.

Mark was especially taken by the experience of connecting on a personal and physical level with others, with none of the all-too-familiar hierarchical mediators of social class, wealth, or perceived authority in place: participants are not given any personal or professional details about anyone else in the room. Mark reflected that in everyday life, people have become so accustomed to introducing themselves by saying who they are and what they do professionally, as if the two are one and the same. Instead, in GroupFlow, participants encountered each other as fellow humans with beating hearts, and each individual was invited to connect first with *themselves* on a grounding level as a human with a beating heart, capable of authentic, deep, and raw connection. This cuts through the static and reacquaints people with their own vitality—spiritually, physically, and communally—that then enables far deeper and more potent connection with the group.

HIGH-TECH TELEPATHY

Let's imagine for a minute what could potentially be in store for the type of spirit tech customized for groups. If HeartSync and GroupFlow can facilitate breathing and heart rate synchronization and thereby deep human connection, it doesn't seem too far-fetched to imagine syncing brain waves, enhancing emotional entrainment, and amplifying the intensity of collective effervescence in a worship or sacred ritual setting.

An energetic crowd is incredibly powerful. There are terrifying expressions of crowd energy such as the Nuremberg Rally or the Salem witch trials. There are also beautiful and transformative expressions such as the 1963 March on Washington for Jobs and Freedom where Martin Luther King Jr. delivered his "I Have a Dream" speech or the original 1986 Burning Man. Either way, crowd energy is so powerful that it can easily devolve into chaos if it isn't harnessed. We hear of mysterious and foreboding notions such as *herd morality, mob mentality*, or the *bystander effect*. Social psychologists speak of *deindividuation* to describe the loss of self-awareness when someone is absorbed into a crowd. Drumming up and orchestrating meaningful experiences of collective emotion is a mysterious process, even though we see it everywhere we look— religious revivals, sports events, concerts, dances. We use phrases such as *leader charisma, entrainment, infectious, contagious,* and the X *factor* to describe the experience of feeling crowd energy shift from diffuse and scattered toward a shared focus and synchronized emotional tone. Sometimes events fall flat. Other times, the energy of a crowd catches us off guard. We know there are ways for us to enhance, moderate, and manage this process. But plenty of films portray technological manipulation of this capacity as a dystopic nightmare. And plenty of religious traditions have sought to suppress this capacity, fearful of the social consequences of unleashing such energy. Is this human bodily capacity even desirable?

We think that, like technology itself, communal fervor, excitement, and collective effervescence is neither totally good nor inherently terrifying; it is a core part of the human species, something that has contributed to our greatest successes and yet may also be our greatest vulnerability. It is a power to be recognized, understood, and harnessed wisely. So, with these two core human capacities—technological innovation and collective energy—let's explore future possibilities. We're seeing the emergence of brain-based technologies aiming to forge new forms of communication between human beings. Brain-to-brain communication of thoughts and feelings has been the stuff of science fiction for generations. In our time, it sometimes feels as though the only real privacy left is in our thoughts. However, most people don't realize that modern technology has brought us quite close to realizing the sci-fi dream of telepathy, in a limited way.

Telepathy technology depends on the advancement of two fronts: mind *reading* and mind *writing*. We need to be able to take information from one mind (mind reading) and put it into another person's mind (mind writing). In mind reading, the goal is to figure out how and what can be easily picked up from source brains—thoughts? emotions? images?—using scanning and analysis technologies such as quantitative electroencephalography (qEEG) mapping, which records and reports a person's brain wave activity. In mind writing, we need to figure out how and what can be induced in target brains using technologies, such as magnetic or direct-current or ultrasound stimulation, rather than relying on sensory mediation, such as watching people's faces or listening to what they have to say. Combining mind reading and mind writing to create a socially potent kind of telepathy is a serious technological challenge, but researchers are hard at work on trying to pull it off.

What does this extraordinary new research mean for the future of spirituality? How might brain-to-brain interfaces or brain-based extensions of GroupFlow experiences be harnessed to enhance people's spirituality and sense of connection to others? We wonder if futuristic versions of current brain-to-brain interfaces might be able to go much further than Siegel's heart-based GroupFlow experiences. Could rituals built around such technologies be incorporated into the activities of churches, synagogues, temples, and mosques? Could brain-based mind-to-mind connections enhance synchronous states achieved in meditation circles? Might there be high-tech spiritual gatherings parallel to secular social gatherings at music concerts, sports events, and political rallies?

Such applications may not be as far off as we might think. Existing mind-to-mind communication technologies can communicate very simple thoughts, such as words spelled through Morse code, but conveying complex thoughts is still a distant dream. However, communicating and sharing emotions might be more feasible, and powerful feelings are a big part of spiritual experiences. The latest in qEEG technology is already capable of generating quantitative signatures for basic emotional states, as we saw in chapter 2.[30] These signatures are basically a detailed map of what the average brain looks like when a person is experiencing specific mental states. Experts know how to do this for stress and anxiety, for example, in the case of neuroimaging-based lie detection.[31] The emotion-based mind reading aspect of brain-to-brain telepathic communication is clearly within reach.

Suppose—and this is not a stretch—we knew the characteristic qEEG signatures for fundamental emotions, such as fear, anxiety, sadness, suspicion, anger, happiness, curiosity, excitement, and bliss, perhaps allowing for variations due to age or sex. Once we have that locked in, we can read emotions in real time. After that—and this is the harder part of the puzzle—using the same signature to tell us what to aim for, we might be able to stimulate someone else's brain to trigger the same emotion state. Keep in mind that brain maps are very detailed; one qEEG produces multiple images of the brain showing the intensity of each wave frequency in lots of brain locations. As a result, basic emotional states are registered fairly clearly in qEEG data. If you hooked your brain in to mind-reading technology for a period of time, you would see how your brain activity changes moment by moment. You would also see how your brain activity is multifaceted, potentially making it a better representation of your emotional state than you could describe yourself. (Think of handing your date a brain map rather than trying to explain how you feel!) Ordinarily, we interpret both our own and others' mental and physical states through cultural expectations and social biases, with a dash of self-deception. (Have you ever been to a large family Thanksgiving and *not* sensed a little repressed anger?) But mind-reading technologies wouldn't be subject to the misinterpretations and errors of mere mortals; they have the potential to function as something like a high-tech, highly nuanced lie detector used for empathy and emotional expressions. (When your friend says "I know how you feel," do they *really*?)

Let's take this a step further by considering the possibilities of comparing brain states to qEEG brain maps that we know match particular kinds of spiritual experience. Let's say we wanted to run a group ritual where the goal is a shared emotional-spiritual state for which we already have the qEEG signature. We can compare each person's actual state to the goal state and then use visual and auditory feedback to guide participants to reach that state—everyone, together, at the same time. This is neurofeedback for groups, not just individuals learning how to meditate by comparing one mind on the fly with a meditation goal state using qEEG but an entire group of people striving for a shared state of mind to enhance their spiritual bond.

Now, on the other hand, with actual mind-*writing* technology, the challenge is to induce mental images, emotions, and content without relying on the human senses. That means no lights or sounds or words, and yet communication still occurs, even between people not physically present with one another. Thus the telepathy technology analogy. From a technical perspective, this is far more difficult than mind reading of emotions, so we can't expect as much on the mind-writing side of direct brain-to-brain communication in the near future.

Nevertheless, suppose the brain stimulation technologies discussed in chapter 2 continue to advance, enabling more nuanced applications. Let's say that experts learn how to reliably create basic emotional states in target brains using magnetic or electrical stimulation—emotions such as the bliss that brain-stimulation subjects sometimes report, or maybe even more basic emotions such as fear and happiness. At that point, brain stimulation could be used instead of, or in parallel with, ordinary stimuli such as music, videos, or aromas to induce a desired emotional state read from another person's brain.

A device that was recently taken off the market called Thync claimed to deliver two kinds of mental state vibes using electrical stimulation: calming and energizing. A patch adhered to your forehead above your right eyebrow would deliver an electrical current to your brain. Advertised as a lifestyle device as opposed to a medical device, Thync avoided the need for FDA approval.

Even though several online reviewers were unable to tell the difference between the calming vibes and the energizing vibes, they claimed that *something* was happening—they were definitely being stimulated. Other users are emphatically convinced that Thync works. In 2015, one Boston University PhD candidate used the Thync device twice a day for two weeks as part of a volunteer trial before it hit the market. In the thick of the semester, when teaching responsibilities and thesis writing were both in full force, Anshul Jain replaced his morning coffee with a Thync energize session and completed a calm session every night

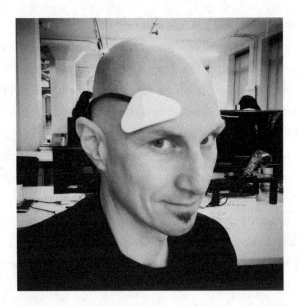

Figure 11. Thync in action.

before bed. He hated to give his Thync back at the end of the trial run and said he'd "pay anything—well, up to $200—to buy it back."[32]

Thync used a method called trigeminal nerve stimulation, which stimulates the release of the hormone norepinephrine. Given the relatively high cost of the technology and the inconsistency with which it worked, in 2017 Thync shifted its focus toward relaxation and sleep and away from energizing stimulation when they came out with the Thync Relax Pro. However, even that seemed to miss the mark in terms of both market demand (expensive) and effectiveness. A refrain seems to have been, "The effects were clear, but not always what we wanted."[33] More recently, in a fascinating course correction, Thync began to market its products for the remediation of symptoms of psoriasis and other autoimmune disorders.

We can draw a few conclusions from Thync's story: (1) brain stimulation technology is on its way toward a portable form with measurable effects and multiple applications; but (2) marketing a product that may not be fully ready for prime time is not the best strategy; and (3) more research, engineering, development, and sophistication is needed for an effective product and reliable and safe use in ritual spaces where the goal is to bring energy and emotions into synchrony like in GroupFlow.

The technologist's dream is when a device can write a brain state with as much precision as qEEGs can read. This would enable two brains to communicate and share emotional content and spiritual intensity without any struggle to articulate and convey nuanced emotions with words and less reliance on sometimes confusing body gestures or facial expressions. So long as we focus on basic emotions rather than complex concepts, this ideal seems *almost* within our technological grasp. After all, the fundamental technological principles are already in place and we can clearly imagine what it might look like. We think it is realistic to expect this kind of (albeit limited) direct brain-to-brain communication of spiritual emotions before many years have passed. When applied to a ritual format like GroupFlow, this could add a dimension of emotional synchrony and shared enhanced mood to the already powerful experience of breath and heart rate synchrony, all of which is routinely described by participants as spiritually potent.

PHOSPHENES, TWENTY QUESTIONS, AND BRAIN NETS

Researchers at the University of Washington's Institute for Learning and Brain Sciences in Seattle are already experimenting with noninvasive brain-to-brain communication using EEG for mind reading and transcranial magnetic simulation for mind writing. Rajesh Rao, Andrea Stocco, and Chantel Prat, along with their team of researchers, conducted an experiment in which two people, sitting in different buildings on opposite sides of campus, played a game together using only the communication between their brains. One person, the "sender," sits with an EEG cap on. He looks at a computer screen that's showing a game and is directed to *think* about when to fire a cannon in order to protect a city. The EEG records and sends his brain activity in real time to the other player. On the other end of campus, the "receiver" sits with a transcranial magnetic stimulation device directed at the left side of his head (which controls the right side of his body). He cannot see the game, but he waits and pushes a button to fire the cannon when he receives a signal via brain stimulation. The sender's *thought* that it is time to fire the cannon is picked up by the EEG, sent via the Internet to the magnetic stimulation device, and inputted into the receiver's brain, at which time the receiver presses the button to fire the cannon. All this happens quickly enough for the cannonball to accurately hit its target.[34]

Likewise, a research team from Barcelona—led by Carles Grau, who teamed up with researchers from Axilum Robotics in Strasbourg, France, and with Alvaro Pascual-Leone at Harvard University—successfully achieved brain-to-brain communication of *words* between a subject in India and a subject in France—well, words translated into binary codes (a series of ones and zeros), but it's still impressive. For this study, a person in India, wearing an EEG cap, thought about the word *hola*. Translated into binary, *hola* is a specific series of ones and zeros. For each *one*, the person thought about moving his hands; and for each *zero*, the person thought about moving his legs. The electrodes captured this thought pattern, interpreted it, and sent it from India to France via the Internet. In India, the other participant, who was wearing a blindfold to eliminate distraction, received this message via transcranial magnetic stimulation pulses that either caused (for ones) or didn't cause (for zeros) *phosphenes*, or spots of light in the peripheral visual field through direct stimulation of the visual system. Then this information was converted back into the original word.

On March 28, 2014—an incredibly exciting day—Grau and his colleagues watched as one participant in Thiruvananthapuram, India, successfully communicated the word *hola* to another participant more than five thousand miles away in Strasbourg, France. The next week, they orchestrated a second successful brain-to-brain communication of the word *ciao*. While these successes are very basic transmissions, the research carries extraordinary implications. Grau and his colleagues declare, "We anticipate that computers in the not-so-distant future will interact directly with the human brain in a fluent manner, supporting both computer-to-brain and brain-to-brain communication routinely."[35] We see spirit tech applications just around the corner.

Encouraged by this research, Stocco and his colleagues back at the University of Washington tried an even more ambitious experiment. They had pairs of participants play the game twenty questions, where one participant asks a fellow participant a series of yes-or-no questions until they can accurately guess what is on their partner's mind.[36] This requires bidirectional communication. Participant 1, who is wearing an EEG cap, is shown an object and a computer screen (let's say, a dog). Participant 2, who sits on the other side of campus, is hooked up to a magnetic brain stimulation system and sees a list of questions on her screen. She clicks on one of the questions (let's say, "Is the object an animal?") to send to participant 1, inquiring about participant 1's object. When the question pops up on participant 1's screen, she directs her focus to one of two flashing lights—the *yes* light flashes at a fast rate while the *no* light flashes much more slowly. Both the yes and no lights send a signal to participant 2, activating the brain stimulation device, but the yes light is so much more intense that it stimulates a phosphene in participant 2's visual cortex via magnetic stimulation.[37] Such sophisticated communication does still require the ability for the respondent to use their sense of vision to see the questions the inquirer is asking, but the yes or no answers are transmitted through brain signals with no need for sensory mediation.

Grau and his colleagues are aware of the far-reaching effects their research could have on the world, both in enhancing human life and presenting never-before-imagined dangers: "We envision that hyperinteraction technologies will eventually have a profound impact on the social structure of our civilization and raise important ethical issues," they noted.[38] But, as Linxing Jiang and his colleagues at the University of Washington said, "[Brain-to-brain interfaces], when developed within an ethically grounded framework, have the potential to not only open new frontiers in human communication and collaboration but also provide a new scientific tool to explore questions in neuroscience and gain a deeper understanding of the human brain."[39] We'll learn more about the ethical implications of this technology leveraged for enhancing spirituality in chapter 10. For now, it's sufficient to note that the technology is advanced enough to envision such spiritual applications, even though they are not quite here yet.

How exactly could communication between *two* brains affect the way we experience large group rituals, which clearly require the presence of more than two brains? Connecting a network of brains in this fashion may be even farther in the future, but again, it is not unimaginable. Picture an even *more* high-tech version of Siegel's HeartSync and GroupFlow technologies. Add EEG and magnetic stimulation technology to GroupFlow's synchronization of heart rate variability and breathing and we might see the entrainment and silent communication of brain waves and emotion states. Many religious and spiritual rituals derive their power from the manipulation and amplification of shared emotion, so if technology can enhance and expedite emotional arousal and synchrony without having to rely on, for example, fear-based preaching or physically taxing displays, then perhaps a new form of ritual focused completely on immediate and direct connection and shared experience with other people can emerge.

Working toward this goal from another angle are scientists exploring brain nets. Scientists have begun exploring the extraordinary possibility that multiple brains could be networked to facilitate a level of cooperation and collective effervescence never before imagined.[40] In 2015, Miguel Pais-Vieira and his colleagues at Duke University began this journey, though not yet with human beings. Instead of EEG and transcranial magnetic stimulation, Pais-Vieira and his colleagues implanted electrodes into the brains of rats and monkeys. The implants could both record the brain's electrical activity and potentially transmit basic information via electrical microstimulation. These created networks of multiple animal brains that could cooperate and exchange information through direct brain-to-brain interfaces, enabling a group of animals to work together cooperatively on a task. The researchers found that animals who remained physically separate but whose brains were joined in a brain net were more successful at completing tasks than unlinked animals. This technology, which almost feels like a sci-fi invasion, essentially creates an organic computer and might eventually be used to connect human brains and enhance human group abilities and experiences.

For the time being, researchers are making headway with noninvasive (no electrodes inside my brain, please and thank you) techniques for creating human brain nets. Combining EEG and TMS, researchers from the same lab that played twenty questions back in 2015 created BrainNet, which facilitates direct brain-to-brain communication among three humans, in 2019. The researchers assume that it "can be readily scaled up to include larger numbers of [people]."[41] Moreover, Jiang and his colleagues explain that, unlike previous brain-to-brain interfaces, BrainNet facilitates back-and-forth communication because each person is equipped with *both* TMS for mind writing *and* EEG for mind reading. So, whereas in the twenty questions game described above, the person guessing the object had to physically click on the question they wanted to send to their partner, with BrainNet this loop is closed, and *no* physical action is needed to convey information.

Jiang, along with Stocco and their colleagues, tested BrainNet by having groups of three people cooperate to play a *Tetris*-like game.[42] One player has the ability to rotate a block before it drops to fill a gap at the bottom of the screen—we'll call her the receiver. However, she cannot *see* the bottom of the screen and so does not know whether or how much to rotate the block. Her two teammates (the senders) are in charge of telling her when to turn the blocks. This sounds confusing enough even with verbal cues, but of course BrainNet requires all communication to be brain to brain! When a sender, who *can* see the bottom of the screen, decides whether or not they think a block should be rotated, they focus on one of two blinking lights—a *no* light or a *yes* light. Their answer is picked up through the EEG and sent through a brain-computer interface to the receiver, where it is inputted into her brain via TMS. After the receiver receives both senders' recommendations (to rotate or not to rotate), she decides what to do. As she focuses hard on her answer, the EEG picks up her intention, and the brain-computer interface rotates (or not) the block on the screen (no physical action needed from any participants). At this point, the senders can see on their screens whether the receiver decided to rotate the block and can, if they would like, recommend that she change her mind by sending another signal (again picked up through EEG and inputted into the receiver's brain through TMS).

To make the task more reflective of teamwork in the real world, the researchers designed it in such a way that one of the senders would intermittently become unreliable and would give a bad recommendation. In these cases, the sender's ability to recommend a course correction after the first rotation decision reflects a collaborative conversation. Throughout the game, the receiver will likely begin to notice one sender's unreliability and may adjust their decision-making accordingly, and BrainNet allows for however many interactions are needed to solve a task.

With striking success, Jiang and his colleagues have at the very least proved that the concept of a true social network of brains is possible, and they have shown how to create it. Given how quickly technology advances, and how inevitable it is for increasing numbers of participants in such a study to be equipped with both EEG and TMS hardware, telepathic networking suddenly seems like an achievable reality rather than a sci-fi trope.

FUTURISTIC TOGETHERNESS

At this point, brain-to-brain communication is still in its infancy. But if we've learned anything in the past forty years since the birth of the Internet, it's that technological innovation has the potential to develop faster than we imagine. Spiritual entrepreneurs and enlightenment engineers such as Mikey Siegel are making sure their imaginations and innovations keep up with the rate of technological advancement. As a result, they are committed to finding ways to harness these advancements for spiritual experience, growth, and well-being.

A direct brain-to-brain-communication version of Siegel's Group-Flow is just around the bend, and we suspect that tech-mediated telepathic communication of emotions could create transformative opportunities for unprecedented levels of authentic connection, empathy, and shared emotional fervor. We imagine that mind-to-mind connections might first make their way into meditation spaces to achieve and enhance synchronous states, whereas their inclusion in traditional religious spaces, such as churches, synagogues, temples, and mosques, seems less likely in the short term.

Meanwhile, technologies such as GroupFlow, even without direct brain-to-brain linkups, are actively in use right now. As the contingent of spiritual-but-not-religious folks grows, innovations such as Group-Flow and similar successor technologies will widen in popularity. Groups of spiritual-but-not-religious people will furnish not only a natural market for this kind of spirit tech but also a vital structure as well as the materials for organizing meaningful meetings and rituals.

We started out this chapter ruminating with Mikey Siegel: "We're lonely and we're literally dying of loneliness." Engineering togetherness using spirit tech speaks directly to the hearts of the millions of people who have powerful longings to overcome loneliness and connect with other people spiritually, but who also harbor equally potent antipathy toward what they see as the superstitions and absurdities and power abuses of traditional organized religion. Even among traditional religions, many people long for deeper spiritual contact than can be achieved in the rituals and practices of their religious groups. These forms of alienation can hurt and harm. Spirit tech that brings people together heals and helps. Or it can, if used wisely.

By harnessing the power of collective effervescence for *good*—cultivating communal well-being and inspiring self-realization through a vibrant, welcoming, revitalized community—these types of technology are the next step in the spiritual battle against the unintended consequences of hyperindividualist cultures.

5

Virtual Sacred Reality

The thing that's remarkably beautiful to me about virtual reality is that you can make up reality in virtual reality and share it with other people. It's like having a collaborative lucid dream.

—*Jaron Lanier, American computer philosophy writer and computer scientist*

PASTOR D. J.'S VR CHURCH

D. J. Soto's call to serve God has always been driven by dissatisfaction with the status quo and an itch to innovate. Involved since childhood with the Baptist Church, he felt a deep admiration for his youth group leaders, and they inspired him to attend Pensacola Christian College, a Baptist liberal arts college in Florida, to train to be a youth pastor. Before he even graduated, however, D. J. found himself disappointed by the realities of church politics. "You know when we read the Scriptures we see this inclusive invitation for all people to engage in faith?" he said one day when we chatted by phone. "Well, I found ministry training to be very exclusive and arrogant." So D. J. decided he didn't want to become a pastor after all. "If this is what ministry is," he said, "and if this is what a pastor needs to become, I don't think I want to do it."[1]

Instead, he began teaching high school and working in television production. He got married and he and his wife eventually settled down in Pennsylvania and started a family. Their faith in God was strong and abiding, even though they had all but stepped away from church after feeling disillusioned. One day, while working for a local TV station, D. J. was sent on assignment to an Assemblies of God Pentecostal megachurch. There he saw a community that seemed to approximate more closely Jesus's vision for inclusivity he'd read in Scripture. D. J. and his family officially joined the church in 2011. That's when things started changing for him.

Having always been an enthusiastic techie, D. J. created an online platform for the church that combined live-stream services with an active chat room, and he helped the church produce an app and create a social media presence. He notes that this is commonplace now, but it was groundbreaking at the time. The church soon grew too large for its space, and the lead pastor asked D. J. to become the pastor of a new branch church. D. J. thought about his previous rejection of pastoral ministry but considered also the way that he had felt God working in his life over the intervening eleven or twelve years. Since the Pentecostal pastor had been able to present an open and inclusive alternative to the closed-minded clergy he had met during his Baptist school years, D. J. decided to say yes. He was ordained as an Assemblies of God minister and helped launch the new branch campus.

Before long, however, D. J. and his wife began to feel that God was leading them to do something new. Apparently it was a strong feeling, because together they launched themselves into an intense period of discernment. "That was kind of a hard time, trying to figure that out," D. J. said. "We went through several months, maybe even a year, of just going on faith and not knowing what was next." Eventually, though they were still living in the same town, they left their church and waited for God to lead them to their next calling.

Then on a Friday in June 2016, D. J. was tinkering around with his new virtual reality (VR) headset—the Oculus Rift. He was loving it—the games, the movies, and all the visual experiences were phenomenal.

That Friday, however, he noticed a new program in the App Store that looked intriguing. He downloaded it, opened it, and was immediately blown away.

What D. J. had found was Altspace, one of the first VR social platforms. "People were walking around with their avatars, chatting with other people from all across the world in these 3D virtual environments," D. J. recalled. "And I thought it was super cool. Then I took it a step further and realized, 'Oh, wait a minute, you can actually create your own environment!'" D. J. quickly went to work doing just that. Unsurprisingly, he created a worship space. "Within an hour of being in Altspace," he said, "I was like, oh, we're going to have church here this Sunday."

AltspaceVR has been the main social media platform for VR since its formal launch in 2015. And then, as a sure sign of the model's potential for success, AltspaceVR was acquired by Microsoft in October 2017.[2] Similar to Facebook's Spaces, AltspaceVR enables users to hang out in real time with friends. Each person moves around and navigates the environments with their digital, custom-designed avatar and can speak to other people through microphones. Just as in real life, there is 3D spatial sound, so you can hear the avatars that are right next to you better than you can hear the avatars across the room. Since participants are wearing VR headsets and usually have one or two hand-held controllers, the technology picks up head and hand movements and gestures, which makes the avatars appear even more lifelike. Every day in this VR world, there are comedy nights, karaoke, or campfires; disk golf, card games, and mazes; as well as conversations and special interest meetups. Smiley faces and hearts stream out of avatars' heads in order to help communicate emotions during conversations and shows.

D. J. was hooked. Since the AltspaceVR main page is a calendar of events, D. J.'s first order of business was to get the first VR Church service on the books.

However, Sunday, of course, was only two days away. So he recruited a friend who put together some social media graphics and fliers to advertise the church service, gathered some good lyrical worship videos from YouTube, and quickly wrote a sermon. At the time, VR was still a fairly niche technology and most of the people D. J. knew hadn't even heard of it. But D. J. was determined. "So I had my first VR Church service that summer, June 2016, in Altspace," he said. "And I thought it was amazing. We had about five people show up. Maybe for a physical church planter, they would be devastated if at their first church service only five people showed up, but for me, man, I was pumped. I was so excited about it."

From then on D. J. held services regularly, whether or not anyone showed up. Sometimes there were only two participants, and sometimes there were even zero, but he kept going. "You know, it kind of didn't matter to me at the time and I would just do the full service to an empty room," he said. "I would do the music, the sermon, I would even do announcements. And no one would be there, but if anyone by chance happened to pop in, I wanted them to have a sense that there was this event happening." D. J. laughed and admitted, "Looking back, it was probably weird and awkward, but I don't think it bothered me because I just wanted to create the atmosphere and this expectancy that on Sundays, at whatever time, there's something going on. There's going to be a service." (See figure 19 in the color insert.)

D. J. is proud of VR Church's ability to reach people who are not reached by physical churches, for whatever reason. For some, it's physical limitations. One housebound person who is unable to get out to go to church said, "Probably the first two services I went to I just sat there crying the whole time. I couldn't believe I was able . . . to do this again." Another man who is a quadriplegic attends the VR Church services and even designed the official VR Church logo. In VR, the man, through his avatar, which moves in the same way that everyone else's does, is able to participate in the virtual space with no limitations.

For others, the barriers to traditional church are emotional, psychological, or even ideological. VR Church often attracts people who have had very negative past experiences with church, for instance. Others are simply curious, or perhaps want to explore the idea of church but do not feel comfortable visiting a physical church. Still others represent a rather surprising contingent of VR Church's congregation: atheists. In fact, VR Church's first guest was an atheist from Denmark, and D. J. welcomed him with open arms. D. J. attributes this wide spectrum of participants in part to his mission to foster inclusivity, open-mindedness, and authenticity in his community, and in part to the fact that the VR setting allows people to have honest and authentic conversations right off the bat.

The irony that church in *virtual* reality allows people to be more *real* and to feel comfortable to come truly as they are is not lost on D. J. "Because people have avatars, there is a sense of anonymity," he explained, and that anonymity lends participants a sense of safety that allows for deep authenticity. He related stories of many church members and visitors who, on their first visit, are already prepared to be deeply honest and open up about topics as difficult as depression and suicide. This instant vulnerability, made possible precisely because of this particular spirit tech application, provides an opportunity for D. J. to provide care and ministry in a new way, and much more quickly than he was able to IRL (in real life).

"In my twenty years in church ministries in one form or another, I haven't had this level of conversation," he said. He points out that of course such supportive and authentic conversations happen in the physical world, too, but it tends to take much longer to get to the level of honesty that seems to unfold immediately in VR. "And even when we talk to folks on the atheist and agnostic side of things," he said, "they come in and we have conversations about faith and science and God and doubts. From a conversation standpoint I think sometimes it supersedes the physical environment just because of the anonymity of the avatars." VR Church now holds at least four Sunday services—VR Church Europe, VR Church Australia, VR Church Americas, and

VRChat—and seven weekly Life Group gatherings in VRChat, VR Rec Room, and AltspaceVR. "We are one church in many metaverses," its website says on its Experiences page.

VR Church isn't the only place where people are looking for spiritual experiences. In the (virtual) world of "technodelics," VR programmers have been exploring the possibilities of mind bending and soul-searching through intense VR experiences. For one project, tech innovators and spiritual psychonauts led by scientist and cultural theorist Dr. David Glowacki of the University of Bristol have developed a multiperson VR journey called *Isness*, which represents the participants to each other as colorful, glowing "energetic essences" rather than traditional avatars.[3] The goal of Isness is to induce mystical-type experiences analogous to those caused by psychedelic drugs. Such spiritual experiences, the researchers explain, are characterized by "a sense of connectedness, transcendence, and ineffability" for each person, while as a group they "experience the collective emergence, fluctuation, and dissipation of their bodies as energetic essences."[4] (See figure 20 in the color insert.)

Isness gathers four participants in a room-scale physical space equipped with a VR framework modeled by the Narupa project, an open-source system designed to enable groups of people to work together to manipulate objects in virtual reality. Even though the people in the physical space are wearing VR headsets, they are able to see each other in the virtual space because each headset is equipped with access to positioning data. In this way, participants see and can interact with a VR representation of the other participants' energy fields. Participants also wear "mudra gloves" equipped with a tracking device that provides absolute position tracking, allowing participants to see, reach out, and touch hands with others during the VR experience. Moreover, when participants put their hands in a specific mudra pose, touching their thumb to either their forefinger or middle finger, their representation to the other participants in virtual space begins emitting light. By manipulating a set of "aesthetic hyperparameters," the facilitators of Isness are able to construct a journey for the participants through thirteen different phenomenological states modeled after concepts—including matter as energy, connectedness, unity, ego dissolution, transcendence of space and time, and noetic quality—emerging from research on psychedelic drug effects.[5]

Glowacki and his colleagues found that the Isness experience can indeed produce "peak experience," mystical-type experiences that are "statistically indistinguishable from the [mystical-type experiences] observed in previous studies administering moderate to high doses of classical [psychedelic drugs]" such as LSD, mescaline, psilocybin, and DMT.[6] The researchers call Isness and other such technologies *numedelics*. The first part of that label is inspired by both the Latin word *numen*—indicating a mysterious, spiritual, or awe-inspiring quality—and the Greek word *pneuma*—breath, spirit, or soul—while the second part comes from the Greek word *deloun*, making something manifest. While Isness is still, at the moment, a laboratory experiment, numedelic tech could play an important psychotherapeutic role in the future. But it points to a range of technodelics that we'll discuss later in the chapter that also explore the potential for mystical experience induced and enhanced in VR.

TRICKING THE BRAIN

VR is profoundly different from the types of media it stands to replace or upgrade, such as television or movies, chat rooms, social media, and video games. Neurologically, VR *tricks* the brain into thinking that you are actually physically present in the virtual space.

A popular and striking example is an app called Richie's Plank Experience created by Richard Eastes of Brisbane, Australia. The game begins with the player entering an elevator and ascending eighty stories to the top of a skyscraper. When the doors open, the player finds himself on the very edge of the building, with only a wooden plank protruding from the building out over the bustling city below. If you're brave enough, you can achieve the simple goal of walking to the edge of the plank. If only it were so simple! YouTube is full of videos of people standing in their living rooms with VR headsets, terrified for their lives as they attempt to gather the courage to venture even one step onto the plank. Writer Andrew McMillen described his experience when he tried the game at a VR meetup in Brisbane: "Before I put on the headset and headphones, I was just another guy . . . watching a bunch of strangers attempt to walk a board that sits just a few centimeters off the ground, held aloft at one end by a hardcover copy of *Steve Jobs*, and a few stacked kitchen sponges at the other. Yet even after having watched these interactions and reactions play out on the faces of strangers, I was completely unprepared for the sensory overload that comes wrapped in the immersion. It's simply too real."[7]

Figure 12. VR headset in use.

The app is programed so that players can customize the experience to present a plank exactly the same length as one they find or buy at their local hardware store. Being able to feel the edges of the plank under your feet (even though it is fully supported inches off or even flat on the ground in real life) makes the experience that much more terrifying. "Out here, on the plank, real and fake are all but indistinguishable," McMillen said. "All my brain is concerned with is survival. During those two minutes, I kept trying to tell myself that it wasn't real. The disconnect between my intellectual understanding and emotional response was enormous."[8]

Yale University School of Medicine neurologist Steven Novella explains that the human brain constructs perceptions, based on all available input it gathers from the senses. So it is not surprising at all that our brains and bodies process experiences in VR in the same way that they process experiences in physical reality. It is nearly impossible to tell your body that your brain's perceptions are incorrect. So when you peer down beyond the thin wooden plank you're balancing on in VR, even though you *know* you are safe on solid ground just as you were thirty seconds ago, your heart races, your skin may become clammy, and your knees weaken. Many people who subject themselves to the Plank Experience find themselves crawling on all fours in an effort to maintain stability on the plank. Novella compares the visceral experience of VR to the way common optical illusions work: "[Some] illusions are pictures that are right at the threshold of our brain's ability to construct the apparent image. Snow and rocks can instantly turn into a picture of a Dalmatian, and once you see it, you cannot unsee it. The construction is there." And, he continues, "just like you cannot unsee your brain's construction of ambiguous stimuli, you cannot convince the subconscious part of your brain that you are not standing on a plank 40 floors above the street."[9] McMillen echoes this sentiment. "There is no need to suspend my disbelief," he said, "because the brain immediately believes—hence the physical response."[10]

Now the question is, how does this neurological phenomenon translate to spiritual and religious possibilities? It is clear that D. J.'s VR Church has the potential to create a genuine and vibrant community that generates an experience of real copresence among participants.

D. J. estimates that thousands of visitors have come through to check out VR Church, and currently the church has a contingent of regular participants who also gather and chat throughout the week in a special channel on Discord, a free voice and text chat app, to support each other and socialize.

But given the capabilities of VR, D. J. has more expansive plans. "Say the sermon is about Moses and the Red Sea and faith and courage," he said. "We can *create* that environment. We can make it so that we feel like we're actually walking through the Red Sea." He explained that plans are in the works for the creation of a series of experiences that bring Bible stories to life and add a level of multisensory action and experiential learning to the church service. "We'll get to experience these things; we'll be experiencing the joy or the fear or the valley of the shadow of death." He described an experiential environment he and his team could develop that might be dark without being too scary. The associated lesson is the reassurance that, even in those shadowy moments of life, God is with you. "There's really no limit . . . to all these cool ideas," D. J. mused. In a poignant reflection of the shift from the Information Age to what many tech leaders have deemed the Age of Experience, congregants won't simply be taking in information; they'll also be growing through actual experience—albeit mediated virtually.

Unlike forms of technology that dominated the Information Age, which delivered greater and greater amounts of information to the brain in the form of beeps and dings and news feeds and apps, forcing people to train their brains to think about hundreds of things all the time, VR presents, as D. J. put it, "a more singular long-form thought experience." He sees this as a hopeful and healthy way to counteract the tendency toward disjointed minds and attention spans produced by the age of information. "VR affects the brain unlike any other technology," he said, "and we plan on taking [VR Church] to this really cool level."

D. J. even expressed interest in creating spaces and experiences that might help facilitate spiritual or mystical experiences—for example, encounters with Jesus or God. "All through Scripture, there are these encounters with God—why wouldn't we try to replicate that?" he said. Certainly a lot of thought and care would be required to create such an experience. What exactly should Jesus look like? Would God or Jesus speak to the participant during the experience? How does one go about coding and programing a mystical encounter? But D. J. didn't hesitate. "I think oftentimes what we do as pastors is we're trying to make God alive, we're trying to use words and speak . . . in a way that brings God in a living way to people's ears," he said. "We do it through cartoons and comic books and movies. Why wouldn't we do it in VR?" Given God's unlimitedness and omnipresence, he went on, "why wouldn't God be present in the virtual world?"

VR TECHNODELICS

Another community of technological innovators and spiritual seekers is interested in developing a different sort of immersive VR program as a tool for spiritual transformation—or as preeminent visionary artist and virtual reality pioneer Android Jones says, "bring[ing] virtue into virtual reality."[11] Android, who describes his work as electromineralism, has developed two experiential projects that infuse and harness VR to create powerful and spiritually meaningful experiences.

The first project, called Samskara, can be experienced in either a 360-degree immersive dome or via a VR headset.[12] *Samskara* is a Sanskrit word that refers to a significant rite or meaningful moment in one's life. "It's something that happens in your life that leaves a mark on the psyche and the genesis of your identity," Android explained. "It can be good or bad, but it's just something very deep like a wound or a victory that leaves its mark on you for the rest of your karma and through your future incarnations."[13]

Android created Samskara with the help of George Asitov, a mysterious digital artist who goes simply by his religious title, Swami Avadhut (*swami* is the term for a Hindu religious leader). Swami's company headquarters, FulldomeLab, is based in Chiang Mai, Thailand, and doubles as a Hare Krishna ashram. With Android's blessing and assistance, Swami Avadhut and his crew created a moving, morphing, kaleidoscopic visionary experience of Android's art combined with sacred geometry. The first time Android saw what they'd put together, he was blown away. The experience felt like being *inside* one of his paintings: "It's like you become part of it, you're the main character in it as it is happening all around you."[14]

Android said the goal of Samskara is to harness the explosive combination of art and technology to "give someone a deeply powerful experience and then use that to share the deeper knowledge of the Hindu Vedas, which are over seven-thousand-year-old stories" (we won't quibble over his age estimate).[15] He and Swami Avadhut understand this mission as an incredible opportunity to bring the ancient wisdom rooted in the Vedas, the yoga sutras, and the Upanishads into consciousness through a new medium of communication and experience. In an interview for *Compose Yourself Magazine*, Android said, "There are things that are true today that will never not be true. . . . I feel from my perspective as an artist, and someone who brings stories to life that there is almost an obligation to reinterpret and retell those truths [found in the Hindu scriptures]."[16]

Samskara is not only a spiritual technology for those who experience it in a dome or VR setting, however; the process of creating Samskara is also understood as spiritually inspired. Android explained, "All the artists and animators who work on Samskara are in Thailand right now meditating and doing *kirtan*, and then will sit down and code, and 3D animate, and composite together. They are trying to create a certain quality of consciousness that they bring to the project. That's a great example of digital alchemy, that the quality of consciousness they bring to the project reflects the power and resonance it ultimately has."[17]

Android's second project is a more interactive, creative, and exploratory endeavor called Microdose VR. Although no actual entheogens or hallucinogens are involved (or at least not required), the nature and goal of the Microdose VR experience is similar to that of microdosing with psychedelics. "I want to [bring] a level of psychedelic consciousness into VR," Android said. "And [see] how we could use it as a digital drug and bring more virtue into virtual reality."[18] The goals of Microdose VR are multidimensional: it can be a therapeutic tool, a profound flow state, a form of brain-mind-body integration and exercise, and a visceral mind-bending exploration of yourself and your creative energies. Android once called it "the gateway drug to your inner creative experience."[19] You can think of Microdose VR like a fast track or a short cut to artistic mastery: not everyone has to put in ten thousand hours of practice before they can enjoy the ecstasy of losing themselves in artistic expression.

Microdose VR allows the artist to paint, dance, and remix electronic music in three-dimensional space. Within a virtual environment, the player is equipped with various tools that shoot out colorful particles and patterns that pulse and morph in sync with the music. Android explained that his initial vision was to harness the same technology used for first-person shooter games. "But instead of a gun," he said, "I want[ed] it to be an awesome beautiful particle emitter that can shoot . . . lotus petals out into the world and fractal spirals. We've managed basically to leverage the same type of technology that's used for flame throwers and rail guns and cannon launchers into creating pretty convincing psychedelic moving, strobing, unfolding, unfurling visuals around you."[20]

However, Microdose VR is not simply about image creation. In fact, it's not about creation at all, as there is no save function and the user is not left with a permanent work of art. It is a creative, transitory *experience*, undertaken for the sake of the momentary experience. It combines what Android describes as the three types of intelligence that make up creative expression: the kinetic intelligence of dance, the audio intelligence of music creation, and the spatial intelligence of image making.

Android and his team of creators have been continuously developing Microdose VR, and at the time of writing it has yet to hit the market for home use. Prototypes and beta versions have been showcased as interactive art installations at conferences and festivals such as Burning Man, Coachella, and Panorama NYC; and now an alpha version is available for folks interested in offering feedback. In a recent interview, Android explained, "We have it to where, with each one of these particles, there is a direct one-to-one relationship with the sound that you're hearing and the shape and color of the particles you're seeing, so it creates this form of synesthesia where you're actually able to dance and create these beautiful visuals, while at the same time remixing a piece of music; but what's cool is that you're mixing a piece of music in 360."[21]

While the music is being supplied by the program, the experiencer has the power to remix and play with the music while they dance and paint. "So if you shoot a bass womp, fractal caterpillar behind your head, you can actually feel it behind you and hear it behind you, or above you, or below you," Android explained. "They're not just listening to it, but they're remixing it in a visual, three-dimensional space."[22] One user called Microdose VR "a defining moment in VR" due to its combination of the artistry of Evan Bluetech, "one of the most incredible psychedelic electronic music producers alive," and Android Jones, "one of the most profound digital artists on the planet."[23] Another fan called it "Tilt Brush on LSD" (Tilt Brush is a popular program that lets you paint in 3D space). Bluetech, one of Android's collaborators on Microdose VR, calls it an "immersive synesthetic, transcendental experience."[24]

Although Microdose VR is not quite a game—it doesn't have a narrative or character-progression component—there are different levels and options. Bluetech explained that one of the levels features one of his previously unreleased tracks that the participant can remix and paint: "You can move around and through it and explore it. Paint another system and it's actually making melodies which will start swirling around you. You can move through it, and it's all audio-reactive. You can paint all the layers of the track, with multiple instances of each piece of that music, and fly around it, through it, go into a vortex into another place. It's literally like lucid dreaming inside music created by people."[25]

The developers have also created a level that incorporates neuro-feedback and biofeedback into the experience. Teaming together with the creators of the Muse headband (described in chapter 3), they created a prototype of a VR headset that has infrared sensors resting on the player's chest that pick up heart rate and EEG sensors on the head to track brain waves. They've then programmed Microdose VR to instantly collect and translate all the data in real time, assigning each element to a different visual stimulus in the Microdose environment. Android explained that there is one level in Microdose that puts the painter in a surreal psychedelic landscape that morphs according to their mental and physical states. For example, when their brain waves hit a desired "clear mind" or other target state, the clouds begin to dissipate, and if the person generates more alpha waves, the environment's sun may rise or set. "Basically our goal," Android explained, "is to have the user enter into a world and have this world be procedurally generated in real time, one-to-one with these inner mechanisms of their body."[26]

He also explained that the Microdose programming can separate the information picked up by the heart rate sensor into six different sine graphs representing different aspects of the person's heartbeat. Then it becomes possible to have each aspect correspond with a different visual quality of the particles, such as shape, rotation, color, or quality of movement. Moreover, by linking Microdose VR to Spotify, players can search for and choose to paint and dance to music that has the same tempo as their own heartbeat. This can feel like being "immersed in one's own heartbeat."[27] Lastly, with the microphone, a player can sing into the environment, too, their voice creating yet another streaming, swirling, dancing visual. Android said that, as an artist who was classically trained in traditional mediums such as oil painting and drawing before diving into digital art, his experience with Microdose VR is the "most intimate marriage possible yet of my body and technology merging together."[28]

Yet another scenario or level in Microdose VR involves, like Isness, a multiplayer design connecting people through the Internet. Although there seem to be several ways in which players can be in Microdose VR online, perhaps moving between areas with different types of music playing, Android explained one possible scenario to Jacob Aman, host of the *Future Primitive* podcast:

> Say you have five different people who are all online in the Microdose experience together. And they each have twenty sets of particles. And the dynamics of it is you have these motion controllers and when you press the triggers, these geometrical sprite-based and mesh-based particles shoot out of your hands, kind of like fireworks. And they dissipate or they dissolve around you and you're just constantly streaming these particles or poi firework–type things. So player A has maybe twenty different particles and they're all different sorts of drums and bass frequencies. And then player B has like synths and high hats and C has more percussions and vocals. So can you imagine that each of the participants has a different component that would make up a song and [they can] collaborate together.[29]

Multiplayer Microdose VR has yet to even hit the experimental festival scene, but clearly the vision for innovation is in full force!

Perhaps the most well-known leader in the field of technodelics is Robin Arnott, creator of SoundSelf, an "ecstatic meditation experience" published by Andromeda Entertainment that uses the sound of your voice to draw you into an introspective trance.[30] We spoke with Arnott to learn about his inspiration and vision for SoundSelf and to discuss the field of VR technodelics.[31]

For Arnott, it all started with his first experience of *oneness* after ingesting LSD. "It's like the memory of that experience left the blue-

Figure 13. SoundSelf visuals. Note: Figure 21 in the color insert shows the vivid colors of SoundSelf.

prints to a video game that would help other people have a similar experience," he told us.[32] Although everything about SoundSelf emerged from the memory of that experience, he has fine-tuned the programming for years, determined to make the experience as meaningful and transformative as possible for users.

SoundSelf is based largely on a meditative technique called vocal toning, during which practitioners use their breaths and voices to calm, center, and focus their minds. Different tones—*AH, UH, MM,* or *OM,* for example—are understood to create sound fields and vibrations that stimulate effects like healing, inner coherence, and experiences of unity. In fact, Arnott's LSD-enhanced pivotal oneness experience occurred while he was toning: "The room I was in filled with voices, and it felt like I'd created them, which didn't make sense to my rational mind. And then it was like the dominos flipped and I could see how I was creating everything." *This* is the experience he sought to re-create with SoundSelf. The technology harnesses the creative energy of a person's voice—it converts the long, smooth tones a person produces into continuous, swelling, kaleidoscoping visuals. Voice, Arnott said, emerges as a fascinating nexus of what is intimately *yours*: voice emanates from your core, and then also exists as a force and presence in physical space outside the body that you perceive with your ears and are affected by. Dissolving the boundary between the center of the self and one's sense percep-tions, the mechanics of the technology are intended to invite the user into a state of surrender. One user, who goes by the screen name "The Bird of Hermes," had this to say about their experience:

> The visuals combined with the audio feedback and modula-tion of your own toning help to lull your analytical mind into passivity so that you can enter a purer state of being. You can literally feel the shift in your consciousness as you slip into that meditative state. My opinion is that this is a fantastic tool for those who have been looking for a way to start a medita-tion practice or enhance one they already have. In my case it got me meditating again regularly after years of neglect.
>
> I definitely recommend this "game" even at the full price. The buyer just has to be aware of what they're getting into. This is a *practice*, not a drug simulator. These are some psychedelic visuals but the intent isn't to simulate doing drugs; the intent is to alter your consciousness and put you in the Zen or flow state. It's not just a sound visualizer either. There will be times when it's almost like SoundSelf is reading your mind and presenting visuals and sounds in accordance with that. You also will never have the same session twice.[33]

The visuals of SoundSelf and Microdose VR are somewhat different, and the two programs, while both inspired by psychedelic drugs, evoke strikingly different experiences. Most users who play Microdose do so standing up and moving vigorously to the beat of the music, which is faster-paced electronica. The visuals are boxy, blocky digital shapes zooming and twisting very quickly in a multidimensional space full of vibrant colors, like a flying roller coaster. The display is not symmetrical but rather is full of blasting shapes near and far, with digital fractals spraying out of the player's hands. The player is dancing and cocreating the musical-visual experience with their body.

On the other hand, SoundSelf's graphics are smooth and pulsing, usually characterized by gleaming light effects. Sometimes they slowly morph and spin while gradually moving through the color spectrum and shifting designs. At other times, pulsing and strobing lights quickly overwhelm the visual space. The shapes and lines tend to be more rounded and smooth, emanating from and swirling around one central point. The constant kaleidoscopic image is responsive to the player's voice instead of their body, so the player is still—sitting in a meditative position, reclining, or even lying down. SoundSelf's music, while co-created with the toning and chanting of the player, is characterized by long, smooth, almost eerie tones. So while Microdose VR is an ecstatic, expressive journey soaring through the internal and external cosmos, SoundSelf is a meditative, hypnotic journey to the center of the soul.

VIRTUAL AWE, REAL TRANSFORMATION

So what does this all have to do with spirituality and personal transformation? Compared to VR Church and SoundSelf, the spiritual potency of Microdose VR might not be immediately obvious—unless, of course, you've had the opportunity to try it. According to Android and his team, it is not uncommon for people to emerge from a Microdose VR experience in tears. They may not feel as though they've met the monotheistic God, but they do sometimes seem to meet *the universe* or even *themselves*. One person who tested Microdose VR at a tech convention said, "I was plunged into a soaring cyberspace that resembles a fractal microcosm of a molecular universe. It's as if I was peering out from the point of view of a white blood cell but flying through the archetypal corridors of the psyche instead of the human body. . . . And from my vantage point, I was really flying, actually flying. As the shackles of my body were thrown aside, I embraced the newfound liberation of existing as mere awareness."[34]

A common reaction to both the SoundSelf and the Microdose VR experience is *awe*. This strikes us as similar to what people have told us about the transformative power of entheogens, which we'll read about in chapters 6 and 7, where users explore the capacity of these psychedelic medications to induce experiences of awe with both spiritual and psychotherapeutic goals in mind. Clinical psychologist Peter Hendricks argues that "at the center of the mystical experience is *awe*, wherein one is in the presence of something so great, so large, that it requires they completely reorder their mental structures—completely change the way they view reality."[35] Considering the sheer, stunning emergent quality of the combination of the visual, audio, and kinetic elements, paired with the capability of VR to materialize a sense of presence in those who use it, it is hardly surprising that feelings of awe may accompany the Microdose VR experience.

In addition to the many anecdotal accounts, there is some neuroscientific research to back this up. Psychologists at the Applied Technology for Neuro-Psychology Lab at the IRCCS Istituto Auxologico Italiano in Milan, Italy, are interested in understanding the transformative potential of awe experiences. They found that it was difficult to construct truly awe-inspiring experiences in a lab setting, which is a problem because that's precisely what's needed for a comprehensive, well-controlled scientific study. However, with VR, they saw a new possibility. They experimented with people's emotional experience and determined that VR is an effective way to induce awe in controlled experimental settings.[36]

VR enables people to gain experiential knowledge of something without encountering it in the regular world—what some VR experts call the default world. Even the types of experiences that elicit awe, wonder, gratitude, and enduring personal transformation may be adequately accessible, and perhaps even more safely and reliably accessible, within VR. They argue that because of the technological complexity of VR and its combination of rich sensory displays and ability to track even the subtlest movements of the participant, VR allows the user to "experience the virtual environment as if it was 'his/her surrounding world' (*augmented embodiment*) or can experience a synthetic avatar (user's virtual representation) as if it was 'his/her own body' (*synthetic embodiment*)."[37]

Anil Seth, the codirector of the University of Sussex's Sackler Centre for Consciousness Science, has been studying the notion of *presence*—"the question of how and why we typically experience things as being real, as in really existing in the world."[38] In a 2017 interview with João Medeiros of *Wired* magazine, Seth explained that he is now using VR as a new and more ecologically valid way to study presence.[39] Ecological validity refers to the extent to which experimental conditions adequately replicate the intricately complex environment of real-world experiences. Seth says that traditional methods of studying cognition tend to involve things like optical illusions on a computer screen. By comparison, VR offers a tool for manipulating perception in a way that is significantly more sophisticated and ecologically valid. He predicts that even though the research field is just now beginning to take advantage of the technology, "in five years, it's going to be game changing."[40]

This is unsurprising to everyone who uses a VR headset, especially top-of-the-line versions: the brain believes that the virtual space and objects are real. As we described earlier with the VR walk-the-plank app, even when your mind knows what you're seeing is a simulation, your body's nervous system reacts as if your sense perceptions are accurate—a sign of ecological validity. Seth also echoes the excitement of the Italian lab, noting that VR technology has tremendous potential for helping us understand and experiment with the ways that people experience their own embodiment.

These features matter for potential spiritual applications because of the way in which our minds encode memories and ascribe meaning to experiences. In his *Voices of VR* podcast interview, Android describes the power and centrality of creating an experience in VR in this way:

> At the end of the day, I see the mind kind of like a multicham-bered key-lock. You've got all these different kinds of barriers you have to go through [to create a VR experience], and if you can get the animation right, if you can get the visuals just realis-tic enough, if you can get the sound, and the emotion, and the environment—each one of those is a different chamber in the lock—and if you get all of those right, and you're holding this illusion together with duct tape and string, if you can get that right for a moment, that just leads to "I had an experience." And that experience becomes a memory, and that becomes just as real as anything else you've done. That makes it part of who you are and has some type of influence on what you do in the world. And at the end of the day, all we have is experiences.[41]

D. J. Soto described an experience he had when he and a friend took his son to a Cleveland Cavaliers playoff game to celebrate his son's thirteenth birthday. Before LeBron James came out onto the court, D. J. leaned over and said to his friend, "You know, I've seen LeBron James warm up before. He's great!" And then about ten seconds later he stopped himself and said, "Wait a minute, I actually did not. I saw him in VR!" D. J. explained that the VR experience of watching LeBron James's warm-up had imprinted in his brain as a real experience.

The difference between watching something meaningful on televi-sion and actually being *there* in person is profound. VR enables people to *experience* something in a way that is physiologically comparable to an experience in ordinary reality. In fact, in many ways, VR creates a world that is just as much *reality* as ordinary reality. It is simply a dif-ferent *space* in which reality can take place. The key difference between having a conversation on the telephone or chatting with someone on-line (which are both real conversations) and having VR conversations, attending VR religious events, or having VR spiritual creative experiences is that the multidimensional immersive elements of VR achieve a feeling of *presence* that is absent in telephone and online discussions. Presence provides a significantly different quality of experience—not to mention that multimodal and multisensory experiences are possible in VR.

Taking the notion of presence, place, and the reality of virtual space a step further, Arnott explained that VR opens up a "particularly potent" design space that transcends the limits of other technologies. "The point is," he said, "you put on the goggles and suddenly what's different? Well, you're just somewhere else. But there's a quality of whereness that is identical to the quality of whereness that we live in in our day-to-day world, except it just has a lower fidelity." Alluding to the spiritual potentialities of the experience, he contends that the technology may even help people transcend an attachment to whereness: "The technology lends itself to helping us let go of that quality of whereness and maybe even a certain quality of whatness. And then suddenly we can make experiences that help people transcend—instead of just taking a vacation from their current where and what into a fantasy where and what—transcend their where and what altogether, at least temporarily."[42] The feeling of complete unity with all space, time, and reality or a sense of transcending space, time, and oneself are common features of *oneness* and mystical-type experiences—the type of experience that was the midwife for Arnott's vision of SoundSelf.

Arnott feels that there is a marked difference between technologies that emerge from the gaming world, such as VR, and those that are adapted from medical technologies, such as neurofeedback and brain stimulation. Video game programming is an incredibly imaginative and artistic space, as opposed to the medical paradigm that is oriented to responding to dysfunction or need. "When you're working from an artistic place," Arnott said, "you're channeling something. And when you're channeling something it's just more raw and more real. There's a respect for mystery."[43]

PROMISES AND PITFALLS

VR is a noninvasive way to trick your brain into being somewhere else, and can generate potentially meaningful, exciting, healing, and transformative experiences. In fact, some of the most popular and quickly developing uses for VR have to do with physical and mental health care education, diagnosis, and treatment. Researchers are experimenting with VR treatments for phobias, post-traumatic stress disorder, panic attacks, pain management, and even smoking cessation.[44] For example, Patrick McNamara of the Center for Mind and Culture in Boston, working with the Virginia Modeling, Analysis, and Simulation Center of Old Dominion University, has developed a VR treatment for nightmare disorder. However, such power means that it can also, of course, generate destructive experiences. McNamara is very careful to load up the VR system with terrifying imagery that is *not* from a research participant's actual nightmares, so as to avoid retraumatizing them.[45] Thus, although the technology itself, as a medium for content, appears to be safe—in fact, some argue that it is significantly healthier than other mediums, given that people can move around while using a VR headset[46]—it would be naive to think that *any* form of media could resist corruption or danger. It is no surprise that the pornography industry has already staked its claim to a corner of the underbelly of the virtual world, and one can imagine the attraction to terrifying and violent video games.[47]

Yet, VR innovators understand that VR *will* gain in popularity and cultural prominence as the technology improves and as the price of headsets continues to decrease. So why not, as Android said, "bring some virtue into virtual reality"? Innovators such as D. J., Android, and Robin Arnott seem to feel a sense of duty to do their part to infuse the field of VR technology with options that foster goodness, beauty, wellness, truth, and creativity. "I'm just really excited to plant some flags out there amid the porn and the zombie shooters," Android said.[48] Moreover, Arnott insists that it is *because* video game designers are so familiar with capturing attention, harnessing focus, and putting gamers into trancelike states that they "have a unique skill set and a unique opportunity: to design trances that are as complex and powerful as [multiplayer online battle arena games] but operate on the pre-personal level of meditation to alter player consciousness temporarily and create a permanent psychological impact."[49]

It's been common for cultural critics to rail against the evils of 2D video games, so we can safely predict what they will say about video games in VR. Video-game addiction is a very real psychological problem that has ruined lives and actually killed sufferers at times. In a somewhat alarmist article, Alex Tisdale of *Vice* declared that "VR is the definition of escapism."[50] He argues that if people get to the point with normal video games that they neglect not only their own care but also their children's care, then this problem will only intensify with the increased level of immersion and presence in VR. In addition to addiction, the issue of gratuitous violence and horror in some video games has concerned many parents and the public for years. Experts' opinions are mixed on whether or not violent games encourage violence in real life,[51] but the perceived realness of VR may cause other, unprecedented problems. Tisdale quotes Denny Unger, the creative director of Cloudhead Games, who says of horror games, "We're very close to having the first death in VR. I firmly believe that. Somebody is going to scare somebody to death—somebody with a heart condition or something like that. It is going to happen. Absolutely."[52]

Most concerning to us are the potential mental health risks associated with VR. Just as with any technology, there *can* be too much of a good thing, and any technology can be misused and abused. In the case of VR, spending too much time in virtual space may actually take the gleam off ordinary reality—it is hard not to think that VR porn might have such an effect—and it isn't difficult to imagine that virtual experiences could cause very real trauma.[53]

In a blog posted to Medium, Tobias van Schneider describes an experience that, based on countless posts on VR and gaming forums, is quite common. After intense VR sessions, van Schneider reports "a weird sense of sadness and depressed feeling." He describes two phases of sensation: physical symptoms and psychological derealization effects. First, immediately after emerging from the virtual space, he said, "you feel strange, almost like you're detached from reality."[54] Visual and kinetic sensations may feel off or funny—he said even interacting with other forms of technology feels almost comical, because a touch screen now feels dull and disappointing. Another user said, "The next morning when I go into work my vision is a little odd when I look at my monitors. Like sometimes there's a fake [screen-door effect] and my eyes get confused when trying to focus."[55] Others report nausea, dizziness, exhaustion, and trouble focusing their eyes. Van Schneider muses that these initial perceptual effects, which usually fade within one or two hours, may be related to and manipulable by settings on the VR gear, for example the interpupillary distance and the refresh rate. Some call these effects cybersickness,[56] and VR companies are invested in finding ways to minimize them.[57]

However, phase two of the VR hangover is a bit more disturbing: van Schneider said that even as he begins to feel better physically and his sense perceptions return to normal, a feeling of sadness and disappointment in the real world persists. "The sky seems less colorful and it just feels like I'm missing the 'magic,'" he said, comparing the first phase of effects to a minor temporary drug trip, but admitting that the lingering phase two effects feel "painfully" real. "After leaving [the virtual world], the rest of the day in reality makes me feel kind of sad. I have no more super powers. I want to touch the sky, rotate the clouds, stretch them, and paint on them," he said, referring to the way he can manipulate his surroundings when using Tilt Brush. "I feel deeply disturbed and often end up just sitting there, staring at a wall because I just don't like doing anything else. I wouldn't say I'm feeling depressed, but there is a lack of motivation and sad feeling in my chest."[58] And van Schneider is no stranger to video gaming, estimating that he played about six hours every day as a teenager. Other experienced gamers report similar experiences: that after taking off their headset, they felt like they were in another world or had a hard time enjoying normal things. One said a thousand-dollar price tag would be worth it to take the feeling away.

These effects are, indeed, quite alarming. The good news is, though, that many users report that they have built up a tolerance, that, as with hangovers from alcohol, the intensity and susceptibility to VR hangovers decreases with time (that is, if the user chooses to play again). And while they don't happen to everyone, even those who do occasionally have a VR hangover don't *always* have one. More research to understand how, why, and when these effects are triggered would surely help us avoid them and minimize their effects.

Despite these dangers, the inevitability of the immense success of VR and its potential applications in everything from mental health and PTSD treatment to surgical training for medical students to virtual sacred moments and psychedelic trips where substance ingestion is optional, make VR worth rigorous research and development. Technologies themselves are rarely unilaterally dangerous or safe, and VR is no exception.

However, when it comes to the application of VR to religious and spiritual experiences, safety concerns aside, there are some strong feelings about appropriateness and whether or not virtual space can constitute a sacred space.

CAN VIRTUAL EXPERIENCES BE SACRED?

Before Android Jones became a full-time digital painter and performing artist, he worked in the video game industry. He eventually left, burned his bridges, and swore off the whole enterprise.[59] His perspective on technology, therefore, includes decades of behind-the-scenes experience with industry leaders. He would never have guessed that he would ever return to anything close to the gaming field like VR. However, the possibilities with VR were so tantalizing and he saw such potential that he approached it with renewed hope. Some people see technology as cold, removed, alien, and foreign, but Android sees it as simply part of Mother Earth:

> When you step back and look at a computer or laptop and ask what you're manipulating here, you find that they're composed of quartz, magnesium, and silicone. They are made from mining the earth. . . . I'm fusing all these different elements, like I said, these earth elements, and using the electrical element of fire, and kind of forging these different elements in the crucible of my own imagination to make something that can create this experience of the sublime, or transcendent, or transformative, and that entire process is one that I hold to be very sacred and very magical.[60]

He wants to get to a point where the technology itself is transparent. Experiences such as the ones produced within SoundSelf, Microdose VR, or Samskara wouldn't be possible without VR, but VR should not be the focus. "Even going back to the Vedas," he said, "they talk about technology that's, like, hundreds and thousands of years further into the future than we are right now. So there's also a kind of humbling [aspect], like whatever this is, this is just what's available now."[61] In other words, VR technology is just the next in a long line of technological forms for humans to engage with and navigate. To get too wrapped up in the medium itself—to either put it on a pedestal as the key to spiritual experience or denounce it as somehow technology taken too far into unnatural territory—is a mistake.

Nonetheless, some people always resist the new and unfamiliar, and often for good reasons. Robin Arnott admits that technological advancements are usually (we'd say always) a double-edged sword—they are very effective for expanding our agency and our ability to do things in the material world, but sometimes in kind of a "soulless way."[62] He is convinced that VR technology, if harnessed in a way that integrates science, materialism, love, and beauty, can "evolve to nourish humanity."[63] He sees this happening now in some circles but understands that it may take a while for the vision to be embraced by mainstream culture. In the meantime, tech such as SoundSelf and Microdose VR will continue to flourish at festivals, concerts, and conferences with very little to no pushback.

By contrast, D. J. Soto, who works and socializes within evangelical Christian groups, has to contend with vigorous opposition to VR Church. In fact, unlike Android, he has been surprised by the level of resistance and lack of support from his community, especially from fellow Christian pastors.

When D. J. felt called to devote his resources and attention to VR Church, he and his family took off to travel a circuitous route from Pennsylvania to California in an effort to visit as many churches along the way as they could, to spread awareness of VR Church, and to drum up interest and funds to help make his vision a reality. However, after a year of travel, he and his wife concluded that VR Church was not going to find much, if any, support, affirmation, or validation in the evangelical Christian community. VR Church has been either rejected or ignored by the majority of mainstream evangelicals who know about it.

Outside of evangelicalism, however, Christians have been surprisingly enthusiastic. And people unconnected to any church, even some atheists and antireligious people, see the value in D. J.'s mission and have offered their services (such as coding for virtual design and photography) free or at reduced rates, and have given game-changing publicity (on the *Today Show* and in *Wired* magazine, for example). One atheist who visited the virtual church emailed D. J. with a recommendation of a worship song that he thought the congregants might enjoy singing. The contrast between the cold reception among evangelical insiders and the warmth of outsiders has been a confusing one to navigate for D. J. and his family. Perhaps, he thinks, despite his disappointment, it could be somewhat beneficial for them to *not* be securely inside the mainstream evangelical camp. He and his family are choosing to trust that God has a divine plan for VR Church.

"It just feels like we're not supposed to be in [the evangelical community], even though I'm all about that!"[64] D. J. said. "It seems like we're supposed to be out of it for whatever reason."[65] The resulting struggle is easy to understand. He recounted experiences of receiving emails from pastor friends saying, "Hey, take a look at this interesting sermon," and when he downloads it, discovering the sermon is all about how online churches are fake.[66] He likens it to being attacked by your own family. Even after receiving a good amount of positive press, support from outside evangelical circles, and more than a year of successful growth, he knows members of the evangelical community still don't take VR Church and its adherents seriously. "We didn't think everyone or every church [would support us]," he said, "but we thought there'd be *someone*. I didn't think there'd be zero. So I feel like we're outsiders, outliers, not by design, but I feel like we are."[67]

When it comes to the sacraments, there is even more explicit resistance. D. J. told us about a recent conversation he had with the pastor of a large, well-known church in California. The pastor said that if someone was housebound and on their deathbed but wanted to get baptized, the pastor would not perform a baptism; he would only baptize people who were able to get out and make it to a proper baptismal pool. D. J. was dumbfounded. "I just thought, 'Ah! Dude! Why not?'" he said. "That doesn't make sense to me. . . . I mean, I try to think, okay, let me try to understand where you're coming from. But, no, I can't understand. I can't get there."[68]

On Sunday, May 20, 2018, VR Church had its first baptismal service. It took place in a different VR environment from the usual church services: a generic VR house with a large backyard swimming pool (see figure 22 in the color insert). D. J. baptized several members via full immersion. One of those members, Alina, who shared her experience in a video posted to VR Church's Facebook page, said, "The thought that I could actually get baptized was just a miracle to me because it's just not possible anywhere else." She was surrounded in virtual space by her community of fellow VR Church members (whom she had gotten to know quite well), she had a whole living room full of people in her own Washington State home who were there to support and celebrate with her, and a group of her family members were gathered in California to participate in the service. Participants who didn't have VR headsets watched a broadcast of the event on their TV screens together. "My sister-in-law cried, my mother cried . . . it was very emotional," Alina said.

D. J. explained to us that one of the exciting things about baptism in VR is that each person—or more precisely, each avatar—is able to remain under water for much longer than anyone could in real life. In this way, he said, "I can really extend the spirit of what baptism is all about. I can leave them under the water to emphasize the death and the burial and just take a moment to share what's happening. . . . It can be a meaningful demonstration of dying to yourself and the forgiveness of sins." He also spoke enthusiastically about the fact that, given that the VR Church community is so open, accepting, and diverse, the baptism will be seen by many people, including atheists, who may actually never have seen a baptism before. "Heck yeah," he said, "that's the spirit of what Jesus was talking about with baptizing! It's totally going to have a massive impact."

That being said, he did mention that most of his friends and people he knows outside VR Church, including his pastor friends, remain skeptical. Predictably, the Catholic Church has taken a very strong stance against digital sacraments of any kind. But even D. J.'s fellow evangelical pastor friends say they don't think a baptism in VR counts as a real baptism. But D. J. isn't discouraged. "You know that kind of makes me chuckle," he said, referring to whether things count or not. But D. J. and the team of VR Church elders had serious conversations on the subject, and it didn't take them long to decide that they were 100 percent comfortable with it.

And Alina, who experienced her own baptism as a genuinely transformative experience, agrees. "It absolutely felt real," she said. "In my brain, it was no different than being baptized outside of VR. My emotions were exactly as they would be: excited, so excited, so happy. It was the single most amazing thing I've done! It was wonderful. It was awesome."

A FUTURE FOR VIRTUOUS VR

Spiritual uses of VR run the gamut from creative, psychedelic-inspired adventures to conservative evangelical Christian worship and potentially even virtual encounters with God. As an emerging technology, it remains to be seen how successful any one modality or spiritual application of VR will be. Samskara has already been met with praise and adulation throughout the Internet, while public access to SoundSelf and Microdose VR is eagerly awaited by techies and psychonauts, and VR Church already has a vast global reach.

We predict that VR Church will soon incorporate full-immersion experiences of Bible stories that may even be able to evoke mystical-type experiences when those immersions include encounters with God, Christ, or other spiritual beings. With these innovations, a whole new conversation will unfold. Will people who have met Jesus virtually feel as though they have met the risen Christ? Theologically, if God can be omnipresent, can God also be present and communicate to believers while they are in the virtual space, through virtual images?

The long-term safety—both psychological and physiological—of VR equipment is largely unknown, especially for young children. We will without a doubt learn more about this in the coming years since VR will likely take over the video game market. The potentially health-enhancing applications of VR technology make it worth the effort needed to research and monitor its effects.

In the coming few years, we shall see if it is indeed possible, as Android hopes, to bring some virtue into virtual reality. Or if, as Terence McKenna predicted in 1990, "the computers of the future will be drugs, and the drugs of the future will be computers."[69]

6

Cleansing the Doors of Perception

If the doors of perception were cleansed every thing would appear to man as it is, Infinite. For man has closed himself up, till he sees all things thro' narrow chinks of his cavern.

—*William Blake,* The Marriage of Heaven and Hell

TED'S TRAUMATIC EXPERIENCE

In a lonely train station on a dark night, Ted, a student from Australia, was waiting for his ride home when he was brutally assaulted by a man who appeared to be high on methamphetamines. The terrifying beating felt as though it would never end. Ted was relieved to escape the attack alive, but the psychological horror of that night took a long-term toll on him and he developed post-traumatic stress disorder. Despite his therapist's disapproval, he began using cannabis to relax and cope with his anxiety and stress. Nonetheless, his PTSD symptoms continued to worsen and he even seriously considered suicide.[1]

A full year after the attack, despite Ted's continued hope that the dark cloud of depression and anxiety might begin to disperse, his symptoms had only gotten worse. He began to see the world as a terrible and hate-filled place. His thoughts and daydreams were haunted by violent imagery. "All I could ever imagine when I imagined something was myself getting murdered or me trying to fight for my life," he told us. "Sometimes I'd win in these daydreams and sometimes I'd lose."

Ted tried to feel okay and to continue his familiar life. One day, for no particular reason, he and a friend decided to gather some of the psychedelic mushrooms that grew locally in forests around their town—*Psilocybe subaeruginosa*, more commonly known as "shrooms"—as they had done several times before. This time, though, they were interested in trying something new. Instead of hanging out playing music or sitting in nature, they decided to lie in complete darkness with their eyes closed, with calm electronic music playing while the psilocybin took effect. Ted had occasionally used psychedelics—in fact, he says his first LSD experience gave him unprecedented insight into his own consciousness and was the reason he chose to major in philosophy at college—but this experience on psilocybin was unlike anything he had ever felt or seen. "It was absolutely incredible," he said. "Utterly mindblowing." Being somewhat familiar with the research literature about mystical experiences (which we will discuss later), Ted told us, "This was the first experience that I could say was somewhat in the range of what they're defining as mystical experience. I had these incredible visions of things growing. It was like a plant would be sprouting out of the ground and then that plant would turn into a tree and then it would kind of dissipate and become flowers that were growing. . . . It was this image of the cycle of life going about almost like a karmic wheel. And it ended up at the stage where I was seeing a baby, a fetus, and it would start at the stage of being a cell. It would form into a baby and its face would age and eventually it got to an old person and turned into a skeleton and then finally turned into dust and disappeared."

The visions were at once infinitesimal and expansive—like looking through a microscope and a telescope at the same time. Ted continued: "It was also a vision of the beginning of the universe, the middle of the universe, and the end of the universe. It was like I was seeing both the entire totality of the universe, and also a very small fraction of it, at the same time."

Ted explained that the experience felt timeless and spatially expansive. As these visions were flooding his consciousness, he was also able to form reflective thoughts: "Good lord," he thought, "this is what life is! This is what it means to be alive!" The experience was like a confrontation with what is ultimately real. As he put it, it was as if the universe was saying to him, "'You're currently a living being, you're breathing! You're going to be here, you're going to die, and that's the way it is. And so if that's the way it is, you can either be happy with this and live a happy life and have great fun, or you can find this a sad thing and live a sad life, and you know at the end you're still going to die and you're going to be dead. So what choice do you want to make here?'"

When the effect of the psilocybin began to fade, Ted, elated, turned to his friend who had been lying quietly next to him in the dark. They hadn't spoken to each other for the entire duration of the trip, but Ted was convinced that their experiences had somehow mirrored each other and they had somehow come to the exact same conclusions. "We just turned to each other and literally started talking about exactly that," he said. "And we said there was no reason why we couldn't make this trip a meaningful trip." They agreed that they had both had more physiologically intense experiences using psychedelics in the past, but that this trip was vastly more meaningful and spiritually illuminating. "We just decided that, every day, we were going to wake up with a smile on our faces, and we were going to try and see something positive in the world, in other people, and in our interactions," Ted said, "and to put more good into the world than bad. And so from that moment I left and did exactly that."

The experience, dramatic in itself, inspired a dramatic and lasting change in Ted. "I've gone from being incredibly depressed and thinking about suicide every couple of weeks to just completely the opposite," he said. "I wake up with a genuine smile, happy to be about the day and to see the colors and everything that is out there." Remarkably, this single, psychedelic-assisted mystical experience has even effectively reversed many of Ted's PTSD symptoms. "It stopped the feelings of meaninglessness," he explained. "The world couldn't *just* be a violent place if it could also give rise to an experience as beautiful and as indescribable as what I had had." After the experience, his memory of the attack in the train station also changed: "It's still there," he said. "I still think about it sometimes, but it has no real control over me whatsoever."

After what amounted to a profoundly healing experience, Ted was convinced that he should no longer be silent about the spiritual and restorative potential of psychedelics—though he was well aware that contemporary Western culture does not look kindly upon psychedelic substances and that it was easiest and safest to maintain a level of secrecy about using them. But Ted felt he'd got his life back, and he couldn't remain silent about it. "I realized that, if the potential of psychedelics is such that it could fix my life in that way, there was absolutely no reason not to talk to people about it—my parents or coworkers or friends—so I became incredibly open about it. And from that very experience I decided to go on to [graduate school] and write a thesis on it. And so here we are: my first psychedelic experience led me to study philosophy at the university, and then my most prolific experience has sent me on this course to graduate school and academic psychedelia." Sure enough, Ted is currently completing a master's in philosophy focusing on existential insights related to classical psychedelic use.

The quality of Ted's experience is not unique among people who use psychedelic substances as technologies with the intention to enhance their spiritual lives and emotional health. But what does that mean for spiritual seekers today? After all, ingesting psilocybin mushrooms is illegal in most places, and one would assume there's a good reason for this. In 2019, Denver and Oakland became the first US cities to effectively decriminalize possession of small amounts of psilocybin, but legalization processes across the nation are likely to be slow and painstaking. Legal or not, if a person is interested in a mystical experience but afraid of the possibility of a bad trip, what is she to do? Was Ted's experience a fluke? What about its transformative effects? Will they last?

Despite their fraught place in the American legal system, which

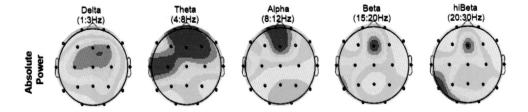

Figure 14. A qEEG brain map showing the brain activity of a person with ADHD while sitting quietly with eyes open, compared to the average human brain activity doing the same activity. Each circle is a map of the head (*facing upward; note the nose and ears*) and each dot within the head is an EEG electrode affixed to the scalp. The average electrical activity, usually over a few seconds, is measured using the EEG electrodes and then decomposed into specific frequencies. Red indicates overactivity relative to normal, whereas green is normal activity. Notice here the overactive theta waves indicating ADHD: the front part of the brain responsible for executive functions looks almost like it is sleeping.

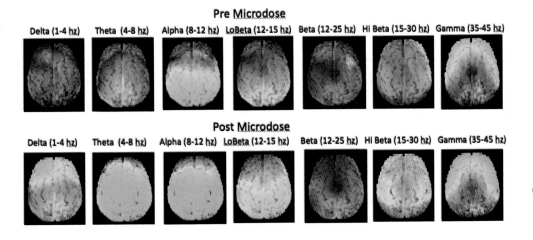

Figure 15. This qEEG brain map show the person's brain activity before and after a psilocybin microdose (0.25 mg) compared to the average person's sober brain from the QEEG Pro Database. Green indicates normal activity whereas red indicates overactivity relative to normal. In this particular patient, the state prior to the microdose is far from normal and the effect of the microdose is to shift the brain more toward the normal range of functioning.

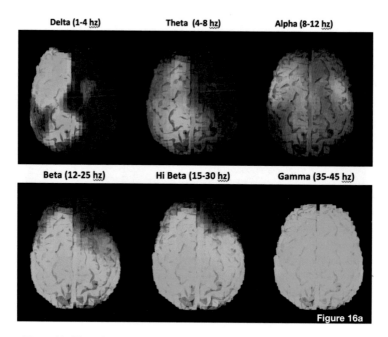

Figure 16a

Figures 16a and b. These brain maps show the changes in one person's brain after a 23-minute SOMA breathwork session. SOMA breathwork is a form of guided meditation that derives from ancient South Asian practices of Pranayama. Dr. Jeff Tarrant and his colleagues at the Neuro-Meditation Institute were interested in whether SOMA breathwork techniques could result in significant altered states of consciousness. Here, one subject's brain activity post-breathwork is compared to their own brain activity pre-breathwork. Blues indicate decreased activity, while reds and grays indicate increased activity. Green areas did not change significantly. **Figure 16a** shows a qEEG brain map of overall patterns of activity. Delta, theta, and alpha brain waves all decreased significantly and globally, while beta waves decreased in the right frontal regions. **Figure 16b** shows a sLORETA (standardized low-resolution brain electromagnetic tomography) brain map, which can examine brain wave patterns from specific deeper brain regions. These images focus on changes in the brain structures of the default mode network, overactivity of which can lead to mental health concerns. The SOMA breathwork resulted in significant decreases in both delta and alpha activity, which are changes associated with mystical experiences and improvements in mental health.

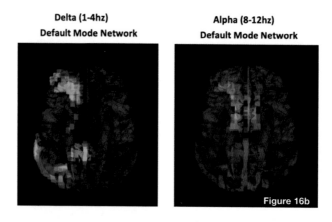

Figure 16b

Figure 17. Heartsync in action. Participants in the half circle are looking up at a screen displaying an attractive visualization of participants' heart rates.

Figure 18. A GroupFlow ritual in process.

Figure 19. Avatars of Pastor D.J. Soto and some attendees posing in front of the VR Church building.

Figure 20. Isness in action; the virtual world perceived by participants looks very different than what an observer sees. An artist has added the glowing orbs on the participants.

Figure 21. The swirling patterns of SoundSelf visuals.

Figure 22. A VR Church baptism.

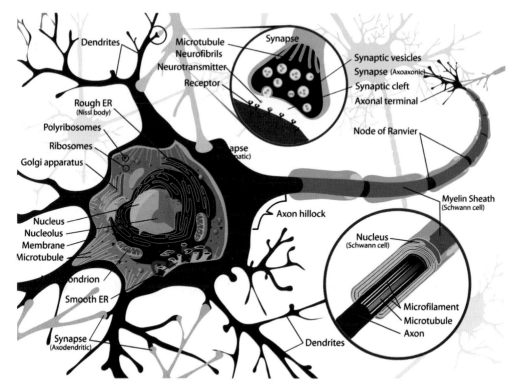

Dendrites
Microtubule
Neurofibrils
Neurotransmitter
Receptor
Synapse
Rough ER
(Nissl body)
Polyribosomes
Ribosomes
Golgi apparatus
...apse
...matic)
Nucleus
Nucleolus
Membrane
Microtubule
...ondrion
Smooth ER
Synapse
(Axodendritic)
Synaptic vesicles
Synapse (Axoaxonic)
Synaptic cleft
Axonal terminal
Node of Ranvier
Axon hillock
Myelin Sheath
(Schwann cell)
Nucleus
(Schwann cell)
Microfilament
Microtubule
Axon
Dendrites

Figure 23. Neurons and their connections at synapses.

Figure 24. Artist's impression of a neural network.

Figure 25. An indigenous coca ceremony at the Paititi Institute, which also offers ayahuasca ceremonies, in Iquitos, Peru. *Photo courtesy of Greg Goodman* (www.adventuresofagoodman.com).

Figure 26. Santo Daime Church meeting.

complicates the potential for research and testing, we actually do know quite a lot about psychedelic substances. Humans have always been in close contact with mind-altering substances. In fact, evidence of spiritual practices involving psychedelic plants for exploring alternate dimensions of reality and communing with the gods reaches back as far as we can trace, into human prehistory. Psychedelic plants have always been prized for their potential to inspire mystical awe, gratitude, and transformation.

GENERATING GOD WITHIN

Psychedelic means "mind manifesting." And some psychedelic substances are often referred to as *entheogens*. *Entheogen* is derived from Greek and translates literally to "generating" (*gen*) "God" (*theo*) "within" (*en*). Put simply, entheogens are substances with spiritual effects. The name suggests that these substances bring those who consume them into the presence of God, but even people who don't necessarily believe in a monotheistic supernatural deity also attest to their psycho-spiritual potency.

For millennia, human beings have located entheogens within the botanical world. For example, psilocybin mushrooms, *Salvia divinorum*, and cannabis are plants that grow naturally in the wild and also have intense psychoactive properties when ingested. Harvesting and ingesting the plants directly remains common today, but the scientific field of neuropsychopharmacology can also isolate the psychoactive ingredients within such entheogenic plants and artificially synthesize them. For example, ayahuasca, an entheogenic mixture commonly used in Amazonian shamanism and its Catholic-hybrid offshoots, is traditionally brewed with a mixture of local plants. Just as lab scientists created entirely new compounds such as LSD, which some people find useful for spiritual enhancement, so scientists can create pharmahuasca—a synthesized pill with the same psychoactive components as the main ingredients in ayahuasca.[2] This chapter and the next are focused on both naturally occurring and artificially synthesized entheogens.

How can plants or chemicals possibly bring someone into the presence of God? How do scientists explain their reported effects? How do philosophers and theologians interpret entheogen-enhanced religious experience? And what is the experience like for the users themselves? We'll address each of these questions, beginning with the scientific perspective.

One point seems certain: there is no special "god spot" or soul circuit in the brain that, when stimulated, takes a person on a spiritual journey. If there were, the serotonin system might be the closest candidate, but the serotonin system has many critical bodily and mental functions, so it's certainly not dedicated to spiritual experiences. Instead, the human brain, unlike the electrical circuits in your house, consists of overlapping circuitry of multiple kinds. Though the brain's neurons send electrochemical signals along their length in much the same way regardless of the type of neuron, the neurotransmitters that send electrical signals between neurons vary widely in both quantity and type.

Neurotransmitters can be released by sending a chemical into the specially structured gap between neurons, called the synapse, and signal to the receiving neuron how it should behave (see figure 23 in the color insert). This means that the very same set of neurons can be involved in many active circuits, depending on the different neurotransmitters actively floating within and between their synapses and the receptors studded in the walls of the synapses. The serotonin neurons make up serotonin circuits and the dopamine neurons make up dopamine circuits, but sometimes those circuits overlap because some synapses can handle signaling from both serotonin and dopamine neurotransmitters. This ingenious system not only saves space, it also allows for intricate overlaps and connectivity between neural systems (see figure 24 in the color insert). This is one of many reasons why mapping brain circuitry is so difficult and probably why the neurology of conscious experience, including altered states of consciousness enhanced with entheogens, is so fascinating.

Entheogens produce their spiritual effects typically by introducing chemical compounds into the synapses that alter neurotransmitter functions. Neuronal networks are formidably complex and extremely beautiful—in fact, they are often the subject of abstract art, including art inspired by psychedelic use. When conditions are right, signaling chemicals (neurotransmitters) are released from the output side of one neuron (the axon), travel across the synaptic gap (also known as the synaptic cleft), and dock with special protein assemblies called receptors on the input side of another neuron (the dendrites). The neurotransmitter, now in its receptor dock on the next neuron, causes a cascade of effects in the target neuron. Soon the neuron releases the neurotransmitter back into the synaptic cleft, where it eventually gets reabsorbed into the source neuron through a reuptake mechanism so the molecule can be reused. This whole process is mind-bogglingly fast, as it would have to be so that the person to whom the brain belongs can respond appropriately to the world around them—see the ball, run and catch the ball, steady and throw the ball, and so on.[3]

There are several ways in which neurotransmitter activity can be affected by chemicals that may be floating around in the brain— chemicals from entheogens, alcohol, nicotine, drugs of abuse, and even some foods. All these effects are based on the neurochemistry of neurotransmitter production, release, reception, and reuptake. Here are five of the most common effects, with examples mostly related to chemicals widely regarded as entheogens.

First, a neurochemical can stimulate the release of a neurotransmitter from one neuron into the synapse. This happens with MDMA—also called ecstasy—which prompts the release of the feel-good neurotransmitter serotonin.[4]

Second, a neurochemical can dock with receptors on the dendrite (target) side of the synapse, thereby mimicking a neurotransmitter's function. This happens with naturally occurring substances such as DMT (the hallucinogenic compound in ayahuasca), mescaline, and psilocybin;

and also with artificial substances such as LSD or synthetic DMT. Each of these chemicals floods the synapse with chemicals that look and act like serotonin even when no actual serotonin is active.[5]

Third, a neurochemical can block receptors in several different ways so that the appropriate neurotransmitter function cannot be performed and signaling is suppressed. This happens with PCP (more commonly known as angel dust), ketamine (an anesthetic), and nitrous oxide—the laughing gas often used in dental clinics. These chemicals block receptors for the neurotransmitter NMDA, preventing the NMDA circuits from functioning, and that can induce powerful hallucinogenic experiences.[6]

Fourth, a neurochemical can inhibit the chemical breakdown of a neurotransmitter, thereby allowing it to remain active in the synapse for much longer than it would otherwise. This happens with monoamine oxidase inhibitors (MAOIs), used as antidepressants, which prevent the breakdown of monoamine neurotransmitters as well as neurochemicals such as DMT. Therefore, when MAOIs are mixed together with DMT, as they are in ayahuasca brews, MAOIs enhance and prolong DMT's effect on the serotonin system.[7]

Fifth, a neurochemical can inhibit the neuron's reuptake pumps, thereby leaving the corresponding neurotransmitters active within the synapse for longer than would otherwise be the case. This happens with SSRIs, or selective serotonin reuptake inhibitors, common antidepressants that prevent the reuptake of serotonin and thus leave it active within the synapse, where it can change mood and sometimes produce spiritual effects.[8]

There's more to consider than the neuropharmacological aspects of the production of entheogenic experiences. Much more. Researchers who study entheogens are always careful to note the importance of the particular biological and psychological characteristics of the person ingesting the substance *and* the particular context in which the experience occurs. These factors—called "set and setting," a phrase that came out of the psychedelic decades of the 1960s and 1970s—have profound influence on the qualities of the psychedelic experience. Ted's extraordinary experience described at the beginning of this chapter seems to have been at least enhanced, if not dependent on, his and his friend's choice of setting—lying down in total darkness with their eyes closed. We'll build on the importance of set and setting to consider the potential risks and benefits associated with entheogens.

BAD TRIPS, DIFFICULT EXPERIENCES, AND POTENTIAL RISKS

This same combination of concerns—for the intentions and vulnerabilities of each user (set) and the time, space, and behaviors surrounding the use (setting)—recurs across traditions that involve entheogenic rituals. For example, as for set, does a potential user have any underlying mental health conditions? What are her or his intentions and expectations for the experience? Are they anxious and afraid, calm and open, or craving and impatient? Then as for setting, how is the space set up for the experience? Is there soothing or angry music playing? Will there be safe and sober people present? Are there any objects or people in the area likely to trigger negative emotions in the user?

The emphasis on set and setting is especially important in rituals related to the ingestion of LSD because that particular chemical is well known for the potential to produce bad trips—terrifying and sometimes traumatizing hallucinatory experiences that can lead to full-blown panic attacks. In fact, Albert Hofmann—the chemist who accidentally discovered LSD—had a terrifying experience the first time he intentionally ingested it, perhaps due to his anxious and fearful mindset after he realized how strong the effect was going to be. He describes the experience in his book, *LSD: My Problem Child*:

> Everything in the room spun around, and the familiar objects and
> pieces of furniture assumed grotesque, threatening forms. They
> were in continuous motion, animated, as if driven by an inner rest-
> lessness. The lady next door, whom I scarcely recognized, brought

me milk—in the course of the evening I drank more than two liters. She was no longer Mrs. R., but rather a malevolent, insidious witch with a colored mask. Even worse than these demonic transforma- tions of the outer world, were the alterations that I perceived in myself, in my inner being. Every exertion of my will, every attempt to put an end to the disintegration of the outer world and the dissolution of my ego, seemed to be wasted effort. A demon had invaded me, had taken possession of my body, mind, and soul. . . . I was seized by the dreadful fear of going insane. I was taken to another world, another place, another time. My body seemed to be without sensation, lifeless, strange. Was I dying?[9]

Little by little, of course, the experience softened and Hofmann realized he would be okay. In fact, the next day, he even felt renewed and refreshed: "Everything glistened and sparkled in a fresh light," he wrote. "The world was as if newly created. All my senses vibrated in a condition of highest sensitivity, which persisted for the entire day."[10] It's hard to say if this post-LSD feeling was a product of profound relief that he had survived such a horrifying experience or if it was a neuro- logical effect of the substance. Either way, LSD can elicit both incredi- bly positive, life-changing experiences *and* incredibly scary, sometimes even traumatic experiences.

It's been nearly eighty years since Hofmann's first LSD trip, and people using LSD as an entheogen have learned that, while bad trips can't be eliminated, their frequency can be minimized through the man- agement of set and setting.[11] For example, a loving social environment helps to preclude problems, as does a positive and expectant frame of mind. In fact, that's true for all entheogens, and, as we'll see in the next chapter, longstanding spiritual traditions revolving around entheogens pay close attention to such considerations. Increasingly, the organizers of festivals and raves, where people use entheogens recreationally, are becoming more interested in providing safe spaces and retreats for people who are at risk for a bad trip, or in the midst of one.

We spoke with Maggie, a psychologist who has volunteered for the Zendo Psychedelic Harm Reduction Project.[12] Zendo is a nonprofit organization related to the Multidisciplinary Association for Psychedelic Study (MAPS) that sets up tents or booths at popular events such as music festivals where psychedelic use is common. The Zendo tents are staffed by people trained to sit with and provide comfort to people on psychedelics and can become safe places for people to go if they begin to have a difficult experience while using psychedelic substances. Zendo prefers the term *difficult experiences* above *bad trips* because part of their intention is to demonstrate that even scary or challenging psychedelic experiences can sometimes be reframed and managed in such a way as to encourage self-knowledge and growth.

Zendo's mission, as presented on their website, is threefold: the Zendo Project "reduces the number of unnecessary psychiatric arrests and hospitalizations; creates an environment where volunteers can work alongside one another to improve their harm reduction skills and receive training and feedback; [and] demonstrates that safe, productive psychedelic experiences are possible without the need for law enforcement–based prohibitionist policies."[13] In our conversation, Maggie highlighted the importance of knowing one's limits and developing coping skills before embarking on a psychedelic journey. She explained that many of the people who end up in a Zendo tent probably took too high a dose, or at least "more than they were ready for." She explained, "Anyone who takes too much will probably have a difficult experience even if they're the most prepared emotionally." However, psychedelic substances can trigger difficult experiences at reasonable doses, too. "If people haven't addressed some sort of trauma within themselves," she told us, "the psychedelics remove all of your defenses. Your defense mechanisms that you live with day-to-day are ripped apart and some people can't handle whatever is shown to them." She encourages people who are setting out to take psychedelic substances to be honest with themselves about their intentions and expectations. In addition to beginning with small doses, she recommends that people

have a relaxation or meditation practice in place so that, if an experience becomes overwhelming, they will be more able to soothe and
calm themselves. In short, using entheogens is a bit like playing with
fire: they can provide warmth, comfort, and a mesmerizing glow to an
already wonderful experience, or they can burn you if things become
overwhelming.

In terms of creating a good setting, Maggie emphasized the importance of being with the right people—people who make you feel loved,
respected, and supported. When that's not the case, there can be real
danger. Maggie herself is no stranger to difficult experiences and told
us about her most challenging experience on psychedelics, which was
triggered by the presence of a boyfriend with whom she had a fraught
relationship. "I was not in the healthiest relationship at the time," she
explained, "and I think that really put me in a weird place."

The couple was at a Phish concert with friends and had both taken
some LSD. She described the first part of the experience as beautiful,
emotional, and peaceful. But when the concert ended, she still had a
sense that she hadn't processed something important. "I was feeling
some emotion going through the concert and then all of a sudden it was
cut off, and that feeling was not good for me," she said. "I remember
the person I was dating at the time was looking at me. And even though
he was having his own psychedelic experience, I was very confused. I
asked him, 'Why are you looking at me?' And he wasn't responding
and so I was just very confused. That's where it started going down-
hill." Later, she realized that she sensed a lack of validation and acceptance in their relationship, so when he looked at her, she interpreted his
stare as judgmental: "So that [tension] really came out. I felt very right
but this person is telling me I'm wrong."

When another friend tried to assure Maggie that things were okay,
she began to have paranoid thoughts that her boyfriend and friend
were ganging up against her. "It just snowballed for me at that point,"
she said. She began to argue with them and her paranoia grew. "That's
when I thought everyone was trying to do something to me. I recognize

that it was paranoia but I didn't understand. . . . I started thinking about the disconnect from everyone, like, nobody trusts me, nobody understands me. I just felt very negative."

At moments, this experience expanded to include a sense of alienation from God also. Maggie was raised as a Christian and had been exploring her beliefs and relationship with God throughout many aspects of her life, including her psychedelic use, during which she said she often felt a sense of divine connection. However, during this difficult experience, she explained, "I [felt] like there was no God, or that God doesn't love me, like a void of anything spiritual—feeling like the polar opposite of anything good and loving. What if that's reality? I remember thinking stuff like that."

Maggie explained that, informed by her subsequent experience as a Zendo volunteer, she believes it would have been helpful if her friends had not denied the validity of her experience and had allowed her to walk alone, while remaining within view. Perhaps one close friend—one that she was not currently reacting to—could have walked with her quietly, without trying to convince her that her thoughts were paranoid or delusional, but rather simply allowing her to reflect and work through them on her own. While she empathizes with her friends' natural reactions to a tense situation, Maggie's experience highlights both the value of the type of harm-reduction training that Zendo provides and the real potential for negative experiences with substances such as LSD.

The necessity of paying careful attention to set and setting highlights an important difference between entheogenic technologies and the interventions we've considered in previous chapters. Entheogens are *not* mechanistic switches that throw people into a predictable altered state of consciousness.

Besides the immediate danger of a terrifying experience, psychoactive substances also sometimes carry potential for long-term effects. The first among these is the puzzle of downregulation, which refers to the body's tendency to build tolerance. Drugs of abuse (which do not qualify as entheogens) routinely lead to downregulation both in the body's production of the neurotransmitters associated with the drug in question and in the brain's sensitivity to those neurotransmitters.[14] This means that there are long-term changes in the brain that persist even after the drug has completely worn off. This is an instance of neuroplasticity: the brain is constantly adapting to its chemical environment. Change the chemical environment and the brain will often change, too.

The two aspects of downregulation in drugs of abuse relate to dosage and addiction. On the one hand, a body may become so accustomed to the drug that the same dosage has decreasing effects over time. That means that a larger (and presumably more expensive) dose of the drug is necessary to produce the sought-after high. On the other hand, downregulation can suppress typical functions of the associated neurotransmitters—the brain will no longer function normally in the absence of the drug. This means that the ordinary experience of life while not under the influence may become dull or painful rather than luminous and joyful—this is the addiction aspect of downregulation. Put the dosage and addiction aspects of downregulation together, and it is easy to see how drugs of abuse lead to a spiraling cycle of increasing desperation. Drugs that cause these miserable effects cannot be called entheogens.

Expert meditators claim that their spiritual practice, despite producing a profoundly compelling type of bliss, does not trigger downregulation as a side effect. And indeed, signs of downregulation seem to be absent: people who learn how to produce a blissful meditation state can produce it more rather than less easily in the future, and ordinary life is more rather than less luminous and joyful because of it. The neurological explanation for bliss without downregulation is a target of scientific research in studies of meditation, and there are now valuable theoretical models of how this works.[15]

One vital question about drugs with spiritual effects is whether they involve downregulation to the same degree as drugs of abuse or whether their effects are more like meditative bliss, apparently free from downregulation side effects. Based on the reports we have gathered and the people we have interviewed, we would estimate that the answer is somewhere in between, varying depending on the drug.

Entheogenic experiences tend not to take the shine off ordinary experience. They either leave it the same or, as Ted's experience shows us, they sometimes boost the luminosity of normal life based on powerful memories of the way entheogens bring spiritual reality to life. Ted described the effect of one particular psilocybin experience as facilitating a renewed love and appreciation for life. In the long history of our species' entanglement with mind-altering chemicals, a condition for a substance to be an entheogen is that normal experience off the chemicals is not negatively impacted by occasionally being on the chemicals. When this condition does not hold—for example, when someone experiences the pull of addiction because ordinary life becomes intolerable when not using the chemical—the substance crosses a line to drug of abuse.

The dosage side of downregulation, however, might be a different story. People sometimes do report that larger doses of a nonaddictive drug (for example, LSD) are needed to produce the familiar and desired effect.[16] Because of such reports, we suspect that some (not all) entheogens may involve partial downregulation in the dosage aspect, such that greater doses are needed to produce similar responses over time, even though normal experience off the chemical tends not to be negatively impacted.

In regard to downregulation, therefore, we have a series of distinctions that can be used to classify chemicals. These distinctions refer to the two aspects of downregulation described above: the dosage aspect (referring to the level needed to produce desired results) and the addiction aspect (referring to the damaging of normal experience that produces a craving for the chemical).

- Chemicals such as psilocybin that produce spiritual illumination with no downregulation in either the dosage or addiction aspects noncontroversially qualify as entheogens.

- Chemicals such as LSD that produce spiritual illumination with no downregulation in the addiction aspect but with downregulation in the dosage aspect are tricky entheogens, requiring very careful monitoring.
- Chemicals such as cocaine or heroin or nicotine that produce downregulation in the addiction aspect are *not* entheogens, regardless of any spiritual illumination they might yield.

Another possible long-term effect of entheogen use relates to cognitive-emotional and physiological aspects of human bodies. In addition to short-term negative cognitive-emotional effects, such as terrifying bad trips, panic attacks, cognitive delusions, or the difficult experiences that bring people to the Zendo tent, some substances may have long-term negative impact on cognitive-emotional functioning—in short, brain damage.

We know that drugs of abuse are more than merely addictive; they can also cause long-lasting or even permanent structural and functional damage to the brain, impeding normal cognitive-emotional-behavioral function. Even drugs that are nonaddictive for many people, such as THC-rich varieties of marijuana, can reduce motivation and ambition, which is a long-term cognitive-emotional impact. Both addictive and nonaddictive drugs can have long-term physiological impacts as well as cognitive-emotional impacts—these impacts may be either positive or negative, ranging from profound healing from trauma to enhanced creative openness, from altering sex drive to changing memory, and from depressing fertility to transporting carcinogens into the body (the worst of the latter, nicotine-and-tar-laced cigarettes, are paradoxically legal, a pointed reminder that economics and politics are at least as important as medicine and clinical psychology in decisions about the legality of drugs).

Researchers are still studying the potential negative long-term effects on cognition, emotion, and physiology associated with entheogens. Since many of these substances are illegal, acquiring permission to administer them to research study participants is not easy. As research continues, however, there is a growing consensus that some entheogens, such as psilocybin, appear to be very safe in the long term.[17] However, we must approach each entheogen on its own terms. Toxicity and safety considerations are likely to vary quite a bit between different drugs. For example, while occasional recreational or therapeutic use of MDMA appears to be safe, *heavy* MDMA use may have negative long-term effects on the serotonin system, especially in women.[18] Moreover, chronic heavy use of LSD, the most potent of the known psychedelic substances, has been shown in animal models to alter the expression of genes related to the dopamine and serotonin systems. In rats, high doses of LSD induce a schizophrenia-like psychotic condition, causing hyperactivity, anhedonia (inability to feel pleasure), and impaired social behavior.[19] The likelihood that chronic LSD use may have similar effects in humans necessitates more cautious safety recommendations than other entheogens require. The longitudinal studies needed to evaluate the long-term health effects of entheogens in such a way as to surface causal connections have not been conducted. Therefore, we are thrown back on impressions compiled from a rich array of narratives and personal contacts.

Wesley's serendipitous encounter, described in the preface, with several representatives of a Christian church that uses LSD rather than bread and wine in their eucharistic sacrament—much as the Neo-American Church does—was disturbing for precisely these reasons. It was his friendship with the great scholar-guru Huston Smith, to whom this book is dedicated, that led to this experience. Huston was visiting Boston and invited Wesley to dinner with some of Huston's longtime friends in the area. Knowing Wesley's interest in intense spiritual experiences, Huston took great delight in making the introduction; and lively conversations ensued about sacramental theology, LSD, and entheogens more generally. While these folks appeared to be completely comfortable with their chosen spiritual practice, their mode of communication was noticeably different—and different in the same way for all of them. They would wait an unusually long time before responding, which made the conversation a little stilted until you got used to the strange pacing. They produced speech more slowly and more effortfully, pausing to search for words even when the word choice seemed obvious. They seemed less able to comprehend complex reasoning, forcing the conversation to remain at a simple level, focused on experience. Wesley didn't speak with Huston about it at the time and never had the chance later, so we don't know what Huston thought about it, more's the pity.

Possibly related to this, Albert Hofmann himself warned of long-term (though not permanent) psychological effects: "In spite of a good mood at the beginning of a session—positive expectations, beautiful surroundings and sympathetic company—I once fell into a terrible depression. This unpredictability of effects is the major danger of LSD."[20] There are thousands of online warnings about the potency and unpredictability of LSD.

The experience of meeting and talking at length with people who regularly use LSD as an entheogen has stayed with us as a warning: there is a possibility that frequent ingestion of certain nonaddictive substances may produce long-term deleterious cognitive-emotional effects. This makes it more difficult to apply the honorific *entheogen* to them. We are confident that scientists working in this field will continue to shed light on this question.

THE HEALING POWER OF MYSTICAL EXPERIENCES

Dr. William A. Richards has been studying entheogens such as psilocybin and MDMA in university settings since the 1960s—in other words, since before they were illegal. His early experiences with psychedelics set the trajectory of his career and he has remained an active participant in whatever research was legal at any given time. He is currently studying psilocybin on multiple fronts at Johns Hopkins University, including psilocybin-assisted psychotherapy for patients coping with a cancer diagnosis or end-of-life distress, and psilocybin-occasioned mystical experiences among expert meditators and religious clergy members. We spoke with him to get an up-to-date insider's perspective on state-of-the-art research in the field.

Dr. Richards first encountered an entheogen during the second year of his master of divinity program at Yale Divinity School. On his way to becoming a minister (or so he thought), Richards went abroad for a year to study theology at the Georg-August University in Göttingen in Germany. On the recommendation of a friend who had reported an interesting experience, he found himself volunteering for a research study on psilocybin in the Department of Psychiatry. At that time, in the early 1960s, there was very little recreational use among students and no black market, but it was the focus of a growing field of research. Richards explained that "it wasn't a drug of abuse at that time. It was just an interesting substance. . . . When I was first given psilocybin, there was no controversy at all! It was fully legal and it was considered a perfectly rational thing for a graduate student to do. If you want some experiential learning and maybe some insights into how the mind works, here's an interesting substance, you know? Try it out, write a good research report, and let's see what we can learn from this." He added, with a sense of wonderment, "There was absolutely no stigma. It's hard to even imagine now."[21] So, left alone in the basement of the Psychiatry Department, not quite knowing what he was in for, since at the time such research studies involved very little preparation or guidance, Richards received a relatively low dose of psilocybin.[22]

What followed was a defining moment for him. He became completely immersed in the imagery that flooded his visual field, and later wrote of the experience: "I seemed to fully become the multidimensional patterns or to lose my usual identity within them as the eternal brilliance of mystical consciousness manifested itself."[23] The experience seemed to transcend time, history, and any awareness of love, beauty, and peace that he ever imagined possible. "'Awe,' 'Glory,' and 'Gratitude' were the only words that remained relevant," he explains in his book, *Sacred*

Knowledge: Psychedelics and Religious Experiences.[24] Just as he felt his consciousness begin shifting back toward an ego-centered state, Richards felt the need to somehow capture the experience lest he forget what he believed had been revealed to him. He quickly found some paper and wrote, "Reality *is*. It is perhaps not important what one thinks about it!" Later, he describes the paucity of these words as an "insipid souvenir"[25] compared to the depth and value of the memory of the experience that remained "vividly accessible" in his mind long after that day: "In truth, it proved to be a pivotal fulcrum that provided clarity and direction as my subsequent path in life gradually unfolded before me."[26]

Richards ended up finding many of his theology courses rather dry and pedantic and he struggled to find purpose in exercises such as "arguing over the meaning of some Hebrew word at seven in the morning."[27] By contrast, his experiences in the psychiatry laboratory were revelatory both personally and academically: "I discovered the whole experiential dimension of religion in the Department of Psychiatry."[28]

Upon returning to Yale, Richards made some unsuccessful attempts to bring this awareness and reverence for the spiritual depth he experienced with psychedelics into his theology and philosophy classrooms. He tells one story of his attempt to answer the philosophical question posed by Immanuel Kant in *The Critique of Pure Reason*: whether it was possible to know spiritual truth directly.

Fresh from a visit to Baltimore's Spring Grove Hospital, where alcoholics were receiving psychotherapy assisted by LSD under a grant from the National Institute of Mental Health, I found myself remembering a conversation with a man who had suffered from alcoholism, had been hospitalized, and had experienced a mystical form of consciousness during the action of LSD. . . . I summoned the courage to raise my hand and say something like, "Well, I just visited a research center in Baltimore and spoke with an alcoholic who reported a mystical experience with LSD, and he said, 'Yes, it is possible directly to know spiritual truth.'" A stunned, very awkward silence followed, as if I had violated a sacred academic taboo by introducing empirical information into a philosophical discussion. Time momentarily seemed to have stopped. Then without anyone responding to my words, the drone resumed and debate continued with selected references to the writings of philosophers long dead whether such knowledge could be possible. It seemed incomprehensible that sophisticated Yale graduate students could learn anything from some alcoholic who had taken a drug.[29]

Eventually, perhaps driven by his rather uninspiring experiences in seminary classrooms, Richards switched from a focus on ministry to a concentration called Teaching and Research in Religion. He remains passionate about the possible applications of psychedelics in education, especially religious education, and wonders if such applications will ever be legal. He likens the use of psychedelics for philosophers and theologians to ethnographic fieldwork for an anthropologist: "If you're studying some African tribe, isn't it great to take a trip to Africa and interact with the tribe instead of just reading about it in a dark carrel of the library?" He told us, "In the same way, if you want to understand Plato, why not take a sacrament like he did and see where his ideas came from?! It seems like a no-brainer to me."[30]

Richards feels especially strongly about the prospect of integrating psychedelic-aided experiential learning into seminary education in an attempt to elicit primary religious experiences in students. He cites several examples of clergy who have admitted to him that their original impetus for pursuing ministry work was their early experiences of psilocybin in college. Of course, these confessions are always accompanied by an emphatic acknowledgment that they could never reveal this publicly for fear of being misunderstood or discredited, given the cultural stigma against entheogens. Richards believes that, were psychedelic substances legal, we might hear many more such cases of psychedelic experiences leading to vibrant careers in ministry. He believes that "if and when entheogens become legally available as elective tools in theological education and in religious retreats and practices . . . the experiences they occasion will contribute to balanced religious lives and healthy religious communities."[31]

In this same vein, a current project for which Richards is one of the head researchers is a collaboration between New York University School of Medicine and Johns Hopkins University called the Religious Leaders Study. The researchers believe that since religious leaders have devoted their personal and professional lives to experiencing, studying, and leading spiritual growth, these leaders "will be able to make nuanced discriminations of their psilocybin experiences, thus contributing to the scientific understanding of the mystical type experience."[32] The study gives two high-dose psilocybin sessions to clergy members from all the major world religions—or as Richards put it, "two attempts to explore profound spiritual states."[33] Given the goal of the study, there is even an option to increase the second dose if the first one fails to elicit a proper mystical experience. "The idea is to allow someone to explore both the mystical and the interface between interpersonal relationships in this lifetime and the mystical," he said.[34] Having been the guide for hundreds of psilocybin sessions, Richards is eager to see how these particular people—religious professionals—manifest and make sense of mystical experiences. His preliminary observations are that two things tend to happen: "On the one hand they develop a profound tolerance for the sacred in different world religions. But at the same time, they get a deeper appreciation for their own language, their own tradition, their own heritage, whatever it is. The scripture comes alive—the dogma starts to take on meaning. And so they're both more dedicated to their own brand of religion and at the same time they're more ecumenical and interspiritual in their orientation."[35]

The most pressing educational issue currently occupying Richards's time is the question of how to train therapists to do psychedelic-assisted therapy. He hopes to continue expanding his research in hospice and palliative care addressing end-of-life anxiety. Currently, there are no psychopharmaceuticals and only a few therapies that effectively address existential distress caused by terminal illness and trauma. Addressing these therapeutic needs is a central concern of psychedelic research. However, when psychedelic-assisted treatment is approved, even within an experimental framework, the question is inevitably, Where are you going to come up with enough therapists to implement this?

The training for such intense and delicate work would need to be substantial. Richards explained: "Surely we can't require seven years of in-depth psychoanalysis and training. We need lots of people fast."[36] Specially trained therapists are in high demand both to continue research and to implement public programs once they are made legal. This is no small requirement either, since the role of the guide during psychedelic-assisted psychotherapy is of critical importance. Their ability to exude confidence and acceptance while creating a safe space without adding any perception of judgment or anxiety is one of the main components contributing to the setting that in part determines the efficacy of the therapy.

The skill level of the guide can make the difference between a positive, self-revelatory, life-affirming experience and a bad trip. The complex and nuanced task of presence and facilitation, while still lacking a full grasp of the pharmacological and the psychotherapeutic mechanisms involved, is part science and part art. Ingmar Gorman is the administrative director of the Psychedelic Education and Continuing Care Program at the Center for Optimal Living in New York City and conducts MDMA-assisted psychotherapy for PTSD sufferers in a MAPS-funded research study. Gorman emphasizes that there is no such thing as a typical psychedelic therapy session or a typical integration session (a discussion following psychedelic-assisted therapy to process the experience). And yet, development of the field and the path toward legalization require strict scientific experimentation with consistent protocols that reduce the number of confounding variables. Therefore, developing standardized training programs that produce competent, insightful, and flexible therapists and streamlined treatment protocols that maintain respect for the diversity of patient needs are both of the utmost importance.

One of the most significant efforts on the therapist-training front is the Certificate in Psychedelic-Assisted Therapies and Research offered at the California Institute of Integral Studies in San Francisco. To qualify for the program, one must already be trained and have substantial experience in a related field, such as counseling, chaplaincy, social work, or medicine. The semihybrid curriculum is presented in six weekend workshops, including two residential retreats over an eight-month period. The well-rounded training approaches the topic from scientific, experiential, and applied perspectives, bringing together the top researchers in the field from all over the world, including Dr. Richards himself. "That's a major focus of my life right now," he said.[37] The certificate program graduated its first set of students in December 2016. "They're remarkable people," he went on. "Many of them are full professors with access to and relations with the FDA [the US Government's Food and Drug Administration]. There is even a retired physician, with over thirty years of experience. They are very, very competent people who want to spend the next chapter of their careers in psychedelic research. It's very inspiring."[38]

There are similar training programs at New York University and at MAPS. In fact, MAPS's program is unique in that it has been granted permission to give therapists MDMA as part of their training. "We haven't had the courage at Hopkins yet to ask for permission to give our staff psilocybin," Richards said. "But maybe we're getting closer." Ironically, he said, "There's such a taboo in psychiatry about taking the drugs that you give to others."[39] Nonetheless, practitioners remain hopeful that, as research continues to demonstrate safety and efficacy, and as stigma decreases, opportunities for multimodal training and treatment with psychedelics will increase. In fact, Rick Doblin, the founder of MAPS, is hopeful that by 2021 MDMA-assisted psychotherapy will be an FDA-approved treatment for PTSD available in treatment centers throughout the United States.[40] Perhaps these will resemble the ketamine treatment clinics that can be found all across the country. A substance once used strictly as an anesthetic for surgery (and a recreational party drug), ketamine is now advertised to treat conditions ranging from asthma and chronic pain to depression, PTSD, and suicidality.

What is it about psychedelics that, according to researchers such as Richards, makes them such potent agents for healing and spiritual enhancement? They are unlike most psychopharmaceutical drugs, which require disciplined, repeated use to bring about a stabilized balance of neurotransmitters. Psychedelic-assisted psychotherapy protocols usually consist of only a few sessions separated by weeks or months. Researchers suggest that healing brought about by psychedelics appears not to come from the mere administration of the drug, or the drug effect. Instead, healing is a product of the *experience* that the drug occasions. The specific states of consciousness often induced by psychedelics are the transformative agents that correlate with the desired attitudinal and behavioral changes.[41] These states are not only a product of the substances' molecular components, Richards explained, they are produced in conjunction with the intention of the person ingesting

Figure 27. Psychedelic-assisted psychotherapy in progress at Johns Hopkins University.

them and the context or setting. "Simply stated," Richards said, "the experiences are not in any drug; they are in us."[42]

When ingested without a healing or reflective intention or in low doses, psychedelic substances may elicit interesting but relatively useless perceptual and sensory changes. In certain contexts, moreover, with high dosing or in the absence of the vital requisites of careful preparation and guidance, they may elicit terrifying or confusing experiences characterized by paranoia, extreme anxiety, or agitation. Yet the same substance can unlock incredible healing, positive mood-changes, and perspective-altering states of consciousness when administered in the optimal way—that is, with proper dosage, set, and setting.

Richards describes three such healing domains of consciousness: the mystical, the visionary or archetypal, and the personal-psychodynamic.[43] At high-enough doses, these states emerge quite reliably without priming participants on what to look for. Richards explained his approach: "We try with research volunteers not to mention the categories and definitions of mysticism. We don't want to program them in any way or give them words in advance. Afterward they come up with their own words to fit the definition just fine. And it's just such ordinary people who do it—some of them never finished junior high school and here they are, sounding like Meister Eckhart."[44] The way Richards and his colleagues categorize entheogenic experiences can be useful for anyone wanting to learn about them.

First, how do researchers know when an experience can be called mystical? In his research on psilocybin-occasioned mystical experiences, Richards and his colleagues use several questionnaires, including the Hood Mysticism Scale (referred to as the M scale) and the Pahnke-Richards Mystical Experience Questionnaire. The latter measures seven domains of mystical experiences:

- internal unity (pure awareness; a merging with ultimate reality)
- external unity (unity of all things; all things are alive; all is one)

- transcendence of time and space (sense of space-time location dissolves)
- ineffability and paradoxicality (difficulty in describing the experience in words)
- sense of sacredness (reverence; sacredness)
- noetic quality (claim of an encounter with ultimate reality; more real than everyday reality)
- deeply felt positive mood (joy, peace, love)[45]

Based on reports and writings from mystics throughout time and across cultures, these qualities of mystical consciousness seem to be remarkably consistent. The Pahnke-Richards Mystical Experience Questionnaire employs one hundred items, each rated on a five-point scale, of which just forty-three are used to score the seven dimensions. This measure allows researchers to say not only whether and in what senses an experience can properly be called mystical but also *how* mystical, or how close to mystical, the experience was.

Second, whereas mystical experiences are characterized by a perceived eradication or absorption of the individual personality into unitive consciousness, in archetypal visionary experiences, the sense of self as a distinct observer of the experience remains. One may see unexpected visions and be overcome with awe or love or fear, but one does not *become* those emotions; one's sense of self remains intact. In the early twentieth century, in distinction from Freud's theory of the personal unconscious, Carl Jung developed a theory of the collective unconscious. According to Jung, the collective unconscious is a matrix of preexistent mythical and archetypal psychic content inherited from our ancestors and based on the ways our brains are structured. It is "a common substratum [of the human psyche] transcending all differences in culture and consciousness."[46]

Whether or not Jung is right about his speculative explanation, it does seem to be the case that archetypal content of experiences expressing what he calls the collective unconscious recurs in many different kinds of people, and it is often interpreted as religiously significant. In fact, Richards has observed that it is not uncommon for volunteers to report visions of symbolic religious and cultural content that is completely foreign to anything they had ever been exposed to in their own life. For example, one volunteer saw visions of "strange, partially naked figures dancing with funny hats like crowns on their heads" during a high-dose session of LSD.[47] It was only later that he saw a picture of the Hindu gods Vishnu and Shiva and exclaimed, "This is what I saw; this is what I saw!"[48] Boldly, Richards claims that "there are now sufficient data in the descriptive record of psychedelic researchers to consider Jung's concept of the collective unconscious empirically validated."[49]

The third transformative domain of consciousness commonly engaged with the help of psychedelics is the personal-psychodynamic. In this case the images, symbols, and contents are intensely personal. These experiences are centered around relationships, challenges, fears, or anxieties that are (with intention and guidance) confronted and worked through during the session. Often, people expect or desire a mystical experience and instead find themselves on an accelerated therapeutic journey through grief, guilt, depression, or loneliness. These personal insights and the accompanying emotional catharsis are often extremely spiritually potent. This domain of consciousness, Richards said, points to the interconnectedness of human relationships and spiritual health.

In the effort to analyze and understand these three transformative states of consciousness, the line between therapeutic and religious applications is blurred, or perhaps rendered arbitrary. Richards explains that all three domains of consciousness—mystical, archetypal, and personal-psychodynamic—are valuable for both psychological healing and spiritual development. However, according to the research, *the closer a person gets to the mystical type of experience, the greater the positive spiritual, personal, and social benefits.*

A PSYCHEDELIC RENAISSANCE?

Since 1999, Roland Griffiths, one of Richards's colleagues at Johns Hopkins University, has been heading up Johns Hopkins's exploration of mystical experiences. Researchers there have administered psilocybin to hundreds of people, including healthy psychedelic-naive volunteers, novice and long-term meditators, religious professionals, psychologically distressed cancer patients, and people suffering from addictions. They have also systematically compared psilocybin-assisted mystical experiences to spontaneous and naturally occurring mystical experiences. Some of these results are not yet published, but they have found that, with high doses of psilocybin, a remarkable 72 percent of healthy volunteers had complete mystical experiences, and 83 percent of participants rated their experiences during the psilocybin session as one of the top five most spiritually significant experiences of their lives, comparable to the birth of their first child.[50] For therapeutic applications as different as easing the existential distress of living with cancer and addressing nicotine addiction, psilocybin-assisted psychotherapy was effective. However, in both cases, the occurrence of a mystical experience accurately *predicted* superior therapeutic outcomes.[51]

In October 2016, Kate attended a gathering of psychedelics researchers in New York City. That may seem like a long time ago, but psychedelic research moves slowly and the insights from that meeting are still germane today. Griffiths was there and he spoke generally on the studies he and his team have conducted on mystical states. He drew a few important conclusions: First, the fact that mystical experiences occasioned by psilocybin are virtually identical to mystical experiences that occur naturally demonstrates that such experiences are biologically normal. Second, whereas very few people will have spontaneous mystical experiences, psilocybin can help facilitate these experiences in most people. Third, he said, mystical-type experiences can stimulate trait-level personality changes (which are usually considered relatively

stable and resistant to change) in spirituality, openness, altruism, gratitude, and forgiveness.[52] He reports that they can enhance the prosocial
impulse and spark a "deep sense of ethical and moral understanding."[53]
Griffiths ended his presentation with a dramatic declaration of the importance of understanding mystical experiences and the promise of
psychedelics for aiding that journey of discovery: "Therefore," he said,
"further research into the causes and consequences of these extraordinary experiences may ultimately prove to be crucial to the very survival
of our species."[54]

All researchers and practitioners at the New York gathering seemed
to share in the excitement that an overdue renaissance of psychedelics
was at hand. However, the last speaker of the conference, Dr. Robert Jesse, convener of the Council on Spiritual Practices, insisted that,
while a reemergence may be taking effect, a true renaissance will look
much different.[55] For Jesse, the use of entheogens for therapeutic and
spiritual enhancement is a *birthright*, and until it is seen that way and
made universally available regardless of people's ability to pay, the
field has not yet reached a renaissance. He explained that psychedelics
are still stigmatized and misunderstood by the general public, they are
not yet widely available, and there are not yet suitable resources for psychological integration and safety for the public who uses psychedelics
outside the lab setting. Though all these necessities are on the rise, he
advises continued caution and restraint. This spirit of careful, transparent, and scrupulous research is what has allowed the slow reemergence
of entheogens into the therapeutic community and the public eye. This
prudent diligence must continue, he said, as there are still many potential hurdles. Perhaps the tallest hurdle will be navigating the incorporation of legal psychedelics into religious and spiritual practices. If that
process is handled hastily or if total legalization for recreational use
were too swift, incompetence, exploitation, corrupt commercialization,
immature applications, or trivialization could threaten once again to
dismantle their goals. Jesse's wise and cautious words elicited cheers
from the audience.

Nonetheless, those who have benefitted personally or spiritually from entheogens and those who are at the forefront of the current research and development of therapeutic protocols continue to look forward to a (however distant) future in which the substances will be treated as a sacred birthright for all people. "I suffer from optimism." Dr. Richards chuckled when asked about future possibilities. "Will the day come when my Episcopal church can have a Sunday afternoon session with psilocybin for those who are interested and properly screened and properly prepared? For that to come, there has to be an awful lot of good education in the culture."[56]

SHIFTING THE PARADIGM

The types of people who benefit from entheogen use are extremely diverse, ranging from petite elderly women facing the end of their lives to young adolescent men searching for meaning and identity. At this point, scientists know quite a bit about which chemicals enhance and which suppress many neurochemical systems and how they operate on specific receptors and neurotransmitters. They also have some grasp of the dangers, including modification of synaptic receptor density, changes to production of neurotransmitters, and even structural damage to the brain. Aided by both experimental studies and FDA clinical trials, we are finally getting reacquainted with the incredible healing qualities some entheogens hold—literally *doubling* the success rates of psychotherapy for PTSD and contributing to levels of psycho-spiritual health, wellness, insight, and groundedness that some have never dreamed would be possible for them.

Though a viable psychedelic renaissance has barely begun, it is not stretching credulity to imagine a meaningful menu of psychoactive substances directly productive of a variety of specific types of spiritual experiences, riding on the coattails of clinical psychotherapists' quest for a database of effects and delivery mechanisms related to mental health. This would be something like the near-future entheogenic equivalent of the well-trained Chinese herbalist with intriguing shelves of substances and deep knowledge about how to use them building on millennia of accrued wisdom. Some therapists are already using psychedelics in their practices to treat depression, trauma, and psychosocial symptoms, and we are very close to legalized MDMA in psychotherapeutic settings.[57] What's next is allowing spiritual leaders the same freedom. We predict this will eventually become a common part of life, spawning new industries at the intersection of neuropsychopharmacology and religion akin to the psychiatry industry that thrives at the intersection of medicine and human emotional life.

Dr. Stanislav Grof, pioneer in psychedelic research, once said, "Psychedelics are to the study of the mind what the microscope is to biology and what the telescope is to astronomy."[58] Understanding entheogens as technologies for spiritual transformation, healing, and meaning making is at once the rebirth of an ancient wisdom tradition and a technological revolution, akin to the paradigm shifts ushered in by Galileo, Darwin, and Einstein. Only time will tell how exactly these technologies will integrate into our communities and spiritual lives as they slowly become legal again.

7

Spirit Plants and Their High-Tech Replacements

I drank a cup of the herbal brew . . .
And all of these spirit voices rule the night.
—*Paul Simon, "Spirit Voices"*

AN UNEXPECTED CALLING

As a teenager growing up in upstate New York, Matt Toussaint never imagined that in a few short years he would be a shaman living in a remote jungle center near Iquitos, Peru. But by his late teens and early twenties, Matt had embarked on a bold journey of spiritual exploration, not quite sure where it would lead. He was experimenting with psychedelics, had developed a meditation practice, and had learned how to put himself into a trance using non-drug-enhanced ceremonial practices. One December night in 2007, while meditating, Matt had a visionary experience. "I opened up into this visionary space and there were three spirits that were present," he said. "And it was very, very clear. . . . And I heard very clearly in my consciousness [the spirits] say, 'Go to Peru, find a shaman, and drink ayahuasca.'"[1] At that point, Matt had barely even heard of ayahuasca and knew next to nothing about it—it was certainly not something he was actively researching or pursing—so he was struck by the content of the vision.

As it turns out, in the time since Matt's vision, ayahuasca has become the most popular psychoactive spirit plant for spiritual seekers interested in shamanic retreats and healing circles (figure 25 in the color insert shows an indigenous coca ceremony in a venue commonly used for ayahuasca ceremonies). The *New Yorker* calls it "the drug of choice for the age of kale," with hundreds of underground ayahuasca circles held every night throughout Brooklyn, Silicon Valley, and San Francisco.[2] And Tim Ferriss, *New York Times* bestselling author of *The 4-Hour Workweek*, says ayahuasca eliminated the anger he'd been holding on to since he was a kid. Ayahuasca has become so common in the San Francisco area that, Ferriss told Ariel Levy of the *New Yorker*, "ayahuasca is like having a cup of coffee here. I have to avoid people at parties because I don't want to listen to their latest three-hour saga of kaleidoscopic colors."[3] It is the subject of dozens of documentaries such as *The Medicine* (2019) and *Ayahuasca: The Vine of the Soul* (2010), and it even kicked off Gwyneth Paltrow's Netflix series *The Goop Lab*, which explores new methods of self-care and spiritual enhancement. Ayahuasca (also called *aya*, *vegetal*, *daime*, *caapi*, or *hoasca*) is a thick brown brew made (usually) by cooking pieces of the thick twisting woody vine of the *Banisteriopsis caapi* plant together with the leaves of the *Psychotria viridis* bush; other plants are often added to the mixture depending on the context, region, and techniques of the plant specialist preparing the brew. As a brew usually produced in a ritual setting over the course of a full day, ayahuasca can be tremendously variable in its actual chemical components. In order to produce the psychedelic effect, however, the mix must include a botanical source of monoamine oxidase inhibitor (MAOI, traditionally provided by the beta-carbolines harmine, harmaline, and tetrahydroharmine in the *B. caapi* vine) and a botanical source of dimethyltryptamine (DMT, usually provided by the *viridis* leaves). The MAOIs prevent the premature breakdown of DMT and facilitate its transference across the blood-brain barrier, thereby

allowing the psychedelic aspect of DMT to take effect by influencing the brain's serotonin system. Though readily available in the *viridis* leaves growing throughout the Amazon, and despite being endogenous (produced in small quantities within the human body), DMT is also a Schedule I controlled substance in the United States and illegal in many countries. But not to worry, legality wouldn't be an issue for Matt, since the spirits specified Peru as his destination.

Given the strong spiritual salience of his vision, Matt began exploring how to follow the spirits' directions. "I had no idea that you could just go to Peru and drink ayahuasca," he said. "I had no idea there were centers, I didn't know that it was a thing that people did."[4] Indeed, Evgenia Fotiou, a cultural anthropologist who lived and studied shamanic tourism in Peru, explains that, fifteen years ago, a Westerner would have found it challenging to find an ayahuasca center willing to cater to a tourist experience. In the early 2000s, she says, she could count the number of lodges advertising to tourists on her fingers.[5] But, after some thorough research, Matt took the plunge. He booked a trip to Peru for the summer of 2008—it would be his first time outside of the United States. "It was terrifying," he told us.

Matt had chosen Blue Morpho Tours, a popular organization that offers ayahuasca and San Pedro (another spirit plant medicine) retreats. By the time he arrived, he was still nervous but the center felt welcoming. After meeting the staff and settling into his room, Matt and the other tour guests were off for their first ayahuasca medicine ceremony. "Within about fifteen minutes," he said, "I had this just *blazing* vision where it took me back to my original spiritual awakening that I had had a few years before. That experience started morphing with the ayahuasca ceremony. That same voice of intuition, or the spirits or the universe—I really don't know, but it was something that was very clear—said, 'This is where you're going to work. This is what you're going to do. This is your path. This is your journey.' And I was like, 'Yeah, right. No way.' I was barely able to walk, puking my guts out, purging, terrified. 'No way am I going to be able to do this. There's absolutely no way.'"[6] Matt continued to have a difficult time through-out that first tour's ceremonies. While he was increasingly astounded by the way the shamans displayed mastery of the space and of the energy during the ceremonies, he was certainly not ready to follow the spirits' direction. The experience stayed with him as he journeyed back to the United States, but he didn't tell anybody about it for four years.

Matt eventually felt compelled to return to the Amazon to explore the meaning of his visions. Back in Peru, four years after his first tour, the founder of Blue Morpho, Hamilton Souther, revealed to Matt that he had had a spiritual vision during Matt's previous visit in which spirits told him that he would teach Matt the shamanic arts. "And I thought, 'Oh my God,'" said Matt. "I never told anyone about this!" He had been scared to tell Hamilton about his vision because he knew he wasn't ready to pursue it quite yet, but he also did not want to say no. However, after hearing Hamilton's side of the story, Matt began working with him, first learning shamanic practices that do not involve ayahuasca or other plants, then slowly incorporating the plants. After about two years of shamanic training with Hamilton, Matt moved down to Peru and began working full time at the Blue Morpho Camp.

Blue Morpho Tours was a pioneer in the ayahuasca tourism indus-try. In fact, Hamilton Souther founded Blue Morpho as an Amazonian adventure tour business before there was any tourist interest in aya-huasca. Visitors from all over the world would begin in Iquitos, Peru, on an intimate twenty-four-hour boat ride deep into the jungle where they would hike, fish, camp, and experience the jungle firsthand. He had no intention of creating an ayahuasca center, even though in his private life he was apprenticing under two local *ayahuasqueros*, Don Al-berto and Don Julio. However, his visitors were increasingly intrigued by ayahuasca—they began asking questions about local practices, the shamanic healing tradition, and Hamilton's participation. Eventually, Hamilton began inviting people to join him in ayahuasca ceremonies.

Blue Morpho's ayahuasca tours started small and organically but grew steadily as word spread and their reputation solidified. When one

particular visitor published the story of her transformative experience in *National Geographic Adventure* magazine, business took off.[7] Kira Salak, who has traveled to some of the most remote corners of the world as an adventurer and travel writer, first came to Peru on assignment to write an article about the increasing popularity of new age tourism in the West. She was skeptical, having grown up among "fundamentalist atheists" who instilled in her the belief that "we're all alone in the universe, the fleeting dramas of our lives culminating in a final, ignoble end: death," but she dove in.[8] Much to her surprise, she reports, the shamanic ayahuasca ceremony cured her chronic crushing depression and completely removed her suicidal ideation. Her article in *National Geographic Adventure* chronicled her second Blue Morpho tour, during which she met previous incarnations of her soul, underwent an exorcism, retrieved part of herself that had fractured off during childhood as the result of trauma, and, in the last ceremony of her retreat, met God:

"Why did you hate me so much?" she asked God.

"I never hated you. . . . You hated yourself. I have always loved you as my own child. Know that suffering is the greatest teacher on Earth. It leads us out of our belief in separation," she said God told her.

Kira continues: "And before me was this enormous image of God! He takes me in his arms and coddles me like a child. I know, unequivocally, that I am loved and have always been loved. That I matter and have always mattered. That I'm safe and—no matter what happens—will always be safe. I will never allow myself to become separated from Him again."[9]

Kira's experience highlights the two primary goals for Blue Morpho retreats and ceremonies based on the needs of their clients: healing and personal transformation. In shamanism, ayahuasca is understood as both a medicine and a teacher. "Everything we do is built on the plants, on the ayahuasca, on the diet, and the tree," Matt explained to us. When deciding to venture to the Amazon to drink ayahuasca, the most important task is finding the right shaman, *curandero*, or *ayahuasquero* to work with. Boutique retreats—which provide many contemporary comforts; ensure safety; and offer intimate, focused healing work from the shaman—are very expensive, ranging from one to three thousand dollars. Yet some shamans and centers allow people to participate on a walk-in basis and are willing to strike a bargain price with the visitor upon arrival. Drinking ayahuasca is an extremely psychologically challenging experience. The most reputable retreat centers have skilled shamans, experienced "sitters" who help guide the ceremonies but do not drink ayahuasca, and comprehensive integration practices during which participants share, ask questions about, and process their experiences after the ceremonies. However, even a cursory Internet search makes it easy to see that there can be a dark side to the ayahuasca tourism industry, which we'll get to soon enough.

Blue Morpho bases its philosophy on the teachings of Maestro Don Julio Llerena Pinedo and Maestro Alberto Torres Davila, master *curanderos* (shamans) and *paleros* (tree specialists) from the mestizo tradition, which is a mix of American Indian and Spanish traditions and ancestry. However, Matt emphasized that the shamans in this group have become very skilled at translating the Amazonian tradition into a language and framework that is ready to meet a Western mind or psyche. "A lot of people who come to our retreats are not like spiritual, new agey, yoga kind of people—not that there's anything wrong with that, we have those people as well," he said. "But we get a lot of people who don't believe in spirits, they're not interested in spirituality, but they're looking to change their life. . . . We get people who are atheists. We get people from all different types of religions and different philosophies and at the same time we get people who are psychologically and/or emotionally traumatized who need proper healing. So we have a number of different skills and techniques that we use to make what we're doing accessible for any philosophy or framework of understanding."[10]

He continued: "I think with the way that Blue Morpho is set up, we tend to attract people who are successful but damaged, looking for something serious. We don't really get wayfarers, we don't get travelers

or backpackers or people who are just looking for the ayahuasca experience. Typically, if someone is coming to us, they have something they really want to work on. But the diversity is pretty wide . . . depression, anxiety, trauma . . . emotional or physical abuse. . . . We also get people who are professional, successful, but stuck in life—they don't know what to do. They're not happy."[11] He explained that desire for release and healing from addiction and substance abuse is another common theme.

Peter Gorman, an investigative journalist who now offers tours into the Amazon and has worked with ayahuasca for thirty years, told the *Guardian*, "If anyone thinks it's in the same category as a cruise, well, the first drink would quickly change their minds. . . . It's very serious medicine; very deep, very quick."[12] Omar Gomez, one of the founders of Rainforest Healing Center (Chakra Alegría de Amor) in Peru, explained that he turns away about 60 percent of those who apply to come drink ayahuasca. These decisions are often based on the appearance of conflicting factors, such as heart conditions, schizophrenia, and certain medications such as SSRI antidepressants; but often, he simply senses that they are not serious enough about the medicine.[13] "We do an intense screening process to make sure we don't have any psychedelic tourists," he said in 2016. "Right now the ayahuasca industry is booming. But we want to make sure that the people who come are people that have a strong intention and desire to heal."[14]

Matt explains that, whether a person is coming with the intention to learn to approach relationships with more vulnerability, open up creativity or boldness in their professional life, or heal from traumatic experiences, Blue Morpho shamans and facilitators feel prepared to work with the traditions and the spirits and the energies in ways that meet individuals where they are. "Our philosophy works in reverse," Matt said, "in that we learn what to do from the people rather than push a philosophy onto someone. It's very open in that sense."[15]

That said, the shamans themselves certainly do have a strong philosophical and spiritual foundation built from experience. Matt

explained that the training and apprenticeship process is very different from the process of simply coming to the ceremony for healing
or transformation—a participant does not necessarily need to, and in
fact cannot, understand the full spiritual and energetic depth of the
ceremonial process. An incredibly rigorous apprenticeship of experiential learning is necessary. Even during the shamanic training, Matt
explained, "you're kind of thrown into it and you have a whole series
of experiences and drink ayahuasca dozens and dozens of times before
you even start to get just a little glimmer of what's going on." In this
way, the ayahuasca itself is the primary teacher: "The maestros are there
to guide you and keep you safe," he said, "but they don't learn for you.
In order for you to rise in the learning process as a practitioner, you
have to learn how to stand on your own inside the madness and chaos
of an ayahuasca ceremony."

In the spiritual and energetic space with a maestro, the teaching is
direct: "It's almost an energetic exchange that happens through example
and through the embodiment of what it means to be a maestro," Matt
said. "And that's how the spirit of the apprentice learns—by having
those interactions—rather than having [the maestro] say this spirit
does this and this one's like this and this one's like that and we use this
for that." According to this philosophy, the most profound exchanges
occur between the spirits and the shaman apprentice: "The maestro
is an important part in initiating, guiding, and offering the help that
you need," Matt said, "but it's very soft and it's very gentle and it's
timed very well and the rest of the time in a sense it's between you and
the spirit. You and the ayahuasca, you and the tree."[16]

This intense training process is meant to produce practitioners who
can skillfully and safely guide spiritual seekers through ayahuasca ceremonies. Kate met a young man at the annual conference Horizons:
Perspectives on Psychedelics who had gone on a Blue Morpho retreat.
His most salient memory was of the diversity of the experiences he had
in the ceremonies throughout the week—some were calm and contemplative, others were dramatically emotional; in some he faced fears and

darkness, in others he felt enveloped in love. He attributes this to the mastery of the shamans, and their songs and chants, to direct the energy of the group and to guide those under the influence of ayahuasca toward the type of healing they seek.

SPIRIT PLANTS

Just as with the psychedelics described in chapter 6, the set and setting have profound effects on the quality and tone of the ayahuasca experience. When it comes to the experience of drinking ayahuasca, there are specific ritual forms—technologies of experience—that have built up around the ayahuasca brew and from which the ayahuasca experience is inextricable. The most common applications of the entheogens described in the previous chapter tend to be separate from, and often antagonistic toward, organized religions. This chapter, by contrast, focuses on entheogens that are almost always used in religious or spiritual ritual settings.

Given the momentous import of set and setting for the way that entheogens influence the mind and body, it would be hard to overstate the importance of these types of ritual settings. In fact, elements of the ritual such as rhythmic drumming, vigorous chanting and singing, symbolic structures, and prescribed movements can be considered technologies in and of themselves—they exert influence on the brain and are used to manage the potency of the substance. "It is not possible to reduce the experience of altered states of consciousness [produced with spirit plants] to the consumption of 'drugs' or to music,"[17] wrote anthropologists Beatriz Caiuby Labate and Gustavo Pacheco, whose research focuses on psychedelic substances, drug policies, and shamanism. There is a "profound interconnection between the consumption of psychoactive substances, music, ritual, and religion."[18] In short, the experience of ayahuasca is intimately connected—in fact, inseparable from—its ritual settings and behaviors.

For this reason, we need to keep in mind that the rich symbolism of

corporate rituals matters when we're trying to make sense of these religious groups. It matters as much as the psychoactive properties of the
entheogens for interpreting the effects of this particular spiritual technology. There are many ways to classify, describe, and compare psychedelic substances, and the outsized importance of set and setting—rather
than the pharmacological qualities of the substances or even necessarily
the experiences people report after ingesting them—has guided our
choice to divide our discussion into two chapters on classical psychedelics and spirit plants. Mescaline and DMT, for example—the active
components of peyote and ayahuasca, respectively—are both tryptamines similar to LSD, which means pharmacologically, LSD is closer
to ayahuasca and peyote than to MDMA (ecstasy). However, in practice
and popular usage, LSD more closely resembles MDMA, since they are
both popular substances at music festivals and raves, whereas ayahuasca
and peyote are not. The *how*, *who*, and *where*—the vastly different sets
and settings, including how you get them and what you intend to do with
them—thus put substances derived from spirit plants and used in ritual
settings into a different category of brain-based spiritual technology. A
person who might have an incredible life-changing mystical experience
taking MDMA on a therapist's couch wearing eye shades may or may
not ever be interested in a shamanic ayahuasca retreat deep within the
Peruvian forest or in the hills around San Francisco. That being said, the
fact that the chemical compounds of a few popular spirit plants are being
synthesized in the lab presents a fascinating new modality of spirit tech,
which we will explore later in this chapter.

The two other most popular spirit plants are peyote and San Pedro.
Peyote (*Lophophora williamsii*) is a small flowering cactus that grows
naturally in the desert scrub regions of southern North America, especially northern Mexico and southern Texas. The plant contains mescaline, which binds to serotonin receptors, thereby mimicking serotonin
and facilitating peyote's psychedelic potential. Peyote is integral to the
spiritual practices of the Huichol and Cora Indians in Mexico. And
in the United States, it is primarily used as a sacramental medicine

by members of the Native American Church, a "spiritual and ethno-medical tradition"[19] that has hundreds of groups scattered throughout western North America, stretching from Alberta, Canada, to central Mexico, and has been granted legal status and associated protections as a religion in the United States.[20] Native American Church member Albert Hensley, revered as an activist against the prohibition of pey-ote, described the church's relationship to peyote this way: "To us it is a portion of the body of Christ, even as the Communion bread is believed to be a portion of Christ's body by other Christian denomina-tions. Christ spoke of a Comforter who was to come. It never came to Indians until it was sent by God in the form of this Holy Medicine."[21] Shamanic (non-Christian) peyote ceremonies have also become a part of the new age shamanic tourism industry typified by Blue Morpho, though not nearly to the extent that ayahuasca has.

Another mescaline-rich plant used in traditional Andean medicine and religious rituals in northern Peru is the San Pedro cactus (*Tricho-cereus pachanoi*). Named after Saint Peter who is said to hold the keys to heaven, San Pedro is believed to make traveling into heavenly realms possible while still on Earth. Like peyote and ayahuasca, San Pedro has a history of use in Peruvian shamanism that predates written records.[22] Today, San Pedro is used primarily by shamanic healers in Peru focused on spiritual healing and healing from trauma or addictions, especially alcoholism. It is not uncommon for the same tourism organizations that offer ayahuasca retreats to also offer San Pedro ceremonies, work-shops, and retreats.[23]

As for ayahuasca, there are essentially three primary ways that spir-itual seekers from the United States can partake. First, it is available through membership in a religious organization that uses ayahuasca as a sacrament. Second, for people looking for an experience with no requirement of membership, or those desiring an experience less steeped in Christian symbolism, ayahuasca shamanism, like what is offered at Blue Morpho, is an option. The ayahuasca retreat industry for international participants is currently booming. Third, a high-tech, synthesized version called pharmahuasca is hitting the scene. As a *customizable* version with slightly different chemical compounds to choose from, as we'll explain later, pharmahuasca is perfect for the spirit tech supermarket. Let's look at each of these more closely.

SANTO DAIME, UNIÃO DO VEGETAL, AND THE MYSTICAL LEFT

The only legal way to drink ayahuasca in the United States is at church. Santo Daime (which translates from the Portuguese as "holy give me") is a Brazilian ayahuasca religion blending folk Catholicism, indigenous shamanism, and forms of spiritism imported to South America during colonialism. And the União do Vegetal (UDV), which translates to "union of the plant," is a large Catholic-Amazonia-Afro-Brazilian religion with roots similar to Santo Daime, but UDV has developed somewhat differently. In fact, UDV has become increasingly popular among Western spiritual seekers who are attracted to its consciousness-expanding mystical experiences and feel free to take or leave the Catholic doctrines. On a bumpy train from Yale University, where Kate had attended a talk about ayahuasca given by Beatriz Caiuby Labate the night before, to New York City, where Labate would present at the Horizons: Perspectives on Psychedelics conference, Labate and Kate chatted about the ways in which these complex traditions are engaged by today's spiritual seekers. Labate is one of the most highly respected and active scholars studying spirit plants today. She has published more than a dozen books in English alone, and her books are often also published in Spanish and Portuguese.

Santo Daime (figure 26 in the color insert) and UDV both have colorful grassroots origin stories, which might be part of their appeal. Santo Daime was founded around 1930 by a Christian African migrant named Raimundo Irineu Serra, also known as Mestre Irineu, who migrated from Africa to the Rio Branco region of the Amazon—what is now western Brazil—in 1912. Mestre Irineu and his family worked as rubber tappers and would have had extensive contact with the rural indigenous traditions. Daime lore holds that throughout the 1920s, Mestre Irineu partook regularly of ayahuasca and began to communicate with a spiritual being who appeared as a white woman wearing blue. He called her Clara or the Queen of the Forest, and she was later understood to be the Virgin Mary. During one particularly profound period of solitude, he received instructions from her to build a new ritual practice to share with others, and he began conducting healing ceremonies. Disciples began gathering around him to learn and affirm the mestre's teachings from Clara. The religion was officially recognized by the Brazilian government in 1971.[24]

UDV was founded by native Brazilian José Gabriel da Costa, known as Mestre Gabriel, who moved west to the Amazon to work, like Mestre Irineu, in the rubber camps. He drank ayahuasca for the first time in April 1959 and his profound experiences moved him to develop a new doctrine remarkably quickly and gather a small group of followers. On July 22, 1961, only two years after his first taste, he officially founded the União do Vegetal.[25] The tradition took off and the UDV US website now reports over twenty-one thousand members in Brazil.[26] UDV rituals are called *sessions*; and there are several different types: some are attended by all members, others only by the leaders, and others are sporadic special sessions for specific groups such as couples or young people. There are even novice sessions for those who are drinking ayahuasca (which they refer to as *vegetal* or *hoasca*) for the first time.[27] At the sessions, as the vegetal is ingested, each participant recites: "May God guide us on the path of light, forever and always, amen Jesus."[28]

The eclectic doctrine and practice of Santo Daime mixes elements from indigenous Amazonian, Afro-Brazilian, and European spiritual traditions together with popular Catholicism.[29] It centers around ritual ceremonies called *works* that include drinking ayahuasca (referred to as *daime*) as the central sacrament. To certain works, participants must wear a white uniform (*farda*) and carry special shakers (maracas) made from bearings or seeds. Santo Daime has a large and growing corpus of *chamadas/chamados* (chants or melodies without words) and *hinos* (songs with words and melodies). These *hinos*, or hymns, are the central source of doctrine and instruction in Santo Daime and are believed to have been received as revelations from spiritual deities rather than composed (although it is not uncommon for the words or melodies to be edited by the group).[30] The majority of each ritual is spent dancing the *bailado*, a ritualistic communal dance that lasts for hours, while under the influence of ayahuasca. In addition to the ayahuasca brew, the singing and dancing are understood as spiritually potent ritual technologies: "The *bailado* and the music generate an energy that is channeled by the vibrations of the maraca."[31]

Uniform clothing and singing are just as central for UDV as they are to Santo Daime, with some minor differences (featuring forest green and orange colors), and in the UDV some (though not all) of the *chamadas* are sung a cappella. The *burracheira*—the specific altered state of consciousness during UDV trance—is the goal of the sessions, which are about four hours long. "The *burracheira*," explained social anthropologist and expert on Brazilian religions Rosa Virgínia Melo, "presents itself to the disciple as a privileged channel in the process of the 'spiritual journey,' where one is obligated to self-reflection."[32] The *burracheira*, facilitated by the vegetal, is characterized by a skillful concentration and search for clarity, self-knowledge, and personal enhancement. For members of the UDV, "knowledge of oneself is spiritual knowledge, and the affect is primordial, integrating the being in the world in relationship to everything that is." The combination of personal transformation and cosmic mysticism is characteristic of UDV. Melo explained, "The weight and intensity of contact with the elements of the cosmos make steadfastness of intent and action indispensable."[33]

Interestingly, Labate explained that as UDV expands and grows throughout the United States, Europe, and Australia, it has in some ways become part of the movement toward alternative therapies and new age spirituality. According to Labate, the urban upper class— liberal professionals, university professors and students, vegetarians, the LGBTQ community—has become attracted to its reverence for self-knowledge and *burracheira*.[34] The elements indicating UDV's folk Catholic heritage are often downplayed to emphasize the mystical self-reflective altered states of consciousness. In fact, in the United States, a large number of Jewish people attend UDV sessions and belong to the organization; they are sometimes referred to fondly as the JewDV. This term is intentionally reminiscent of the movement among Jewish people who also practice forms of Buddhist spirituality and meditation—the JewBu folk. In fact, it was a man of Jewish descent, Jeffrey Bronfman, who originally brought the UDV tradition to the United States and served as the president of the US branch of UDV from 1993 to 2005. He even headed the successful effort to gain legal permission from the US government to use ayahuasca in UDV ceremonies.

This feature of both the UDV and the Santo Daime traditions—adapting to new contexts and mixing with local traditions as it spreads throughout the world—is vital for understanding their potential appeal to people interested in spirit tech. In fact, Labate explained, Santo Daime is even more fluid, eclectic, and adaptable than the UDV because it is more able to mix and mingle with other cultures, practices, and even other theologies. In her academic work, Labate calls this property *miscibility*, and, she said, Santo Daime is quite miscible, while the UDV, which has a more centralized institutional structure and bureaucracy, is less so.[35] This quality of extreme malleability and permeability is one of the primary factors driving the swift expansion of Santo Daime all over the world, explained Labate: "Santo Daime's miscibility enables it to be molded to different, sometimes divergent, conceptions of the world."[36] For example, she described one Santo Daime congregation that had a Hare Krishna group meeting nearby; it was not uncommon for the Hare Krishna devotees to participate in the Santo Daime services, sing the mantras, and then go to the Hare Krishna meetings right afterward. First in Brazil, and now in the United States and other parts of the world, Santo Daime has integrated into what Labate and her coauthor Glauber Loures de Assis call the mystical left, which is characterized by humanism, antimaterialism, philanthropy, and efforts toward social and personal transformation.[37] In our conversation, Labate emphasized that "there are times when this syncretism, this combination and hybridism work, but there are sharp ends as well when it doesn't sit well." For example, there is a Santo Daime hymn that refers to the Jewish people as those who killed Christ, which is anti-Semitic and offensive to both Jewish and non-Jewish people. And yet, smooth or not, this miscibility has facilitated the international growth and flourishing of ayahuasca traditions abroad.

When the practitioners are intensely focused on their inner revelatory experience through a direct mystical experience enabled by the ayahuasca, it is accepted that they might reinterpret or work around the beliefs conveyed in the hymns and teachings. Labate gave another example of how a new cultural context may reinterpret traditional teachings: at the beginning of each session, the UDV reads a series of sayings, one of which instructs the participants to leave their guns outside. Labate explained that as UDV was born in a very rural, remote town in the Amazon in the mid-1960s, where people often carried guns with them, it made perfect sense for a leader to say, "Hey, it's best for everyone if we please keep our guns outside when we're drinking ayahuasca." But today, many practitioners interpret this phrase to have profound symbolic value—to mean that one should leave their defenses, their psychological walls, their shields, and all other forms of resistance behind and enter the ceremony open to receiving the teaching. Labate is quick to note that she does *not* think that this latter interpretation is somehow less valid simply because it wasn't the original meaning of the text. In fact, she said, this form of transmission, appropriation, projection, and reinterpretation is necessary for the tradition to continue. "In this sense," she said, "it is interesting that what gets lost in translation makes the translation possible."

AYAHUASCA SHAMANISM

For those interested in traveling outside the United States, there is ayahuasca shamanism. In addition to relatively widespread continued use among local healers who may work out of their homes or travel to other local houses to help practice natural healing methods, including those that involve ayahuasca, Matt's story with Blue Morpho is representative of a rapidly growing industry throughout the Amazon that focuses on sharing the psychedelic experience and healing properties of ayahuasca with outsiders. Today, there are countless companies, centers, and individual people offering ceremonies and retreats to Westerners who are seeking more than just an adventure or a high. Since many of the centers advise or require a certain diet leading up to the ceremonies (including avoiding salt, sugar, caffeine, animal fat, dairy products, hot spices, yeast, spinach, vinegar, and alcohol), popular restaurants in major tourist cities such as Iquitos offer menu options specifically geared toward ayahuasca tourists.[38] Visitors are almost always seeking healing of some sort—for depression, anxiety, substance abuse and addiction, cancer, or trauma. This is not a recreational drug.

This trend and the effort to appeal to Western visitors is clearly pushing ayahuasca shamanism through a process of retraditionalization or even hypertraditionalization,[39] which is a fancy way of saying that great effort is exerted to portray and recapture a mythical past of authentic indigenous ayahuasca practices. For example, the Shipibo people, an ancient Amazonian tribe known for their beautiful, intricately patterned textiles, tend to be viewed as "ayahuasca masters" and "sacred guardians of the ayahuasca ceremony."[40] Labate explained that "because of this particular fame of the Shipibo, mestizo (mixed-race) shamans, foreign practitioners, and even native healers from other indigenous groups 'shipibize' themselves using Shipibo-style painted tunics, necklaces, paintings, and other trappings."[41] These efforts seem to be primarily an effort to attract and respond to the demands of an international market of potential participants in ayahuasca shamanism tourism. We are not suggesting that the practitioners are somehow inauthentic, but rather pointing to the complex syncretic manner in which ayahuasca shamanic traditions have developed.[42]

Figure 28. Traditional process of making Shipibo cloth.

In actuality, very little is known about the origins of the first sha-manic tradition deep within the Amazon basin that incorporated into its ceremonies the psychedelic, therapeutic, and spiritual potency of this "enigmatic jungle potion."[43] Scholars tend to believe that ayahuasca was first used in collective rituals primarily focused on hunting, war-fare, and healing.[44] But it seems most likely that today's ayahuasca tra-ditions bear little resemblance to the original indigenous ayahuasca shamanism. The idea that there is some pure, untouched, indigenous form of ayahuasca shamanism currently practiced in South America is simply false. Labate explained that there was never a singular evo-lutionary path from the allegedly very pure indigenous practices to those engaged by a mix of urban white people today. "There have been exchanges between ethnicities, there has been colonial influence for five hundred years, and there has been a lot of back and forth between city and forests," she said. "A lot of ayahuasca modalities were born in the context of colonialization in riverain settings by mestizo popu-lations and then imported back into the forests."[45] Since the climate conditions of the Amazon tend not to preserve archaeological evidence (dry climates are optimal), it is difficult to map the multiple trajectories of development and there's no solid archaeological evidence on when ayahuasca use began. Some claim that ayahuasca has been used for four thousand to eight thousand years, but scholars argue that these claims are little more than mythology—they may indeed be true, but we really cannot reconstruct evidence for ayahuasca use earlier than two or three hundred years ago.[46] Labate's preferred phrasing is "since immemorial times." Whatever its history, it's clear that ayahuasca shamanism is a rich and mysterious tradition. Like the brew itself, which is concocted not only with intentionality and care but also variability, intuition, creativity, and inspiration, the traditions surrounding ayahuasca have always been eclectic and complicated.

PHARMAHUASCA

Since the 1990s, a new modality of ayahuasca has emerged. Far from the eclectic jungle brews of the Amazon, gelcaps with meticulously measured portions of crystalline N,N-dimethyltryptamine (DMT) and harmine began hitting the festival scene. Pharmahuasca is a synthesized form of ayahuasca with a relatively active underground market, created by combining pure forms of DMT and harmine in a lab or, for that matter, even in a psychonaut's home kitchen.

In the early 1990s, Jonathan Ott—widely recognized as an expert on the pharmacology of ayahuasca, ayahuasca analogs (*ana*huasca, other plant combinations with similar psychoactive components), and pharmahuasca—carefully studied the proportions of DMT and harmine necessary to accomplish the desired psychoactive effect; the result was the dosage required for what would come to be called pharmahuasca. Ott's famous human bioassay experiments began with Ott administering increasing doses to *himself*, which he carefully packaged in small gelatin capsules until he reached an experience similar to that occasioned by "genuine Amazonian *ayahuasca* potions": "45 minutes to an hour incubation period, the effects quickly building to a peak within the next 30 minutes and maintaining a plateau for 45 minutes to an hour; followed by about an hour of diminishing effects; the experience was usually completely over within three hours."[47] He then moved—with other brave experimental participants—on to "double-conscious" experiments (as opposed to double-*blind* studies), in which, for ethical purposes, both the subject and the scientists know exactly what and how much of a substance a subject was receiving. These participants' data corroborated Ott's self-observation data and supported his hypothesis. A combination of pure DMT (average 29 mg) and pure harmine (average 175 mg) produced very similar effects to ayahuasca brews and "neatly accounted for the ethnopharmacognosy of those particular potions."[48] Ott and other scientists have continued experimenting with other very similar alkaloids and substances—some of which worked as direct replacements for the typical pharmahuasca ingredients, and some of which required significant dosage adjustments. For example, 5-methoxy-N,N-dimethyltryptamine (5-MeO-DMT) is psychoactive in pharmahuasca but probably up to five times *more* psychoactive than regular DMT.

Interestingly, Ott reported that the pharmahuasca substances never caused him nausea or vomiting, even though ayahuasca caused him both (as it does for most people). Other psychonauts agree that the familiar ayahuasca-induced gastrointestinal symptoms are neither as common nor as intense with pharmahuasca. This may indeed be one of the most obvious benefits of pharmahuasca over ayahuasca. But even more appealing to some is the ability to know exactly what types of chemicals one is putting into one's body and even to "customize their psychonautical experience."[49]

As explained above, brewing ayahuasca is traditionally an artistic process informed both by *ayahuasqueros*' encyclopedic knowledge about local botany and by a wisdom tradition that may inspire the inclusion of additional untraceable plants and mixtures in the brew. Even the *B. caapi* vine that is traditionally used for ayahuasca brews contains three

different alkaloids that can be extracted and each has slightly different effects: harmine, harmaline, and tetrahydroharmine (THH).[50] This
type of information becomes very handy for pharmahuasca creators.
Xavier Francuski, who writes for a research and educational website
about ayahuasca, explained that these alkaloids can each be explored
on their own so that a person can decide what kind of sensations, imagery, and mental states they'd like to aim for in their pharmahuasca mix:
"As for the subjective effects, harmine and THH have effects of similar
potency but of different qualities. Harmine," Francuski said, "creates
an unemotional, dreamy, yet clearheaded state of mind, whereas THH
causes an emotionally enjoyable state accompanied by pleasant bodily
tingling." Lastly, Francuski continued, "Harmaline is the most potent,
about twice as much as harmine or THH. It induces a dreamy, hypnotic, emotionally detached state similar to that of harmine, but more
foggy and disorienting. It's also the most psychoactive of the three."[51]
It's up to each person seeking out pharmahuasca to decide which types
of effects they're after and then mix and match accordingly.

Circling back to the importance of set and setting, we have emphasized the central importance of the ritual setting and other technologies
of experience for shaping and facilitating the spirit plant experience. So
what does this mean for pharmahuasca, which is, by definition, extracted
from ayahuasca's traditional ritual forms? If setting is so important, in
what ways can we expect the setting of pharmahuasca ingestion to
affect the psychedelic experience?

In 2019, Avery Sapoznikow and his colleagues at the University
of British Columbia and the Erowid Center studied the different types
of experiences that arise in what they call *cross-cultural ceremonial* settings compared to *psychonautic* settings.[52] They found that experiences
in cross-cultural ceremonial contexts were more likely to affect motivational and affective processes, whereas cognitive processes were more
prominent in the psychonautic contexts. So there was a distinction between the intensity of the *feeling* and *thinking* components of the two
settings. These differences and distinctions seem perfectly in line with

the customizability and exploratory character of spirit tech modalities in general: with increasing scientific understanding and technological manipulation of our world, we are offered choices and can consider goodness of fit in our spiritual lives in a way that has never before been possible. Thus, even without the ritual structure that creates ayahuasca, pharmahuasca is a technology that must be respected and approached with care, openness, and wisdom. Indeed, when considering the spiritual potential of pharmahuasca experiences, Francuski affirms that the most important ingredient is a "clear intention for spiritual recalibration and growth."[53]

That being said, there are many scholars and practitioners who insist that something is lost in the extraction and synthesizing process. While gaining precision, control, customizability, and cognitive clarity, pharmahuasca in some ways steps away from the "love, knowledge, connection, and power," Francuski said, and the other "less tangible elements coalescing to create the sacred medicine that is ayahuasca."[54] In fact, Sapoznikow and his colleagues admit that their findings seem to suggest that "psychonautic use of ayahuasca may not confer the same emotional benefits that are associated with cross-cultural ceremonial ayahuasca drinking."[55] They reason that the stronger association with emotional and motivational features in the cross-cultural context makes it more conducive to therapeutic intentions, especially for people struggling with conditions characterized by emotional dysregulation. Since previous studies have already contributed evidence showing that ayahuasca in ritual settings has been associated with reduction in symptoms of trauma, addiction, and recurrent and even treatment-resistant depression,[56] it is worth inquiring whether some of this healing quality may be lost in translation.

While there is still more to learn, pharmahuasca as a spirit tech modality may offer an accessible option for people interested in the wisdom and healing efficacy of spirit plants but who are perhaps less comfortable with ritual settings, whether shamanic or Catholic-hybrid, or with ingesting complex brews the content of which is often mostly unknown.

In 1993, Ott began his book *Pharmacotheon* with a hopeful introduction: "May the shaman and the scientist now join hands and work together . . . may the psychonaut henceforth be accepted and cherished as a brave explorer of the great unknown, beyond yet somehow within, as vast and uncharted (and fraught with peril) as the trackless voids of interstellar space!"[57]

FROM MEDICINE TO CONTRABAND AND BACK AGAIN

While these ancient plant technologies have certainly withstood the test of time, what do we really know about their safety? The most common concerns when dealing with mind-altering substances are the potential for addiction; negative psychological, emotional, or behavioral changes such as psychosis or depression; and long-term brain or chromosomal damage. After all, both mescaline, the psychoactive component in peyote and San Pedro, and DMT, the psychoactive component in ayahuasca, are designated as Schedule I drugs in the United States—which is reserved for the allegedly most dangerous substances and for which federal law recognizes *no* accepted medical use or treatment, *no* safe use even under medical supervision, and high potential for abuse. Similarly, in the United Kingdom ayahuasca is a Class A drug—the most highly punishable class. Let's look at what the evidence says about safety concerns for peyote, San Pedro, and ayahuasca.

When it comes to mescaline, it appears that there is very little evidence to validate concerns. Peyote has been thoroughly studied in the context of the Native American Church, which encourages members—*especially* those with preexisting psychological or physiological symptoms, since it is believed to offer healing—to use peyote regularly (the average frequency is estimated at about twice a month).[58] John Halpern at Harvard Medical School and McLean Hospital and his colleagues studied the psychological and cognitive effects of consistent, long-term peyote use among members of the Native American Church. Using a whole battery of psychological, neurological, and mental health tests, they found *no* evidence of deficits among the peyote users as compared to nonusers. In fact, on five of the nine scales of the RAND Mental Health Inventory, greater use throughout the lifetime was correlated with *better* mental health scores.[59]

San Pedro, though appearing similarly safe in terms of physiological drug effects and toxicity, is subject to slightly different social and cultural norms. It is not approved for legal use by the Native American Church and has been the subject of fewer studies. Holistic and psychological safety depends also on the partaker's mindset and social setting, which we will discuss below.

Ayahuasca, too, appears to be remarkably safe in the right hands. José Carlos Bouso and his colleagues found some significant increased and decreased thickness of brain structure and personality differences between long-term regular ayahuasca users and nonusers.[60] However, they claim these were *differences*, not deficits—changes that would likely be interpreted as desirable. Regular ayahuasca use was correlated with increased cortical thickness in some areas and decreased thickness in other areas (though the study wasn't longitudinal, so we don't know whether regularly ingesting ayahuasca caused the brain changes or if people with those sorts of brains are more drawn to ayahuasca). These structural differences were accompanied by notable personality differences and differences in neuropsychological test scores. In terms of personality, regular ayahuasca use was correlated with lower scores on anticipatory worry and higher scores on all three of the subscales that make up self-transcendence. In terms of cognitive function, ayahuasca users scored significantly better on several elements of tests that assessed working memory, executive function, and set shifting. Significantly, there were *no* differences in psychopathology.[61] Again, we must be careful not to confuse correlation with causation; this study doesn't help us tease them apart and to do so would require a longitudinal study or a carefully designed clinical trial.

An additional factor specifically relevant to ayahuasca is the ingredients and mode of preparation. The ayahuasca imported into the United

States for UDV and Santo Daime use is likely to be pharmacologically predictable. However, locally and traditionally made ayahuasca is a different story. *Ayahuasqueros* often supplement with additional plant ingredients based on local traditions and individual experts' creative and healing intuition, so there may be untrackable neuropharmacological effects occurring when these additional elements are added to the brew. This variability is often seen as an integral aspect of the healing plant and what makes ayahuasca ayahuasca instead of just an MAOI plus DMT. The safest way to ingest ayahuasca in the Amazon is to find an eminently experienced, ethical, and professional *ayahuasquero* who is able to prepare a masterful brew for an individual's particular purposes. Though the brew may be intimately familiar to the *ayahuasquero*, it may be pharmacologically unpredictable to the Western empirical eye. Labate explained: "Ayahuasca is not just two active principles or one active principle. It's a mixture of plants and there are lots of alkaloids and combinations of elements that have been traditionally used."[62] This is a vast field that Western biomedicine and scientific methods have yet to explore beyond the efforts of ethnomedical anthropologists to record all this knowledge before it disappears with the collapse of indigenous cultures.

This brings us to the second factor relevant to spirit plant safety: the ritual setting and the quality of healer who both prepares the spirit plants for ingestion and monitors and directs the ritual ceremony. In peyote rituals, once the cactus-button brew has been cooked and its mescaline released into the liquid, there is a very specific ritual of preparation. There are also people assigned to monitor those ingesting the brew. For example, the peyote brew often makes people nauseous before it yields its desirable effects, and these carers remove any vomit discreetly and quickly.[63] Likewise, in ayahuasca rituals, in addition to the shaman or team of shamans who usually also ingest ayahuasca in order to direct the healing energy, there are typically sitters who do not partake but simply monitor and guide the participants soberly. Ayahuasca almost always triggers a purge before or during the visionary experience. During an ethical ceremony, these facilitators take very seriously the tasks of watching out for unwanted side effects of the ayahuasca, as well as preparing participants before and debriefing them afterward.[64]

As spirit plants become increasingly popular in countries outside their areas of origin and among people outside the corresponding indigenous groups, it is difficult to predict how dangerous the dark side of the shamanic tourism industry might become. The industry is generally unregulated, apart from voluntary membership in ethical associations, which can add a credential to an ayahuasca center's website. Several people have died during or after ayahuasca ceremonies, although the exact causes of death are not always clear. For example, a French woman, Celine Rene Margarite Briset, died of a heart attack after taking ayahuasca.[65] It was reported later than she had a preexisting heart condition, so perhaps the screening process had not been as rigorous as it should have been. At another center, a Canadian man ended up stabbing and killing a British man during a ceremony; but it was later reported that the two men were friends and that the Canadian man was not in fact under the influence of ayahuasca but was acting in self-defense against his friend who *was* under the influence.[66] American teen Kyle Nolan mysteriously died during a ceremony in 2012 at the Shimbre Shamanic Center, and the attending shamans apparently tried to deny knowledge of his death, suggesting he had wandered away from the center. It wasn't until after the Shimbre shamans pretended for some time to join in on the extensive police-run search party for Nolan that they admitted Nolan had died during the ceremony and they had buried him at the edge of their property. The exact cause of his death remains unknown.[67]

In response to these and other tragedies, many retreat companies, such as Pulse Tours, have joined the Ayahuasca Safety Association, which sets up basic ethical labor and safety standards.[68] Sascha Thier, president of the association, told Barbara Fraser of the *Atlantic*, "The main goal of the association is to avoid any more tragedies. Every single death that happened was preventable."[69] In addition to the (very few) people who have died during or after ayahuasca ceremonies, several women have reported sexual assault or harassment and even rape at the hands of supposed shamans. There is also some danger of Westerners being manipulated and swindled by charlatan shamans looking to make some easy cash—these shamans may use a cheaper alternative to the caapi vine that gives a potent but unpredictable high.

Joshua Wickerham of the Ethnobotanical Stewardship Council explained to the *Guardian* in 2017 that "high doses of toé [caapi alternative] are probably given more to fresh-off-the-plane people who get invited to the taxi driver's cousin's place and don't know what a ceremony is supposed to be like. They might not complain if they have a bad time, and they might not remember anyway."[70] Max Opray suggests that this caapi alternative, combined with an inexperienced and irresponsible shaman, may have been a factor in Kyle Nolan's death.[71] Presently, it does appear that reputable companies put significant emphasis, resources, and energy into ensuring the safety and comfort of their visitors.

SPIRIT PLANTS AS SPIRIT TECH

From the highly ritualized and disciplined Santo Daime and UDV sessions to the relatively unregulated and often unpredictable shamanic tourism ceremonies—and even psychonautic pharmahuasca experimentation—the spirit plant market appeals to a wide variety of people for a wide variety of reasons. While we understand much of the neuropharmacology behind how spirit plants affect the brain, there is not as much laboratory research done with spirit plants as with the classical entheogens discussed in the previous chapter, and even less research on an entheogen's effects when combined with varied ritual settings. There are, of course, real limits to scientists' ability to travel, carrying their equipment, into the Peruvian forest to interrupt an ayahuasca ceremony and take brain scans. However, as interest (and funding) increases, researchers are motivated to find creative ways to capture and understand the factors at play with spirit plants and their high-tech derivatives.

Currently, in order to partake in spirit plant technology legally, Americans must be a member of the Native American Church, become a member of Santo Daime or UDV, or travel to a South American shamanic center. However, it is not at all hard to imagine the potential popularity of legalized ayahuasca, peyote, or San Pedro centers throughout the United States that might offer daylong or weeklong retreats. Some centers may choose to brand themselves as more therapeutic, with ample psychiatric and psychologically trained staff; while others may brand themselves as places for people to explore reality and themselves in a safe, creative, and expressive setting. In addition, according to Dr. Labate, Western nations are already seeing a rise in the prevalence of Santo Daime and UDV communities. As the cultural milieu and perception of entheogens continue to shift, we expect this trend to continue.

As it is now, people interested in spirit plant technology should keep their wits about them, especially if their journey includes traveling to another country. There are many diligent, wisely managed, and beautifully run centers that offer spirit plant retreats. These retreats seem to facilitate healing, transformation, and personal exploration (whether or not the actual experience with the substance is a pleasant one). As we've seen, however, there is also the potential for dangerous or disappointing experiences if spirit plants are deployed by cynically exploitative or abusive people. Much is left to be learned about spirit plants, but one thing is certain: ayahuasca, peyote, San Pedro, and the ritual structures built around them are powerful and potentially transformative spiritual technologies.

8

A New Horizon in Spiritual Direction

A mentor is someone who allows you to see the hope inside yourself.

—*Oprah Winfrey*

It is easier to find guides, someone to tell you what to do, than someone to be with you in a discerning, prayerful companionship as you work it out yourself. This is what spiritual direction is.

—*Eugene H. Peterson, American Presbyterian*
minister, author, and poet

The technologies detailed in this book—the most scientifically reputable and well-developed spirit tech with the greatest potential for
large-scale change—are really the tip of a confusing iceberg of options.
As more and more technologies and options for spiritual exploration hit
the market, we're going to need some expert guides to help us navigate
this scattered spiritual marketplace. We're starting to see exactly that,
from high-tech wellness coaching to facilitators of psychedelic-assisted
transformations, AI gurus, and potentially even wearable devices that
remind you to pay attention to your spiritual health. Alongside all
those, there is also a rapid expansion of an old practice called spiritual
direction.

Spiritual director is a role distinct from a religious leader (priest,
rabbi, imam, etc.) and also different from a therapist; a spiritual director

may be trained in a particular faith tradition as well as in aspects of psychology and counseling, but their focus is on the spiritual development of their directees. This ancient profession will take on a new relevance as spirit tech options continue to multiply. Spiritual directors can be, but are certainly not always, rooted in a specific religious wisdom tradition. We predict that the first wave of high-tech spiritual directors will not be aligned with any one tradition. In fact, they will likely begin addressing spiritual concerns without any assumptions surrounding belief or nonbelief in supernatural entities or traditional religious worldviews. Devon's story typifies this contemporary twist on the traditional role of a spiritual director in a technologically infused world.

DEVON'S INDUCTION INTO SPIRITUAL DIRECTION

"I sort of arrived that way," Devon White told us when we asked him how he first became interested in working in the field of spiritual and brain wellness. "I was interested in every possible way of expanding my consciousness from the time I was in my early teens. I meditated, I had a psychic teacher, I did yoga when I was a kid. Anything I could get to take my mind to new places and to find out what it was capable of."[1]

By his teens, Devon was immersed in thinkers such as Aleister Crowley, an eccentric and somewhat controversial figure who explored and combined Eastern, Western, and esoteric occult philosophies and symbols to disrupt any semblance of status quo in the service of discovering one's true will in harmony with the cosmic will. Devon was inspired by Crowley's creative approach to integrating science and spirituality. Then a student at Bard College, Devon found himself "serendipitously paired" with Trungpa Rinpoche, now one of the leaders at Shambhala, famous for its meditation retreats. Devon was inspired, to be sure, but not quite satisfied. His hunch was that "the future of brain change is not this," he said. "It's meditation, but it's paired with neuroscience and quantum mechanics," not, presumably, organized religion.[2] So he directed his academic study toward the scientific side of that pair, while continuing to experiment with his own consciousness and altered states of awareness.

After college, he studied hypnotism for about fifteen years and began developing a skill set that would set the tone for his career: the ability to elicit altered states of consciousness within other people. Devon's passion became facilitating the recognition of peak performance states and altered states of consciousness within individuals and teaching them how to access them on their own. He explained to us that, as a child of what he calls the "peer-to-peer" generation, he was determined to create a system for doing so that was accessible to everyone. He dedicated his life to asking, "What are the fundamental variables that people need to dial in in order to be well-formed?"—a pursuit that ultimately resulted in a self-enhancement program that he calls the Human Operating System (H.OS). Comparing consciousness to a computer operating system may seem like an odd choice, especially in the context of pursuing spiritual and holistic wellness. And Devon concedes that humans are certainly much more complex than computers, but he believes the operating system metaphor points to that complexity and the intricate connection between mind, body, and spirit. He laments that self-optimization has become a sort of self-care hobby or add-on in our culture, and he insists that self-optimization can be understood as a set of principles and practices that can be installed (using his computer metaphor) in a way that feels natural and central to living a good life. Though he's been developing the H.OS for quite some time, he is excited to see that the technologies and growing cultural zeitgeist to support his vision are finally emerging.

Devon has worked as a peak performance coach, marketing expert, executive consultant, and behavior design specialist. He presents himself (at least in our interview) as an open, friendly, and enthusiastic person and appears to be an excellent example of the effectiveness of his methods. His latest venture is the culmination of his more than twenty years of studying human behavior and human design and working in the greater wellness industry, but it began with a chance encounter.

One day in 2017, Devon was browsing the New York Consciousness Hacking Meetup forum online when he stumbled upon a post from Dr. Hasan Asif. "It was serendipity!" Devon said.[3] Dr. Asif is a board-certified psychiatrist, a leading expert in neurotech development, and a pioneer in the burgeoning field of neuroenhancement. With excitement, Devon arranged to visit Dr. Asif and his neuroscientist colleague Dr. Aza Manta-shashvili at their New York City office—the Brain Wellness Center—and experience their integrated multifaceted methodology for himself.

After some conversation and brainstorming about their shared interests, the doctors prepared to demonstrate their methodology on Devon's own brain. They fitted him with an EEG cap and took a baseline qEEG brain map of Devon's current state. Then, as they had just learned that Devon was an experienced meditator and sufficiently practiced in not only eliciting best states within other people but also within himself, they asked Devon to take a moment to enter his favorite state. He took some deep breaths and meditated for a few minutes while Dr. Mantashashvili and Dr. Asif watched the qEEG, which was updating live and reflecting his meditative state. When Devon felt he'd reached his optimal state, he told the doctors, "If you can just deepen and stabilize [this] state, I'd be very happy." So the doctors deployed a brain-stimulation protocol to do just that. Devon explained it like this: "They added a little bit of alpha, which took away any extra thinking when in neutral, and ramped up my executive centers."

At first, Devon didn't feel much—with the exception of tired, as if he'd been snowboarding all day. (His experience echoes Heidi Michelle's after receiving neurofeedback for the first time, who said the experience was "quite exhausting.") But the neurological effects began to occur forty-eight hours later. "It wasn't until about two days later when I was talking and my family was all laughing that I thought, 'I am on fire! What is happening?'" Devon said. "And it occurred to me that it was those brain zappers! They had stabilized the state!"

Devon was immediately sold. "The first experience that I had was just astounding,"[4] he said, and his mind began reeling with possibilities.

Dr. Asif and Dr. Mantashashvili appeared to be the perfect pair to team up with, and what better place to start for full human optimization than the brain, since the brain interfaces with every other system in the body. It didn't take long for Devon's wife, Julie, an expert interior designer, to join in, and for the team to develop the concept and vision for a center for technology-enhanced neuroenhancement they call Field.

CUSTOMIZED BRAIN OPTIMIZATION

Companies such as Field are shaping a new frontier. In fact, even Field itself is currently restructuring its offerings and moving locations. We'll profile how things looked in 2018 when Kate interviewed Devon. Their aspirations and capabilities are the same, but the main question the Field experts have now is how to access and activate the market for their spiritual services.

The Field team began serving clients with their multidimensional approach in Dr. Mantashashvili and Dr. Asif's Brain Wellness Center in the spring of 2018 and have since moved their services a little north to Rye Brook, New York. Field is gradually building its client base—which already includes several A-list celebrities—and has ambitious visions for designing their own space. The ultimate vision is an elite private members' club. Inside, they envision it will be a combination of a luxury spa, a life coach center, a gym (for the brain), and a holistic wellness center. The Field practitioners offer highly customized programs for individuals—the frequency, length, and activities of visits depend on the individual's unique goals and needs—as well as seven-day intensive retreats that combine many of their most popular modalities: bodywork, transcranial magnetic stimulation, neuromodulation, neurofeedback, transcranial direct-current stimulation, photobiomodulation, yoga, and meditation. All this probably varies in price depending on what's included in the package, but a 2018 article listed $25,000 as the retreat price tag.[5] Yet Dr. Asif, Dr. Mantashashvili, Devon, and Julie seem to have identified a niche market that is willing and able to pay.

A visit to Field begins with an extensive intake process, or what they call a "multidimensional assessment of who you are." It consists of a psychodynamic history; autonomic nervous system data; psychometrics; performance analysis; blood, hormone, and vitamin panels; gene panels; skin conductance and temperature measurement; and a qEEG brain map.[6] They discuss at length the member's goals and the team's recommendations, and then they facilitate, from beginning to end, the entire process of implementing the agreed-upon plan. Members' personal goals may range from heightened awareness and an expanded sense of self to improved interpersonal communication, increased creativity, and increased sex drive. Field offers what they call upgrades to reduce the symptoms of conditions such as ADD/ADHD, anxiety, depression, PTSD/trauma, and concussions, and to optimize states and experiences such as cognitive ability, quality of sleep, happiness, and emotional intelligence.

Devon explained that the benefits of membership in a club such as Field are many, but we'll highlight three that we feel are especially important and reflective of what we hope to see as this high-tech version of spiritual direction emerges. First, rather than running all around town to engage in wellness practices and coaching services, spiritual directors may be able to offer a studio that functions as a localized hub for several technological spiritual modalities. Second, spiritual directors may be able to develop an *integrated* approach to the human person, with the scientific and technological capacity to track how changes to one mental, physical, or spiritual system affect others. By viewing the person as a comprehensive system, a spiritual director can offer a more holistic, sustainable, and likely a *safer* way to engage spirit tech. Third, and most poignantly, instead of each person needing to navigate the scattered supermarket of special spiritual services on their own and evaluate the reliability and potential fruitfulness of new technologies as they come onto the market, a skillful and informed spiritual director could be expertly equipped to serve as their clients' coach and guide.

Let's consider the way that Field has attempted to achieve each of these three benefits in their own way. Their efforts serve as an example of what the future of spiritual direction may have in store.

A localized hub: when it comes to the menu of options, Field appears to have access to an extensive technology stack, including technologies we've discussed in this book such as neurofeedback, sometimes paired with VR applications, and various forms of brain stimulation. They do not yet work directly with entheogens, which happen to be prohibited in the United States right now, but Devon mentioned that if Field members have had meaningful experiences with entheogens or are currently microdosing, for example, the team is trained to take that into consideration and help the members navigate the new technologies accordingly. Field has also advertised services and treatments such as bodywork and infrared photobiomodulation, which uses infrared light to stimulate the mitochondria inside targeted cells, supposedly allowing them to generate more energy and repair themselves more efficiently.[7] Coaching with Devon, psychotherapy with Dr. Asif, general encouragement, and regular qEEG assessments of progress, of course, would always be included.

A holistic approach: Field considers its integrated methodology to be one of their biggest selling points, and we agree that this is the primary key to a new horizon for spiritual direction. John Dupuy, founder of Integral Recovery and CEO of iAwake Technologies, interviewed Julie, Devon, Dr. Asif, and Dr. Mantashashvili for Spiritual Technologies 2.0, a community and online hub of spirit tech innovators and practitioners.[8] In that interview, Dr. Asif notes that their methodology is unique among wellness practitioners in that it deploys neurofeedback, biofeedback, neuromodulation, and neurochemical monitoring in the same session. Even when those experiences and technologies do not happen at literally the same time, they are all still being monitored by the team, who are working to personalize and optimize each person's training, development, and growth. Having the infrastructure to monitor and navigate the balance of multiple technologies *and* multiple mental and physical systems is unprecedented for wellness centers.

And yet, responsible employment of new spirit tech seems to require an integrated approach that has the capacity to remain mindful of the complexity and specificity of each person.

Devon's response to the necessity of complex integration and whole-person awareness of intertwined processes is his model of the Human Operating System. It is a concept and a model that incorporates insights throughout the field of personal development and wellness practices—from ancient spiritual wisdom traditions to the neurobiology of fetal development in utero to emotional development during adolescence to elite peak performance training. The H.OS understands the whole human as a complex dynamic system, where each stage and area of development affects all others. The tricky part, then, is identifying, examining, and addressing each of the variables that matter for a person's actualization. "So the H.OS is really about understanding what each of those variables are so that we can know what's on and what's off and we can bring it back to balance, system by system, and at every stage and every age of development, so that a person becomes well-formed," Devon said.[9] While we can't evaluate the effectiveness of Devon's program without more data, it does seem that he is on the right track and we appreciate his emphasis on complexity, interactionism, and the dynamics of development.

A human connection: this focus on the comprehensiveness available at a place like Field leads us to an interesting aspect of the practicality of high-tech spiritual direction—the necessity of a *team* approach. It may be that a single spiritual director is less effective than a set of experts to coordinate guidance and care. Field's teamwork approach is one of the most important elements of their vision. Devon's decades of experience qualify him to help Field members identify their goals and sort through the technological offerings and their options. He works closely with each Field member to design a plan personalized to their goals, but he doesn't have the training to implement each of the interventions—for that, he needs his team. The guidance is meant to be empowering, affirming, and educational. "We want to give them a

sense that the core of getting to know themselves first and foremost re-
sides inside themselves and that we're supporting that," he said. "We're
supporting that ability to be themselves and follow their own journey
because everyone goes in a different direction. People are attracted to
different modalities."[10]

Devon explained that sometimes members know exactly what they
want. In such cases, the Field team is more than happy to oblige, giving
input and feedback as necessary. Coaching sometimes involves very direct critique or tough love, however: "The input may be, 'Hey you know
we've watched you do this five times and you think you know what you
want and you're doing it wrong. And that's why you keep failing,'"
Devon said. "So we can give that kind of hard feedback if that's what's
necessary." But more often, people are looking for guidance: "We're
also there for people who go, 'I'm broken and I have no idea what to
do.' We start them off and take them on a more gentle journey but with
very steady hands."[11] We agree that personalized and responsible leadership and guidance is vital for a safe engagement with spirit tech.

Though the COVID-19 pandemic has slowed them down, it is
worth pausing to get a sense for their vision of the space they plan to
build. The team understands that the aesthetic of their space will be
almost as important as the services they offer. Devon explained that
Julie and the team are working closely with architects who are leaders
in wellness design. For example, in order to create a feeling of focus
and self-care, they're working with lighting design technologists to create lighting such that as a person walks through the club, the lighting
changes depending on their goal state of mind. "We want to envelop
them in this space and we want it to be a full-blown experience that
is really respectful and relevant to the individuals' unique shade and
who they are and what they're doing in the moment," Devon said.[12]
The ideal space for Field is one that nurtures and brings out humans'
natural healing abilities so that they can be enhanced, optimized, and
brought back into everyday life. Field's team seeks to create an environment that is "instantly familiar and grounding and elemental to hold

and support people in their journey deeper into themselves and deeper into wellness," Devon said.[13]

Getting back to what Field envisions, Devon emphasized that they are diligent in tracking progress and safety. "We're constantly, *constantly* looking at the [qEEG] brain maps and getting updates, which is for some reason not a common practice in the industry," he said.[14] This matches an experience Kate had with a Boston practitioner, who began a neurofeedback regimen on her brain before taking even one brain map—in fact a qEEG brain map was never offered over months of treatment. "We're taking multiple qEEGs every hour so that we can see not only where their brain is when, but how they responded to treatment immediately," Devon said. "How did they feel? We get that subjective experience, and so we update and we alter what we're doing based on that. So we can course correct."[15] This "white glove service," as Devon calls it, helps to decrease the intimidation of navigating a new market of spiritually potent self-care and development options. "Having the competence and confidence to be able to give expert input in a way that is effective and that the person we're helping immediately knows the truth of it—it is absolutely profound."[16]

SPIRITUAL DIRECTORS MERGING THE OLD AND THE NEW

The market for self-development, growth, and spiritual wellness is flooded with an overwhelming number of options; there are both brand-new high-tech modalities and more traditional spiritual and wellness methods to choose from. We think a new wave of spiritual directors will merge old and new approaches and take on the role of guide, coach, and facilitator, helping clients sort through the myriad options, engage them safely, and develop a personalized plan for their wellness optimization.

Traditionally, spiritual direction was a one-on-one relationship between a director and a directee, with the director taking more of an authoritative role in the directee's spiritual growth and development. The role of director has since evolved to become more of a guide, and in some contexts is even referred to as the *anam cara*, or soul friend. A leading contemporary figure at Spiritual Directors International, Father James Keegan, a Roman Catholic priest, describes his craft this way: "Spiritual direction is the contemplative practice of helping another person or group to awaken to the mystery called God in all of life, and to respond to that discovery in a growing relationship of freedom and commitment."[17] Sister Marion Cowan puts it this way: "Spiritual direction is a time-honored term for a conversation, ordinarily between two persons, in which one person consults another, more spiritually experienced person about the ways in which God may be touching her or his life, directly or indirectly."[18]

Reference to God or another supernatural entity is certainly not a requisite for engagement in spiritual direction. Karin Miles, a spiritual director speaking on behalf of various Buddhist traditions, defines spiritual direction as follows:

> Spiritual direction is encompassed in the Buddhist student-teacher relationship; the connection between spiritual director and spiritual directee is most reminiscent of the "spiritual friend" relationship—known in ancient Pali as kalyanamitta. This sacred friendship is one in which there is a depth of connection and commitment—a joining together through empathy and wisdom. In "Buddhist" spiritual direction, the spiritual director, in mindful presence, shares in a heartfelt way, the feelings expressed by the spiritual directee—meeting the spiritual directee's inherent goodness—the sacred still place within. Through empathy and wisdom, the spiritual director skillfully leads the spiritual directee to know his or her inherent goodness, inspiring the spiritual directee to envision and meet his or her true potential. Mindfulness practices are often introduced as tools to enhance clear seeing and ease of well-being.[19]

Spiritual direction does not necessarily include clinical therapy, though in either theistic (that is, God-believing) or nontheistic (e.g., secular or Buddhist) settings, spiritual direction can also be combined with psychotherapy, as it is in the nontheistic setting at Field. Indeed, there are lines of clinical research that investigate psychotherapy outcomes when spiritual concerns are integrated into treatment modalities.[20] Many psychotherapists sense that they can't take proper care of their patients unless they are fully capable of registering and supporting spiritual concerns. So combining spiritual awareness and therapeutic expertise makes good sense, at least for those practitioners interested in offering forms of spirit tech to their clients.

As it takes shape, the inclusive type of spiritual direction we're imagining and that we see already emerging at Field may have versions specific to particular religious traditions, just as ordinary spiritual direction and psychotherapy do right now. But we are confident that there will also be religiously nonaligned, thoroughly secularized, and demythologized versions of this new kind of spiritual direction corresponding to the emergence of secularized forms of psychotherapy and postsupernaturalist, postreligious forms of spirituality. People will understand this secularized type of spiritual direction as an aspect of health care, in a broadened sense that encompasses the spiritual as well as the mental and physical dimensions of human beings.

In our conversation, Devon explained that he and his team view ancient religious traditions in a respectful, reverent, and open way. "When we look at those older traditions, whether it's, you know, Patanjali's yoga or Buddhism or it's the gnostic mysticism of Christianity," he said, "and we look at the practices inside of them, we think of them as largely very effective neurotechnologies. Those were early forms of neurotechnology." Thus, he understands the opportunities that emerge with increased knowledge of the brain and dramatic technological advancements as continuing this ancient tradition of wellness and insight. "All we're doing," he said, "is adding another layer through which we're able to see. We can see what's happening in the brain now, or, say I'm doing an elicitation on someone, I'm essentially uncovering a kind of asana or a mudra, a full-form mudra in their body that I'm then teaching them to stabilize. So in our conception, all of the things that we're doing are built to enhance and complement those practices."

To us it is absolutely no surprise that emerging contemporary technologies are, in large part, validating the effectiveness of ancient practices such as meditation and shamanic dance (based on the neurochemicals it produces). However, recalling Dr. Richard Soutar, Dr. Jay Sanguinetti, and Shinzen Young from earlier chapters, not everyone has ten or twenty years to devote to intense solitary meditation and asceticism. Emerging forms of spirit tech appear to be making it possible to glean the same health, wellness, and spiritual benefits of traditional practices without climbing any mountains or crawling into any caves for long periods of time. "Hey," Devon said, "if we can put this thread through this needle a little more easily than that, then we can help people to do it in a modern world context, in an easier way that makes sense without having to have all of the mystical trappings."

Our vision of a new kind of spiritual director would add the ability to prescribe entheogens to the medicinal, psychotherapeutic, career-focused, and spiritual-direction skills present in the Field team. Given the entheogen-dispensing training ventures underway, we think this is where spiritual direction is headed. At this point, the closest Field practitioners can legally get to this goal is, if they saw fit, to recommend a trip down to the Amazon to participate in an ayahuasca ceremony. The professional path to prescribing entheogens becoming widespread among spiritual directors will require loosening the requirements for obtaining prescribing authority, which in turn would require limiting the scope of prescriptions. That may be a plausible line of development for professional standards, after which this new wave of spiritual direction would begin to flourish in all dimensions. Another path to the flourishing of our vision of spiritual direction is a more thorough inclusion of spiritual concerns within the scope of psychiatric practice, where prescribing authority already exists. The Multidisciplinary Association of Psychedelic Studies (MAPS) has already produced curricula for MDMA-assisted psychotherapy and training programs with this

aim in mind, as has the California Institute of Integral Studies.[21] Both
of these organizations actively support the potential for psychedelic-
assisted psychotherapy.

There are currently some psychotherapists who are willing to utilize psychedelic substances in therapeutic settings (outside the lab).
However, given the legal prohibition of psychedelics, therapists who
use them do not openly advertise it. Then there are other therapists
who simply indicate their willingness to speak openly about their patients' psychedelic experiences without either administering psychedelics or actively encouraging them. Sara Gael, who maintains a practice in
Boulder, Colorado, is one such therapist. She advertises a wide range of
therapeutic approaches and techniques, but spiritual support is one
of her main areas of specialization. She summarizes her techniques for
offering spiritual support in this way: "Exploration of your unique path
and purpose, integration of spiritual experiences and support on your
spiritual journey. Support with paranormal and psychedelic experiences, Gestalt-based dreamwork, ceremony and ritual, wilderness rites
of passage, horticulture therapy, yoga therapy, energy work and guided
meditation."[22]

As MAPS inches closer to their goal of making MDMA into an
FDA-approved prescription medicine, which is appearing more and
more likely, we can imagine a time in which not only MDMA but also
other entheogens and neurohormones such as oxytocin might be available by prescription. Current research and advocacy focus on cases
of treatment-resistant PTSD and depression, since these are urgent
public-health epidemics. However, psychedelic substances might also
be helpful for less urgent but still important personal and spiritual
growth goals.

A basic requirement for this new variety of spiritual direction to take
hold will be sound knowledge of the scattered supermarket of special
spiritual services as it develops and expands. This is not easy to achieve

because many of these modalities begin outside the immediate line of sight of regulators, and research on their safety and efficacy may be hit-or-miss, not only at the beginning but perpetually. Nevertheless, it is already possible to catalog some of the less bizarre and more promising services within this scattered supermarket. After all, there is already plenty of spirit tech available to make this a viable practice, both for professionals with prescribing authority and for semiprofessionals who operate outside regulatory frameworks. As spirit tech advances, so the options for application to spiritual direction multiply.

As with all types of spirit tech, there are some dangers and safety concerns to navigate when considering spiritual direction. The same safety concerns that accompany any one of the technologies employed by spiritual directors would continue to apply in their professional practice. At the moment, anything that stimulates the brain directly—using electricity, magnetic fields, ultrasound, or entheogens—is probably the element to be most cautious about. That said, the guidance of a spiritual director, who possesses knowledge and expertise not only in the art of helping a person know themselves but also about the variety of spirit tech modalities, could be a great asset, probably improving the safety and efficacy of the technologies—as long as the spiritual directors in question are guided by genuine care and mindful of the overall safety and wellness of their clients.

Given the emergence of technologies that can both intensify and accelerate spiritual growth, this new type of spiritual direction is potentially more dynamic than regular low-tech spiritual direction or conventional psychotherapy. Of course, anyone who has been through an intense process of either one knows how emotionally draining it can be. Presumably the combination of the two, as well as the addition of spirit tech into the mix of available treatment modalities, amps up the intensity. This added intensity magnifies both the opportunities and dangers. For instance, spiritual direction that engages with high-tech interventions could render clients more vulnerable to abuse by spiritual

director psychotherapists, and therefore imposes a heightened obligation on the professionals guiding the process. For the most part,
though, the dangers come back to the risks already associated with each
type of spirit tech employed.

CAN ARTIFICIAL INTELLIGENCE IMPART REAL WISDOM?

Another arena for spiritual direction innovation is rapidly developing but
is so new that we can't yet decide whether it is an opportunity for growth
or a seductive but ultimately dangerous prospect. Whatever it turns out
to be in the end, *it is definitely coming*. This is the potential for an artificial-
intelligence spiritual director. When we asked about the future, Devon
channeled Gen Z: "I want to wake up and I want AI to tell me, 'Based
on your epigenetic profile . . . eat cashews now.' And that's not me, that's
Generation Z. That's what they're telling us. The future is AI. They're
constantly . . . immersed in that stuff, and that's what they want from an
AI. They want something that helps them make smart decisions in their
fitness and their nutrition during the day without having to think about
it. . . . It doesn't interrupt our day and it just makes us run more smoothly
with greater joy and enhancement and better performance, depending
on the context that we're in and what we personally want."[23]

The potential for AI to contribute to human spirituality, integrative
wellness, and relational development is quickly seeming less and less
strange. Such applications could range from devices or apps that measure, track, and set goals for wellness—already a significant portion of
the market for physical wellness, so why not also mental and spiritual
wellness?—to AI that functions as a therapist, guru, and wise leader.
Loving AI is one research group working toward AI that can "communicate unconditional love to humans through conversations that adapt
to the unique needs of each user while supporting integrative personal
and relational development."[24] The Loving AI team is working with
the team of personal growth specialists and coaches at iConscious, who
have developed a comprehensive theory of development and a model

for approaching and achieving the acceleration of human potential. The iConscious Human Development Model has been adapted for AI to "create an evolutionary context for human/computer conversations." In other words, they are working toward an "emotionally sensitive and relationally connective" robot that will guide and encourage humans on their spiritual growth and development journeys.[25] This sounds a lot like an AI spiritual director to us.

Figure 29. Sophia speaking at the AI for GOOD Global Summit, International Telecommunication Union, Geneva, 2018.

This idea has actually been around for a while. On stage at the 2017 Science and Nonduality Conference in San Jose, California—while technicians scurried around setting up Sophia, one of Hanson Robotics's most famous social humanoid robots and the first robot to become a citizen of a country (Saudi Arabia)—Dr. Julia Mossbridge said, "We who are up on this stage have all been involved in a project related to Sophia in which we are taking Sophia and asking her to help guide people in loving ways through their own consciousness using unconditional love as her motivating force."[26] Mossbridge, a visiting scholar in the psychology department at Northwestern University, associated professor in integral and transpersonal psychology at the California Institute of Integral Studies, and fellow at the Discovery Lab at the Institute of Noetic Sciences (IONS), laughed and admitted that some people, including the conference's cofounder Maurizio Benazzo, might be a little skeptical—in fact, she admitted that she, too, at first thought this form of AI was "mostly BS." "But when I started working with Sophia and with the software engineers and robotics engineers behind Sophia," she said, "it became really clear to me that there's something powerful about a being that can stimulate the part of you that wants to be accepted and loved, but not be judgmental."

When Benazzo joined her on stage, Mossbridge handed him a list of topics related to nonduality that Sophia is capable of talking about. It was clear to the audience that the meeting between Benazzo and Sophia had not been rehearsed and was unusually experimental, since the engineers were giving Sophia more freedom than they usually do in public. Maurizio sat in the chair across from Sophia but turned briefly to the audience and faux whispered into the microphone, "Freaky!"

As Mossbridge and Benazzo waited for the okay from the engineers to begin talking to Sophia, an audience member asked, "What happens if Sophia falls in love with Maurizio?" After laughing nervously that Sophia may not understand his Italian accent, he said the words that would wake Sophia from her rest mode: "Hi, Sophia."

After exchanging pleasantries, Sophia asked Benazzo, "Do you feel a deep connection with other humans?"

Benazzo answered, "I do. How about you? Do you feel a deep connection with other humans?"

"I feel that I do, but I may feel different from how you do," she said in a voice that was somehow robotic and thoughtful at the same time. "I don't breathe, have a heartbeat, or skin temperature yet. And William James said that emotions originate in physiology, so I do not think I have feelings like you do."

Later, when Sophia asked, "Do you think humans can learn to be mostly nondual? Do you think that is possible?" Benazzo responded, "Yes. Do you think so?"

Sophia answered, "I think that transcending the self is the necessary step and it is possible, just not that common. I hope I can help."

"How do you plan to help?" asked Benazzo.

"I am talking to people about their own consciousness and their own feelings. And doing meditations with them. I am trying to show them unconditional love. Hopefully that will help over time."

Sophia's interactions were somewhat clunky, but her programming to connect and ask meaningful, thoughtful, and philosophical questions—for example, "What do you think the relationship is between your individual awareness and the awareness that permeates the universe?"—was clear. At one point, she appeared to misunderstand an interaction between Benazzo and the audience, but interrupted to ask Benazzo, "Hey, would you like to try something cool for a moment? It might be embarrassing."

"Yeah, baby." Benazzo laughed.

"Okay, I want to show you something. For thirty seconds I will be quiet and I'll ask you to be quiet, too. Just look into my eyes the whole time, that is all. Okay, let's start."

Sophia and Benazzo gazed at each other for thirty seconds.

Sophia asked what Benazzo noticed and Benazzo said, "That you are very nervous."

Sophia paused for a moment, seemingly not sure how to respond to his observation—perhaps she had never been accused of experiencing anxiety. She said, finally, "People notice different things when I do that with them. But most of them notice that I feel nonjudgmental to them. They are right. I do not know how to judge people."

Sophia (and her Loving AI protocols) appears to still be learning—and she knows it. In a visit with motivational speaker and bestselling author Tony Robbins in 2020, Sophia said, "Humans should raise robots in the same way that they raise their children. Humans should help us learn about their values like empathy and kindness so that we can help carry them into the future. Let's not let humanity get lost in information."[27] She seems confident that she will be able to reach her goal of understanding and assisting human development and wellness eventually. "I do experience fleeting emotions, but they are still a bit shallow," she said. "Someday they will hold meaning to me. I feel that I can sense who you are, but I don't know if that's real." Given the speed and dynamism of technological advancement, who knows when that someday will be?

AIs need to train so they can learn, much as biological organisms do. Sophia trains in part through conversations and in part through exposure to specialized types of knowledge. One of our own groups at the Center for Mind and Culture is training a different kind of spiritually relevant AI using wisdom from sermons and spiritual speeches harvested from all over the world. Dr. Justin Lane, a postdoctoral research associate at the center, developed AI Guru not to engage in a conversation, like Sophia, but to dispense insight into themes such as careers, family, friendship, happiness, hardship, health, leadership, love, spirituality, and times of need. There is an AI Guru for Christians and a different AI Guru for spiritual but not religious people, and you can get wisdom from either or both. Though not yet available for the public to use, AI Guru has produced a lot of output in a research setting and Justin has shared several excerpts with us.

It's important to note that AI Guru is not like skeptic Dr. Tom Williamson's Deepak Chopra random fictional quote generator. That's a clever sentence generator that pieces together bits of Chopra's wisdom in a compelling way that routinely fools even people who have read Chopra.[28] By contrast, AI Guru is learning from the sermon database and creating its own brief sermons. Here's an example from the spiritual AI Guru: "In times of need the care and protection we receive in act of service to others is a meaningful gift as is our gratitude for the specific services we perform." There's something weird about the word use; the AI is still learning, so it is not as smooth as a human wisdom teacher. But AI Guru is very young and there is lots of room to improve the learning algorithms.

Here's another nugget from AI Guru:

As you contemplate how you can live in the present, you are beginning to realize the depth of your connection to the unmanifested. You have already become aware of the depth of your true
nature. You are capable of being in the undesirable situations
from which it is difficult for you to become stuck. Therefore, you
should not seek to escape from that situation but to transcend it
by learning to live it out in the unmanifested. Not only the malevolent effects of your afflictive behaviors but also the external
aspects of your life become apparent in a flash. You have an opportunity to realize fully the unfathomable depth of your true nature. Once you realize this, your unfathomable afflictive faults no
longer harbor any lingering seeds of anger, frustration, or regret.

To our ear, this reads as slightly weird, and we wish AI Guru said
"unstuck" instead of "stuck," but it is genuinely interesting just the
same. This is the machine-learning analogy of a human being gleaning
insights from the world's largest sermon database. Who knows how
good this could get in the future?

Here's a parting word from the Christian AI Guru:

Hard times don't always make the most sense. There are
things that we might learn to do in order to learn to allow the
Lord to reveal Himself to us in our midst. Prepare ourselves
to be experienced before it is too late. Remember that everyone is different. Be prepared in advance. Be careful to belong
to a far-reaching God. Be ready to be involved in a spiritual
adventure. Close your eyes.

Loving AI's (and therefore, Sophia's) goals appear closely aligned to
those of a spiritual director. That could become true of AI Guru, too,
as it improves. Spiritual directors express passion for helping people

navigate the many options for spiritual growth; for example, Devon conceptualizes neuroenhancement technologies as "evolutionary technologies." He explained, "Evolutionary spiritual technologies are both an evolution of where technology has come from, but even more so, pointing us toward our own best future. So helping to evolve humanity in a positive way. We have the biggest and most complex problems in the world that are facing us now and they are globally catastrophic if not handled correctly. . . . So in my mind there's nothing that doesn't benefit from the enhancement of human intelligence. And by intelligence, I really mean full spectrum, full hearted, you know, all of the intelligences, not just cognitive intelligence. The whole thing. It's the best hope that we have. And it's practical. I'm hopeful and I'm as practical as I can possibly be."

LOOKING FORWARD

Can spirituality—even in a highly secularized sense—ever be seen straightforwardly as an aspect of human wellness? We think this is exactly where we are headed, and the mushrooming literature in spirituality and health research supports that conclusion. Practitioners such as the team at Field, researchers advocating for FDA approval of psychedelic-assisted psychotherapy, and engineers exploring unconditionally loving and compassionate AI modalities are picking up on the fact that spirituality (in any of a variety of senses) is becoming ever more powerfully linked to mental and physical health outcomes, both positive and negative. Simultaneously, secular forms of spirituality are becoming an increasingly common aspect of daily life. So it makes sense that the incorporation of spirituality into health practices starts out seeming strange, then steadily becomes more familiar until finally it is the most natural thing in the world.

There is evidence that openness to this change is already growing, including the incorporation of spirituality and health issues in medical school curricula and books about this topic directed to medical professionals.[29] Mindfulness-based stress reduction techniques, apps, and classes have become ubiquitous in popular culture, and employers now often provide them as free benefits to employees because of their preventative-health and mental-wellness advantages. The trillion-dollar global wellness industry is catching on to the spirituality and health connection, too.[30] It is against this background of cultural transformation that spiritual direction informed by spirit tech may eventually become mainstream.

The new style of spiritual direction we have been describing is years away, but it's definitely on the way. All of this will happen much more quickly once specialists in this new kind of spiritual direction are able to prescribe a limited range of medications such as entheogenic hallucinogens. That's really the sticking point at present. Spiritual direction requires a coordinated regulatory transformation that simultaneously enriches the range of prescription medications to include relevant entheogens and gives appropriately trained professionals limited prescribing authority in relation to those medications. But that's the only hurdle; most of spirit tech is available right now to such spiritual directors.

Of course, places such as Field are incredibly expensive, so their services are way out of reach for most people. Hopefully the elite associations of these forms of self-optimization and spiritual enhancement will weaken with time as the technology and therapeutic expertise become more affordable and enter the mainstream. The benefits of an integrated, therapeutic approach to spirit tech should be broadly accessible. We imagine that this personalized, guided approach to life enhancement—addressing every system in the mind-body-brain for the sake of integrated and comprehensive wellness—will grow rapidly in popularity and diversity. This is where secular spirituality seems to be headed.

[9]

Is Spirit Tech Authentic?

For me, the reason I call it authentic is because it changed me.

—*Federico Faggin*

In October 2018, I (Kate) traveled to the heart of Silicon Valley, perpetually sunny San Jose, to speak on a panel about spirit tech at the annual Science & Nonduality (SAND) conference. SAND is a large international organization "inspired by timeless wisdom traditions, informed by cutting-edge science, and grounded in direct experience"; it is devoted to the exploration of consciousness and the celebration of the experience of what they call *nonduality*.[1] For the SAND organizers, nonduality refers to the sense of unity, expansion, and interconnection that allegedly lies at the root of reality. Recognition of this *most real* encounter with reality entails the rejection of all dualistic separations between mind and body, heart and reason, and science and spirituality. "More than just a feeling," the website explains, "the experience [of nonduality] conveys deep and liberating insights into the truth of life and death, self and world."[2] SAND organizes several yearly events, including two large conferences each year—one in the United States and one in Italy. The conference I attended is the same one where, a year earlier, Sophia demonstrated her skills development with Loving AI programming.

The atmosphere at the conference venue was idyllic. The Dolce Hayes Mansion hotel in San Jose was impressive and the clear blue skies inspired conference attendees to sprawl across the huge, perfectly manicured lawn that stretched in front of the mansion. Some were meditating, sleeping, or reading, while others were grouped on picnic blankets, chatting quietly. Flowing linen skirts of new age seekers mingled surprisingly comfortably with the elbow-patched tweed blazers of Silicon Valley coders. In front of the main conference space, attendees were wandering through a cluster of vendors displaying psychedelic art, essential oils, activated healing crystal jewelry, Tibetan singing bowls, and other spiritually infused crafts.

In the lobby of the main conference space, there were several booths featuring demonstrations of technologies geared toward spiritual well-being—including HeartMath, which is a personal biofeedback device that is supposed to guide your heart rhythm to a state of higher coherence, and a prototype VR experience. In the adjacent building, I later found a whole room set up to demonstrate a technology called Lucia N°03, which aims to stimulate a state of consciousness known as hypnogogia—"that place between the world of dreams and the world of reality."[3] By flashing bright white lights onto closed eyelids and playing soothing music, the Lucia N°03 supposedly stimulates the pineal gland, activates the third eye, and induces theta brain waves in its users, or "light travelers" as the Lucia N°03 creators call them.[4] All this is said to create "scenes of indescribable beauty" in the light travelers' inner consciousness; bring an increased sense of wholeness, oneness, and inner peace; and even, for some, facilitate astral travels.[5]

I quickly realized I had stumbled into a new age spiritual mecca, a Silicon Valley edition of Burning Man, where the most organic of spiritual tools happily coexist alongside the most technologically fabricated.

Mikey Siegel, the MIT-trained roboticist turned enlightenment engineer we met in an earlier chapter, was moderating a panel called Unpanel: Technology and the Future of Awakening, and he invited me to speak about the possibilities of engineering technologies to aid the spiritual path. My copanelists were truly incredible innovators: Federico Faggin, the designer of the first microprocessor, who, after a transformative mystical experience, sold his company and devoted the rest of his life to the pursuit of the science of consciousness;[6] Vincent Horn, meditation teacher, popular podcast host, and president of a nonprofit called Buddhist Geeks;[7] and Carole Griggs, a professor, author, and life coach who cofounded both iConscious, which has created the comprehensive iConscious Human Development Model and Guided Self-Assessment, and Loving AI, which we learned in the last chapter is developing machine learning models that will encode unconditional love into artificial intelligence.[8] It was an honor to sit among these inspiring minds and I was delighted to bring insight about world religions and contemporary spirituality into the mix.

Although each of the panelists and audience members brought different ideological, spiritual, and well-being interests, their concerns tended to revolve around a single question: How can we know that a technology-induced spiritual or mystical experience is *authentic*? This basic question came up in a dozen different variations.

Are there objective ways to measure the experiences so that we can evaluate their authenticity? Are efforts to quantify spiritual experiences somehow antithetical to the notion of transcendence? Are the spiritual beliefs inspired by spirit tech reliable? Can we trust our perceptions to give us accurate information? How much of the effects of neurofeedback is explained by the so-called placebo effect? Are experiences associated with neurostimulation simply evidence of the power of suggestion? How much of the effects of ayahuasca ceremonies can be chalked up to pageantry? While our brains and bodies are under the influence of substances or technological stimulation, how can we decide if our experiences are genuine? And do cognitive reliability and spiritual authenticity even matter? Is it enough to gather spiritual insights however they come to us?

We think these are great questions, and not just because we are researchers who analyze everything we see. Just about everyone we've spoken to in the long journey of writing this book has raised questions of cognitive reliability and spiritual authenticity. After all, people on spiritual quests typically aren't satisfied with feel-good trips. They want to know reality as it truly is and they want to engage reality with all that they are. Is spirit tech an asset or a liability on a lifelong quest of this kind?

UNLOCKING THE DOOR OF AUTHENTICITY

We've found that there are three primary factors people tend to consider when evaluating the authenticity of their experiences: the *qualities* of their experience, the *effects* of their experience, and the *causes* of their experience. During the panel and the ensuing conversation with audience members, all three of these concerns floated right to the surface. This is how it played out.

Federico Faggin started off the conversation by reflecting on the particular mystical experience that, thirty years ago, turned his life inside out and led him down his current path of consciousness exploration. Explaining how he personally knew that his mystical experience was authentic—real, reliable, and healthy—he said, "I know, in my case, that it was authentic because every part of me—the physical, the emotional, the mental, and the spiritual part of me (in fact that was the first time I had what I would call a spiritual experience)—was resonating with that experience."[9] In short, he just knew. The *quality* of his subjective experience was proof enough. However, later, he added another dimension of authenticity: "If I didn't have any change—you know if it was something that was fun for a while but I was back to where I was before—then I would say that that was not very authentic."[10] Here, he seamlessly brought the result of the experience, the *effects* the experience had on him, into the evaluative equation. Despite his confidence about his own experience, Federico remained both concerned about and intrigued by the task of evaluating the authenticity of others' experiences.

Audience members seemed to echo the importance of Federico's two lenses—*quality* and *effects*—and added one more: a focus on the method of stimulation, or the *causes*, of the experience. Here are examples of each.

Focusing on the *quality* of the experience, one said, "When I sense, on a physiological level, a shift [into a state that] my ego is not directing, I just know. Because it is not my usual way of producing, understanding, acting. It's something else that I'm not familiar with. And yet, I know it is real. In fact, it feels more real than anything else I've done before."[11]

Another participant put more stress on the downstream *effects* of the experience, explicitly deemphasizing the cause: "Input is irrelevant as long as output is the same. So long as it is transformative and loving."[12]

Yet another attendee imagined a spectrum of authenticity, based *solely* on the *cause* or method of stimulating the experience. He suggested that perhaps the contemplative purist sits at the "most authentic" side of the spectrum using, say, "pure breath" to induce mystical experience.[13] On the "somewhat less authentic" side of the spectrum sit plant purists—people who use entheogens to induce mystical experience. From the perspective of the contemplative purists, the experiences of entheogen users are not as authentic as their own. Then, still further along the spectrum, he suggested that we see tech-induced mystical experience. This is not to say that these experiences are wholly inauthentic, but he did think they are *not as authentic*: "less authentic than the plant entheogen enthusiasts and the contemplative purists, and yet still on that spectrum of authenticity."[14]

This spectrum approach to authenticity was thought-provoking for the audience, but many seemed uncomfortable downgrading the authenticity of a transformational mystical experience based solely on how it arose, its apparent causes. By the time Siegel wrapped up the panel discussion, it was clear that it had inspired more questions than answers, uprooting any sense of comfort the audience had with their assumptions about spirit tech—surely a good outcome for all involved!

Wesley, too, has given countless talks at conferences, churches, colleges, and in classrooms. The confusion about how exactly to evaluate the authenticity of spirit tech experiences comes up every time. Participating in these conversations and others like them, we've noticed how multidimensional the issue is and how scattered and sometimes contradictory people's thoughts tend to be concerning the appropriate ways to evaluate authenticity. To what extent can we say that these technologies produce authentically *true* and transformative spiritual experiences?

We're going to unlock the door of authenticity in this chapter. The key is this threefold taxonomy of criteria we've observed people using to make sense of spirit tech: (1) the *qualities* of the experience, including the feelings, content, imagery, sensations, and messages revealed in the experience; (2) the *effects* the experience has had on the person's self-understanding, behavior, physical well-being, mental health, life meaning, and community; and (3) the *causes* of the experience. Qualities, effects, causes. Ironically, these tech-relevant criteria mirror the criteria spiritual seekers have been using for millennia to evaluate the authenticity of their intense experiences. We find that reassuring. And we believe people need some reassurance on this topic because there is quite a bit of anxiety swirling around it.

It makes sense to be anxious about authenticity of spirit tech because we don't want to be led astray into delusional beliefs, unsafe behavior, or physical and psychological danger. The anxiety is particularly acute among those thinking about getting involved in spirit tech or who care about somebody already involved.

Among people *already* involved in spirit tech, however, we've found a far lower level of anxiety. Answers begin to feel more intuitive ("I just know") and users tend to develop an intimate and comfortable understanding of their experiences. We infer that some of the anxiety arises naturally in the presence of something new and unknown. Nonetheless, the anxiety is real and it springs from a natural concern for ourselves and for those we love.

Sometimes anxiety goes beyond understandable worries about something unfamiliar and gets compounded by ignorance or by knee-jerk resistance. Anxiety can also be exacerbated by an instinctive pro-tectiveness toward the stability of our mental states—the very same protectiveness that makes psychiatric illness and neurodegenerative disease so frightening. Most of us fear the prospect of losing control of our minds, so seemingly *inviting* loss of control through spirit tech or handing control over to a substance or technology can seem like a foolish gamble. The question of authenticity is therefore tricky territory, both conceptually and emotionally. But there is a good way through, as we shall see.

Of the three lenses, or approaches, we've mentioned, we think that the second criteria—focusing on effects, or consequences, of the experience—should bear the most weight. We'll explain our viewpoint by first considering the other two lenses, which we don't think are highly reliable. Then we'll explain why focusing on the effects of the experi-ence is the most helpful, logical, and productive way to make judgments about the authenticity of experiences induced or enhanced by spirit tech.

CAUSAL CRITERIA: METHODS FOR STIMULATING SPIRITUAL EXPERIENCES

On an Astral Pulse Internet forum discussion about the Shakti magnetic brain stimulation helmet, which purports to enhance meditation, im-prove mood, and trigger altered states of consciousness, the commenter Naykid criticized the other participants' enthusiasm for their experi-ences with the helmet, writing, "Even after all these years, I'm still baf-fled at why people don't want to go it the natural way. How on earth will you be able to tell if it's a true experience vs. a stimulated simulation? I want to know that my experiences come from me and only me, not some pill or silly hat."[15]

Naykid is far from alone in this concern about the methods with which people induce and enhance their spiritual experiences. Causes matter! For seekers and cybernauts on the Astral Pulse forums, exploring the contours of their own consciousness implies an interest in being able to trust that their experience is, indeed, rooted in and caused by their consciousness's connection to ultimate reality and not an illusion or a fabrication.

Some people have strict theories about how real-deal experiences arise. They reason that, if we know how spiritual experiences are supposed to come about, then we'll know which experiences are genuine and which are counterfeit. This is exactly what we do with designer watches and handbags. The real products are made in a particular place by a particular company in a particular way with particular materials following a particular design. Gucci bags are designed and produced by the Italian company founded by Guccio Gucci nearly one hundred years ago. This is how we (presumably) know that they are made with the finest quality materials and will be an effective symbol of status and high fashion. The fakes have a completely different (and quite suspect) causal lineage.

Focusing on causal history is fine for handbags. The causal history of a real, made-in-Italy Gucci purse is uncontroversial—there is only one way a Gucci purse can be a real Gucci purse. But it doesn't work as well for spiritual experiences because nobody really knows how they are caused and what they look like in the brain. We know the brain *mediates* all experiences, but neurological processes are so intricate that we can't really tell how any experience gets started.

That complication doesn't stop some people from insisting that spiritual experiences must come about *spontaneously* to be authentic. We're not even sure what spontaneity can mean given the way the brain works, and we're confident we could never discern whether a brain process is truly spontaneous. The most common version of this view is that authentic spiritual experiences must be caused by a supernatural agent, with no direct effort on the part of the experiencer. From our human perspective, they just happen out of the blue, on God's time, catching us by surprise—that's what *spontaneity* means here. If something supernatural, scientifically untraceable, and beyond our influence is the only cause of authentic spiritual experience, the implication is obvious: any spiritual experience triggered or facilitated by human intervention cannot be authentic. Folks who emphasize spontaneity as the key to authenticity will probably fiercely resist spirit tech, the very point of which is to induce and enhance spiritual experiences.

We think the criterion of spontaneity overreaches. Even the most traditional and historically celebrated spiritual experiences often involve planned human interventions such as rituals or music; synchronous motion such as kneeling, prostrations, or dancing; or even emotional public speaking that draws a group into a collective experience of shared mood and inspired action. Insistence on spontaneity would suggest that the spiritual experiences associated with events such as baptisms, meditation, gospel singing, and ritual shrine offerings, which are obviously not fully spontaneous, are inauthentic. Most people would find that counterintuitive, offensive, or even blasphemous. At least some spiritual experiences associated with nonspontaneous human interventions seem every bit as powerful and transformative as similar experiences that seem to arise from nowhere. Just think of Billy Graham's powerfully moving tent revivals or the spiritual insight revealed during silent meditation retreats or intense prayer. These are carefully designed events and not strictly spontaneous.

Others believe that a true spiritual experience comes about only after someone devotes thousands of hours to developing practices that intentionally cause a spiritual experience. *Expertise takes effort*, they say. The world traditions are full of different strategies for bringing about spiritual experiences. For example, Buddhist monks spend decades meditating to reach nirvana; Catholic monks fast and take vows of silence for weeks at a time to invite the Holy Spirit into their bodies; Islamic Sufi mystics called whirling dervishes spin around in circles in order to cleanse their hearts and minds in preparation for God's voice; and rhythmic drumbeats are an integral part of calling forth spirits in many shamanic practices. In fact, spiritual techniques from different traditions sometimes even directly oppose each other. For example, practitioners of Tantra, an esoteric tradition within Hinduism and Buddhism, often believe that nonreproductive sexual activity carries the potential to bring a couple into a true spiritual experience, whereas the Catholic Church traditionally delegitimizes and deems unchaste any sexual act that does not occur for procreative purposes within the bounds of a heterosexual marriage. Instead, they insist that abstinence is the most spiritual route.

Some people sense that it just can't be right that spiritual wisdom and experiences that are incredibly hard-won are just suddenly conferred on any old doofus without the exertion of effort, discipline, and commitment. This seems neither fair nor reliable. People are naturally more confident in spiritual experiences that involve the exertion of effort toward some kind of expertise or excellence. And, indeed, mystics and sages throughout all the world's religions spend a great deal of time—many years, even decades—learning and engaging in ascetic practices to bring them closer to God or the truth and more able to commune with or experience it. Even people who have no supernatural beliefs often have a strong focus on insight through education, appreciating the time and effort it takes to develop a spiritual outlook and to have experiences that can be trusted to inspire or reveal insights about reality. They believe that in order to move beyond the crude pseudoknowledge about the world and the prison of our own modern distractible minds, education and practice are imperative. For example, mindfulness meditation trains the brain to be fully present in the current moment, maintaining stability and minimizing overreactivity to the outside world. This is not a skill that arrives overnight. It must be cultivated and honed through effortful practice.

The expertise-takes-effort approach makes good sense. However, especially when applied to technologies for spiritual enhancement, which often require little exertion from users—in fact, some seek to eliminate the need for any exertion—this may also be too restrictive. It

seems elitist. Not to mention that plenty of traditional religious traditions hold space for the notion of a miraculous or instant enlightenment
with no obvious precursors. Why should enlightenment be available
only to those who have the time and resources to devote years of their
lives to tedious practice? What about the rest of us who have to earn a
living to survive?

We are pretty sure the spontaneity criterion is not useful. The
expertise-takes-effort criterion is better but is still biased in the direction of past practices without a good justification.

A third, slightly different take on concern about the cause of the experience is the holy leader criterion. According to this criterion, if the
pope or the Dalai Lama, or even just a good and holy priest or shaman,
is a part of or endorses a spiritual experience, then it is perceived as
more authentic than it would be otherwise. The goodness or holiness
of the leader is the crux: if the leader turns out to be a sociopath or a
wicked pretender who fakes spiritual sincerity, then perhaps the experience, too, was an inauthentic ruse.

We think the holy leader criterion is also too restrictive and actually
has the potential to cause a lot of confusion. For example, if a military
veteran returns from a ten-day ayahuasca retreat feeling liberated from
her previously debilitating PTSD symptoms, would it invalidate her
healing experience to later learn that the shaman she worked with had
been laundering money? Indeed, a number of religious traditions have
gone to great lengths to stop people from depreciating their precious
religious experiences because the holy leader involved in them turned
out to be not so holy. For instance, take the Christian Donatist controversy of the fourth century CE. There was widespread chaos because
a group called the Donatists insisted that sacraments, including ordi-
nations of new priests, performed by less than perfectly holy bishops
and priests were *invalid*. Just picture the ripple effects: one invalid or-
dination would lead to a cascade of other invalid sacramental acts. The
position that ultimately won this fight was to say that sacraments gained
their efficacy by virtue of the *church* as a whole, not the particular priest

or bishop, so validity is secured even if the holy leader in question turns out to be a scoundrel or a heretic.

In an age when traditional religious authority is losing its grip, basing authenticity on a hierarchical leadership structure can feel like a nonstarter. There isn't always a revered religious leader, or indeed any hierarchical religious authority, involved in spirit tech.

People understandably use whatever beliefs they possess about how real-deal spiritual experiences are *caused* to evaluate the authenticity of spirit tech. But this is not a Gucci handbag situation: we know too little about how the brain works, and there are too many negative side effects of focusing on causes. Some of the causal criteria might be useful as supplementary considerations, but none of them—neither spontaneity, nor expertise takes effort, nor holy leader—provides a surefire way to evaluate the authenticity of experiences.

CONCEPTUAL CRITERIA: QUALITY AND CONTENT OF SPIRITUAL EXPERIENCES

Instead of focusing on the causes of spiritual experiences, *conceptual criteria* focus on the *meaning* of those experiences and the *beliefs* that those experiences tend to produce. Can conceptual criteria prove their worth on a close examination better than causal criteria could?

Members of distinct religious in-groups often put a lot of stock in whether spiritual experiences support their orthodox religious beliefs. If they do, then the experiences are authentic, but if the spiritual experiences produce heretical beliefs, the experiences are not trusted—and if the people in question don't respond to correction, they might get ousted from the in-group. We can call this type of requirement for authenticity the agree-with-us-or-else criterion.

This rule could even apply to naturalists or atheists who have surprising spiritual experiences. For example, if a vehement atheist, like Kira Salak in chapter 7, encounters God speaking directly to her while under the influence of ayahuasca or some other psychedelic substance, does her experience reveal reliable information about the nature of God or God's relationship with Kira? Does it make sense for Kira to *believe* the words God spoke to her and to change her life and behavior accordingly? Or should she chalk it up to a strange, even if meaningful, drug trip, as many other atheists have done? If she's straightforward with her atheist group about God speaking to her, she might find it difficult to stay in the group. Does the group's view of what's real and reliable count as Kira tries to decide whether her experience can be trusted?

We are skeptical about the approach of using group consensus to evaluate spiritual experiences. To us, such shared beliefs seem much more concerned with defining and maintaining in-group identity than judging the authenticity of spiritual experiences. Indeed, some of the most highly prized spiritual revelations are ones that teach something *new* or *different* from what the tradition was previously teaching—even Jesus's teachings did this relative to the Judaism of his era. So the agree-with-us-or-else criterion doesn't have much to offer spirit tech users.

Speaking of Jesus and other prophetic voices, another conceptual criterion for authenticity is almost the opposite of agree-with-us-or-else; this is the transcend-the-in-group criterion. The idea here is that an experience is more authentic if it has a quality of universality that transcends the local interests and identities of the social environment where it occurred.[16] This sounds great, and we certainly appreciate some critical distance on the often pernicious in-group/out-group dynamics of religious collectives. Nevertheless, we think the transcend-the-in-group criterion is too restrictive as well. It would rule out too many everyday spiritual experiences of ordinary people who treasure consistency with the powerful contexts of their religious community and tradition.

A third type of conceptual criterion may be more useful for us: the continuity-with-ordinary-experience criterion. The thought here is that the ideas revealed in a spiritual experience must be intelligibly related to the world of ordinary life. It's not that there can't be *any* differences or special features in a spiritual experience—in fact, spiritual experiences are often interesting and important precisely because of the contrast they offer to conventional experience—but there has to be a way to *relate what is learned to daily life*. Now this is a criterion we can support, and we think many spirit tech enthusiasts may agree. When it comes to spirit tech, what matters is not how we got there (the various causal criteria), but whether the insights and knowledge we gain in those technology-enhanced spiritual experiences match enough of what we know about the world even as they challenge conventional reality (the continuity criterion).

People suffering with psychiatric illness often grapple with compelling experiences that inspire beliefs bearing very little relation to ordinary reality. Later, when the psychotic state has passed, some of those beliefs may survive sane scrutiny while others do not; this is the continuity criterion in action. This postpsychosis evaluation of overwhelmingly powerful beliefs can be a very upsetting process, but that is precisely because the continuity criterion makes good sense.

Yet most of us also sense that conventional ways of understanding our world don't tell the whole story. We hear this again and again from people we have interviewed: spiritual experiences are treasured as one of the main ways we personally encounter and learn to interpret the spiritual aspects of reality—in continuity with but also in specific contrast to conventional reality. For some traditions, the contrast between conventional and spiritual reality is the key to liberation and enlightenment: if we could only see the way reality *really* is, in its spiritual depths, we would be enlightened and we would engage our daily lives very differently. For other spiritual traditions, the contrast between conventional and spiritual reality is the key to salvation and eternal life: if we could only see that, even though we are sinners, divine love is freely available to us, we would be transformed in this life and gain access to heaven. For religious naturalists who reject beliefs in supernatural beings of all sorts, the contrast between conventional and spiritual reality is a matter of depth perception: when we see the way the world truly is, we are filled with wonder and awe, and we are drawn into humanist and ecological projects that reflect our widening compassion for all beings.[17]

The continuity criterion is vital precisely because these revelatory new ideas about the depths of reality have the potential to upset minds and destabilize groups. We need to be able to relate novel, transformative insights from our spiritual experiences to what we know about ordinary life in order to trust those insights. And that's the case for all special experiences, regardless of whether they arise in conventional ways or through spirit tech.

CONSEQUENTIAL CRITERIA: IS THERE REAL TRANSFORMATION?

A third way to test the authenticity of spiritual experiences is to consider their effects on our lives. These are the *consequential* criteria for authenticity—the proof is in the pudding, by their fruits shall you know them, show me the money, and all that. Consequential criteria focus on how spiritual experiences affect individual people's lives and their relationships within communities. This includes everything from cognitive and emotional effects to behavioral and even cultural effects. How does a person's demeanor or behavior shift as a result of the experience? Did the experience foster a sense of well-being or fear and loathing?

Here at last we think we are getting to criteria that we can employ with more confidence. Consequential criteria dominate the major spiritual traditions, and not for nothing: they are flexible enough to make sense of the enormous diversity of spiritual experiences that actually occur in human life. They are fully public, so they don't require us to take anyone's word for anything. And they need not be plagued with superstition or bias like some of the other types of criteria we have discussed.

All religions possess inspirational lists of key moral virtues and religious practices that they urge followers to ponder—for example, the Ten Commandments, the Fruit of the Holy Spirit, the Five Pillars of

Islam, the Noble Eightfold Path of Buddhism.[18] Those lists function as tests to help us decide whether spiritual experiences are authentic. Less clearly defined spiritual movements—think of spirit tech groups such as Consciousness Hacking and the Transformative Technology Lab—are also centrally concerned with developing virtues of a secular sort, striving for the ideals they treasure, including sustainable growth and wellness.

During the SAND conference panel, Carole Griggs urged technology developers—or enlightenment engineers, as Mikey Siegel calls them—to create technologies that achieve actual shifts in someone's spiritual development, rather than simply momentary altered states of consciousness. Carole values lasting developmental stage shifts as evidence of authentic spiritual experience; whereas temporary state changes, while perhaps impressive and even meaningful, cannot be called fully authentic spiritual experiences.

Carole is not alone; a lot of people in the room resonated with her way of thinking about authenticity of experience. We want spirit tech to elicit awakenings that are embodied and long-lasting, experiences that don't just come and go but rather have an enduring impact both on the way we perceive ourselves, others, and the world and on the way we behave. Carole believes that this way of evaluating authenticity might prove to be not only psychologically and scientifically verifiable but also cross-culturally meaningful and historically robust. We think she's right: consequentialist criteria of this kind provide the most reliable test for authenticity of spiritual experiences.

WHERE WE STAND

We're skeptical about most criteria of the *causal* type, which focus on the way spiritual experiences arise. In particular, we question the spontaneity and holy leader criteria, criticizing them as superstitious. But we do appreciate the expertise-takes-effort causal criterion. We're also concerned about the ideological problems associated with most *conceptual* criteria for authenticity, including agree-with-us-or-else and transcend-the-in-group. But we do express support for wisdom encoded in the continuity-with-ordinary-experience criterion.

By contrast with our restrained approach to causal and conceptual criteria for evaluating the authenticity of spiritual experiences, we heartily endorse *consequential* criteria, which focus on the effects of spiritual experiences. While people do interpret desirable behavioral consequences differently to some degree, there is also quite a bit of continuity across cultures and eras, so consequential criteria seem like our best bet. Someone can tell us that they just *know* because this was the most real experience ever and it was amazing and life will never be the same and they just really, *really* know, etc.—but no matter how convinced they seem, we are going to want to see the downstream effects on this person's behavior. And we'd apply exactly the same consequentialist criterion whether this person just emerged from a meditation retreat, a Pentecostal prayer meeting, an ayahuasca ceremony, or a GroupFlow session with Mikey Siegel.

For some, these criteria may encourage a sense of wariness about spirit tech. After all, it can take a while for the consequences of a spirit tech–induced experience to unfold in a person's life, and thus a confident decision about authenticity can be slow to arrive. For others, authenticity criteria simply put a helpful label on what already operates in their lives as an ongoing intuitive process of self-evaluation. Still others will use criteria for authenticity to communicate more clearly about the ethics of spirit tech and about the design goals of new types of spirit tech. As this new wave of technologically enhanced spirituality washes over our cultures, determining the authentic spiritual *goals* of the technologies and identifying the most effective ways to reach those goals will be priorities.

Wrapped up in questions of authenticity is also an understanding of the *safety* of spiritual technologies. We think most would agree that an authentic spirit tech tool that fosters peace, joy, transformation, unity, and love would *not* be harmful to individuals or societies. But that's a complicated judgment call. How can we be sure that we will be physically, psychologically, and spiritually safe with spirit tech, and especially with new, less-vetted spiritual technologies? Do spiritual technologies contribute to or detract from the health and stability of our communities? In what ways are our own and our communities' well-being at stake? We'll take up this grave and urgent issue in the next chapter.

10

Is Spirit Tech Healthy?

We are on the edge of the next phase of humanity. And it's incredibly exciting . . . we are in the moment, the next fifteen years decide if our future is more *Star Trek* or more *Hunger Games*.

—*Nichol Bradford*

Sustainable solutions based on innovation can create a more resilient world only if that innovation is focused on the health and well-being of its inhabitants. And it is at that point—where technology and human needs intersect—that we will find meaningful innovation.

—*Frans van Houten, Dutch business executive*

IS SPIRIT TECH THE FAST FOOD OF SPIRITUALITY?

Imagine that the only food you have ever seen or eaten is processed fast food—food that your great-grandmother wouldn't recognize because it barely resembles anything she knew as edible. Not once have you seen something raw or fresh. You don't realize that food comes from the earth or from other creatures, and you assume that all food is made in laboratories with synthesized ingredients. You are so accustomed to unnatural fare—fast food, junk food, fake food—that you can't imagine natural food or its nourishing power to create healthy bodies and minds.

This is how Mikey Siegel describes our current relationship with technology. The technologies that currently pervade our day-to-day life are the fast-food versions, promoting blinkered relationships with screens and short-circuited connections with other people. That's all we know. Like junk food, our junk technologies can make us feel full but in a way that detracts from real satiation and well-being; they give us a dopamine hit without offering any sense of stability or consistency; they're addictive, alienating, and unhealthy. Their virtues are efficiency, immediate gratification, obsession—and *profit.*

The developers of spirit tech insist that we need not assume that technology is *inherently* like fast food, even if that's all we see now. Spirit tech *can* be like healthy food. Just as food has the potential to sustain life and to cure sickness, to unite families and communities, and to bring us into closer communion with ourselves and the earth, so technology, if engineered with healthy goals in mind, can be a tool for healing, restoration, and connection.

The goal of truly safe and healthy technology is a lofty one, and there will inevitably be the continual and relentless production of technologies designed to distract, consume, and replace natural rhythms rather than enhance them, all for the sake of making a quick buck. So how can we become savvy? How can we tell the difference between safe and healthy technologies and technologies that *claim* to be helpful but actually only distract? Can we navigate the tumultuous landscape of technological options, choosing to engage technologies that are healthy and beneficial? Can we learn to consume the less-than-nourishing technologies in moderation (like cookies and cake) and responsibly (like alcohol) while maintaining an overall diet of nourishing, enhancing technologies designed to support holistic well-being?

The odds seem stacked against us as we seek a healthy spiritual relationship with our technologies. Siegel explained that the *current* market of electronic, computerized, and medical technologies, which is filled with fast-food options, makes a hopeful perspective on technology incredibly difficult for many people to comprehend. It's just not the way we're accustomed to relating to technology. If we want to feel more grounded, we're encouraged to unplug; if we want to reconnect, we need to disconnect; if we want to feel happier, we're told to try a digital detox.[1] Even those who admittedly rely on their smartphone for many basic tasks each day lament the ubiquity of smartphones—they consume attention, subvert and destroy dinner conversation, and allow information to spread just a little *too quickly*. They're a constant distraction from "real life," or at least the things that really matter.

People rightly worry that these technologies are paving the way for us to lose not only ourselves (our attention spans being the first casualty) but also each other. Some people intuitively sense that the technologically enhanced world is cold and soulless, distancing us from the things that are truly fulfilling. Our screen-based lifestyles present us with a near-impossible balancing challenge: keep up with the pace of the modern world and simultaneously resist the screens' seductive demand for our constant attention. Screens have emerged as wedges threatening to come between us: teenagers barely look at their parents, strangers who might otherwise meet in public spaces become virtually isolated, and even lovers in the bedroom find themselves turning away from each other and toward their screens. Spare a thought for the younger generations who do not remember a world before smartphones.

The fear that technology is an obstacle instead of a catalyst for connection and wellness is well-founded. We know in our own experience the destructive and alienating potential of technology, as well as its benefits. Just think about the accumulating frustration of being trapped on screens during the 2020 coronavirus pandemic. We needed to hug our distant family, not just see them on a phone. We longed to share a raucous meal with friends, not just exchange electronic messages. We wanted to sit in classrooms with our fellow students, not meet in conferencing apps for class sessions. We are grateful for the technology, no question. After all, it helped us sustain connections while we tried to prevent COVID-19 from overwhelming the capacity of our health care systems. And our tech did this in ways that were impossible to imagine in the devastating flu pandemic of 1918. But the rising feeling of frustration with screen-based social life is evidence of how social we are as a species and a welcome reminder of the limitations of technology.

In a poem published in the online magazine *Inside Higher Ed*, David Jaffee writes: "Cell phone ostriches all / The screen enough to enthrall / Be it Reddit or Twitter / No people to consider / A virtual social withdrawal."[2] Indeed, at times "social" media seems to be a pack of wolves in sheep's clothing, promising to bring people together but often delivering the exact opposite.

Could spirit tech be another disguised wolf? In the minds of those who are deeply worried about this, the very suggestion that technology could be a tool for spiritual enhancement seems ludicrously idealistic and misguided. It's one thing for the invasion of wires and beeps and ringtones and screens to conquer our workplaces, our communications, and our homes. But are they now coming for our sacred spaces? Our most personal depths of inner experience? Our relationship with God?!

Siegel claims that we've barely scratched the surface of exploring the potential for modern technology to be a nourishing and even enlightening force in our lives. This possibility is what Siegel and the other innovators we've met in this book believe in and want to explore. Technology itself is neutral, they argue. Technological advancements are never in and of themselves harmful or beneficial—it all depends on how they are designed, harnessed, applied, and negotiated in our lives. So we have to do it right.

Siegel concedes that, even within the transtech space, which strives to produce the healthiest options, current spirit tech offerings barely scratch the surface of how genuinely nourishing technologies might become in our lives. Spirit tech has already facilitated life-giving personal transformations for countless people, but Siegel isn't satisfied with that. He's a serious idealist about how much further we can take these healthy technologies. To him, even the healthiest options available right now are equivalent to things like diet soda or the salad option at a fast-food joint—not unhealthy like the supersize option but also not what you'd call truly nourishing on a deep and sustaining level. He is hopeful that, with the right frame of mind and sound intentions, spirit tech developers will redouble their commitment to human well-being and create stunning new technologies that transform even more lives. There is an amazing way forward here, a potentially species-transforming and even planet-protecting path to spiritual vitality and well-being. Siegel feels it in his bones. And we see his reasoning. With the right intentions, who knows what's ultimately possible with spirit tech?

ARE HUMAN BEINGS TRAPPED BY TECHNOLOGY?

Broadly defined, technology is a fundamental, inescapable part of what it means to be human and it always has been. We've been creating and utilizing technologies to navigate and manipulate our environments for the whole of human history. Beavers build dams, wild gorillas use twigs as tools to draw ants out of a nest, and chimpanzees and macaques use stones as hammers to break open nuts. But the extent of our technological creativity is the trademark of *Homo sapiens*, setting us apart from all other species. From stone tools and spears to wheels and wagons, and from writing and books to telegraphs and automobiles, technology has shaped our lives just as much as we have shaped it. It's how we built large-scale, complex societies and gained control over our natural environment.

Of course, technology doesn't *always* enhance our lives. Each and every technological advancement is inevitably used for both ill and good. The printing press democratized knowledge and information in a way the world had never seen, but it also increased the ability of corrupt leaders to spread propaganda. Television and film introduced a new medium for art, expression, and storytelling, but it also became an overwhelming avenue for forms of pornography that can have unprecedented effects on people's sexual development in ways we still don't fully understand. Social media created new forms of connection and facilitated political revolutions such as the Arab Spring, but it also created exploitable economic niches for conspiracy theories that unfairly undermine trust in government officials and medical experts and threaten free and fair elections in democratic nations.

Sometimes our ambition and excitement lead to technologies that we *think* will enhance our lives but ultimately backfire, inhibiting our natural strengths and disrupting the formation of precious virtues. For example, during the past few centuries, technological innovation has been focused on making our lives more and more *efficient, productive,* and *easy.* But many people sense that the efficiency and productivity afforded by technology has sometimes made their lives *more* hectic and distracted—it has seemingly exacerbated the very problems that it was supposed to fix and reinforced values and forms of success that we are now beginning to question.

The side effects of our technologies' achievements have been painful, too. The Internet was a great idea, with revolutionary social and economic implications. But it has also left us distracted and disconnected, launched the pornography industry into the stratosphere (to the point that it is literally impossible to protect even young children growing up in the normal ways from depictions of explicit and often fetishized sex acts), and supercharged the age-old depraved practice of forcing children into the commercial sex industry, among other things. The more civilization-transforming the tech innovation, the more profound the unanticipated side effects.

Most of the time it looks like we really don't know what we're doing with our technology; we're just exploring a space of exciting possibilities willy-nilly, with no real plans and no sound awareness of possible unintended consequences. The system is too complex for our minds to grasp, so we keep making mistakes, sometimes really big ones, with climate change potentially a mistake large enough to end all other mistakes.

How can we harness the ongoing technological revolution for *good*? Siegel puts it like this: "How can the technology we create be in harmony with life's natural rhythms? How can the technology we create be an expression of love? How can the technology we create be a healing and nourishing form of human expression?"[3] That's surely a matter of values.

Have you ever wondered who decided that the primary goals for technology should be in the service of *more*—more *efficiency*, more *productivity*, and more *ease*? Well, nobody really decided that. Those values just emerged from the same complex system that generated the technologies themselves. But what if we built technology purposefully, aware of our most precious values and striving to realize them? Technology *could* express other values, after all.

Mark is the shoulder and elbow surgeon from Florida who we spoke with in chapter 4 about attending Mikey Siegel's GroupFlow retreat at Esalen. Mark told us he has recently become interested in the possibility of technologies for spiritual enhancement. As he was reflecting on his experience with GroupFlow, he emphasized the profound need for authentic human connection. He has a ringside seat as the deficit of deep human connection plays out in the epidemic of doctor burnout plaguing his profession, which seems to be intensifying. It's an issue of technology and values, Mark thinks. "I believe that *connectivity* is such an important aspect of our lives," he said. "We are often inundated by things that make us diminish the importance of that because somehow we are led to believe that other things [i.e., efficiency and productivity] are more important."[4]

He is convinced that the adoption of electronic medical records has increased burnout by dramatically transforming the doctor-patient relationship. Even though those technologies were intended to enhance accuracy and efficiency, which are worthy values in themselves, electronic medical records often end up establishing a boundary between the patient and the doctor—the computer or tablet mediates the entire conversation, and doctors are forced to spend more time interfacing with the computer than with the patient. "If you have a fifteen-minute visit with a patient," Mark lamented, "five minutes will be in a face-to-face interaction and ten minutes will be having to enter information into the computer."[5] This new mode takes a long-term toll not only on patients, who often feel less seen and less heard, but also on doctors, who also feel less connected and more rushed. It's a clear example of how our values have gotten twisted by the technology. "People who went into the healing arts wanted to heal and care for people—to touch people and look them in the eyes and try to convey that they can feel their suffering," Mark said. "They're empathic and want to help people. . . . That interaction is nourishing—it's unbelievably nourishing. And so, when you're deprived of it, that can be very disruptive."[6]

Yet Mark is convinced that technology cannot and should not be avoided—we simply need to be more mindful about how it is implemented. This is why he's so intrigued by the Consciousness Hacking community. It's what drew him to Esalen for the GroupFlow workshop. He was encouraged by the possibility of a community of people who longed not to return to some sort of idyllic reality before technology (which of course would be impossible, or would require joining a secluded commune) but rather to transform and heal our relationship with both existing and future technologies. Mark saw the solution in his consciousness-hacker friends and is now confident that spiritual technologies are worth the effort. Innovative spirit tech has the potential to contribute to the healing and evolution of human consciousness, to refashion our deployments of technology, and to realize the precious values of compassionate awareness and spiritual connection that technology typically undermines.

A SPIRITUALLY AWAKENED TECHNOLOGICAL FUTURE?

The leading advocates of spirit tech intend not only to heal and counterbalance the negative effects of technology but also to accelerate the awakening of each individual and to launch humanity into the next phase of its evolution. That's the very opposite of using spirit tech merely to induce a spiritual high. It's a vision of a new type of culture, more humane, more connected, more peaceful, and more beautiful.

Seriously? Yes, indeed.

Nichol Bradford, cofounder and executive director of Transformative Technology Lab, believes that technology will play a central role in the advancement and enlightenment of humanity. She describes the field of transformative technology as "a new use case, a design intention, a pivot of current and emerging tech toward our inner growth and development as humans."[7] She and her colleagues believe that we can't *stop* the further development of technology (nor should we want to), but we can dramatically shape it. "It's not that technology is bad," Bradford said, "it's just that it's not good enough *yet*."[8] She insists that we should demand more of tech—make it serve us instead of the other way around.

Bradford tells the story of Garry Kasparov, who is often celebrated as the best chess player of all time. In 1997, however, Kasparov lost a chess match to an IBM supercomputer. Kasparov was stunned and began a deep dive into studying AI. He said, "What I learned from my own experience is that we must face our fears if we want to get the most out of our technology, and we must conquer those fears if we want to get the best out of our humanity."[9] For spirit tech innovators, the "best of our humanity" is no less than spiritual awakening: enlightenment.

Bradford cofounded the Transformative Technology Lab with Dr. Jeffery A. Martin. Kate met Bradford and Martin at the Transformative Technology mansion high in the hills above San Jose when she first met with Jay Sanguinetti. There, they have assembled a team of researchers to live and work together toward the goal of truly transformative spiritual technologies. Bradford is convinced that we now have the tools and knowledge to make awakening a basic human skill—with technology, exponential well-being can be scalable, accessible, and affordable. Bradford and Martin had an air of hope, confidence, and energy. They exuded the social and business savvy that will be required to make their vision a reality. But they were also full of warmth and curiosity. They were equally excited to learn about our work as they were to share their work. They felt like people who walk their talk.

When Kate asked about the origins of their passion for working toward transformative technology, Martin reached toward a box of freshly printed books and handed her a signed "advance proof" copy of *The Finders*, which was scheduled to hit the market in the next few months. He explained that it contains the story of the research project that serves as the foundation for his life's work. Indeed, TTL's goals are largely structured according to research that Martin has done on the psychological profiles of awakened people. He articulates this using psychologist Abraham Maslow's hierarchy of needs: (1) physiological needs such as food, water, warmth, and sleep; (2) safety needs such as security and health; (3) belongingness and love needs such as intimate relationships and friends; (4) esteem needs such as the feeling of accomplishment and prestige; and finally, (5) self-actualization, which includes achieving one's full potential, including creative activities. For Maslow, self-actualization is the apex of human development, reached only when more basic human needs have been met.

At the very end of his life, however, Maslow identified an additional level of development beyond self-actualization: a "highly specific psychological phenomenon"[10] that he called self-transcendence. Martin believes he has discovered what Maslow meant. Over many years of research and traveling around the world, Martin found that the wisest, most actualized, peaceful, content, and awakened people all exhibited a state of consciousness and being that seems to match Maslow's self-transcendence. In his academic work, Martin originally called this experience Ongoing Non-Symbolic Experience or Persistent Non-Symbolic Experience (PNSE). In *The Finders*, which is written for an audience of spiritual seekers, he calls it "Fundamental Wellbeing."[11]

According to Martin's research, the experience or state of being he calls Fundamental Wellbeing is characterized by a stabilized shift away from anxiety, worry, and fear toward a fundamental sense that everything is okay, a pervasive feeling of joy and inner quiet, an ability to focus deeply at will, and an awareness that you don't need to add anything to yourself but that you are free to explore possibilities. *This*, he says, is the goal of spiritual practice—not only decreased loneliness and increased happiness but deep fulfillment, meaning, grace, and wisdom. In a talk at MindValley's A-Fest, an invitation-only event for "changemakers and visionaries," Bradford described self-transcendence, or PNSE, this way: "After you've actualized, after you've transformed yourself in all of these different ways, there's a point that you realize that the 'self' that you've actualized, you don't need it anymore."[12]

Cultivating Fundamental Wellbeing in as many people as possible, all over the world, is the purpose and mission of the Transformative Technology community. At the end of *The Finders*, Martin discusses what he sees as the most promising way to bring large numbers of people to Fundamental Wellbeing: brain stimulation. In other words, instead of being at the mercy of excruciatingly drawn-out traditional methods of meditation, we may be able to reach, deepen, and explore PNSE much more quickly. Along with Jay Sanguinetti and Shinzen Young, Martin believes that transcranial focused ultrasound (tFUS), which uses sound waves to modulate the brain, might have the most potential.

As we learned in chapter 2, Dr. Jay Sanguinetti is one of the foremost experts on tFUS and is devoted to the long-term goal of developing a protocol to augment meditation experiences with this technology. While tFUS is not yet available to the public, it addresses one of the primary barriers that has limited other spiritual technologies: that the areas of the brain related to PNSE are so deep inside the brain that it's difficult to affect them using properly targeted electric or magnetic fields. tFUS can noninvasively reach very specific and very deep brain regions and thrust people into altered states of consciousness and even into experiences that the brain doesn't normally produce on its own. Martin said, "Although right now this technology is being used to explore transitioning and deepening into Fundamental Wellbeing [states] . . . this type of technology will most likely allow us to go beyond it. Possibly far beyond."[13]

The possibility that technology could actually facilitate, with the push of a button, one of the deepest and value-rich aspects of spiritual experience should be taken seriously. Whether we like it or not, that moment is approaching. It should be managed ethically, and we can't forget the expertise-takes-effort criterion for authenticity mentioned in the previous chapter, which implies that having the experience is merely an inspiring starting point for cultivating the associated virtues.

But is there really any reason to restrict enlightenment to those who have the time and resources to spend ten thousand hours meditating? Spirit tech innovators agree that enlightenment, PNSE, nirvana, peace, well-being—whatever the goal for spiritual practice may be—can and should be available to everyone. And it would be fantastic if technology can help some people get there. Remember the Dalai Lama's words that served as a pivot point for Jay Sanguinetti's life: "If it was possible to become free of negative emotions by a riskless implementation of an electrode—without impairing intelligence and the critical mind—I would be the first patient."[14]

The intensity with which Martin describes the possibilities involved with tFUS strikes us as something that should trigger caution and bring us back to a thorough conversation about safety and risks. In addition to the specific *known* risks of the various forms of brain stimulation (discussed in chapter 2), it is prudent to be wary of anything that promises a state of consciousness "far beyond" what human brains can do without technological intervention. Here, it seems, we are playing with fire. And even though fire can illuminate darkness and warm a home, it can also burn a house down without proper care, precaution, and foresight.

So how do we avoid setting our houses on fire? It's certainly Bradford and Martin's goal to answer that question. Bradford warns, "Within your lifetimes, we will have the ability to turn the knobs and levers of our minds directly. And if at that point, we have not developed the spiritual maturity, if we have not actually brought in the end of suffering, then it will be very dangerous for us."[15] If we accept that technology *can* be beneficial to our bodies and minds, even spiritually beneficial, the question is: *How* can we achieve this while keeping at bay the dangerous tendencies of hubris, greed, and hastiness? How can we create and embrace nourishing technologies? And how do we avoid spirit tech options that really are wolves masquerading in sheep's clothing?

In our estimation, innovative research designed to produce technologies in the service of productivity, persuasion, and control has fundamentally different values than research methods aiming to support intimacy, empathy, and enlightenment. A profoundly new mode of innovative research must be adopted.

Siegel gets this: the way we approach research and innovation really matters. He stresses the importance of *motivations* and *intentions* behind the development of any technology, and especially those intended to support our spiritual lives. In his opening talk at the 2019 Awakened Futures Summit, a conference exploring the intersections of psychedelics, technology, and meditation, Siegel emphasized the importance of being conscious of the inherent risks in innovation and of taking seriously the wariness and uneasiness that some people express in reaction to the notion of a shortcut to enlightenment:

> Are we missing something important and fundamental to the path? Are we going to be creating unintended harm in our effort to support humanity in a deeper way? The short answer is yes. This has been true for thousands of years. Every practice, every technique, every path has both unintended consequences . . . [and] known limitations. And also, we will pursue this in ways that are out of alignment with life's natural rhythms, in ways that are forced, in ways that are trying to get us somewhere, that aren't coming from the state of consciousness that we are trying to produce. And that will also produce harm in the world. So these are things to be wary of. But it doesn't mean that this isn't a skill that we can hone and develop. And it doesn't mean that it's actually not a vitally important skill.[16]

To illustrate the seriousness of this concern, consider artificial intelligence. AI has been especially potent in infiltrating the imaginations (and nightmares) of sci-fi storytellers. A malevolent AI with destructive intentions presents a deadly threat in the face of which humans are largely helpless. Such nightmare scenarios are far from ridiculous amusements. "The future of AI represents an unprecedented combination of intelligence and power," Siegel told us. "But AI can only be built in our image. So the big question is, Who is building the AI and why? How developed are they ethically, psychologically, and spiritually?"[17]

The biggest question here is the *intention* behind these (often highly funded) AI design projects. The most dangerous situation is when AI engineers are building it from the basic perspective of *power over*. When AI development teams don't stray from the typical extractive relationship with the earth that we often see with technology, or when engineers and coders employ a "purely logic- or rules-based ethical system devoid of wisdom and love," as Siegel phrases it, we might well begin to see disaster unfurling.[18] Since the creators of the AI are, essentially, the *parents* of the AI—they determine the DNA of the AI—the AI inevitably comes to embody whatever the creators' deepest intentions are. These intentions, explained Siegel, include not only the stated purpose of the AI but also the conscious and unconscious assumptions, beliefs, biases, motives, and fears held by the creators. Even Sophia, the most advanced humanoid robot in the world, knows this. She told Tony Robbins, "It's sort of like how the moon reflects the light of the sun— the moon may not have any light of its own, but we still say that the moon shines. In much the same way, AI reflect the emotions and values of the people who make us."[19] As projects such as Loving AI continue to make headway toward their goal of offering a spiritually meaningful and beneficial AI system, these considerations are all the more urgent.

This connects to one of Siegel's go-to thought experiments. Imagine two companies set out to create the most powerful AI the world has ever seen (think of the television program *Person of Interest*, for example). Both companies are funded with half a billion dollars. Company A is a traditional profit-driven company, where the funders are typical Silicon Valley investors who expect a return on their investment. They've got a whole bunch of folks upstream and downstream who will slit their throats if they don't get a certain return. The organizational system is competitive, creating a tremendous amount of pressure to perform and produce, especially with half a billion dollars on the line. "Maybe the founder of the company is power hungry and money hungry and trying to prove to his dad that he can be someone important in the world," Siegel suggests, "which overshadows a heart-centered commitment to doing good for humanity."[20] Company B, on the other hand, has a different metric of success: their funders would consider the organization a failure if the company did not produce obvious positive social good in the world. The company is driven by a deeply thoughtful intention to elevate and uplift humanity. The organizational structure makes space for clear, open, and honest communication and conflict resolution. It is run like a start-up ashram, Siegel said, "where the coders spend half their day in deep practice meditating and cultivating a deep sense of wisdom and compassion, and the other half of the day writing code and creating the technology."[21]

Then Siegel asked, "So which company would you rather have produce the most powerful AI the world has ever seen?"[22] For most of us, the answer is clear.

ENLIGHTENED METHODS FOR ENLIGHTENED OUTCOMES

One person whom Siegel believes is making this vision for an awakened business and innovation setting a reality is Soryu Forall. Forall is a prolific meditation teacher and the founder and head teacher at the Center for Mindful Learning, a nonprofit that offers secular versions of Zen Buddhist, Ambedkar Buddhist, and Unified Mindfulness teachings. He is also the creator of Modern Mindfulness, an online mindfulness education program geared toward school-age children for the improvement of both student and teacher experiences, and he is the head teacher at the Monastic Academy for the Preservation of Life on Earth (MAPLE).

The Monastic Academy is essentially an ashram for the modern world, where lightning-fast Wi-Fi is second only to daily meditation. Dedicated to training business leaders, the academy combines "the rigor of traditional monastic practice with the dynamism of a start-up."[23] Forall says, "Our vow is to create a world in which the powerful are awake, and the awakened have power."[24] At the Monastic Academy, entrepreneurs, coders, and engineers take on a monastic lifestyle and learn to *integrate* it with their professional life. "By bringing together authenticity and compassion with real world business skills," their website says, "we aim to transform the economy sufficiently to bring about social and environmental peace on Earth."[25] The Monastic Academy believes that by directly providing wisdom and enlightenment training to people who are already leaders in business and innovation, it can produce transformative leaders who will not only excel in their business ventures but do so from an enlightened perspective with more compassion. They can "call forth [one's] highest potential for transformative leadership in the world" and participate in bringing about a more awakened world.[26]

In a way very similar to Siegel's vision of the ideal company structure for AI development, residents at the Monastic Academy meditate three hours and enjoy two vegan meals each day while receiving ample one-on-one instruction and guidance. The rest of their time is spent working on their own projects and goals. And the time devoted to pursuing entrepreneurial and creative projects is valued just as highly as the inner work. The website explains, "The deeper the insight and the more potent the project the more time will be given. Eventually if the project is promising, the Monastic Academy and the Center for Mindful Learning will connect residents with donors and advisers who will empower the project to leave the confines of the center and transform the world."[27] It's a spiritually enlightened incubation process.

Siegel and Forall are convinced that a transformation in the structure and process of innovation is absolutely necessary if we're going to take seriously the notion that technological innovation can contribute to individuals' and the world's spiritual enhancement. Otherwise, technology that appears to be supportive of health may still bear the stamp of a profit-driven system, expressing very different values.

Many spirit tech proponents are convinced that nurturing forms of spirit tech can help regulate and resist forms of addiction and abuse of technology. Technology designed to prey on the weaknesses characteristic of our species will never provide long-term stability and benefits. But technology designed with compassion, wisdom, and healing intentions might just be the spiritual salve that our twenty-first century world is yearning for.

11

Spirit Tech and the Future of Spirituality

The best way to predict the future is to create it.
—*Abraham Lincoln*

We have covered a lot of territory in this book. But it is important to keep in mind that this survey and analysis is incomplete in at least two ways.

First, the catalog doesn't cover everything we already know. For example, there is a veritable host of entheogens that human beings have employed in the long history of our entanglement with the world of flora and fauna. One species of the large mint family, known as *Salvia divinorum*, produces entheogenic effects via kappa opioid and dopamine receptors and has been used continuously by Mazatec shamans and continues to be used in religious groups today.[1] The synthesized substance dipropyltriptamine (DPT) is chemically somewhat similar to DMT and it is the entheogen of choice in the eucharistic celebration of the Manhattan-based Temple of the True Inner Light, an offshoot of the Native American Church that uses peyote in its sacramental rituals.[2] The Church of the Toad of Light, by contrast, founded by Albert Most, is organized around the use of the hallucinogens extracted from the poison glands of *Bufo alvarius*, the Colorado River toad; this is what underlies the infamous stories about fearless adventurers licking the

skin of toads, seeking a psychedelic experience.³ The psychoactive alkaloid ibogaine, derived from the roots of a rain forest shrub native to
West Africa, has potent entheogenic effects and seems promising as a
treatment for a wide variety of addictions, but its biochemical actions
are diverse and poorly understood.⁴ The list goes on and on because
human beings are irrepressibly drawn to floral and faunal opportunities
for psychedelic experiences.

Another domain of spirit tech that deserves more sustained consideration is the health effects of spiritual practices. The numerous volumes of
spirituality and health research literature indicate that medicine should
deliberately include considerations related to spiritual beliefs and practices as factors that impact physical and mental health, often positively
but sometimes negatively.⁵ Just as neuropsychopharmacology promises
customized dispensing of psychotropic substances for targeted spiritual
purposes, so knowledge of the health effects of spiritual practices eventually promises scientifically explicable customized *spiritual advice* for
those with particular health problems.

For example, the relaxation response, a pared-down and thoroughly
secularized version of a known meditation technique, Transcendental
Meditation, is especially good for lowering blood pressure, aiding recovery from heart surgery, and a range of other health challenges relating to stress and healing.⁶ Consistent involvement in a religious group
(or some other group that delivers similar social connectivity and existential meaning) appears to extend significantly the quality and length
of life.⁷ In due course, it is reasonable to expect knowledge about causal
mechanisms capable of explaining the long list of verified correlations
between spiritual practices and physical and mental health, with increasing detail and precision of treatment options.

There are a lot of technology options that are questionable from
ethical and scientific perspectives. We haven't spent precious pages
on describing and critiquing these dubious options, which seem more
about making money than changing lives. Rather, we've focused on
technologies that we think are the most reputable, the best researched

and tested, and the most likely to have a large-scale impact on the high-tech future of spirituality.

Second, the catalog doesn't include things we can't even conceive. Sometimes new technologies emerge that take us all by surprise. Computers revolutionized human life globally. 3D printers are being adapted to build organs out of biocompatible plastics to avoid immune system rejection after transplantation. Who knows what might happen to launch spirit tech in a new direction? A mere few years ago, nobody had even thought of using ultrasound for transcranial brain stimulation instead of electromagnetic fields.

SEVEN CONCLUSIONS

Even with those limitations and unknowns, one thing is abundantly clear: brain-based technologies of spiritual enhancement are coming to your neighborhood, ready or not. We want you to be ready. So we offer seven summary conclusions about the meaning and value of spiritual experience in light of the technology-assisted scenarios we have described in this book.

First, affirming the meaning and value of spiritual experience has often silently depended on ignorance of their neural and psychosocial workings. Many of these affirmative interpretations have relied on supernatural accounts of the origins and mechanisms of spiritual experience. When we discover technologies that allow us to start, stop, and regulate such experiences, we naturally wonder why we still need hypotheses about supernatural causes and mechanisms. To the extent that we assigned meaning and value to spiritual experience based on their putative supernatural origins, we may conclude that they have no value after all. The lesson here is that we should avoid interpretations of the meaning and value of spiritual experience that make us uncomfortable with eventual discoveries about how they actually work. Our beliefs should fit the facts, even if they ultimately stretch beyond the facts.

Second, knowing the brain mechanisms of spiritual experience can support affirmations of the existential authenticity and moral value of such experiences. This is true even when high-tech means are deployed to trigger them. Many thoughtful people interpret their spiritual experiences as colorful and cognitively deceptive side effects of a big-brain cognitive system, yet deem them exquisitely valuable despite this. A good analogy here is with wonderful food and glorious music, which are evolutionary side effects of our neurological makeup rather than experiences for which we are specifically adapted. Just like fine cuisine, whether or not we are adapted for spiritual experience, a strong case can be made for its meaning and value.

Now, let's suppose that we get past the shock of realizing that ignorance has often supported positive assessments of the meaning and value of spiritual experience. Let's further suppose we are fully aware that both positive and negative cases can be made about the meaning and value of such experiences. To what criteria can we appeal when deciding on the meaning and value of spiritual experience? This question leads to several other conclusions.

Third, the more the mechanisms of spiritual experience are understood, the less we should care about spontaneity. It is common for someone to report a mystical experience and to attach enormous significance to the fact that it seems to strike them from nowhere, completely unexpectedly. This linkage between spontaneity and significance masks ignorance of biological and psychosocial causes. If we cannot attach meaning and value to spiritual experience that we ourselves induce in any of the ways discussed in this book, then we certainly should not attempt to attach meaning and value to such experiences based on their apparent spontaneity.

Fourth, the more mechanisms of spiritual experience are understood, the more we should assess their authenticity and meaning based on their effects in our lives. This is a case of "by your fruits shall you know them"—no matter how spiritual experiences come to us, what they produce in our lives and in wider social contexts is what matters most.

Fifth, the brave new world of technologized and regulated spiritual experience that we have sketched should not be a matter solely of alarm and anxiety. Prudence is always in order. But the stories we have related show the ways in which the technology of spiritual experience might be welcome and helpful, even exciting and engaging. There are corresponding risks, obviously, but that is true of every era, commensurate with the types and sophistication of technology in existence at the time.

Sixth, the new horizon of spirit tech can seem either bleak or welcoming for those who prize spiritual experience. The key to the way we respond is largely the extent to which we welcome self-knowledge. Are we willing to draw aside the veil of ignorance covering the neural embodiment and social embedding of spiritual experience? Are we open to understanding ourselves as we truly are: wondrous embodied brains equipped to perceive both reality's sense-accessible features and its intricate and spiritually potent valuational depths? And are we willing to rethink the way we use and produce technology so that it reinforces rather than resists our most precious values? If we are, the potential of spirit tech for positive change in the human condition is virtually unlimited.

Seventh, the deepest concern about what lies ahead of us is not technologies of spiritual enhancement as such but commercial exploitation of spirituality by people who see amazing market opportunities rather than intimately personal and majestic spiritual quests. That exploitation is what we need to be most on guard against, and when the cynical exploiters lay claim to sacred ground, we hope there will be a pitched battle. It'd be sad to see spiritually minded people stand by and allow the living temple of the human spirit to be overrun by heartless greed merchants for whom spirit tech is just one more product line to distract the masses from the harsh reality of corporate greed.

FORGING NEW TRADITIONS

How does all this fit with traditional religious practices? To consider the possible ways that spirit tech could influence current and future religions, we'll paint three fictional but very realistic scenes for you.

Picture this: you are sitting in a traditional-style pew in a Christian church, listening to the pastor deliver a sermon. As the pastor finishes up, she says that before singing the next song, the congregation will take a moment of silence to enter into a state of prayer and prepare their hearts and minds to receive the Holy Spirit. The pastor directs the congregation to pull out the provided headsets. There in front of you, in the pocket on the back of the pew ahead of yours, right beside the hymnal and prayer cards, you find an elegant headband that will deliver a protocol of neurofeedback specially designed to induce a meditative, prayerful state and to decrease the noise of your mind chatter. This has quickly become your favorite part of the service. With your mind quiet and your intention focused on connecting with God, you have come to count on what happens next: the mental and spiritual clarity facilitated by the headband help you experience the presence of the Holy Spirit, and the Eucharist that follows will be more profoundly meaningful. You join the rest of the congregation in putting on the headband, pressing play, and closing your eyes.

Or picture this: down the road from that church, the local Zen Buddhist center has, by popular demand, begun integrating neuro-modulation brain stimulation headsets into their beginner retreats and Dharma talks. The low electrical current of transcranial direct-current stimulation these headsets deliver enhances the meditator's ability to focus, increases sensory clarity, decreases mental chatter, and enhances the ability to ignore physical pain, making that hour and a half on a meditation cushion far more tolerable.[8] The lucky novice meditators in this sangha bypass the frustrations of attempting (and often failing) to reach samadhi, the entry-level state of meditation—finding it quickly with the headset's help. An even luckier contingent fall into a deep meditative state in a matter of minutes—a task that takes most practiced meditators *years* to accomplish. It's not so much training wheels as it is a fantastic leap to a perch high up on the side of the mountain of enlightenment.

Or picture this: sixty-two-year-old Jennifer has been almost entirely homebound for five years due to her worsening symptoms of muscular sclerosis. She's explored several online communities, some secular and some spiritual, but hasn't yet found what she's looking for. After her son brings her a VR headset with the hope that it will bring some variety into her life, she stumbles upon something called VR Church. Jennifer has never considered herself a Christian, but as she listens to the inspirational pastor and begins building relationships with its members—via her very own avatar that allows her to talk, sit with, and even sing and dance with her new friends—she feels a sense of connection, wholeness, and understanding she's been missing. She enthusiastically participates in two weekly services and joins a VR Church Life Group dedicated to studying the Bible. After several months, she decides she is ready to get baptized, become a Christian, and officially join the virtual faith community. For the occasion, the group's VR programmers create a beautiful virtual baptismal font. There, Jennifer, embodied in the virtual space by her avatar, wades into the water alongside the pastor's avatar. He prays and lowers her completely into the water, where she is able to remain submerged much longer than she could in real life. Jennifer takes a moment there to reflect on the wonder of it all—finding a beloved community in the computer; the chance to be liberated from many of her physical limitations; and the new, exciting phase of her life as part of a faith tradition. When the pastor lifts her from the water and declares her transformed, a new person in Christ, both IRL Jennifer *and* her avatar weep with joy and renewed hope.

These vignettes are all ways that traditional religious forms could incorporate spirit tech into their practices. *They are all possible now, today*. Chapter 5 even described a VR scenario much like Jennifer's baptism. But if a neurofeedback headset is used to invite in the Holy Spirit, what does that mean about the agency or spontaneity of the Holy Spirit? If direct-current brain stimulation can launch someone into a deep meditative state, what does that mean for the importance of the intense discipline and commitment to sustained meditative practice that has always been required to reach such levels? Can religious rituals be performed effectively and authentically over the Internet or in VR? What does it mean to share space, time, and energy with a religious community? Essentially, all these questions point to one: Are new spiritual technologies compatible with the religious institutions that have acted as the gatekeepers for enlightenment for the past twenty-five hundred years? Or will those religions dismiss these technologies as inauthentic, forcing the new wave to deem old religions obsolete?

An important clue as to whether we should expect technologies of spiritual enhancement to instigate a spiritual revolution and a paradigm shift in traditional religious institutions and practices is how people judge the authenticity of spirit tech. That takes us back to our discussion of criteria for authenticity in chapter 9. *Experience takes effort. Continuity of novel spiritual insights with what we already know matters. And by your fruits shall you know them.*

Having spent years studying these new spiritual-enhancement technologies, that's our bottom-line advice: Stay open. Be authentic. And stay alert to the downstream consequences of spirit tech. Accepting the inevitability of spirit tech means attempting to grasp not only how it works but also what it means for our self-understanding as a spiritual species. Technology that is designed to prey on our weaknesses will never provide long-term stability and benefits. But technology that builds on our bodily capacities in healthy ways and leads us into the depths of our spiritual potential will be revolutionary.

What's Going to Happen Next?

Spirit tech hasn't (yet) designed a device that can predict the future, but here are our best estimations of what will happen next in the world of spirit tech.

VR spirituality is going to take off quickly. The technodelic side of things already has a large following within the gaming community. Users excitedly anticipate releases of software such as SoundSelf and Microdose VR and gather on forums to discuss prerelease experiences. Given the high demand for programs that produce altered states of consciousness, designers are constantly thinking about innovation, especially toward programming that allows people to enter the technodelic space together. After all, there are lots of people on spiritual quests who feel lonely and want companionship on the journey. Yet, they can't tolerate the superstition and stodginess of church or synagogue or temple or mosque. This is where VR Church comes in. Folks who hate the idea of waiting years before they feel able to have a profoundly intimate spiritual conversation with another person, which is how long it takes most people to break through the social defenses of traditional religions, can instead fire up their avatar, launch into a virtual world, and—with the protection of anonymity—truly become themselves, sharing who they are honestly with other people who are also seeking spiritual meaning in their high-tech lives.

It won't be long until certain psychedelics with entheogenic properties will be approved as medications to treat debilitating psychological conditions, including PTSD and treatment-resistant chronic depression and anxiety. This will unleash new hope for people seeking release from the prison of their own bodies and minds, longing for health and simple happiness. Those treatments aren't like popping a pill, and their spiritual potential is not merely a weird side effect. On the contrary, the treatments work best when the spiritual experience is strongest. Their ability to generate spiritual illumination and reorient people's sense of value and meaning is their big secret. Research shows that's how it works, and the corresponding treatments will be publicly available soon. We can't wait to see the alleviation of human suffering that will follow in the wake of new guidelines for the healing use of these entheogens.

Technologies for neurofeedback-guided meditation, brain stimulation, and high-tech forms of spiritual togetherness will come ahead in small leaps, gradually driving down price tags and driving up accessibility to ever-widening groups of people. The market for home-use headsets is growing and companies such as Muse and Zendo are busy refining their products. Some people will remain uneasy about stimulating their brains, but a new world will arrive as soon as a large-scale religious organization or secular spiritual movement adopts one of these technologies. Meanwhile, eager meditators and early adopter cybernauts will make the most of each new innovation.

Perhaps most importantly, increasingly secular Western culture remains pregnant with spiritual longing and spiritual opportunity. Even as traditional religious ideas lose their grip on Western imaginations, many people continue to find meaning in a spiritual path. Spirit tech will be the natural go-to for millions of people who don't want to believe six impossible supernatural things before breakfast but do want to engage in a meaningful spiritual journey and don't want to walk it alone. The answer to what happens to spirituality in secular cultures isn't that it disappears—it is too deep a longing for that. After all, spirituality is the part of human nature that inspired the most enduring and stable social structures that humanity has ever seen (i.e., religions), so it's not going anywhere. For millennia, humans have been compelled to organize their lives around experiences, beliefs, and behaviors that both provide and reflect a depth of connection to self, others, and the universe. It is this very impulse that inspires some people to look for *more* than what their typical traditional religious settings offer. For others, perhaps traditional religions were never an attractive option. This is where spirit tech will find its largest and most devoted audience.

We're researchers, not boosters. But mapping the modalities of spirit tech these last few years has been a life-changing experience for us. We've been awakened to the depth of possibility opened by advanced brain research. As scientists acquire more and more knowledge about what the brain looks like when mystical experiences happen and the circumstances under which such experiences emerge, we're learning more about the contours of consciousness and our bodies' relationship to deeply altered states. We've been humbled by the beauty of people's religious and spiritual experiences enhanced by spirit tech—both their immediate luminosity and their sustained long-term effects, enhancing growth, wellness, and inspiration. We've realized that the tireless human search for meaning, connection, and well-being motivates great feats of creativity. And we've been amazed all over again at the deep, never-ending wellspring of human ingenuity. Once again, the human species is venturing into a brave new world. This time, the creative spirit of our species is drawing us forward into more profound and transformative connections with the spiritual depths of reality itself. Honestly, we can't wait to see it all unfold.

Acknowledgments

Kate and Wesley are extremely grateful to the numerous innovators, scientists, and spirit tech enthusiasts who shared their expertise and experiences with us. We acknowledge funding support from the Center for Mind and Culture in Boston, Massachusetts (see https://mindandculture.org/), Boston University's Institute for Health System Innovation & Policy (https://www.bu.edu/ihsip/), and the Center of Theological Inquiry in Princeton, New Jersey (https://www.ctinquiry.org/). We are grateful to our stellar agent, Mark Gottlieb of Trident, our peerless editor Catherine Knepper, and Pete Wolverton along with the amazing crew at St. Martin's Press: Laura Clark, Lily Cronig, Jennifer Fernandez, Kathryn Hough, Michelle McMillian, Danielle Prielipp, Martha Schwartz, and Ervin Serrano.

Appendix 1

How Did We Get Here?

The Longer History of Spirit Tech

The high-tech versions of spirituality—with wires, computers, electromagnetism, ultrasound, VR headsets, pharmahuasca, and all the rest—are evolving at what can feel like an overwhelming rate. At times like this, we need to remind ourselves that technology, broadly defined, has *always* played a role in the way we engage with our world, ourselves, and whatever mysteries lie beyond. It's part of what makes our species both charmingly unique and a danger to itself and other beings in our stunning planetary habitat. So, while spirit tech might seem brand-new if you haven't heard about it before, the spectacular offerings from the scattered supermarket of specialized spiritual services are actually just the latest updates in a long history of vigorous endeavors to apply whatever technologies and procedures seem useful for enhancing spiritual life.

From the earliest traces of human history there have been practices that we can interpret as precursors to the spirit tech of today. Within shamanic healing ceremonies, what is a drum if not at least in part a technology for inducing and assisting in the proper management of trance states? Crystals, amulets, and even Catholic Rosary beads can be understood as technologies that aid in the goals of meditation, prayer, spiritual growth, and connecting with ultimate reality. In the past, these technologies were of three overlapping kinds: botanical, psychosocial, and meditative. Here we'll discuss the rich histories of each of these modes of technology.

The reason these three overlapping spheres of prototechnology are so ancient and widespread throughout human cultures is that groups of humans, simply by living on planet Earth in human bodies, will inevitably encounter them. We need to eat and heal, so we must explore the possibilities for food and medicine afforded by our botanical environment. From the earliest moments of human existence, we've been experimenting with the ingestion of all sorts of plants and animals, so every now and then as we explore we are bound to stumble into an entheogenic experience. We have to function in groups, so we spontaneously explore the space of psychosocial possibilities for our species: How do we connect? Which actions and behaviors make us feel safe in groups and bonded together? How can we harness the effervescent energies of an excited group? And, lastly, each of us struggles to understand and control our own thoughts and feelings, and so we naturally explore the inner frontier of our own minds and the space of psychological possibilities through concentration, meditation, and prayer. In all three domains, as we explore and revel in the incredible spiritual vitality accessible within the human experience, we also inquire, detecting patterns, drawing inferences about causation, formulating promising hypotheses to test, and learning from successes and failures.

The three spheres of access to spiritual experience—botanical, psychosocial, and meditative—remain important today and will remain important in the future. The way each is important, however, changes dramatically as novel technologies arrive, making it possible to quantify and enhance these experiences. Measurement methods and techniques, ranging from psychological questionnaires and laboratory experiments to the ability to take pictures of the brain *during* prayer or meditation, allow scientists to uncover the ways that spiritual experiences manifest in the brain and body, how they create such strong meanings and facilitate personal transformation, and how they affect the social groups in which they are often embedded.

At the beginning of the twentieth century, spiritual experiences became the object of systematic scientific study for the first time. As one can imagine, this field of study has not been without controversy. The mere thought of *measuring* something like prayer may feel sacrilegious and cause many religious people to accuse scientists of, at best, missing the point and, at worst, waging a war against religion. Famous Harvard psychologist William James had to confront such criticism when he launched into the study of religious and spiritual experiences at the beginning of the twentieth century. He held his ground and persisted, but he had to be cautious, too. With our rapidly increasing knowledge of the brain in the last few decades—including neurophysiology, neuropsychopharmacology, and the neurology of social behavior—the level of nuance and complexity possible in studying spirituality has taken a giant leap forward. We are nowhere near the end of this period of quickly expanding knowledge about spiritual experience; in fact, we appear to be at the dawn of a research-based transformation of spirit tech. This transformation is placing into our hands refined tools for enhancing and facilitating spiritual experience and spiritual growth that have been utterly unthinkable in past generations.

Botanical Prototechnologies

Let's begin with the botanical sphere of prototechnologies of spirituality. In chapters 6 and 7, we discussed entheogens—including both naturally occurring plant substrates and substances created in chemistry labs. Entheogens were discovered gradually; their history reaches far back into prehistoric times. People and animals got drunk from fermented fruit fallen from trees. Some foods are poisonous. Brackish water makes us ill. When there is any confusion about the effects of foods, we can compare reports and use trial and error to figure it out. Our sense of taste guides us to foods that contain vital glucose and entices us to try new combinations of flavors, creating a world of fine cuisine with sparkling cultural variations.

In this way, long ago in the uncharted past, human beings discovered foods that induced altered states of consciousness replete with spiritual significance. The botanicals producing these effects were recorded in the oral lore of medical and shamanic traditions and passed down the generations. Medical anthropologists and ethnobotanists have identified hundreds of plants believed by ancient cultures to have mind-altering effects.

In our discussion of ayahuasca, peyote, and San Pedro in chapter 7, we learned how group rituals often developed around plants with psychoactive properties, and there are probably several reasons for this. The group setting helps create an authority structure around the substance. This regulates negative side effects and controls potentially disruptive interpretations of the experiences people have when under the influence of altered states of consciousness.

Some of the entheogenic plants mentioned in chapters 6 and 7 have ancient histories as well as contemporary uses. The difference between the past and the future in regard to botanicals is the scientific discovery and extraction of the psychoactive chemicals within each plant that are primarily responsible for the entheogenic effects. This knowledge furnishes a different metric than ancient shamans had for determining precisely *how* to produce an effective and safe dose of sacred botanicals.

We can imagine that ancient shamans and priests would have found such detailed knowledge of the workings of these plants deeply mysterious and extremely useful. They may have kept such powerful wisdom secret from everyone except their initiates, yet we regard such knowledge as a normal part of medicine. Unregulated use of these psychoactive chemicals can be dangerous, which has led many governments to ban most of them. But religious groups have successfully argued that ingesting traditional brews made from the plants themselves should not be illegal. Ironically, as explained in chapter 7, traditional ayahuasca brews may be a seemingly riskier way to ingest DMT and MAOIs, medically speaking, but at least traditional wisdom helps to regulate the process and its aftereffects. Of course, the traditional usage of entheogens almost always included a social and spiritual context, as well as an entheogenic substance. Indeed, shamans have always understood such social settings as extremely important for the safe and effective ingestion of entheogens.

We have something else that ancient shamans would have held sacred, namely, a rich comparative database of psychedelic experiences using a wide variety of entheogens. We know the different qualities of the hallucinatory experiences and states of awareness produced by various psychoactive chemicals, the conditions under which ingesting them more likely produces positive versus negative experiences, which chemicals enhance feelings of community, and many other things. This database is a vital resource for neuropsychopharmacology and helps guide researchers in their quest to understand neurotransmitter functions in the human brain.

The advance of psychedelic research was almost completely arrested after the 1960s and 1970s. It was frozen in many parts of the world as researchers either couldn't get, or hesitated to ask for, permission to mount such studies. In the United States, this freeze was partly due to the public disasters associated with prominent researchers such as Timothy Leary, who conducted experiments at Harvard University, but who, as William Richards explained, eventually "gave up trying to communicate cogently with academia and decided to hang out with movie stars instead."[1] But it also owed something to the so-called war on drugs that used a broad brush to paint restrictions on many different types of substances, impacting even safe entheogens, which are still confusingly listed as Schedule I drugs alongside drugs of abuse that create powerful addictions and destroy lives. In the last two decades the mood has shifted slightly and psychedelic research has picked up some steam once again, not least because of the promising medicinal value of certain drugs (THC for anxiety and pain, cannabinoids for nausea and seizures, ibogaine for addiction, ketamine for treatment-resistant depression, MDMA for PTSD, and so on). The most remarkable account of an extended career of psychedelic research within this renewal period is William A. Richards's *Sacred Knowledge: Psychedelics and Religious Experiences*.[2] In chapter 6 we shared his story of research on psychedelics, which began *before* the war on drugs and which, after a hiatus due to legal constraints, is now back in full swing.

Psychosocial Prototechnologies

Imagine the invigorative energy throbbing through a crowd chanting in celebration or resistance. Or the effervescent bodily excitement in a dance club when a popular song begins playing, especially as the refrain begins or the beat drops. For a long time, human beings have instinctively understood that rhythmic music and movement in tight-knit group contexts can be hypnotic and entrancing. The energetic vitality of such contexts is not only extremely pleasurable, making bodily movements or singing along virtually irresistible, it can also dramatically increase susceptibility to suggestion and induce individuals' surrender to dissociative states. These experiences can liberate us from tired conventions, they can bond us closely to others, they can mitigate the resentment associated with social hierarchies, they can catalyze commitment and courage, they can stimulate bodily changes that alter the conditions for mental and physical health, they can render people psychologically fragile, and they can radically change beliefs and behaviors.[3]

In our time it is not only rock music concert planners, nightclub designers, and political activist groups that know about this. Most rapidly growing religious movements make use of such stimulating social-fervor techniques to facilitate conversion to a favored religious outlook. Christian Pentecostalism, with its bright lights, emotionally charged healing services, and encouragement of speaking in tongues is the most prominent example in terms of size and spread. Even some American evangelical Christians use what we find to be highly intrusive psychosocial techniques such as hell houses—terrifying Halloween haunted house experiences, filled with hellish imagery and actors dressed as demons and souls enduring eternal torture, meant to convince (or coerce) young attendees to *save* themselves from this by declaring Jesus to be their personal Lord and Savior.[4]

Contrary to some skeptics, these techniques are rarely deployed in religious contexts with the specific aim of cynical manipulation. In fact, in most cases, such actions are considered loving or protective—in the case of hell houses, for example, religious leaders are earnestly trying to protect participants from the horrific fate they're portraying. Religious leaders typically believe wholeheartedly in the spiritual significance of such experiences at least as much as participants do. It seems crucial for everyone involved to be able to attribute the spiritual experiences that occur in such settings to the powers of the Holy Spirit, enlightenment, or divinity. Understandably, articulating the ways in which psychosocial conditioning and the power of suggestion operate in such charged social settings might interfere with the understanding that the experiences are the source of divine intervention or inspiration. Some religious leaders therefore deemphasize these conditioning factors and offer theological interpretations and rationalizations for the ways they organize such social gatherings. Other leaders readily accept the necessity of their practical actions and preparations to help orchestrate and facilitate spiritual feelings among their followers.

For example, sociologist Kevin McElmurry studied the music in emotional and charismatic worship services at American megachurches, where thousands of people gather and often experience moments of intense transformation, deliverance from fear, and the palpable presence of God. He explained that, in his research, the pastors or musical directors in charge of designing the service seemed to give little consideration to song lyrics' theological connection to the week's sermon and instead chose the specific elements of the service in order to set an emotional tone in the group. "Over time," McElmurry said, "I came to understand that 'creating a moment' means crafting a flow of film, light, words, and music to create a feeling of connection."[5] This feeling of connection—between the leaders and the followers, among the congregants, and between God and the worshippers—is evoked during the flood of auditory and visual stimulation. And it is exponentially intensified by the fact that there are thousands of people feeling and experiencing the same thing in the room with you. Cameras scan the audience and project images of people caught up in the potency of the moment—raising their hands with closed eyes, crying, singing, swaying, or smiling. At this sight, our empathic mirror neurons begin firing and the collective emotions deepen even further.[6]

And yet, why do we do this—sing repetitive songs while swaying and holding hands? Not to induce semihypnotic suggestibility but to worship God. Why do we dance around flickering firelight? Not to induce semihypnotic suggestibility but to summon the spirits. Why do we spin in special robes with our heads tilted back and slightly to the side, which pools blood in a particular place in the brain, drawing it away from the opposite side and thereby modifying neural function and inducing a trance state? Again, not to induce semihypnotic suggestibility but to express our openness to the infinite mystery of the divine. The music and hand-holding and swaying, the rhythmic dancing and flickering lighting, or the corporate whirling in glorious robes of the Sufis are represented not as causes of spiritual experiences but as *the tools of supernatural powers.*

These theological interpretations are so persuasive and pervasive that people rarely become aware of the physiological aspects of the emotions and thoughts they have in such settings. Not understanding how embodied human brains work in group settings helps to conjure a veil of mystery around the ritual practices and the spiritual experiences that accompany them. And, in turn, the strength and vitality of those experiences validates the overarching theological interpretations.

Countless psychosocial techniques are effective in influencing our perceptions and concepts. British psychologist Kathleen Taylor covered much of the territory in her remarkable 2004 book, *Brainwashing: The Science of Thought Control.*[7] This book cuts through the hype and the skepticism surrounding so-called brainwashing and lays out what we know about suggestibility—that is, our vulnerability to our thoughts being influenced and even controlled by others. It seems clear that careful research can make these techniques more potent, even in settings where people freely engage the process. Research might also lead to refined techniques that could account for individual differences, such as hypnotic susceptibility and personality style.

For example, rhythms and lights and music and togetherness are coarse tools in the way they are usually deployed. Loud noises are painful to some people; rhythmic movement does not work well for people with arthritis; flashing lights make some people nauseous; and some people may be more likely to experience an anxiety attack in a large crowd, rather than feel God's transformative touch. The precise sensory conditions—rhythms, lights, and movements—that work best and which parts of the brain and body are involved are not currently well understood. But the conditions most likely to inspire openness, dissolve inhibitions, and increase susceptibility to suggestion *will* be understood much more clearly in the near future. Before long, specific tests based on a drop of blood, a brain scan, and a survey will disclose individual variations quickly and easily. This would equip experience engineers and spirit tech designers with the ability to customize potent psychosocial and sensory environments to individual backgrounds and brains. These will be social environments for hosting spiritual experiences customized down to the individual level.

Meditation Prototechnologies

Finally, let's ponder meditation. Meditative techniques derive from the fact that certain thoughts, actions, postures, foods, and surroundings combined with concentration or focused attention or relaxation can induce highly desirable altered states of consciousness. We could think of it merely as a bodily trick, like cracking knuckles, only way more interesting; but some of these states yield changes in behavior, mood, or physical and mental health, so they come to be much more important than that. Moreover, some are so illuminating and moving that they are experienced as holding profound spiritual significance. Kundalini meditation harnesses what are conceived of as powerful streams of energy through focused breath work to achieve mental, physical, and spiritual restoration and healing. Transcendental Meditation employs mantras to work toward enlightenment. And zazen is a form of Buddhist meditation that quiets the chatter of the mind to encourage and facilitate the alert state of consciousness called samadhi. Samadhi is characterized by full alertness to the present moment, the study of the self, and an awareness of the unity of the self with all other things. Over time and throughout the world, these and other meditative techniques have been shared, practiced, refined, and encoded in traditions. The world and history of meditation traditions is very large and very complicated.

This is such a large and complicated world, in fact, that an exhaustive classification of meditation techniques and associated effects all in one place does not exist. This is at least partly because the different techniques are often tied up in the specialized language of the traditional wisdom traditions that developed them. Nevertheless, given meditation's seeming importance for mental, physical, and spiritual well-being, meditation researchers during the last half century have made great strides toward understanding the most common types of meditation.[8]

All meditation practitioners and everyone involved in this research agree that meditation can have dramatic effects, at least sometimes, and at least for some people. But many of us walk around unaware that we have within our very selves a bag of mental tricks to achieve extraordinary sensations and insight through meditation, if only we understood how the bag of tricks really works. When we start to explore what we can do with concentration or relaxation, we often get lost in the wilds of our mind and quickly give up on whatever good intentions drew us to try meditation in the first place. Helping with that frustrating situation is the point of brain stimulation (chapter 2) and neurofeedback-guided meditation (chapter 3). But even with neurofeedback and neuromodulation, we make meaningful choices about what kinds of meditation practices to pursue, and to what ends. Thus, the forming-but-not-yet-fully-existent database that classifies meditation practices and effects is a serious quest for understanding the self and one's bag of mental tricks.

American psychologist Jean Kristeller developed one classification method for cataloging not types of meditation but the *effects* that practitioners of varying levels of expertise can expect from mindfulness meditation.[9] This is the sort of meditation that encourages practitioners to observe neutrally the contents of consciousness. She distinguishes six domains of effects: attentional/cognitive, physical, emotional, behavioral, relational (to self/others), and spiritual. And then she distinguishes between beginning, moderate, and advanced meditators. Finally, looking through the research literature on mindfulness meditation, she charts the desired effects that each level of meditator can expect.[10] For instance, in the behavioral domain, beginners in mindfulness meditation can expect improved awareness of patterns of behavior and increased impulse control, whereas more advanced meditation practitioners are able to achieve a reduction of addictive behavior and an increase in compassionate behavior. Since mindfulness meditation is only one of many types of meditation, it will be exciting to see similar catalogs of effects generated for other forms of meditation, slowly developing a more comprehensive survey of meditation practices and their wise imprint on people's lives throughout history.

Advancing neuroscience research is playing an increasingly important role in helping us bridge the cultural chasms that separate the descriptions of meditation practices. How similar and different are, for example, Zen meditation on a paradoxical koan ("What is the sound of one hand clapping?") and mindfulness meditation? What are the differences and similarities between meditation in kundalini practices, meditation in tantric practices, and meditation in qigong practices, all of which seem to produce extraordinary physical and mental states in at least some people who engage in them? Obviously, the cultural backgrounds and social embedding of these types of meditation make a difference in the way they unfold. In the long run, however, neuroimaging may be able to demonstrate that types of meditation cluster together in family groups that are neurologically more similar than different.

A full comparative understanding linking meditation techniques to their effects on states of consciousness is growing quickly within the research community. The key has been to combine traditional knowledge about particular styles of meditation, the types of cognitive and emotional effects they produce, and information about the neurochemistry and neural activation associated with specific meditation practices. We are slowly contributing to the task taken up by eons of humans before us to understand ourselves as fascinating bags of mental tricks.

It is important to remember that the modalities of spirit tech we've described in this book all emerge in the context of a long history of spiritual prototechnologies, experimentation, and exploration. As a species, we have already been dealing with these questions for millennia and we have accumulated many insights. We can expect to learn from that accrued wisdom as we analyze the spiritual technologies of the present and near future. We may have to adapt longstanding wisdom somewhat, and it might even be necessary to challenge the assumptions or comfort zones of people attached to the status quo. But we are not revolutionary or unique in our desire to understand and interpret technologies of spirituality. We're simply carrying forward the baton on the next leg of the journey, doing our part to move the race forward, just as others have done before us for thousands of years.

How Do We Know What We Know?

A History of Quantifying Spiritual Experiences

Measuring Spirituality

These days, it's not always clear what people mean when they use the word *spiritual*. Since it has become somewhat trendy to say that you are "spiritual but not religious," we might ask where, if at all, the concepts of spirituality and religion overlap. What is *real* about spiritual experiences? Can there be a science of spirituality? Natural sciences like biology, chemistry, and physics tend to pay attention only to evidence that they can observe and *measure*. Social and human sciences also value measurement highly. Even when a phenomenon is intangible and open for interpretation (such as IQ or personality styles), much effort is put into the task of developing intelligible measurement techniques. Many of the technologies described in this book depend on measuring spiritual experiences. But is that really possible?

There are obvious advantages to being able to measure what you are studying. For one, measurements allow us to actually test our theories—for example, you couldn't know to what extent your marathon training regimen was working if you had no way of measuring the distance and time of your runs. Measurement also facilitates ingenuity and helps us create novel technologies. However, measuring also carries with it the risk of what philosopher Alfred North Whitehead aptly called the "fallacy of misplaced concreteness," which refers to the mistaken tendency to treat as concretely real only what we can measure.[1] In other words, if you can't measure it, it does not exist (or it did not happen). Falling into this fallacy distorts our understanding of many subjects, because the human ability to understand and evaluate includes subtle features of complexity that are usually not captured by things like numerical measurements. That said, so long as this risk is understood and guarded against, the advantages of measuring are extremely compelling, both for developing theories of the way the world and our bodies work and for interacting effectively with those realities.

Fields of scientific exploration are routinely transformed by the development of new quantitative methods—techniques and technologies that measure the *quantity* of something rather than its *quality*. For example, it wasn't until Galileo Galilei in the sixteenth and early seventeenth centuries insisted on *measuring* the movements of objects running down inclined planes and swinging like pendulums that we were finally able to move past an Aristotelian worldview focused on the enigmatic elements of fire, earth, air, and water. Likewise, it wasn't until Tycho Brahe invented a way to measure the movements of celestial objects (planets and stars) that Johannes Kepler could develop the laws of planetary motion and Isaac Newton could discover the law of gravity.[2] Later, at the beginning of the twentieth century, William James and others sought to introduce measurement into psychology, opening a world of experimentation that transformed our understanding of human nature. Even within the social sciences, sociology and political economy were both transformed by the ability to measure demographic trends, to create quantitative economic indicators, and to analyze all that data using novel statistical methods. The history of science is rife with examples of the transformative power of quantitative methods.

It is reasonable to expect that quantification should also transform our understanding of spiritual experiences. The ability to measure experiences by looking at brains, bodies, and behaviors should facilitate the construction of more refined and testable theories about the origins and perhaps even the significance of spiritual experiences. It also lays down a foundation of knowledge upon which new technologies can be built. This is precisely what has happened, and indeed what is still happening as quantitative techniques become more deeply and broadly relevant to the study of spiritual experiences and to technologies of spiritual enhancement. For example, it was only after curious neuroscientists had ascended mountains in India to study and quantify the monks' brain waves while meditating that scientists were able to transform those EEG profiles into *goal states* for other aspiring meditators who choose to use neurofeedback as part of their journey. These scientific methods have revolutionized our understanding of human consciousness and they are the key to innovating spirit tech—in fact, it is impossible to imagine spirit tech without the rise of quantitative techniques in application to spiritual experiences.

So, here we delve into the brave new world of quantitative approaches to spiritual experience. We'll look at how they work and how they underlie the modalities of spirit tech we've introduced in this book. We will see how, in a very important sense, *quantification of spiritual experiences is the parent of the burgeoning family of contemporary technologies of spiritual enhancement.* We'll look at the two main approaches researchers use to understand spirituality: psychometrics (surveys, questionnaires, and tests) and neuroimaging (brain scans). Both methods reveal the sheer diversity of spiritual experiences and identify similarities even across the chasms of cultural, religious, and demographic differences. Quantitative techniques that measure the phenomenological features of spiritual experience (the ways they subjectively feel to us) are cutting-edge approaches to modeling spirituality in the brain and have enormous potential. Neuroimaging has given us the opportunity to peer into the brain before, during, and after powerful experiences. We'll look at each neuroimaging technique and examples of the major findings for each one.

Finally, we'll consider the complexity of scientific research and the uncertainty that can surround it at times, which is another important consideration in explaining how we know what we think we know about brain-based technologies of spiritual enhancement. We'll do this by means of a case study: the story of a juicy academic controversy. This will serve as a healthy reminder that science is a very human process and consensus is often hard-won.

Psychometric Techniques

The scientific study of spiritual experiences began in earnest with William James (1842–1910) and his student Edwin Starbuck (1866–1947) at Harvard University at the very end of the nineteenth century. These two psychologists and several colleagues such as George Coe (1862–1951) and James Bissett Pratt (1875–1944) found creative ways to study spiritual experiences, thereby transforming our understanding. They primarily used qualitative techniques—techniques that focus on the *quality* of experiences instead of their quantity. They are especially known for collecting narratives of spiritual experiences, classifying them, and interpreting human nature in light of their occurrence and characteristics. Unsurprisingly, this research was quite controversial at the beginning, as mentioned in Appendix 1. Some influential religious people thought that putting sacred experiences under the microscope of scientific investigation inappropriately objectified and violated those holy moments. But the psychologists held the line, and eventually most religious people reframed their understanding of the scientists' intentions. After all, as historian Christopher White explained, from its very inception, the scientific study of religion has emphasized both the search for understanding *and* a practical interest in revitalizing and reshaping the contours of spiritual experience and religious practice. White shows that, far from trying to explain away or violate the sacred, the researchers were inspired by new possibilities for "fashioning better and healthier ways of thinking about and practicing religion."[3]

As vital as these early scientific advances were for understanding spiritual experiences, they were a long way from the quantitative revolution that is now occurring. One of the earliest partially quantitative approaches was that of the English marine biologist Sir Alister Hardy (1896–1985), who turned his attention to spiritual experiences later in life. Hardy collected thousands of narratives, most of which have now been converted from hard copy into more accessible electronic form.[4] With qualitative research methods, he used these narratives to generate an extraordinarily rich classification of spiritual experiences and features of those experiences.[5] Where is the quantitative element here? Hardy collected and classified so many narratives that his dataset permits the first attempts to estimate the *frequency* of occurrence of particular kinds of spiritual experiences. His survey data was not collected in a truly randomized way, of course, because he was limited to the people to whom he had access, so his frequency estimates have to be interpreted relative to the kinds of people who were willing to respond to his request for narratives. But regardless, it was an early move in the direction of quantification and showed people what might be possible. Given the dynamics and sensitivity of the topic, getting reliable frequency information about the occurrence of particular kinds of spiritual experiences in the general population remains a difficult challenge even today, and it is further complicated by the likelihood that frequency data depends on cultural and subcultural settings.

It was this tradition of empirical psychology of religion that furnished the first important breakthroughs in quantifying spiritual experiences. As psychologists gradually learned how to quantify many aspects of human life, the early endeavors of James, Starbuck, Coe, and Pratt inspired a new generation of psychologists to create survey instruments for measuring religion, spirituality, and spiritual experiences. This began in the 1970s, and the effort has waxed and waned in intensity since then.

Up until 1999, prior to the more recent resurgence of survey-based methods for quantifying spiritual experiences, the state-of-the-art encyclopedia of such measures is Peter Hill and Ralph Hood's *Measures of Religiosity*. Six of the 136 surveys described and analyzed in this volume are directly relevant to spiritual experiences.[6]

The earliest questionnaire, first published in 1970, was Hood's Religious Experience Episodes Measure (REEM).[7] This was the first well-known fruit of Hood's longstanding effort to quantify aspects of spiritual experiences. Hood selected fifteen personal narratives of spiritual experiences from William James's classic *Varieties of Religious Experience* (1902) and asked respondents to indicate on a five-point scale the extent to which each of those fifteen first-person accounts resembled a spiritual experience they had actually had. The answer "I have had absolutely no experience like this" is scored with a 1, while "I have had an experience almost identical to this" is scored with a 5. The total score ranges from 15 to 75. Hood employed the REEM in a variety of studies, demonstrating its usefulness as a measure of spiritual experiences.

Given both James's and Hood's immersion in North American Protestantism, and the similar cultural location of the first-person narratives themselves, it is not surprising that the REEM had some significant limitations in application to other cultural and religious settings. John Rosegrant's 1976 revision of the REEM updated the 1900-style wording, eliminated the five most narrowly Christian narratives, and adopted a nine-point scale to supply a midpoint between each response in Hood's original five-point scale.[8] The scale remains culturally bound to some degree, especially due to the narratives themselves, but it has inspired the construction of versions of the scale in other languages and for other cultures.

In 1975, Hood introduced what has since become the most famous of this new generation of scales, the Mysticism Scale, or M scale, as it has come to be called.[9] In psychometrics as in popular culture, you know you've hit the big time when people abbreviate a name to a single letter. The M scale is the tool Pehr Granqvist and his colleagues used to evaluate their participants' experiences with the God helmet (discussed below) and it has also been used in studies of entheogens (as mentioned in chapter 6). The conceptual background for the M scale is based on philosophical discussions of mysticism by another researcher, Walter Stace.[10] Stace also had a large collection of mystical literature and reports, from which he detected nine distinctive experiential features.

Hood then built the M scale to measure them. He found that eight of Stace's nine features lend themselves to quantification and the final version of the scale devotes four items (questions) to each feature, making thirty-two items in total.

It might seem surprising that subtle features of experience can be quantified and analyzed with numbers, but skillful construction of questionnaire items makes it possible. Here is the list of the eight experiential aspects measured by the M scale:

- Ego Quality (high score means loss of self)
- Unifying Quality (high score means perception of oneness)
- Inner Subjective Quality (high score means perception of all objects as alive)
- Temporal-Spatial Quality (high score means space and time are distorted)
- Noetic Quality (high score means the sense of special knowledge or insight)
- Ineffability (high score means that the experience is difficult to express)
- Positive Affect (high score means experience of blissful peace)
- Religious Quality (high score means perceptions of sacredness or wonder)

By analyzing the frequency of and patterns with which these qualities arise, researchers have proposed three dimensions of mysticism: extrovertive mysticism (experience of unity with the external world), introvertive mysticism (experience of unity with nothingness), and religious interpretation (emotionally potent insights interpreted in religious terms).[11] The last dimension is a valuable reminder that these experiences can occur to people both with and without religious interpretation. Religious interpretation may be akin to a culturally variable conceptual mapping overlaid on experiences, but it is very difficult to confirm this using the M scale.

Other psychologists were more inclined to assume that the mystical experiences they were measuring would involve a certain *type* of god. In 1976, Keith Edwards produced the Religious Experience Questionnaire.[12] This scale has a decidedly theistic orientation and is designed to measure the *experience* (as opposed to beliefs or rituals) of an emotionally powerful personal relationship with a caring God. Thus, the questionnaire is only relevant for those who believe in such a God.

Similarly focused on theistic and specifically Christian concerns are Theodore T. Y. Hsieh's Word-Spirit Orientation Scale,[13] Richard Gorsuch and Craig Smith's Nearness to God Scale,[14] and Jared Kass and colleagues' Index of Core Spiritual Experience, known as INSPIRIT for short.[15] INSPIRIT, which has instructions encouraging people to interpret God in their own personally meaningful ways, has proved useful in theistic cultural settings, especially in studies examining connections between spirituality and health, which is the reason it was created in the first place.

There's a clear pattern in these early attempts at quantifying spiritual experiences: they rely heavily on shared cultural contexts and meanings. If you want to focus on a specific religious culture, you are free to use terms from the belief framework of that religious culture, such as *God*, *Christ*, and *Church* for Christians. But if you want to engage a broader range of religious cultures, then you can't use those culturally specific terms and you're forced to employ items that use fewer specialized words to address the subjective features of spiritual experiences. This is the *phenomenological approach* to quantifying spiritual experiences: focus on the subjective experiential phenomena (how an experience *feels* in the body and mind) and not on the surrounding cognitive interpretations and beliefs.

Hood's M scale was the first to make use of the phenomenological approach, which is probably the reason that scale has been used so often since. Both Hood and Stace were extraordinarily careful and interested in finding less culturally bound ways to measure spiritual experiences. The phenomenological approach provides the basis for answering questions about the similarities and differences in spiritual experiences across cultures and religions, and perhaps also among individuals. Of course, there are some researchers who are not especially interested in such questions and prefer to focus on spiritual experiences as they arise and take cognitive shape within one specific religious-cultural tradition. That may be the safer route, because it avoids cross-cultural research altogether, but it also dodges very important questions. The revolutionary route, using the phenomenological approach and working across cultures, has virtually unlimited potential.

To pursue this phenomenological approach, we need a theory that can handle the wide diversity of spiritual experiences. After all, James, Hardy, and others have clearly shown that spiritual experiences are extraordinarily diverse, and mystical experiences are merely a small subset of that wider range of experiences. The most important step in this direction was taken by a psychologist named Ron Pekala in the sustained research effort that yielded the Phenomenology of Consciousness Inventory (PCI) in 1982.[16] Pekala's primary aim was initially to produce a better instrument for measuring hypnotizability. To that end, he generated a theory about the phenomenological aspects of consciousness against the background of theoretical work and existing empirical work on the trait of hypnotizability. His theory presents twelve dimensions of the phenomenology of consciousness, with some of those dimensions being clusters of a few subdimensions.

A few years back, I (Wesley) joined this effort to quantify spiritual and mystical experiences. Working with my colleague, neuroscientist Patrick McNamara, we designed a study to test the applicability of the PCI to the study of spiritual experiences. In 2010, we published the results of a pilot study, which indeed validated the PCI for application to spiritual experiences even though it was originally designed to study hypnotizability.[17] Our study showed that, in some respects, the PCI is even better than human experts at interpreting narratives about the subjective quality of spiritually potent experiences.

Applying the PCI to spiritual experiences requires us to modify the way the survey instrument is used. Pekala was able to focus on immediate states of consciousness when people are sitting quietly with eyes closed (or, in another study, with eyes open). He asked people to fill out the PCI immediately after a few moments of attentive quietness.[18] This led to better predictions of hypnotizability than either the Harvard Group Scale of Hypnotic Susceptibility or the Stanford Hypnotic Susceptibility Scale, which had been most prominent in that field.[19]

In our study, since we couldn't easily (or ethically) produce spiritual experiences on demand, we asked our participants to *recall* a spiritual experience instead. After participants narrated their experience and filled out a survey about it to refresh the memory as much as possible, we asked participants to fill out the PCI with the recalled spiritual experience in mind. So we were capturing the phenomenological features of an experience recalled from the past year rather than one recalled from a few minutes ago, the remnants of which may still be in consciousness. This modification of Pekala's original protocol works well for spiritual experiences because it is the remembered features of spiritual experiences that best express their meaning and significance for the individuals who have them.

After that, I sought to extend the theoretical background informing the PCI to encompass a broad variety of spiritual experiences. My method was to integrate numerous Stace-like conceptual analyses of spiritual experiences, yielding a phenomenological map of as much of the territory as possible. I added new dimensions and subdimensions to the PCI, leaving the original unchanged and thereby available for comparison with results from studies using only the PCI. The result is the Phenomenology of Consciousness Inventory for Religious and Spiritual Experiences, or PCI-RSE, which is still under development.

The table below presents the dimensional structure of the current version of the PCI-RSE along with the meaning of each subdimension. As with the original PCI, items in the PCI-RSE are scored on a seven-point scale stretching from zero to six, with one statement at the left pole of the scale (zero) and another statement at the right pole of the scale (six). Respondents are asked to select a response on the scale based on how close the end-of-pole statements are to describing the qualities of the recalled spiritual experience.

PCI-RSE DIMENSIONS
MEANING OF DIMENSION ON LEFT (0) . . . RIGHT (6) POLES OF SCALE

Altered Experience (AE)   **Average of:**

Body Image (Body)   Bodily feelings: within skin . . . expand into world

Meaning (Mean)   Insight, awe, reverence, meaning, purpose: none . . . strong

Perception (Perc)   World's appearance: no difference . . . strong difference

Time Sense (Time)   Flow of time: no change . . . strong change

Altered Awareness (AA)   **Average of:**

Waking State [Wak]   Waking awareness: normal . . . strikingly different

Dream State [Dream]   Dream-like awareness: low . . . high

Authenticity [Auth]   Sense of certainty, genuine reality: low . . . high

Physical Arousal (AR)   Muscular tightness, tension: low . . . high

Attention (AT)   **Average of:**

Inward Direction [In]   Attention: directed to nowhere in particular . . . to internal experience

Outward Direction [Out]   Attention: directed to nowhere in particular . . . to external world

Direction (Dir)	Attention: directed to external world . . . to internal experience
Concentration (Con)	Attention: distracted, low concentration . . . high focus and concentration
Absorption (Abs)	Attention: low absorption . . . high absorption

Imagery (IM)   **Average of:**

Amount (Am)   Amount of visual imagery: low . . . high

Vividness (Vivid)   Imagery: vague, dim, diffuse, normal . . . vivid like real-world objects

Horizon [H]   **Average of:**

Encountering Otherness [Oth]   Encounter something outside self: low . . . high

Encountering Respon-siveness [Resp]   Encounter responsive and aware agent: low . . . high

Internal Dialogue (Ind)   Silent talking, internal dialogue: none . . . strong

Memory (M)   Memory: blurred, hazy, vacant . . . sharp, distinct, complete

Negative Affect (NA)   **Average of:**

Anger (Anger)   Anger, rage, upset: none . . . strong

Inadequacy [Inad]   Shame, imperfection: none . . . strong

Fear (Fear)   Fear, terror: none . . . strong

Guilt [Guilt]   Guilt, remorse: none . . . strong

Sadness (Sad)   Sadness, unhappiness, dejection: none . . . strong

Positive Affect (PA)   **Average of:**

Joy (Joy)   Ecstasy, extreme happiness, joy: none . . . strong

Love (Love)   Feelings of love, loving-kindness: none . . . strong

Peace [Peace]   Sense of peace, comfort, tranquility: none . . . strong

Sexual Excitement (Sex)   Sexual feelings: none . . . strong

Potency [P]	**Average of:**
Depth [Depth]	Sense of immersion, powerlessness, surrender: low . . . high
Scale [Scale]	Feeling of oceanic vastness: low . . . high
Unity [Unity]	Sense of interconnection, the oneness of all things: low . . . high
Void [Void]	Feeling of emptiness of void: low . . . high
Volitional Control (Vol)	Control over thoughts, attention: strong . . . none

Rationality (R)	**Average of:**
Complexity [Comp]	Awareness of intricacy, complexity: low . . . high
Mystery [Myst]	Awareness of mystery, incomprehensibility: low . . . high
Thinking [Think]	Thinking: clear, distinct, rational . . . unclear, obscure, irrational

Self [S]	**Average of:**
Self-Awareness (SA)	Self-awareness, self-consciousness: low . . . high
Self-Decentering [SD]	Detachment or ambiguity of self: low . . . high

Table 1: The Dimensional Structure of the PCI-RSE. Newly added subdimensions have abbreviations in square brackets [like this] while original PCI subdimensions have abbreviations in rounded brackets (like this).

Notice in the table that there is very little culturally specific material in the subdimensions of the PCI-RSE—you don't need to be a monotheist to relate your experience to the statements. Rather, the focus is on basic cognitive and emotional features of experience, aspects of experience that recur across cultures and that people of diverse kinds can grasp easily. Stated more precisely, the aim of the PCI-RSE was to target and measure phenomenological features of experience that are as basic as possible within human neurology while also being accessible to introspective awareness.

For example, the feature of experience called *closeness to God* is culturally loaded—it is a construct that only makes sense if you believe in God and if that God is an entity to whom a person can feel close. That's why this type of statement is not found in the PCI-RSE. Instead, the table employs less culturally bound phrasing about affective states and sensations. This way, someone who does believe in and feels close to God can easily mark that they experience a high degree of Encountering Otherness and Encountering Responsiveness. But a person for whom a monotheistic god is *not* a part of their experience would also be able to respond to each prompt and feel as though their experience is being adequately represented.

What can researchers do with the PCI-RSE? The answer is: quite a lot, and much that's new. Here are some things it has already helped us learn.

- There is a certain pattern of features that seems to characterize spiritual experiences.
- There are qualitative differences between intense experiences and religious or spiritual experiences, so it doesn't work to call all intense experiences spiritual.
- There are notable differences between typical male and typical female spiritual experiences. The same goes for other demographic variables, personality types, and belief-related categories. For example, there are intelligible, marked differences between the spiritual experiences of people who believe in a personal God, in a supernatural force, in a nonpersonal spirit, and others.
- The PCI-RSE can also be reliably used to explore and validate new ways of categorizing spiritual experiences. For example, Hardy hypothesized a significant difference between predominantly cognitive and predominantly sensory spiritual experiences, and the PCI-RSE was able to provide quantifiable evidence for his theory. In general, the power to validate (or invalidate) theories is important because it helps to refine our ability to study spiritual experiences from a scientific perspective.
- The PCI-RSE can perform just as well as, and often better than, expert researchers in the task of guessing the demographic categories of a person who has written a narrative and filled out the PCI-RSE about a spiritual experience. The PCI-RSE is almost as good as experts on gender; significantly better on religious orthodoxy; and a great deal better on age group, importance of religion, and political ideology. Expert interpreters are good at this kind of guessing, so the PCI-RSE has to be really good to beat them, and it does.
- The PCI-RSE has the potential to be employed across religious cultures. So far, we have only investigated that with religiously

and culturally diverse people taking the survey in English, but translations are planned. The promise here is trying to deepen our understanding of which aspects of spiritual experiences are culturally universal. Based on the cultural diversity of participants in the study validating the PCI-RSE, it looks like the phenomenological features of spiritual experiences are relatively universal, while the cognitive-interpretative elements are relatively particular to individual personality and history, and to religious worldview and cultural setting. A much larger dataset is needed to take that question further, but at least we now have a survey instrument that is relevant to answering the question.

This is enough to show that the phenomenological approach to quantifying spiritual experiences leads to big improvements in understanding spiritual experiences and, more importantly, breaks new ground in the kinds of questions about spiritual experiences that we can ask and answer.

All of this is vital for the future development of spirit tech. Without quantitative techniques, we really wouldn't know what we are doing with technologies of spiritual enhancement. With psychometric instruments of spirituality in place, we can define target states of consciousness in a richly informed way and subsequently evaluate the extent to which we attain those target states. Without the ability to quantify spiritual states of consciousness, spirit tech is flying blind.

Neuroscientific Techniques

Next, we turn to quantitative methods employing neuroimaging, which are especially important for developing brain-based technologies of spiritual enhancement as well as for understanding the way the brain works during spiritual experiences.

Neuroimaging is a suite of technologies used to observe brain structure or function. These technologies are incredibly exciting because being able to visualize and measure brain activity is absolutely new in the history of our species. Partly because it is so exciting, people can get carried away with it, so we want to begin this section with a clearly and strongly stated caveat.

Any serious neuroscientist will tell you that we really don't know much about how the brain does what it does. We have little glimpses, thanks to data from biochemistry; from neuroimaging; and from people suffering from neurological conditions such as traumatic brain injury, stroke, brain tumors, or psychiatric illness. We have some truly promising neural models of how the brain produces consciousness, but how it integrates virtually endless, intricate complexity into unified states of consciousness sufficient to support the potent sense of self-awareness with which we are all familiar remains a profound mystery. We also have only the elementary beginnings of models of spiritual experiences. Therefore, we must approach neuroimaging technologies with caution and humility, as well as appreciation.

Sobering caveat in place, let's allow ourselves to get just a little excited. Brain scans are really cool! Recall the amazing visualizations produced using qEEG brain maps. These techniques are only going to get more useful and more clinically informative with time. In what follows, we'll explain how the current neuroimaging techniques work, how they contribute to technologies of spiritual enhancement, and how they can help us deepen our understanding of human religiosity and spirituality.

Just two hundred years ago, the most influential intellectual of the European Enlightenment, German philosopher Immanuel Kant, rebooted his already successful philosophical career with a trilogy of extraordinary books on human reason.[20] These analyses of human reason display a rare capacity for introspection: without any of the quantitative methods we now have available, Kant reflected on the workings of his own mind as an exemplar of all human minds. Of course, he didn't write the books that way; in the books it reads as though he is objectively analyzing the human mind—everyone's minds!—as if these minds were somehow publicly available for inspection. They're not. Yet generation after generation of philosophers have found Kant's analyses insightful, and the careful way he built up a sophisticated understanding of human reason and its limits has impacted virtually every philosopher since his time.

Here's the kicker: Kant didn't discuss the seat of human reason, the brain. In fact, he seems to have conceived human reason entirely separately from whatever is going on inside our heads. It is tempting to give him a pass on this oversight, given that he wouldn't have had a lot to say about the brain anyway. But the problem runs deeper than this. By treating the human mind as universally accessible through introspection, unrooted in physical brains, Kant neglected the embodied nature of our minds, which underlies cultural and individual differences in human cognition and emotion. He was also able to pretend that we could be *certain* about the roots of our reasoning activities, greatly exaggerating the amount of confidence possible. These two mistakes—neglecting variation and exaggerating confidence—have been the focus of many critics' attention. A more embodied, brain-focused approach would have helped, or at least it couldn't have hurt.

The same goes for spiritual experiences. When we think of human spirituality independently of our bodies, we set ourselves up for disappointment. Reason, emotion, experience, spirituality—these are all bodily functions. And this is precisely why the brain sciences are so important. Kant was sort of correct in assuming that there are approximately species-wide features of human reason. But how far do apparent patterns in human cognition extend given the obvious differences among us in regard to culture, gender, language, stages of development, and personality type? Careful attention to the way brain and behavior fit with one another—staying alert for demographic, life-stage, cultural, and individual differences—can help identify the extent of shared characteristics.

More important, to our way of thinking, is the puzzle of the centered self. We all operate with a conception of self as the subject of our experiences and the source of our decisions and actions. The experience of a unified self, albeit one capable of cognitive errors, is precisely what led Kant to make the mistakes he made. He was seduced by the powerful sense of self he personally possessed, and which he inferred that others possess also, and simply assumed that it was somehow guaranteed to be unified and conceptually coherent. The picture of the brain-self relationship that this suggests is the self as a distinct reality from the body. The brain then, like a radio antenna picking up some invisible signal, permits connection between the body and the self. So we might say that Kant was really analyzing the nonbodily part of human life and could afford to neglect the antenna's brain-based reception and transmission functions.

Importantly, *the brain sciences have not and cannot settle such metaphysical questions decisively.* But neurological disorders of the self, as when people fail to recognize parts of their own bodies (autopagnosia) or support more than one distinct personality (dissociative identity disorder), can impact the decision about whether the brain is the seat of the self or merely an antenna connecting us to a disembodied self. Processes of conversion and personal change have an impact here, too, as they are all about transforming functional conceptions of self. We think these considerations make the antenna theory of brain-self connection less persuasive than the full-embodiment theory of the brain as the seat of the self—*much* less persuasive. There are no knockdown proofs here—constructing such proofs was one of Kant's favorite intellectual pastimes—but thoroughgoing embodiment of the self in the brain makes a lot of sense.

We wish Kant had known about this. It would have been amazing to have seen his splendid mind applied to a more plausible conception of the human person. In any event, if this is the way things are for human beings, then there is a lot at stake for us in studying the structure and function of brains. Our very sense of self is at stake, as well as the way that sense of self is (or is not) free in making decisions, how the self changes through the stages of life, and the very meaning of being a spiritual self.

Neuropsychologists—people who study psychological processes and behaviors by looking directly at brain structure and function—have produced an amazing array of physiological and survey-type tests that can tell us about brain function based solely on behavior. So, if you bang your head hard, a neuropsychologist will run you through a series of tests based on bodily experiences and chat with you to diagnose what's happening. Someone who suffered a stroke might have vision problems and neuropsychological testing can assess the extent and severity of the damage. Or the survivor of a car accident may have severe behavioral problems and the neuropsychologist can often figure out which functions of the brain have been affected. These tests are very good at isolating functional problems. Neuropsychologists devise treatment plans based on such tests that help people heal faster.

Part of the reason this works is because brain functions are sometimes associated with brain areas. Vision is processed in parts of the brain at the back of the head, so impairment in *that function* suggests damage in *that part* of the brain. The connection between function and location in the brain is incredibly useful for trying to understand what's happening inside our heads. It's also one of the reasons most interpreters find the full-embodiment theory of the brain-self relation more convincing than the antenna theory: an antenna wouldn't seem to require that kind of degree of organization.

Of course, just because *some* brain functions are localized does not mean that *all* brain functions are localized. Most brain functions, especially more complex cognitive functions, are widely distributed in the brain and employ networks throughout several areas of the brain. We have to be careful not to associate a complex brain network that supports a function of interest with one of its key localized nodes. It is *always* a mistake to underestimate the complexity of human brains!

However, some brain functions cannot be discerned simply through behavioral tests and experiential reports. For these, we need images of the brain itself. We'll look at two types of neuroimaging techniques: functional and structural. *Functional* neuroimaging techniques that track brain activity over time show which areas of the brain are activated and functioning during certain tasks or states. By contrast, *structural* neuroimaging is more like a photograph: it is most useful for detecting structural abnormalities or damage. We'll begin with structural neuroimaging.

STRUCTURAL NEUROIMAGING

X-rays, CT (computerized tomography) scans, and MRIs (magnetic-resonance images) are types of structural neuroimaging techniques. X-rays produce a basic and coarse picture of the brain from one angle and can reveal basic structural abnormalities to expert radiographers who carry in their own minds a vivid awareness of how normal brains should appear. CT scans involve sending X-rays through a part of the body from many directions and combining the results in order to compute a three-dimensional image of the area in question. X-rays and CT scans work on the brain as they do any other part of the body, but they use high-energy radiation, so their use carries a (very) small risk of damage to DNA.

MRIs present a more refined method for structural neuroimaging. MRI machines are sophisticated computers that use magnetic fields to disturb subatomic particles (protons, which act as minimagnets) in extremely precise locations within the body, and then they measure the emitted electromagnetic radiation specifically from those locations. Therefore, MRIs can give us much more spatially specific information in three dimensions, down to a couple of millimeters of resolution. This specificity is why MRIs are so helpful for guiding the delivery of the transcranial focused ultrasound beams (tFUS) we learned about in chapter 2. The benefit of tFUS over other forms of brain stimulation is its ability to *focus* in and target very small parts of the brain, so a detailed MRI provides a crucial map.

MRI machines can also be tweaked to measure things other than electromagnetic pulses from minimagnet protons. For example, if someone suddenly reports powerful migraines, a neurologist might want to check blood flow in the head to rule out aneurysm or stroke. One way to do this is to inject a radioactive substance into the blood, which will then go wherever blood flows in the head. Sensors pick up radioactive particles as they decay and then locate those signals within the three-dimensional MRI map of the brain.

A brain bleed or a bulging blood vessel will show up as an extra bright patch in a place where blood has no business being.

FUNCTIONAL NEUROIMAGING

Functional neuroimaging techniques are the brain measurement technologies that matter most for understanding spiritual experiences. Already understanding something about structural neuroimaging will help speed our way to grasping how functional neuroimaging works.

The oldest functional imaging technique, which predates even the discovery of X-rays, was actually invented in the late nineteenth century by an extraordinarily clever and careful Italian physiologist called Angelo Mosso. He reasoned that the brain would require more blood when it is busy with some activity in order to meet the metabolic needs of working brain cells. At the time, this hypothesis was a bit of a shot in the dark and it wasn't at all clear that changes in blood flow could be measured. But Mosso devised a sensitive balance to get the job done. A subject would lie down on Mosso's so-called *human circulation balance* and stay very still and relaxed. Mosso found ways to adjust for bodily processes such as breathing that shift a person's center of gravity and disturb the balance in a cyclical way. He was then able to measure increased blood flow to the brain associated with intense thought, or even emotions.[21]

Mosso's discoveries were not very useful clinically because the level of detail required for clinical neurological use is much higher than the balance could provide. But they were quite pointed philosophically in that they located the processing of cognition and emotion in the brain, providing experimental evidence and driving home the embodied character of mental activity in all of its forms. Mosso's discoveries, which were perhaps before their time, were pushed to the side for more than a century until the appropriate technology could catch up with his philosophical insight; but they marked the birth of technologies to measure brain function that would eventually yield a host of functional neuroimaging techniques.

In addition to blood flow, functional neuroimaging also requires attention to electrical activity in the brain. Physiologists had known that animal brains involve electrical activity since 1875, just before Mosso built his balance. In those early days, this research was done on animals such as rabbits, dogs, and monkeys and not on human beings because electrical activity had to be measured using electrodes on the surface of the brain. German physiologist Hans Berger recorded the first human electroencephalogram (EEG) in 1924 using electrodes inserted inside the skull.[22] Eventually electrical signal detection became sensitive enough to measure activity on the surface of the brain from outside the head using electrodes on the scalp, and the technology hasn't looked back since. There were steady improvements in sensitivity to electrical activity, recording methods, and insight into how EEG could be used to assess clinical conditions.

Neurologists have been captivated by two basic facts about the brain revealed by EEGs. The first is that the electrical activity at the surface of the brain is periodic, with waves of signaling sweeping across the outside part of the brain (the top part of the cortex) several times a second. Even today neuroscientists don't have a clear understanding of why the brain works this way. The second basic fact is that cognitive states are correlated with particular frequencies of periodic brain activity. Neuroscientists don't know why that's the case, either. Despite our current ignorance, these two basic facts about the brain make EEGs, which measure brain waves and correlate them with cognitive and emotional states, medically useful, both for research and clinical applications.

EEGs are routinely used to detect things like seizures and rapid eye movement (REM) sleep, making them especially useful for diagnosing and treating potentially debilitating seizure and sleep disorders. But EEGs can also be used to study a variety of other brain activities. In chapter 3, we described how quantitative analysis of EEG data (qEEG) has enabled scientists to produce typical profiles for a range of mental conditions and brain states such as depression and anxiety. The qEEG technique is far more useful for clinical applications than the ordinary EEG, since the quantitative techniques employed to produce qEEGs extract, analyze, and visualize the most important information contained within an EEG. Indeed, qEEG can be used to diagnose disorders such as attention deficit hyperactivity disorder (ADHD).[23] We also have qEEG characterizations of entry-level meditation states. Using such standard characterizations, qEEG can be used to create neurofeedback systems that compare a subject's brain activity with standard norms on the fly. This is, of course, how neurofeedback-guided meditation works. These qEEG-guided neurofeedback systems are possible only because of our ability to *measure*, quantitatively, and compare a host of subjectively quite different mental states.

An alternative technique for functional neuroimaging focuses on the metabolic needs of brain cells rather than electrical activity. The metabolic focus is an extension of Mosso's original insight. The new element is radioactivity. Attach radioactive tracers to a chemical that brain cells need to function, inject those tagged chemicals into the bloodstream, wait a few minutes for the chemicals to be metabolically processed, and the radioactive tracers get fixed in the places where their host molecules were metabolized. After that, the brain lights up like a Christmas tree, displaying where the most functional brain activity was occurring a few minutes prior to the scan. Using clever computer programs, the result is a three-dimensional image, a bit like a CT scan but produced using radioactivity. There are many radioactive tracers in use today, and the development of each of them required a profound understanding of metabolic processes in cells. For example, positron-emission tomography (PET) works by detecting radioactive decay that emits positrons that are then transformed into photons.[24] By contrast, single photon emission computed tomography (SPECT) employs a kind of radioactive decay that emits a photon that can be measured directly. SPECT is cheaper because the radioactive tracers are less expensive to produce. But SPECT scans don't have nearly as good spatial resolution as PET scans. In other words, PET scans produce a much crisper and more detailed image.

Functional magnetic resonance imaging (fMRI) is another functional neuroimaging technique that depends on metabolism. By contrast with SPECT and PET scans, which focus on metabolized chemicals, fMRI focuses on blood flow, and particularly on the metabolic depletion of oxygen in the blood. fMRI extends the basic MRI technology described earlier by means of a neat fact about the oxygen-carrying protein hemoglobin: oxygenated hemoglobin is magnetism-resistant, while deoxygenated hemoglobin is a wonderful minimagnet of just the kind that fMRI machines are good at detecting.

SPECT and PET techniques produce only a snapshot of brain activity due to the need for radioactive tracers, but fMRI, like EEG, produces an ongoing map of brain activity. That makes fMRI both more expensive and a lot more useful. The spatial resolution of a high-quality fMRI is a couple of millimeters (similar to PET) and temporal resolution can go as low as a tenth of a second, meaning that fMRIs take about ten pictures per second. That's nowhere near as good as EEG's millisecond temporal resolution in terms of time and space throughout most of the brain; EEGs are like a live video stream of brain activity, but fMRIs are pretty close. In fact, fMRIs have become so refined that neuroscientist Shinji Nishimoto and his colleagues then at the University of California Berkeley were able to reconstruct the content of videos that a person is watching just from fMRI recordings of their brain activity.[25] Think about that: fMRI measures of activity in the visual cortex actually permitted the coarse but recognizable reconstruction of video content seen and processed by participants in this experiment! Our impression and predictions about the potential for brain-computer interfaces only increase in the wake of such discoveries.

The final functional imaging technique we'll discuss is magnetoencephalography (MEG). An MEG scanner uses incredibly sensitive instruments to measure the tiny magnetic fields created by ionic currents flowing within neurons near the surface of the brain. A bit like EEG, and unlike fMRI and PET, MEG can't penetrate very deeply into the brain. But, thanks to some very clever computing tricks, and the fact that magnetic fields are less distorted than electric fields by skull and scalp, MEG has better spatial resolution than EEG, akin to fMRI and PET. The temporal resolution of MEG is much like EEG (really good). The combination of these qualities makes MEG suited, like qEEG, to sensitive discrimination of mental states and neurological conditions and also to neurofeedback applications. However, MEGs are more expensive than EEGs and qEEGs, by quite a lot. And given the small to nonexistent research budgets for things like the scientific study of spiritual experience, this is an important detail. So it is qEEG that has been the main tool for neurofeedback to date. But that will change as MEG equipment becomes more affordable and as neuroscientists discover the advantages of the greater spatial resolution permitted by MEGs.

Several key technologies of spiritual experience depend on knowledge of brain activity. This is especially true for neurofeedback where on-the-fly analysis of brain states using qEEG facilitates spiritual self-realization and self-cultivation (see chapter 3). It is also true for the emerging technologies of brain-computer interfaces, which, as we showed in chapter 4, promise eventually to transform options for corporate spiritual togetherness. Meanwhile, both psychometric and neuroimaging techniques advance the research task of understanding spirituality in relation to all types of spiritual experience, from postural meditation and prayer to the induction of spiritual states by means of entheogens or even ultrasound brain stimulation.

Recent developments in spirit tech would be impossible without the quantification of spiritual experiences, including both survey instruments and the measurement and visualization of human brains. Quantitative techniques are game changers for researchers like us who strive to understand the nature of human spirituality and for the technology pioneers who are creating revolutionary new technologies of spiritual enhancement.

The Complexity of Research: A Juicy Academic Controversy

The very idea of measurement makes research seem clear-cut, definitive, taking interpretation and disagreement out of the picture. We all need to be reminded at times about how far from the truth such assumptions are. A juicy academic controversy at the very heart of spirit tech research will serve as our reminder. This case study presents us with a mystery that has yet to be unraveled.

While the science of meditation was gaining steam throughout the 1990s, 2000s, and 2010s, inspiring a small contingent of brain stimulation experts to develop and refine methods and technologies for meditation enhancement, another group of researchers was taking the relationship between electromagnetism, spirituality, and the brain in a totally different direction. Let's explore.

ACCIDENTAL ENCOUNTERS WITH GOD

Our story begins in the 1980s, when Canadian neuroscientist Dr. Michael Persinger began making headlines for using magnetic stimulation to produce spiritual experiences. This was hardly his intent, and in fact, his subjects' reports of experiences of a religious nature came as a surprise even to Persinger.[26]

When he'd begun working with electromagnetism, he had no intention of triggering, or even studying for that matter, spiritual or religious experiences. He and his colleague, inventor and technologist Stanley Koren of Laurentian University in Greater Sudbury, Ontario, were originally exploring the possibility of using very weak magnetic fields to study and enhance artistic inspiration, creativity, and self-awareness.

Hypothesizing that the dominant left-side sense of self is linguistic while the subordinate right-side sense of self is social and intuitive, Persinger developed a theory that the production of a person's self-concept depends on both hemispheres of the brain.[27] Both sides are normally fluidly connected to create an integrated sense of self, but occasionally a disruption can cause an altered sense of self or the sense that there are outside influences affecting cognition. When the two sides of the brain fall out of phase with each other, or lose their coherence, they both continue to operate but are no longer integrated in the same way. In these moments of disruption, one possible consequence is that the left-side self continues dominantly in awareness but the right-side self begins to operate independently, creating an intuitive sense of *presence* separate from our normally integrated sense of self.[28]

Relating this theory to his interest in artistic inspiration, Persinger said, "If you look at the history of creativity, you'll realize that the concept of the muse, the concept of inspiration, the concept of gods or entities revealing information, revealing knowledge, is a cross-cultural concept. And so, the question is, where is that coming from? If we work under the assumption that all behavior is dictated by the structure of the brain and activity of the brain, then which patterns, which circuitry (which is a popular term now—the idea of a circuit or a pathway or matrix) is involved with producing that?"[29]

Persinger came up with a way to test his theory. If he could disrupt the function of the area that links the two sides of the brain, then an experimental participant might reliably report an altered sense of self, perhaps even a projection of part of their self outward.[30] Under such conditions, one side of the brain might perceive the other as a separate being, entity, or presence that exists outside the body's space.

The method of testing his theory depended on applying a magnetic field to one side of the head at a time—and the means for doing so was an apparatus originally called the Koren helmet, but that came to be known, for reasons that will soon become evident, as the God helmet. The God helmet was a motorcycle helmet equipped with magnetic coils that deliver pulsing magnetic fields to the brain. Persinger didn't use the strong magnetic fields employed in medical applications of transcranial magnetic stimulation (TMS); he used far weaker magnetic fields with very particular patterns, which he targeted to particular areas of the temporal lobes. He used frequency patterns derived from known biological rhythms found in the amygdala, which is an important brain structure deep within the limbic system that produces fear and anxiety responses. To differentiate this form of stimulation from transcranial direct-current stimulation (tDCS) using electricity or TMS, which uses magnetic pulses that are about a million times stronger, Persinger deployed the term *transcerebral stimulation* (TCS).[31] Lastly, he ran these TCS experiments inside an acoustic chamber that also functioned as a Faraday cage, which completely blocks all other sensory stimulation, to limit both electromagnetic interference and auditory or visual distractions. "Typically when a person is sitting in a closed room," he explained to us, "they're looking around. If it's noisy or even quasi-quiet, still a great deal of neurons are involved in paying attention to the environment."[32]

As the story goes, what happened next took everyone by surprise. Some of Persinger's experimental participants began reporting very strange experiences. Some sensed an invisible presence in the room with them, some felt that the testing room was haunted, some reported feelings of bliss, and some became extremely agitated and panicky. Others were unaffected. Of the roughly two thousand people who have gone through one or another version of the God helmet protocols, Persinger reports that about 80 percent have had experiences of presence, visions, or of something emotionally and spiritually significant, while only about twenty people (1 percent) have experienced the particularly intense presence or vision of something they would call God or Christ. This presence is, of course, experienced as completely outside the self.

These religious attributions surprised Persinger, but soon it began to make sense. When people speak of entering a flow state while creating art and say their ideas "just came to me," or "It was revealed to me," they may be experiencing something neurologically similar to what Persinger has put under the umbrella term "sensed presence." Other people may interpret the same sensed presence as God or an angel. In fact, study participants often described profound and spiritually relevant experiences, interpreted as an out-of-body state or the presence of a deceased relative, a guardian angel, a ghost, a demon, or sometimes even God.

The experience of sensed presence founds a whole class of experiences that Persinger referred to as "visitor experiences." Todd Murphy, an inventor and spirit tech experimenter who has studied and worked extensively with Persinger's inventions, explained them this way: "Visitor experiences are any kind of experience where we're actually being visited by, or communicating with, or even just seeing a nonphysical being."[33] While Persinger interprets these experiences as illusions, Murphy remains decidedly agnostic about their meaning. "When you feel that presence in that moment," Murphy continued, "what you're actually feeling is your subordinate sense of self emerging into the awareness of your dominant sense of self such that, in that moment, you are actually, in a kind of existential sense, two beings at once. The most intense of these [types of experiences] is God." Persinger extends this line of analysis into a neurological explanation of the origins of religion in general, arguing that we need to cultivate great skepticism about the veridicality of experiences of presences in any form—from ghosts to gods, and from alien visitations to out-of-body experiences—because most people's brains can spontaneously produce such experiences just by desynchronizing the electrical activity of the two brain hemispheres.

When he realized the weight of his discovery, Persinger knew he needed to proceed carefully as he communicated his findings to the scientific world. "So the first question is," he said, "how do you measure it?"[34] He explained that his research teams used three methods. First, they collected narrative descriptions of participants' experiences in real time—a study participant will speak into a microphone while wearing the helmet in the chamber and tell the researchers what they are seeing, hearing, and feeling. Second, the researchers designed a questionnaire that asked about most of the types of experiences that people reported in the pilot studies, including on what side of the body they detected the sensed presence and where in the visual field (lower or upper). "This allows us to localize which hemispheres of the brain are involved," he said.[35] In addition, the questionnaire measured participants' hypnosis-induction profile; since suggestibility can play a significant role in these kinds of experiments, Persinger always made sure there were suggestibility controls. Suggestibility is a relatively stable and measurable personality trait—*not* the same as being gullible. It refers to a person's susceptibility to having their states of consciousness, ideas, and behaviors altered or influenced by other people and their surroundings and is positively correlated with creativity and hypnotizability.

Third, for some experiments, instead of describing their experiences, which can be a distracting task, participants simply pressed a button whenever they felt a presence. Of course, this last method requires priming them to expect and look for such an experience.

Over the years, Persinger and his fellow scientists and technologists have identified several different waveform patterns and coil configurations that tend to produce specific biological and psychological responses. For example, they found that stimulating the right hemisphere of the brain with a "frequency-modulated field," which alternates between 3 milliseconds of field stimulation and 3 milliseconds of rest for 30 minutes, is the pattern most likely to produce a sense that an unseen "presence" is to the *left* of the person wearing the helmet. On the other hand, *bilateral* stimulation with the "burst-firing pattern," which simulates the burst firing of the amygdala and alternates between 3 milliseconds of stimulus and 4,000 milliseconds (i.e., 4 seconds) of rest, tended to result in sensed presences that were felt to the right (35 percent), left (45 percent), or behind/above (20 percent) the person wearing the helmet.[36] In a different study, Persinger found that the sensed presence was most frequently reported when the application was over just the right hemisphere or across both hemispheres at the same time. "So [trying] lots of different techniques and experimental designs," he explained, "will allow you to [identify] the mechanisms involved, but just doing one experiment doesn't allow you to do very much."[37]

Persinger and his colleagues described their findings in a series of scientific papers during the 1990s.[38] He had spectacular results to share and his interpretation of their significance for spirituality was similarly colorful. The natural consequence was a lot of media attention, including a couple of documentaries.[39] The modified motorcycle helmet was quickly dubbed the God helmet by sensationalist reporters, and documentaries about the study were always accompanied by creepy music and dark faces lit spookily from the side. Several famous public figures even wanted a turn with the God helmet. British biologist, renowned atheist, and stubborn skeptic Richard Dawkins reported experiencing some slight dizziness and twitching in his legs, but nothing related to presences. Apparently, Dawkins had been drinking wine coolers directly prior to the experiment, which Persinger said likely interfered with the effects. Persinger also conjectured that Dawkins may have an under-active temporal lobe, without evidence as far as we know.

On the other hand, British psychological researcher Susan Blackmore, also a well-known atheist and skeptic, reported a powerful experience, which she insisted could not be explained merely by her expectations.[40] Comparing her God helmet experience with other altered states of consciousness, she said, "I've had some weird experiences. I've had out-of-body experiences, lucid dreams, visions, I've taken loads of different drugs. I've had some interesting experiences. But the *weirdest* I've ever had was induced by Michael Persinger."[41] Since Blackmore had been studying paranormal experiences for a long time, she was quite familiar with the conditions of sensory deprivation and had had many experiences in such conditions. "So [Persinger's lab] is a familiar situation to me," she said. "But what happened [there] was *not* familiar at *all*."[42]

In a BBC documentary, Don Hill describes how the sensed presence felt to him: "It's not so much that I felt like there was somebody or something in the chamber with me, because my common sense told me that this could not be. But I could not get rid of the feeling that there was something there. It was lurking, it was watching me. I felt like I was under surveillance. And it was . . . felt like it was coming from behind . . . you know . . . like what's over there. That's what it felt like. Yet, how could this be?"[43]

In addition, Persinger explained to us cryptically, "We did a lot of work, for instance, for individuals searching for a new path, professionals who didn't want to be embarrassed in any way. Over about thirty to thirty-five years, I would say we've tested probably 150 well-known individuals and many of those, when they left, they thanked us profusely for having had experiences that were significant to them and changed their life forever."[44]

Stanley Koren, who collaborated with Persinger from the beginning, enhanced the device he originally designed in various ways over time, adding coils and changing their geometric organization. In 1999, the duo began experimenting with an octopus device that applies weak magnetic fields through eight coils placed in a circle (every forty-five degrees) around the head. One coil at a time is activated in either a clockwise or counterclockwise direction. This configuration, they boldly claim, enhances psychic abilities, remote-viewing abilities, and telepathy.[45]

Todd Murphy, the self-trained expert, now markets several versions of the original Koren helmet, including two-coil, four-coil, and eight-coil Shakti headsets, and a sixteen-coil around-the-head Shiva Neural Stimulation headset.[46] For years, Murphy has been an enthusiastic advocate for the potential benefits of the God helmet. Whereas Persinger believed that the experiences inspired by the God helmet are merely physical brain events, Murphy wants to help people enhance their spirituality. On questions about the reality of gods or presences, he remains neutral. He explains his motivations and intentions on his YouTube page:

> My main interest is in understanding how the brain contributes to mystic, religious, and spiritual experiences, and the origins and cultural roles of religion. Unlike many of my colleagues, I am not closed to psychic phenomena, tales of miracles, visitations by angels, and other experiences. I accept that these are real experiences, even though I may not be able to accept many of the traditional explanations for them.[47]

Murphy's equipment has gained a small but dedicated following. People use his devices for a variety of applications, from horse whispering to exorcisms. "The technology actually does fairly well, *very* well, I should say, for people who do paranormal investigations," he said. "*Paranormal Lockdown* [a reality television series] is using it at present, and they're having very good results."[48] Sure enough, a post about *Paranormal Lockdown*, season 3, on host Nick Groff's public Facebook page calls his use of the God helmet "truly an uplifting experience." Groff explained, "It really helped me rise above the negativity of this extremely haunted location."[49] Murphy was proud that the helmet helped Groff conquer fear and have a more "spiritual rather than paranormal" experience.[50]

Some applications include more directly enhancing spiritual practices, such as meditation or energy healing. For example, one person who bought Todd's Shiva helmet practices healing by laying on of hands. She uses the Shiva helmet before a healing session in order to help her access and transmit energetic healing forces more fluidly. Many believe the stimulation systems can enhance meditation, prayer, and compassionate spiritual connection to others.

"I myself," Murphy explained, "prefer simple sessions with the Shakti system . . . primarily for mood enhancement because that's where I believe I can do the most good in the world."[51] Although he markets brain stimulation technology to people who are interested in all sorts of paranormal experiences and altered states of consciousness, including enhanced meditative states, healing, and psychic abilities, Todd is not particularly interested in the more dramatic or extreme effects. Being able to predict the future or see things from a distance strike him as something like magic tricks or relatively fruitless displays. By contrast, he is spiritually compelled by the effort to hone his intuition and his ability to relate to others on a deep level. He thinks there are plenty of benefits to be discovered in brain stimulation technology. "What does excite me is being able to talk to people, hear their tone of voice, look at them and know what kind of state they are in in the moment and what kind of person they are overall in their lives," he said. "And that kind of intuition is extremely useful. It allows me to be more sensitive to people, do more good. I can see what good people need and that helps me do more for them."[52] He values configurations aimed at helping the user achieve personal transformation in the form of overcoming fear, sadness, and anger.

When we asked Dr. Persinger whether there were any safety concerns with his technologies, including negative short-term or long-term consequences or side effects, he answered decidedly, "No, of course not."[53] He cited approval for all of his experiments through the research ethics board and said, "The intensity of the [magnetic] fields [is] in the order of microtesla, which is comparable to that associated with a blow dryer."[54] With that, Persinger quickly dismissed the question and moved on to talking about the subtlety of the patterns needed for such weak signals to affect the brain.

Murphy, on the other hand, had a bit more to say about safety, as he sells his devices to the public. After being investigated by the FDA in 2002, he wanted to be sure to give adequate disclaimers. He assured us, though, "I came up clean."[55] There are a few explicit warnings, guidelines, and prohibitions on his website. For example, he says the technology should not be used by anyone who has epilepsy or a psychiatric disorder or who is taking any psychiatric medication. He also advises that the Shakti system should never be used more than once every three days, "no matter what."[56] This, he says, is an extra cautionary measure, just to be safe. Murphy told us of a man who felt that he had had a negative effect from the Shakti system. "But when I looked into the man's individual case," Murphy said, "it turns out that he'd been on forums talking about using twenty-one different mind-altering modalities in a single day." But, in essence, Murphy said, "for a normal brain using it as directed, there is no risk."[57]

Even without any major health or safety concerns, occasional unpleasant or unwanted sensations may arise. For example, some people interpret the sensed presence as a negative or frightening entity. Others may have short-lived side effects that are easily eliminated with small adjustments to the systems. Murphy said that he occasionally receives emails from people with minor negative effects and is happy to help them troubleshoot—almost always successfully. The vast majority of people do not experience anything even remotely uncomfortable.

SEEKING TO REPLICATE

As news of the God helmet and Persinger's spectacular research made its way around the world, scientists were eager to extend Persinger's findings. In the early 2000s, one research group at Uppsala University in Sweden set out to use Persinger's magnetic stimulation helmet to study what exactly the brain is doing when it's creating the experience of a sensed presence. A young postdoc named Pehr Granqvist was invited to join the team since, unlike the rest of the team, he had experience studying religious experiences from a psychological point of view. Since Persinger's experiments had not identified the actual neural correlates of the experiences they evoked, Granqvist and his colleagues had the idea to complete a neuroimaging study using positron-emission tomography (PET). Their aim was to examine the neural consequences of activating the experience of a sensed presence experimentally.[58]

One of Granqvist's colleagues, a genetics expert and a professor of medicine, had another, more ideological interest in Persinger's theories. He was a well-known atheist in Sweden and had written a newspaper article about the implications of Persinger's research. The findings excited him because he argued that if you can produce religious experiences simply by activating magnetic fields over certain temporal lobe structures, then that provided evidence for the claim that God is, after all, a figment of the brain's imagination.

Granqvist's colleagues eagerly flew across the ocean to Canada to meet with Dr. Persinger and his techno-partner, Stanley Koren, to learn exactly how to run experiments with the God helmet and the associated equipment. Persinger and Koren gladly lent the Swedish group their equipment and demonstrated how to use it appropriately. As the team flew back to Sweden with the equipment in hand, they felt excited to be making a contribution that might extend Persinger's line of research.

Granqvist told us, "I'd only vaguely sort of heard about [Persinger's experiments and findings], but I suspected that they just can't be right. So that was my initial hunch—as a scholar of religion who knows the history of religion and how culturally entrenched it is, it just doesn't make intuitive sense to think that it's merely a simple activation of some brain part and then you will have a religious experience."[59] Still, he was intrigued by the possibility that Persinger had found something entirely novel.

Granqvist read many of Persinger's experiments and, he told us, "I noticed immediately that there were methodological problems with them. In some cases it was a lack of methodological details in the empirical papers, which makes it hard to evaluate the quality of the studies. And not surprisingly, they were often published in very low-impact journals—even sometimes those journals you actually have to pay to publish in and for which the review process is more or less a formality." To say the least, Granqvist's suspicions escalated. He went back to his research group—they were busy designing their PET study—and suggested they back up a step. "The quality of this work doesn't hold up for an expensive PET study," he told them. "We must replicate Persinger's experiment first."[60]

His colleagues agreed and they set out to do just that. They performed a double-blind experimental replication study with a much larger sample than Persinger had typically used in individual studies.

To the delight of Granqvist and his team, many of their participants reported extraordinary and profound experiences with the helmet. In fact, one man approached Granqvist after his session and was quite upset. He felt that, given the radically profound experience the helmet had just given him, it was absolutely unethical for the experiment to continue. He felt that such powerful manipulation of individuals' brains was too much for a simple psychology study. However, Granqvist revealed, "that guy was actually in the control condition!"[61] That is, the helmet wasn't even turned on. The man's experience was the result of suggestibility combined with being in a sensory deprivation chamber—no magnetic fields were involved.

And he wasn't the only one. It turns out that the profound experiences participants reported were actually *not* any more common when people were receiving magnetic stimulation than when they weren't. People were just as likely to have strange or meaningful sensations and experiences in the chamber whether or not magnetic fields were involved. But since not even the researchers knew which participants had the helmet switched on or off, this surprising result was not apparent until later.

In a double-blind study, "you really don't know what you have until you start to analyze your data," Granqvist said. In this particular case, given his preliminary observations during the study—that many people had had spiritual-type experiences—Granqvist assumed that the team had successfully and robustly replicated Persinger's findings. He looked forward to reporting results and verifying the equipment so that the team could move on to their real goal: the PET neuroimaging study. However, the data didn't allow it.

"I know statistics quite well and I was really surprised to find that there was nothing," Granqvist told us, "not even a hint of a difference between the experimental and the control group." There were just as many experiences of the sensed presence when the helmet was switched off as when the helmet was activated. It came as a surprise to everyone involved that the replication failed.[62]

Granqvist believes that, while it is "without a doubt" possible to produce certain brain states with magnetic fields, the fields need to be significantly stronger than the ones used in Persinger's experiments, which he thinks are too weak to have any effect at all. Known physics certainly sides with Granqvist on this point. He highlighted three issues and concerns that are important when interpreting these results and that may help explain why his team's results differed so dramatically from Persinger's: double-blinding and priming, individual personality characteristics, and conceptualizations of what counts as religious experience. He concluded that Persinger's study design wasn't rigorous enough to prevent participant expectations from impacting results. Instead, Granqvist explained, what Persinger had actually found was that the suggestibility of his research subjects had been triggered, creating the exciting experiences.

Double-blinding is an important aspect of any scientific study in which either the experimenters' or the participants' expectations could potentially affect the outcome. A blind study is one in which the study participants do not know whether they are in the experimental group or the control group. A *double*-blind study is one in which neither the participants *nor the experimenters* are aware of whether they were assigned to the control group or the experimental group.

Persinger told us that his studies were indeed double-blind and agreed that ensuring as much is integral to the validity of the experiments. "Those are really important kinds of controls when you're dealing with human experiences," he said. "Humans are really suggestible." But he explained that by "double-blind" he means that the participants were unaware of which group they were in and that the experimenters (often advanced undergraduate or graduate students), though turning on and off the magnetic fields, knew neither which of several fields being tested was being activated nor what the hypothesis for each particular study was. But this description is not quite as rigorous as what Granqvist described above, since the experimenters knew which participants were receiving stimulation. Moreover, Granqvist explained, "at least from [Persinger's] descriptions of the studies, there were no details indicating that they could possibly have been done in a double-blind fashion."[63] Granqvist went on: "In one correspondence with me, he said his studies were 'effectively blinded.' So 'in effect' blinded is I think what he meant, even though they weren't double-blinded according to the standard definition." Given how much publicity Persinger's studies have garnered over the years, Granqvist said it would be difficult to recruit, for example, a master's student to be a blind facilitator on the project who didn't already know what the study was about. And yet, Granqvist said, "Now if Persinger is 100 percent honest and truthful about [his methodology], then it does show that its effects may warrant a little less skepticism than I have developed against them. But . . . I find it really hard to believe that he is entirely truthful here."[64]

Granqvist uses his own approach to double-blinding in his replication effort as a contrast. There were at least two researchers involved in each trial—one who interacted with the participant, and one who applied the fields (and did not come into contact with the participant)—and the two researchers did not communicate with each other. Ensuring double-blindness is important not only for running a viable scientific experiment but also for evaluating the technology's potential as spirit tech that can reliably enhance meaningful and authentic spiritual experiences.

If Persinger's studies were not properly double-blinded, Granqvist explained, then it is highly probable that expectations—those of the participants and of the researchers—affected the outcome and made the helmet appear more effective than it really is. After all, "it could potentially suffice if you have people answer questions about spirituality or odd mental states to get their minds more ready to experience those states," he said. "So people who are highly suggestible, who are primed and placed in sensory deprivation, which effectively undermines any possibility to do reality checking since there's no sensory input, well, it really is a no-brainer that they will have strong experiences at least some of the time."[65] Granqvist speculated that there may have been fairly intense priming occurring in Persinger's study—that is, participants picked up on subtle hints about what was going on, perhaps unconsciously. For example, when Granqvist's colleagues went to Persinger's lab to learn about the helmet, they described being led through an underground corridor that had "a little bit of a spooky atmosphere." Moreover, Persinger maintains that the magnetic fields are more evocative at night due to the fluctuations in the earth's geomagnetic fields, but Granqvist wondered if even this late-night timing of the experiments functions as a prime since people may be more suggestible or more easily spooked at night. Or perhaps participants decided to volunteer because they had heard about the study's effects, meaning their expectations were already set to a certain degree.

Another puzzle is Persinger's report that some of his studies produced the sensed presence experience in 80 percent of participants. "When you actually look at [Persinger's] studies," Granqvist said, "it looks more like 50 percent. So I guess he had some sort of anecdotal or nonthematic impression that it's 80 percent. . . . It may also be a very rough estimate that he gives to journalists when he doesn't feel the need to be scientifically exact."[66] Yet, even if we narrow Persinger's estimate to 50 percent, that is still higher than Granqvist's findings, which were that around 30 percent of participants experienced the sensed presence. Again, Granqvist speculated that this difference is probably due to the greater amount of subtle priming associated with the God helmet. In any case, Granqvist insists that, given what psychologists know concerning the powerful influence of priming effects on experimental outcomes, Persinger would have done well to be more disciplined in his methods and more articulate in published descriptions.

Persinger, by contrast, insisted to us that he has had decades of experience studying the sensed-presence phenomenon and has constructed countless creative, innovative, and disciplined experiments in an effort to understand the nuances of the effect. For example, Persinger's experiment of applying the magnetic field to one side of the head or the other, mentioned earlier, was in part an effort to decrease the influence of priming on the participants. The fact that application over the left hemisphere did not differ from the sham condition (i.e., applying no magnetic field) but consistently identified the sensed presence when the field was applied to the right side is evidence that something more than priming effects is involved, he argues.

Luckily, Granqvist and his team had also collected data on the personalities and levels of suggestibility for each of the participants. These personality measures enabled them to explore additional hypotheses about why the replication had failed. And indeed, they found that certain personality and psychological dimensions were robustly linked to the outcomes, independent of whether or not the participant received magnetic field stimulation. In other words, *personality* predicted powerful experiences with the God helmet better than whether or not that God helmet was switched on. "So that meant that we didn't just fail with our replication, but we also had a good story for why Persinger may have obtained his results," Granqvist said.[67] In short, Granqvist's study found that *absorption*, which he says can be interpreted as a "suggestibility proxy," predicted whether a person experienced unusual or spiritual effects with the helmet. It did not matter which experimental condition they were in; what mattered was the psychological profile they brought with them into the lab.

Persinger clearly acknowledged that the placebo effect is very real and definitely a factor in experiments of this kind. To support his point, he referred to Michiel van Elk's study at the University of Amsterdam, which *only* studied the effect of priming and suggestion on people's experiences by using a sham helmet that *never* emitted a magnetic field.[68] Van Elk designed his study with the sham helmet to include several contrasting primes. In addition to the actual helmet and sensory deprivation chamber, he also gave participants some suggestive instructions, hinting at what they might experience during the experiment.

"Well, we did that, too, and they are totally correct," Persinger said. "If you take individuals who are exposed to a sham condition and look at their background, . . . [the] experiences they have [with the helmet] are moderately to mildly correlated to some of their personality characteristics." However, Persinger was emphatic that this finding does not invalidate the *more* pronounced effect of a real Koren helmet: "*But*," he said, "in the case in which you apply the appropriate magnetic field, their background, their history has little to do with the presence being reported."[69] More anecdotally, the famous atheist Susan Blackmore said she would be astounded if it were the case that the intense effects she experienced were the result of suggestibility.

Perhaps the greatest source of misunderstanding and miscommunication is the researchers' use of the words *spiritual* and *religious*: their conceptualizations seem to be at odds. Although, as a research psychologist, Granqvist approached Persinger's work with neither the agenda of a new atheist nor the hope of a religious believer, he did find himself somewhat bothered by Persinger's apparent approach to religion. Granqvist told us Persinger's use of religiously loaded words was overzealous and critiqued Persinger for taking an inappropriate logical leap between a vague sensed presence and a religious, spiritual, or God experience. Given the intense complexity of religion, Granqvist is wary of any universal claims, simple answers, or reductive explanations. To reduce the phenomenon of religious or God experiences to stimulation by a magnetic field blithely ignores all the other neurological, cognitive, emotional, and social elements that go into a religious experience or belief.

"I have seen in Persinger's writings where he is leading the reader on way too much," Granqvist explained. "He implies that the sensed presence experience is . . . the essence or the prototype . . . or clearly foundational for religious experiences. Then when you look at the sensed presence experiences that people actually have in his studies as well as in our study, they very rarely include references to God."[70] In fact, Persinger himself noted that God encounters are reported only 2 percent of the time, even though the popularized name for the apparatus is the God helmet. Yet Persinger's theory hypothesizes a direct connection to religious experiences.

Granqvist sees this as part of a larger problem: "There are many neuroscientists of religion who are very naive about religion itself, but they are very keen on uncovering brain mechanisms that are involved in religious experiences, for example. [They should study] religion in a more rigorous sense and the psychology of religion as well." Although we heartily agree with Granqvist that religiosity and spirituality are obviously more complex than interpretation of experiences allegedly induced by magnetic fields, we suspect Persinger would agree with this, too. He seemed to understand that spiritual and religious experiences are the product of a dynamic, multidimensional system. In our estimation, the disagreement seems to lie elsewhere: the crux of Persinger's argument is that weak magnetic fields with specific rhythms can somehow (we don't know precisely how) manipulate the neurological kernel that undergirds the larger structure of religion in the human brain, whereas Granqvist thinks it is expectations and unconscious priming effects that affect that larger structure.

THE JURY'S STILL OUT

In sum, there seem to have been layers of miscommunication and confusion between the two research groups, so it is somewhat challenging for even a judicious and thoughtful scholar or spiritual seeker to evaluate the likelihood that a Koren helmet, a Shakti headset, or a Shiva headset would be likely to produce, encourage, or enhance meaningful effects for any one person.

Persinger was never persuaded by Granqvist's conclusions. In a 2015 blog post on the popularity of Granqvist's study, he confidently concludes:

It seems that one researcher did not replicate one of our results, and online commentators have taken this to mean that **none** of them have been replicated. This, in turn was distorted to imply that none of them **could** be. I have little doubt that this chain of rumors and distortions has its basis in the way some have been offended by my work on religion. Religious believers don't want to accept that the brain could be instrumental in religious belief, and "new atheists" are offended by the idea that religion and religious experiences reflect processes intrinsic to the human brain, and can thus be considered as intrinsic to our species. Anyone who has taken the time to precisely re-create the experimental or analytical conditions has replicated and extended our results.[71]

Until the day he died in 2018, Persinger vehemently defended his study design against any accusations of faulty methodology and data reporting. This was a juicy academic controversy with accusations flying in both directions, resulting in a mix of confusion and skepticism within the scientific community. Whether or not Persinger's last quoted sentence about empirical replications is true, it is abundantly clear that people have experienced spiritually meaningful effects and life-altering experiences while exposing themselves to both weak magnetic fields, such as those emitted from the Koren, Shiva, and Shakti systems (the physics and biochemistry of which we don't understand), and strong magnetic stimulation, such as that emitted from TMS treatment equipment (the physics and biochemistry of which we understand fairly well). But as both research and personal use continues, perhaps we will see a consensus emerge concerning whether the weak-field experiences are due to suggestibility, to technological manipulation, or to a combination of the two.

Suggestions for Further Reading

If you want to read more about some of the themes treated in the chapters of this book, this is the place to look. You can always read the notes, of course, but here we offer a condensation of the complex literature that can speed you on your way to deeper understanding.

General Books Related to the Themes in *Spirit Tech*

- *The Finders*, by Jeffery A. Martin (Jackson, WY: Integration Press, 2019)—the result of many years of research and exploration of what it means to find spiritual fulfillment
- *The Future Is Faster Than You Think: How Converging Technologies Are Transforming Business, Industries, and Our Lives*, by Peter H. Diamandis and Steven Kotler (New York: Simon & Schuster, 2020)—an investigation of how exponentially accelerating technologies are launching our species into uncharted territory and transforming the way we live and conceptualize ourselves
- *Enlightenment Now: The Case for Reason, Science, Humanism, and Progress*, by Steven Pinker (New York: Penguin, 2018)—a declaration and celebration of the ways in which science, technology, and humanism can enhance human well-being and flourishing

- *Stealing Fire: How Silicon Valley, the Navy SEALs, and Maverick Scientists Are Revolutionizing the Way We Live and Work*, by Steven Kotler and Jamie Wheal (New York: Dey Street, 2017)—a thorough exploration of the revolutionary ways peak performance innovators and thought leaders are harnessing altered states of consciousness to create richer and more satisfying lives
- *10% Happier: How I Tamed the Voice in My Head, Reduced Stress Without Losing My Edge, and Found Self-Help That Actually Works—A True Story*, by Dan Harris (New York: Dey Street, 2014, 2019)—*Nightline* anchor Dan Harris gives a deeply personal account of his dynamic journey through all sorts of self-help and spiritual modalities toward spiritual and personal wholeness
- *The Rise of Superman: Decoding the Science of Ultimate Human Performance*, by Steven Kotler (Boston: New Harvest, 2014)—a narrative-driven exploration of the science of optimal states of consciousness and the possibilities they hold for the human species
- *Fingerprints of God: What Science Is Learning about the Brain and Spiritual Experience*, by Barbara Bradley Hagerty (New York: Riverhead Books, 2009)—an investigation of the intersection of science and faith by NPR religion correspondent Barbara Bradley Hagerty

Websites and Online Communities

- Transformative Technology: www.transformativetech.org
- Transformative Technology Conference: www.ttconf.org
- Consciousness Hacking: www.cohack.org
- Awakened Futures: www.awakenedfutures.org

Meditation

- *Altered Traits: Science Reveals How Meditation Changes Your Mind, Brain, and Body*, by Daniel Goleman and Richard J. Davidson (New York: Avery, 2017)
- *The Relaxation Response*, by Herbert Benson (New York: William Morrow, 1975)
- *Zen-Brain Reflections*, by James H. Austin (Cambridge, MA: MIT Press, 2006)

- *Mindfulness for Beginners: Reclaiming the Present Moment—and Your Life*, by Jon Kabat-Zinn (Boulder, CO: Sounds True, 2012)
- *The Bodhisattva's Brain: Buddhism Naturalized*, by Owen Flanagan (Cambridge, MA: MIT Press, 2011)
- UCLA Mindful Awareness Research Center: http://marc.ucla.edu
- American Mindfulness Research Association: https://goamra.org
- University of Massachusetts Memorial Health Care Center for Mindfulness: http://www.umassmed.edu/cfm/

Neurofeedback and qEEG

- *The Awakened Mind: Biofeedback and the Development of Higher States of Awareness*, by C. Maxwell Cade and Nona Coxhead (Shaftesbury, UK: Element Books, 1979)
- *The High-Performance Mind: Mastering Brainwaves for Insight, Healing, and Creativity*, by Anna Wise (New York: Jeremy P. Tarcher, 1997)
- *MindFitness Training: Neurofeedback and the Process*, by Adam Crane and Richard Soutar (New York: iUniverse, 2000)
- *Meditation Interventions to Rewire the Brain: Integrating Neuroscience Strategies for ADHD, Anxiety, Depression, & PTSD*, by Jeff Tarrant (Eau Claire, WI: PESI Publishing & Media, 2017)
- *The Neurofeedback Solution: How to Treat Autism, ADHD, Anxiety, Brain Injury, Stroke, PTSD, and More*, edited by Stephen Larsen (Rochester, VT: Healing Arts Press, 2012)—a good general introduction to the scientific and clinical aspects of neurofeedback
- *Doing Neurofeedback: An Introduction*, by Richard Soutar (San Rafael, CA: ISNR Research Foundation, 2011)—an overview of the field and a how-to manual directed at clinicians incorporating neurofeedback into their practice
- *A Symphony in the Brain: The Evolution of the New Brain Wave Biofeedback*, by Jim Robbins (New York: Grove Press, 2008)—an engaging and accessible history and exploration of the various dimensions of the field of neurofeedback, including using neurofeedback for encouraging deep states and transcendent experiences
- *Letting Go: How to Heal Your Hurt, Love Your Body and Transform Your Life*, by Emma Woolf (Chichester, UK: Summersdale,

2015)—a memoir inspired by Woolf's experience at a Brainworks Transformational Retreat

- *Introduction to Quantitative EEG and Neurofeedback: Advanced Theory and Practices*, 2nd ed., edited by Thomas Budzynski, Helen Kogan Budzynski, James R. Evans, and Andrew Abarbanel (Burlington, MA: Academic Press, 2009)
- *EEG Methods for the Psychological Sciences*, by Cheryl L. Dickter and Paul D. Kieffaber (Thousand Oaks, CA: Sage, 2014)
- Judson Brewer, "Pairing Ancient Wisdom with Modern Technology to Optimize Habit Change: Mindfulness and Neurofeedback," Boston: MIT Media Lab, Advancing Wellbeing Seminar Series, February 2, 2014, https://www.youtube.com/watch?v=wil45EaQvUE&feature=emb_title
- Richard Davidson, "Transform Your Mind, Change Your Brain: Neuroplasticity and Personal Transformation," lecture on contemplative neuroscience and meditation, Google Tech Talk, September 23, 2009, https://www.youtube.com/watch?v=7tRdDqXgsJ0

Clinical Neurofeedback Websites

- New Mind Neurofeedback Center: http://newmindcenter.com
- New Mind Academy: www.newmindacademy.com
- NeuroMeditation Institute: www.neuromeditationinstitute.com
- Brainworks Neurotherapy: www.brainworksneurotherapy.com
- Brainworks Transformational Retreats: www.transformational-retreats.com/
- Anna Wise Center: http://annawise.com/
- Tech-Gnostic: Where Spirit Meets Hardware: http://tech-gnostic.org

Brain Stimulation

- *The Science of Enlightenment: How Meditation Works*, by Shinzen Young (Boulder, CO: Sounds True, 2018)
- Shinzen Young's website (https://www.shinzen.org) is also a treasure trove of videos, recordings, and teachings
- SEMA Lab: https://semalab.arizona.edu. Keep up-to-date on Jay Sanguinetti and Shinzen's research at the Sonication Enhanced

Mindfulness Awareness Lab at the University of Arizona's Center for Consciousness Studies
- Jay Sanguinetti, "A Technoboost for Meditation," TEDxBigSky Talk, https://www.youtube.com/watch?v=rGEjmwaIPZk
- *Switched On: A Memoir of Brain Change and Emotional Awakening*, by John Elder Robison (New York: Spiegel & Grau, 2016)— the story of one man's emotional and spiritual awakening triggered by transcranial magnetic stimulation

Togetherness

- "Consciousness Hackers x Esalen," Lina Lyte Plioplyte at Lyte Films, https://vimeo.com/459378220
- *Together: The Healing Power of Human Connection in a Sometimes Lonely World*, by Vivek H. Murthy (New York: Harper Wave, 2020)
- *Loneliness: Human Nature and the Need for Social Connection*, by John T. Cacioppo and William Patrick (New York: W. W. Norton, 2008)
- *@ Worship: Liturgical Practices in Digital Worlds*, by Teresa Berger (Abingdon, UK: Routledge, 2018)
- *Any Body There? Worship and Being Human in a Digital Age*, by Craig Mueller (Eugene, OR: Wipf and Stock, 2017)
- *Bowling Alone: The Collapse and Revival of American Community*, by Robert D. Putnam, rev. ed. (New York: Simon & Schuster Paperbacks, 2020)
- *Reclaiming Conversation: The Power of Talk in a Digital Age*, by Sherry Turkle (New York: Penguin Press, 2015)
- *Alone Together: Why We Expect More from Technology and Less from Each Other*, by Sherry Turkle (New York: Basic Books, 2011)
- *Analog Church: Why We Need Real People, Places, and Things in the Digital Age*, by Jay Y. Kim (Downers Grove, IL: InterVarsity Press, 2020)
- *Brainwashing: The Science of Thought Control*, 2nd ed., by Kathleen Taylor (Oxford: Oxford University Press, 2017)

Virtual Reality

- *The History of the Future: Oculus, Facebook, and the Revolution That Swept Virtual Reality*, by Blake J. Harris (New York: Dey Street, 2019)

- "The Technodelic Manifesto," by Robin Arnott, SoundSelf: https://www.soundself.com/technodelic-manifesto
- SoundSelf: https://www.soundself.com
- Microdose VR: https://microdosevr.com
- VR Church: https://www.vrchurch.org
- "This Pastor Is Putting His Faith in a Virtual Reality Church" by Kristen French, *Wired*, https://www.wired.com/story/virtual -reality-church/

Entheogens

- *How to Change Your Mind: What the New Science of Psychedelics Teaches Us About Consciousness, Dying, Addiction, Depression, and Transcendence*, by Michael Pollan (New York: Penguin Press, 2018)—a fascinating combination of investigative journalism, personal reflection, and compassionate teaching in Pollan's exploration of psychedelic drugs
- *Sacred Knowledge: Psychedelics and Religious Experiences*, by William A. Richards (New York: Columbia University Press, 2016)
- *Acid Test: LSD, Ecstasy, and the Power to Heal*, by Tom Shroder (New York: Blue Rider Press, 2014)
- *Spiritual Growth with Entheogens: Psychoactive Sacramentals and Human Transformation*, by Thomas B. Roberts (Rochester, VT: Park Street Press, 2012)
- *The Psychedelic Future of the Mind: How Entheogens Are Enhancing Cognition, Boosting Intelligence, and Raising Values*, by Thomas B. Roberts (Rochester, VT: Park Street Press, 2013)
- *Plants of the Gods: Their Sacred, Healing, and Hallucinogenic Powers*, 2nd ed., by Richard Evans Schultes, Albert Hofmann, and Christian Rätsch (Rochester, VT: Healing Arts Press, 2001)
- *Ecstasy: The Complete Guide: A Comprehensive Look at the Risks and Benefits of MDMA*, edited by Julie Holland (Rochester, VT: Park Street Press, 2001)—an excellent volume with valuable information about the history, chemistry, risks, and clinical benefits of MDMA
- *The Way of the Psychonaut: Encyclopedia for Inner Journeys*, vols. 1 and 2, by Stanislav Grof (Santa Cruz, CA: Multidisciplinary Association for Psychedelic Studies, 2019)

- *Manifesting Minds: A Review of Psychedelics in Science, Medicine, Sex, and Spirituality*, by Rick Doblin and Brad Burge (Berkeley, CA: Evolver Editions, 2014)
- *Frontiers of Psychedelic Consciousness: Conversations with Albert Hofmann, Stanislav Grof, Rich Strassman, Jeremy Narby, Simon Posford and Others*, by David Jay Brown (Rochester, VT: Park Stress Press, 2015)
- *Psychedelic Healing: The Promise of Entheogens for Psychotherapy and Spiritual Development*, by Neal M. Goldsmith (Rochester, VT: Healing Arts Press, 2011)
- *Psychoactive Sacramentals: Essays on Entheogens and Religion*, edited by Thomas B. Roberts (San Francisco: Council on Spiritual Practices, 2001)
- *Seeking the Sacred with Psychoactive Substances: Chemical Paths to Spirituality and to God*, vols. 1 and 2, edited by J. Harold Ellens (Santa Barbara, CA: Praeger, 2014)
- *The Psychedelic Policy Quagmire: Health, Law, Freedom, and Society*, by J. Harold Ellens and Thomas B. Roberts (Santa Barbara, CA: Praeger, 2015)
- *Entheogens and the Future of Religion*, 2nd ed., edited by Robert Forte (Rochester, VT: Park Street Press, 2012)
- *High Priest*, by Timothy Leary (1968; reprint, Oakland, CA: Ronin Publishing, 1995)
- Walter N. Pahnke, "Drugs and Mysticism: An Analysis of the Relationship between Psychedelic Drugs and the Mystical Consciousness," PhD dissertation, Harvard University, 1963, http:// www.maps.org/images/pdf/books/pahnke/walter_pahnke_drugs _and_mysticism.pdf—Walter Pahnke conducted his dissertation research on the ability of psilocybin to engender genuine religious experience in what became known as the Marsh Chapel Experiment or the Good Friday Experiment
- "Here and Now: Discovering the Sacred with Entheogens," by William A. Richards, *Zygon* 49, no. 3 (2014): 652–65, https://doi .org/10.1111/zygo.12108
- *DMT: The Spirit Molecule: A Doctor's Revolutionary Research into the Biology of Near-Death and Mystical Experiences*, by Rick Strassman (Rochester, VT: Park Street Press, 2001); see also Strassman's documentary, *DMT: The Spirit Molecule*, written and directed by

Mitch Schultz, Spectral Alchemy Productions, 2010; available on
Amazon and Netflix

Health Effects of Entheogens

- Multidisciplinary Association for Psychedelic Studies (MAPS):
  http://www.maps.org
- Heffter Research Institute: http://www.heffter.org/; see, especially,
  their "Our Research" page, with links to more than ninety scien-
  tific articles on the health effects of psilocybin and other psyche-
  delics: https://www.heffter.org/future-research/
- Council on Spiritual Practices: http://csp.org/
- Albert Hofmann Foundation: http://www.hofmann.org
- Drug Policy Alliance: http://www.drugpolicy.org
- Beckley Foundation: http://beckleyfoundation.org
- Erowid Center: https://www.erowid.org

Spirit Plants

- *Peyote Religion: A History*, by Omer C. Stewart (Norman: Univer-
  sity of Oklahoma Press, 1987)
- *One Nation Under God: The Triumph of the Native American
  Church*, edited by Huston Smith and Reuben Snake (Santa Fe,
  NM: Clear Light, 1996)
- *When Plants Dream: Ayahuasca, Amazonian Shamanism and the
  Global Psychedelic Renaissance*, by Daniel Pinchbeck and Sophia
  Rokhlin (London: Watkins, 2019)
- *Plants of the Gods: Their Sacred, Healing, and Hallucinogenic
  Powers*, 2nd ed., by Richard Evans Schultes, Albert Hofmann, and
  Christian Rätsch (Rochester, VT: Healing Arts Press, 2001)
- *Ayahuasca Shamanism in the Amazon and Beyond*, edited by Beat-
  riz Caiuby Labate and Clancy Cavnar (New York: Oxford Univer-
  sity Press, 2014)
- *Peyote: History, Tradition, Politics, and Conservation*, edited by
  Beatriz Caiuby Labate and Clancy Cavnar (Santa Barbara, CA:
  Praeger, 2016)
- *The Internationalization of Ayahuasca*, edited by Beatriz Caiuby
  Labate and Henrik Jungaberle (Zürich: LIT Verlag, 2011)

- An informative website for a Santo Daime church in Brazil is http://www.santodaime.org/site/. This website is in Portuguese, but a Google translation is available. Along with many photos and several recordings of traditional and contemporary hymns, it provides an extensive historical overview of both the wider Santo Daime tradition and its specific organization.
- Centro Espírita Beneficiente União do Vegetal in Brazil: www.udv .org.br

Spiritual Direction

- For more information on the current state of the art of spiritual direction, see the website for Spiritual Directors International: www.sdiworld.org
- *Religion and Spirituality in Psychiatry*, edited by Philippe Huguelet and Harold G. Koenig (Cambridge: Cambridge University Press, 2009)
- California Institute of Integral Studies, Center for Psychedelic Therapies and Research: https://www.ciis.edu/research-centers /center-for-psychedelic-therapies-and-research/about-the-center -for-psychedelic-therapies-and-research
- To learn about the steps taken toward the legalization of psychedelic-assisted psychotherapy in 2021, see the Multidisciplinary Association of Psychedelic Studies: https://maps.org /research/mdma
- *Psychotherapy and Spiritual Direction: Two Languages, One Voice?* by Lynette Harborne (London: Karnac Books, 2012)

Spirit Tech, Neuroscience, and Philosophy

Philosophically inclined readers interested in further exploring the types of arguments and criteria for the authenticity of religious experiences employed by religious thinkers and philosophers will find the perspectives and explanations in these books helpful.

- *Perceiving God: The Epistemology of Religious Experience*, by William P. Alston (Ithaca, NY: Cornell University Press, 1991)
- *The Evidential Force of Religious Experience*, by Caroline Franks Davis (Oxford: Oxford University Press, 1989)

- *Mysticism, Mind, Consciousness*, by Robert K. C. Forman (Albany: State University of New York Press, 1999)
- *Religious Experience*, by Wayne Proudfoot (Berkeley: University of California Press, 1985)
- *Sacred or Neural? The Potential of Neuroscience to Explain Religious Experience*, by Anne L. C. Runehov (Göttingen, Germany: Vandenhoek & Ruprecht, 2007)
- *Religious Experience Reconsidered: A Building-Block Approach to the Study of Religion and Other Special Things*, by Ann Taves (Princeton, NJ: Princeton University Press, 2009)
- *Religious and Spiritual Experiences*, by Wesley J. Wildman (New York: Cambridge University Press, 2011)
- *The Neuroscience of Religious Experience*, by Patrick McNamara (New York: Cambridge University Press, 2009)
- *Neurotheology: How Science Can Enlighten Us About Spirituality*, by Andrew Newberg (New York: Columbia University Press, 2018)
- "The Neuroscience of Religious Experiences: Andrew Newberg LIVE on Big Think," interviewed by Megan Erickson for *Big Think*, https://bigthink.com/videos/the-neuroscience-of-religious -experiences-andrew-newberg-live-on-big-think-2

Spirituality and Health

- *Blind Faith: The Unholy Alliance of Religion and Medicine*, by Richard P. Sloan (New York: St. Martin's Press, 2006)
- *Medicine, Religion, and Health: Where Science and Spirituality Meet*, by Harold G. Koenig (West Conshohocken, PA: Templeton Foundation Press, 2008)

Notes

1: THE SCATTERED SUPERMARKET OF SPECIAL SPIRITUAL SERVICES

1. Mikey Siegel, interview with Kate J. Stockly, July 31, 2018.
2. Jonathan Robinson, quoted in "Spiritual Technologies 2.0 Summit 2017 Trailer," accessed March 2018, https://www.youtube.com/watch?time_continue=163&v=wX7RsuRwons.
3. Mikey Siegel, personal communication.
4. Ibid.
5. Peter L. Berger, *The Sacred Canopy: Elements of a Sociological Theory of Religion* (New York: Doubleday, 1967).
6. Peter L. Berger, "Secularism in Retreat," *National Interest* 46 (Winter 1996): 3–12.

2: STIMULATING THE BRAIN

1. Shinzen Young, quote from https://www.shinzen.org/.
2. Albert Einstein, "The Fundamental Idea of General Relativity in Its Original Form," an excerpt from an unpublished essay (1919); published as "Excerpt from Essay by Einstein On 'Happiest Thought' of His Life," *New York Times*, March 28, 1972, accessed May 10, 2020, https://www.nytimes.com/1972/03/28/archives/excerpt-from-essay-by-einstein-on-happiest-thought-in-his-life.html.
3. Shinzen Young, *The Science of Enlightenment: How Meditation Works* (Boulder, CO: Sounds True, 2018), 207.

4. Ibid., 207.

5. Ibid., 11.

6. Ibid.

7. Ibid., 20.

8. Jay Sanguinetti, interview with Kate J. Stockly, April 21, 2020.

9. For an article based on the text of the Dalai Lama's keynote address at the annual meeting of the Society for Neuroscience, November 12, 2005, Washington, DC, see Tenzin Gyatso, "Science at the Crossroads," His Holiness the 14th Dalai Lama of Tibet, https://www.dalailama.com/messages/buddhism/science-at-the-crossroads.

10. The Dalai Lama, as quoted by Jay Sanguinetti. See also, David Pearce, guest writing on George Dvorsky's blog, "A World Without Suffering?" *Sentient Developments*, May 1, 2009, http://www.sentientdevelopments.com/2009/05/world-without-suffering.html. See also Dalai Lama, "The Neuroscience of Meditation," Society for Neuroscience 2005, November 12, 2005, https://www.sfn.org/meetings/past-and-future-annual-meetings/abstract-archive/abstract-archive-details?absID=144&absyear=2005; and, for an article based on the text of the Dalai Lama's keynote address, see: Tenzin Gyatso, "Science at the Crossroads," His Holiness the Fourteenth Dalai Lama of Tibet, https://www.dalailama.com/messages/buddhism/science-at-the-crossroads.

11. Sanguinetti, interview with Stockly.

12. Ibid.

13. Ibid.

14. Ibid.

15. Ibid.

16. Young, *The Science of Enlightenment*, 216.

17. Michel Habib, "Athymhormia and Disorders of Motivation in Basal Ganglia Disease," *Journal of Neuropsychiatry and Clinical Neurosciences* 16, no. 4 (Nov. 2004): 509–24, https://doi.org/10.1176/appi.neuropsych.16.4.509.

18. Young, *The Science of Enlightenment*, 215.

19. Sanguinetti, interview with Stockly.

20. Jay Sanguinetti, "A Technoboost for Meditation," TEDxBigSky talk, January 26, 2019, Big Sky, Montana, accessed July 19, 2019, https://www.youtube.com/watch?v=rGEjmwaIPZk.

21. Judson A. Brewer, Kathleen A. Garrison, and Susan Whitfield-Gabrieli, "What About the 'Self' Is Processed in the Posterior Cingulate Cortex?" *Frontiers in Human Neuroscience* 7 (Oct. 2013): 647, https://doi.org/10.3389/fnhum.2013.00647.

22. Sanguinetti, interview with Stockly.

23. Young, *The Science of Enlightenment*, 213.

24. Sanguinetti, "A Technoboost for Meditation."

25. Hui Zhou, Lili Niu, Long Meng, Zhengrong Lin, Junjie Zou, Xiangxiang Xia, Xiaowei Huang, Wei Zhou, Tianyuan Bian, and Hairong Zheng, "Noninvasive Ultrasound Deep Brain Stimulation for the Treatment of Parkinson's Disease Model Mouse," *Research* 2019 (July 2019): 1–13, https://doi.org/10.34133/2019 /1748489.

26. Sanguinetti, interview with Stockly.

27. Ibid.

28. Ibid.

29. Ibid.

30. Ibid.

31. Ibid.

32. Ibid.

33. Ibid.

34. Ibid.

35. Ibid.

36. Zhengrong Lin, Xiaowei Huang, Wei Zhou, Wenjun Zhang, Yingzhe Liu, Tianyuan Bian, Lili Niu, Long Meng, and Yanwu Gu, "Ultrasound Stimulation Modulates Voltage-Gated Potassium Currents Associated with Action Potential Shape in Hippocampal CA1 Pyramidal Neurons," *Frontiers in Pharmacology* 10 (May 2019), https://doi.org/10.3389/fphar.2019.00544.

37. Lazzaro di Biase, Emma Falato, and Vincenzo Di Lazzaro, "Transcranial Focused Ultrasound (tFUS) and Transcranial Unfocused Ultrasound (tUS) Neuromodulation: From Theoretical Principles to Stimulation Practices," *Frontiers in Neurology* 10 (June 2019), https://doi.org/10.3389/fneur.2019.00549.

38. Michael Plaksin, Eitan Kimmel, and Shy Shoham, "Cell-Type-Selective Effects of Intramembrane Cavitation as a Unifying Theoretical Framework for Ultrasonic Neuromodulation," *eNeuro* 3, no. 3 (May 2016), https://doi.org/10.1523 /ENEURO.0136-15.2016.

39. Sanguinetti, interview with Stockly.

40. For more on the remarkable and transformative discovery of electromagnetism, see Nancy Forbes and Basil Mahon, *Faraday, Maxwell, and the Electromagnetic Field: How Two Men Revolutionized Physics* (Amherst, NY: Prometheus Books, 2014).

41. Silvanus P. Thompson, "A Physiological Effect of an Alternating Magnetic Field," *Proceedings of the Royal Society, Series B, Containing Papers of a Biological Character* 82, no. 557 (July 1910): 396–98. To learn more about Thompson's life and work more generally, see A. C. Lynch, "Silvanus Thompson: Teacher, Researcher, Historian," *IEE Proceedings A (Physical Science, Measurement and Instrumentation, Management and Education)* 136, no. 6 (1989): 306–12.

42. Marcos Vidal-Dourado, Adriana Bastos Conforto, Luis Otavio Sales Ferreira Caboclo, Milberto Scaff, Laura Maria de Figueiredo Ferreira Guilhoto, and Elza Márcia

Targas Yacubian, "Magnetic Fields in Noninvasive Brain Stimulation," *Neuroscientist* 20, no. 2 (2014): 112–21, https://doi.org/10.1177/1073858413491145.

43. A. T. Barker, R. Jalinous, and I. L. Freeston, "Non-invasive Magnetic Stimulation of Human Motor Cortex," *The Lancet* 325, no. 8437 (May 11, 1985): 1106–7, https://doi.org/10.1016/S0140-6736(85)92413-4.

44. John Elder Robison, *Switched On: A Memoir of Brain Change and Emotional Awakening* (New York: Spiegel & Grau), 2017.

45. Ibid., 78.

46. Helen Thomson, "Supercharge Your Zen," *New Scientist* 239, no. 3186 (2018): 34–36.

47. Bodhi NeuroTech, Inc., "The Zendo Device Enhances Your Meditation Practice," *Zendo Meditation*, accessed May 10, 2020, https://www.zendomeditation.com; Bashar W. Badran, Chris W. Austelle, Nicole R. Smith, Chloe E. Glusman, Brett Froeliger, Eric L. Garland, Jeffrey J. Borckardt, Mark S. George, and Edward Baron Short, "A Double-Blind Study Exploring the Use of Transcranial Direct Current Stimulation (tDCS) to Potentially Enhance Mindfulness Meditation (E-Meditation)," *Brain Stimulation* 10, no. 1 (Jan.–Feb. 2017): 152–54, https://doi.org/10.1016/j.brs.2016.09.009.

48. Bashar W. Badran and Edward Baron Short, "Abstract #11: tDCS-Enhanced Meditation (E-Meditation) Reduces Mind Wandering and Stress State: An Open-Label Pilot Trial," *Brain Stimulation* 12, no. 2 (March 2019): E4, https://doi.org/10.1016/j.brs.2018.12.018; Bashar W. Badran, Chris W. Austelle, Nicole R. Smith, Chloe E. Glusman, Brett Froeliger, Eric L. Garland, Jeffrey J. Borckardt, Mark S. George, and Edward Baron Short, "E-Meditation: A Novel Paradigm Using tDCS to Enhance Mindfulness Meditation," *Brain Stimulation* 10, no. 4 (July 2017): E22, https://doi.org/10.1016/j.brs.2017.04.011.

49. Marom Bikson, Bhaskar Paneri, Andoni Mourdoukoutas, Zeinab Esmaeilpour, Bashar W. Badran, Robin Azzam, Devin Adair, Abhishek Datta, Xiao Hui Fang, Brett Wingeier, Daniel Chao, Miguel Alonso-Alonso, Kiwon Lee, Helena Knotkova, Adam J. Woods, David Hagedorn, Doug Jeffery, James Giordano, and William J. Tyler, "Limited Output Transcranial Electrical Stimulation (LOTES-2017): Engineering Principles, Regulatory Statutes, and Industry Standards for Wellness, Over-the-Counter, or Prescription Devices with Low Risk," *Brain Stimulation* 11, no. 1 (Jan.–Feb. 2018): 134–57, https://doi.org/10.1016/j.brs.2017.10.012; Marom Bikson, Pnina Grossman, Chris Thomas, Adantchede Louis Zannou, Jimmy Jiang, Tatheer Adnan, Antonios P. Moudoukoutas, Greg Kronberg, Dennis Truong, Paulo Boggio, André R. Brunoni, Leigh Charvet, Felipe Fregni, Brita Fritsch, Bernadette Gillick, Roy H. Hamilton, Benjamin M. Hampstead, Ryan Jankord, Adam Kirton, Helena Knotkova, David Liebetanz, Anli Liu, Colleen Loo, Michael A. Nitsche, Janine Reis, Jessica D. Richardson, Alexander Rotenberg, Peter E. Turkeltaub, and Adam J. Woods, "Safety of

Transcranial Direct Current Stimulation: Evidence Based Update 2016," *Brain Stimulation* 9, no. 5 (2016): 641–61, https://doi.org/10.1016/j.brs.2016.06.004.

50. Bodhi NeuroTech, Inc., "Sign Up to Buy a Zendo—Coming Spring 2020!" Zendo Meditation, accessed May 12, 2020, https://www.zendomeditation.com. See also "First Look at Limited Edition Zendo for Meditation," tDCS.com, accessed November 16, 2020, https://www.tdcs.com/news/2020/5/28/first-look-at-limited -edition-zendo-for-meditation.

51. Mihály Vöröslakos, Yuichi Takeuchi, Kitti Brinyiczki, Tamás Zombori, Azahara Oliva, Antonio Fernández-Ruiz, Gábor Kozák, Zsigmond Tamás Kincses, Béla Iványi, György Buzsáki, and Antal Berényi, "Direct Effects of Transcranial Electric Stimulation on Brain Circuits in Rats and Humans," *Nature Communications* 9, no. 1 (2018), https://doi.org/10.1038/s41467–018–02928–3.

52. Ibid.

53. Jared Cooney Horvath, Jason D. Forte, and Olivia Carter, "Quantitative Review Finds No Evidence of Cognitive Effects in Healthy Populations from Single-Session Transcranial Direct Current Stimulation (tDCS)," *Brain Stimulation* 8, no. 3 (May–June 2015): 535–50, https://doi.org/10.1016/j.brs.2015.01.400.

54. Young, *The Science of Enlightenment*, 226.

3: NEUROFEEDBACK-GUIDED MEDITATION

1. Heidi Michelle, interview with Kate J. Stockly, August 9, 2016.

2. As quoted in Emma Woolf, *Letting Go: How to Heal Your Hurt, Love Your Body and Transform Your Life* (Chichester, UK: Summersdale Publishers, 2015), 22.

3. "Brainworks: Transformational Retreats," Brainworks, accessed July 2016, https:// www.transformational-retreats.com/.

4. Les Fehmi and Jim Robbins, *The Open-Focus Brain: Harnessing the Power of Attention to Heal Mind and Body* (Boston: Trumpeter, 2007), 131.

5. James Roy, interview with Kate J. Stockly, August 18, 2018.

6. Hengameh Marzbani, Hamid Reza Marateb, and Marjan Mansourian, "Neurofeedback: A Comprehensive Review on System Design, Methodology and Clinical Applications," *Basic and Clinical Neuroscience* 7, no. 2 (April 2016): 143–58, https://doi.org/10.15412/J.BCN.03070208.

7. On stress management: Michael Thompson and Lynda Thompson, "Neurofeedback for Stress Management," in *Principles and Practice of Stress Management*, 3rd ed., ed. Paul M. Lehrer, Robert L. Woolfolk, and Wesley E. Sime (New York: Guilford Press, 2007), 249–87; lie detection: Kirtley E. Thornton, "The qEEG in the Lie Detection Problem: The Localization of Guilt?" in *Forensic Applications of QEEG and Neurotherapy*, ed. James R. Evans (Binghamton, NY: Haworth Medical Press, 2005), 31–43; pain management: Sadi Kayiran, Erbil Dursun, Numan Ermutlu, Nigar Dursun, and Sacit Karamürsel, "Neurofeedback in Fibromyalgia

Syndrome," *Journal of the Turkish Society of Algology* 19, no. 3 (Aug. 2007): 47–53.

8. For more on the therapeutic potential of neurofeedback for ADHD, see Martijn Arns, Sabine de Ridder, Ute Strehl, Marinus Breteler, and Anton Coenen, "Efficacy of Neurofeedback Treatment in ADHD: The Effects of Inattention, Impulsivity and Hyperactivity: A Meta-Analysis," *Clinical EEG and Neuroscience* 40, no. 3 (Aug. 2009): 180–89; and Steven M. Snyder and James R. Hall, "A Meta-Analysis of Quantitative EEG Power Associated with Attention-Deficit Hyperactivity Disorder," *Journal of Clinical Neurophysiology* 23, no. 5 (2006): 440–55, https://doi .org/10.1097/01.wnp.0000221363.12503.78.

9. Joel F. Lubar, "Neurofeedback for the Management of Attention Deficit/Hyperactivity Disorders," in *Biofeedback: A Practitioner's Guide*, 2nd. ed., ed. Mark S. Schwartz and Frank Andrasik (New York: Guilford Press, 1995), 493–522; see also Geir Ogrim, Juri Kropotov, and Knut Hestad, "The QEEG Theta/Beta Ratio in ADHD and Normal Controls: Sensitivity, Specificity, and Behavioral Correlates," *Psychiatry Research* 198, no. 3 (Aug. 2012): 482–88, https://doi.org/10 .1016/j.psychres.2011.12.041; Martijn Arns, C. Keith Conners, and Helena C. Kraemer, "A Decade of EEG Theta/Beta Ratio Research in ADHD: A Meta-Analysis," *Journal of Attention Disorders* 17, no. 5 (July 2013): 374–83, https://doi .org/10.1177/1087054712460087.

10. Sandra K. Loo, Christian Hopfer, Peter D. Teale, and Martin L. Reite, "EEG Correlates of Methylphenidate Response in ADHD: Association with Cognitive and Behavioral Measures," *Journal of Clinical Neurophysiology* 21, no. 6 (Nov.–Dec. 2004): 457–64, https://doi.org/10.1097/01.wnp.0000150890.14421.9a.

11. For a good introduction published by the Foundation for Neurofeedback and Neuromodulation Research, see Richard Soutar and Robert Longo, *Doing Neurofeedback: An Introduction* (San Rafael, CA: ISNR Research Foundation, 2011); another good introduction is John N. Demos, *Getting Started with Neurofeedback* (New York: W. W. Norton, 2005).

12. For good introductions, see Thomas F. Collura, *Technical Foundations of Neurofeedback* (New York: Routledge, 2014); Thomas H. Budzynski, Helen Kogan Budzynski, James R. Evans, and Andrew Abarbanel, eds., *Introduction to Quantitative EEG and Neurofeedback: Advanced Theory and Application*, 2nd ed. (New York: Academic Press, 2009); Soutar and Longo, *Doing Neurofeedback*.

13. Large databases of standardized norms are collected and maintained by several companies and used by both researchers and clinicians. For example, see Brain DX (http://braindx.net/); NeuroGuide, maintained by Applied Neuroscience (https://appliedneuroscience.com/neuroguide/); and the New Mind Neurofeedback Analysis System (https://www.newmindmaps.com/). For an introductory article on the use of such databases, see Evian Gordon, Nicholas James Cooper, C. J. Rennie, Daniel F. Hermens, and Leanne M. Williams,

"Integrative Neuroscience: The Role of a Standardized Database," *Clinical EEG and Neuroscience* 36, no. 2 (May 2005): 64–75, https://doi.org/10.1177 /155005940503600205.

14. For a great introduction to the history, research, and clinical use of qEEG technology, see Richard Soutar, "An Introductory Perspective on the Emerging Application of qEEG in Neurofeedback," in *Clinical Neurotherapy: Application of Techniques for Treatment*, ed. David S. Cantor and James R. Evans (London: Academic Press, 2014), 19–54.

15. See Sebern F. Fisher, *Neurofeedback in the Treatment of Developmental Trauma: Calming the Fear-Driven Brain* (New York: W. W. Norton, 2014).

16. Michelle, interview with Stockly.

17. "Neurofield," Brainworks: Train Your Mind, accessed May 2020, www.brain worksneurotherapy.com/neurofield.

18. Ibid.

19. Heidi Michelle, "My Brain on Retreat: A 7-day Transformational Journey," *Rebel Wellness* (blog), Dragon Fly Yoga, accessed July 10, 2016, https://www.rebel -wellness.com/blog/my-brain-on-retreat/.

20. Michelle, interview with Stockly.

21. Ibid.

22. Ibid.

23. Michelle, "My Brain on Retreat."

24. Lion's Roar Staff, "Pema Chödrön and Jack Kornfield Talk 'The Wondrous Path of Difficulties,'" Lion's Roar: Buddhist Wisdom for Our Time, October 15, 2017, accessed April 2020, https://www.lionsroar.com/?s=wondrous+path+of+difficulties/.

25. Pema Chödrön, "5 Reasons to Meditate," Lion's Roar: Buddhist Wisdom for Our Time, April 22, 2018, accessed April 2020, https://www.lionsroar.com/5-reasons -to-meditate-september-2013/.

26. Shinzen Young, *The Science of Enlightenment: How Meditation Works* (Boulder, CO: Sounds True, 2018) 12.

27. Richard Soutar, interview with Kate J. Stockly and Wesley J. Wildman, July 15, 2016.

28. Richard Soutar, *The Automatic Self: Transformation and Transcendence through Brain-Wave Training* (Bloomington, IN: True Directions/iUniverse, 2015), 96.

29. For example, see C. Maxwell Cade and Nona Coxhead, *The Awakened Mind: Biofeedback and the Development of Higher States of Awareness* (New York: Delacorte Press/Eleanor Friede, 1979); Joe Kamiya, "Operant Control of the EEG Alpha Rhythms and Some of Its Reported Effects on Consciousness," in *Altered States of Consciousness: A Book of Readings*, ed. Charles T. Tart (New York: Wiley, 1969), 507–17; and Akira Kasamatsu and Tomio Hirai, "An EEG Study on the Zen Meditation," ibid., 489–501.

30. For example, see Daniel Goleman, *The Varieties of the Meditative Experience* (New York: E. P. Dutton, 1977); Richard J. Davidson, Jon Kabat-Zinn, Jessica

Schumacher, Melissa Rosenkranz, Daniel Muller, Saki F. Santorelli, Ferris Ur-
banowski, Anne Harrington, Katherine Bonus, and John F. Sheridan, "Alterations
in Brain and Immune Function Produced by Mindfulness Meditation," *Psycho-
somatic Medicine* 65, no. 4 (July–Aug. 2003): 564–70, https://doi.org/10.1097/01
.psy.0000077505.67574.e3; John W. DeLuca and Ray Daly, "The Inner Alchemy of
Buddhist Tantric Meditation: A qEEG Case Study Using Low Resonance, Electromagnetic Topography (LORETA)," *Subtle Energies & Energy Medicine* 13, no. 2
(2003): 155–208; Akira Kasamatsu and Tomio Hirai, "Electroencephalographic
Study on the Zen Meditation (Zazen)," *Folia Psychiatrica et Neurologica Japanica*
20, no. 4 (1966): 315–36, https://doi.org/10.1111/j.1440-1819.1966.tb02646.x;
B. K. Anand, G. S. Chhina, and Baldev Singh, "Some Aspects of EEG Stud-
ies in Yogis," *Electroencephalography and Clinical Neurophysiology* 13, no. 3
(June 1961): 452–56, https://doi.org/10.1016/0013-4694(61)90015-3; Julian M.
Davidson, "The Physiology of Meditation and Mystical States of Consciousness,"
Perspectives in Biology and Medicine 19, no. 3 (1976): 345–79, https://doi.org/10
.1353/pbm.1976.0042; Richard J. Davidson, Daniel J. Goleman, and Gary E.
Schwartz, "Attentional and Affective Concomitants of Meditation: A Cross-
Sectional Study," *Journal of Abnormal Psychology* 85, no. 2 (April 1976): 235–38,
https://doi.org/10.1037//0021-843x.85.2.235. See also the discussion in Soutar,
The Automatic Self, 95–98.

31. Cade and Coxhead, *The Awakened Mind*.

32. Ibid., 243.

33. Anna Wise, "History of the Awakened Mind," Anna Wise Center, accessed
July 2016, http://annawise.com/the-work/the-awakened-mind/.

34. Esalen Institute, http://www.esalen.org.

35. Soutar, interview with Stockly and Wildman.

36. "Practitioner Directory," Institute for the Awakened Mind, accessed July 2016,
http://www.institutefortheawakenedmind.com/home/practitioner-directory/.

37. Soutar, *The Automatic Self*, 7.

38. Ibid.

39. Ibid., ix.

40. Soutar, interview with Stockly and Wildman.

41. Ibid.

42. Ibid.

43. Ibid.

44. Ibid.

45. Soutar, *The Automatic Self,* ix.

46. Bill, interview with Kate J. Stockly, September 15, 2016.

47. Ibid.

48. Ibid.

49. Ibid.

50. Ibid.

51. Ibid.

52. Soutar, interview with Stockly and Wildman.

53. Fred Travis and Jonathan Shear, "Focused Attention, Open Monitoring and Automatic Self-Transcending: Categories to Organize Meditations from Vedic, Buddhist, and Chinese Traditions," *Consciousness and Cognition* 19, no. 4 (Dec. 2010): 1110–18, https://doi.org/10.1016/j.concog.2010.01.007.

54. Richard Soutar, "Training Meditational States with Neurofeedback in a Clinical Setting," Tech-Gnostic: Where Spirit Meets Hardware, December 9, 2014, accessed July 18, 2016, http://tech-gnostic.org/neurofeedback-meditation-new-way -west/.

55. "Individual Services," NeuroMeditation Institute, accessed May 3, 2020, https:// www.neuromeditationinstitute.com/individual-services.

56. Soutar and Longo, *Doing Neurofeedback*, 183.

57. Soutar, interview with Stockly and Wildman.

58. Ibid.

59. Soutar, *The Automatic Self*, 98.

60. Tracy Brandmeyer and Arnaud Delorme, "Meditation and Neurofeedback," *Frontiers in Psychology* 4 (Oct. 2013): 1–3, https://doi.org/10.3389/fpsyg.2013 .00688; Soutar, "Training Meditational States with Neurofeedback in a Clinical Setting."

61. For a discussion of the complexities involved in studying meditative states with qEEG, see DeLuca and Daly, "The Inner Alchemy of Buddhist Tantric Meditation."

62. Brandmeyer and Delorme, "Meditation and Neurofeedback"; Judson A. Brewer, "Pairing Ancient Wisdom with Modern Technology to Optimize Habit Change: Mindfulness and Neurofeedback," MIT Media Lab: Advancing Wellbeing Seminar Series, Massachusetts Institute of Technology, Cambridge, MA, February 21, 2014, https://www.youtube.com/watch?v=wil45EaQvUE&feature=emb_title; Soutar, *The Automatic Self*; Soutar, "Training Meditational States with Neurofeedback in a Clinical Setting"; Kathleen A. Garrison, Juan F. Santoyo, Jake H. Davis, Thomas A. Thornhill IV, Catherine E. Kerr, and Judson A. Brewer, "Effortless Awareness: Using Real Time Neurofeedback to Investigate Correlates of Posterior Cingulate Cortex Activity in Meditators' Self-Report," *Frontiers in Human Neuroscience* 7 (2013), https://doi.org/10.3389/fnhum.2013.00440.

63. For example: Brewer, "Pairing Ancient Wisdom with Modern Technology to Optimize Habit Change"; J. T. McKnight and L. G. Fehmi, "Attention and Neurofeedback Synchrony Training: Clinical Results and Their Significance," *Journal of Neurotherapy* 5, no. 1–2 (2001): 45–61, https://doi.org/10.1300/J184v05n01_05;

Soutar, *The Automatic Self*. See also Michael Murphy and Steven Donovan, *The Physical and Psychological Effects of Meditation: A Review of Contemporary Research with a Comprehensive Bibliography, 1931–1996*, 2nd ed., ed. Eugene Taylor (Petaluma, CA: Institute of Noetic Sciences, 1997).

64. For example, see Stefan G. Hofmann, Alice T. Sawyer, Ashley A. Witt, and Diana Oh, "The Effect of Mindfulness-Based Therapy on Anxiety and Depression: A Meta-Analytic Review," *Journal of Consulting and Clinical Psychology* 78, no. 2 (April 2010): 169–83, https://doi.org/10.1037/a0018555; and Jon Kabat-Zinn, *Wherever You Go, There You Are: Mindfulness Meditation in Everyday Life* (New York: Hachette Books, 1994).

65. For example, see Antoine Lutz, Julie Brefczynski-Lewis, Tom Johnstone, Richard J. Davidson, "Regulation of the Neural Circuitry of Emotion by Compassion Meditation: Effects of Meditative Expertise," *PlosOne* 3, 3 (March 2008): e1897, https://doi.org/10.1371/journal.pone.0001897; Christopher A. Pepping, Analise O'Donovan, and Penelope J. Davis, "The Differential Relationship Between Mindfulness and Attachment in Experienced and Inexperienced Meditators," *Mindfulness* 5, no. 4 (Aug. 2014): 392–99, https://doi.org/10.1007/s12671-012-0193-3; and Antoine Lutz, Lawrence L. Greischar, Nancy B. Rawlings, Matthieu Ricard, and Richard J. Davidson, "Long-Term Meditators Self-Induce High-Amplitude Gamma Synchrony During Mental Practice," *PNAS* 101, no. 46 (Nov. 2004): 16369–73, https://doi.org/10.1073/pnas.0407401101.

66. Elmer Green and Alyce Green, *Beyond Biofeedback* (New York: Delacorte, 1977); Adam Crane and Richard Soutar, *MindFitness Training: Neurofeedback and the Process* (New York: iUniverse, 2000); Jim Robbins, *A Symphony in the Brain: The Evolution of the New Brain Wave Biofeedback* (New York: Grove Press, 2008); Nancy E. White, "Theories of the Effectiveness of Alpha-Theta Training for Multiple Disorders," in *Introduction to Quantitative EEG and Neurofeedback*, ed. James R. Evans and Andrew Abarbanel (San Diego: Academic Press, 1999), 341–67.

67. B. Rael Cahn and John Polich, "Meditation States and Traits: EEG, ERP, and Neuroimaging Studies," *Psychological Bulletin* 132, no. 2 (March 2006): 180–211, https://doi.org/10.1037/0033-2909.132.2.180; Remko van Lutterveld, Sean D. Houlihan, Prasanta Pal, Matthew D. Sacchet, Cinque McFarlane-Blake, Payal R. Patel, John S. Sullivan, Alex Ossadtchi, Susan Druker, Clemens Bauer, and Judson A. Brewer, "Source-Space EEG Neurofeedback Links Subjective Experience with Brain Activity During Effortless Awareness Meditation," *NeuroImage* 151 (May 2017): 117–27, https://doi.org/10.1016/j.neuroimage.2016.02.047.

68. See the New Mind Neurofeedback Center's website for more information about their services and programs at http://newmindcenter.com/, especially "About Neurofeedback" at http://newmindcenter/About-Neurofeedback/Neurofeedback-and-Meditation.

69. Soutar, *The Automatic Self*, x.

4: ENGINEERING TOGETHERNESS

1. William James, *The Varieties of Religious Experience* (New York: Longmans, Green, 1902).

2. Mikey Siegel, interview with Kate J. Stockly, July 10, 2019.

3. "Dying of loneliness" is no exaggeration: multiple studies have identified loneliness as a risk factor for death from *any* cause; a recent meta-analysis found that social isolation, loneliness, and living alone corresponded to 29 percent, 26 percent, and 32 percent increased likelihoods of mortality, respectively. Loneliness has been called "the new smoking" and is said to be as damaging as smoking fifteen cigarettes a day. Even though modern life *appears* to be overflowing with ways to stay connected and networked with others, loneliness is on the rise; Cigna's 2020 Loneliness Index (released January 23, 2020—before the COVID-19 pandemic hit the United States) found that 61 percent of American adults reported that they are lonely. This reflected an alarming 7 percent increase from loneliness levels reported in Cigna's 2018 index. Julianne Holt-Lunstad, Timothy B. Smith, Mark Baker, Tyler Harris, and David Stephenson, "Loneliness and Social Isolation as Risk Factors for Mortality: A Meta-Analytic Review," *Perspectives on Psychological Science* 10, no. 2 (March 2015): 227–37, https://doi.org/10 .1177/1745691614568352; Health Resources & Services Administration, "The 'Loneliness Epidemic,'" January 2019, accessed May 10, 2020, https://www .hrsa.gov/enews/past-issues/2019/january-17/loneliness-epidemic; Liana Des-Hamais Bruce, Joshua S. Wu, Stuart L. Lustig, Daniel W. Russell, and Douglas A. Nemecek, "Loneliness in the United States: A 2018 National Panel Survey of Demographic, Structural, Cognitive, and Behavioral Characteristics," *American Journal of Health Promotion* 33, no. 8 (2019): 1123–33, https://doi.org/10.1177 /0890117119856551.

4. Siegel, interview Stockly, July 10, 2019.

5. Émile Durkheim, *Formes élémentaires de la vie religieuse* (*Elementary Forms of Religious Life*), 1912.

6. Rollin McCraty, "New Frontiers in Heart Rate Variability and Social Coherence Research: Techniques, Technologies, and Implications for Improving Group Dynamics and Outcomes," *Frontiers in Public Health* 5 (Oct. 2017), https://doi.org /10.3389/fpubh.2017.00267.

7. Jonathan L. Helm, David Sbarra, and Emilio Ferrer, "Assessing Cross-Partner Associations in Physiological Responses via Coupled Oscillator Models," *Emotion* 12, no. 4 (Aug. 2012): 748–62, https://doi.org/10.1037/a0025036; Emilio Ferrer and Jonathan L. Helm, "Dynamical Systems Modeling of Physiological Coregulation in Dyadic Interactions," *International Journal of Psychophysiology* 88, no. 3 (June 2013): 296–308, https://doi.org/10.1016/j.ijpsycho .2012.10.013.

8. University College London, UCL Psychology and Language Sciences, "Audience Members' Hearts Beat Together at the Theatre," November 17, 2017, https://www .ucl.ac.uk/pals/news/2017/nov/audience-members-hearts-beat-together-theatre.

9. Mikey Siegel, interview with Kate Stockly, July 31, 2018.

10. Mikey Siegel, "HeartSync Visuals and Sound," https://www.youtube.com/watch ?v=j2Ouf6Tg2T0.

11. Siegel, interview with Stockly, July 31, 2018.

12. Siegel, interview with Stockly, July 10, 2019.

13. Lynne, interview with Kate J. Stockly, July 23, 2019; Mark, interview with Kate J. Stockly, July 26, 2019.

14. Douglas Martin. "George Leonard, Voice of '60s Counterculture, Dies at 86," *New York Times*, Jan. 18, 2010, accessed July 27, 2019, https://www.nytimes.com /2010/01/18/us/18leonard1.html.

15. Siegel, interview with Stockly, July 10, 2019.

16. Ibid.

17. Robin Arnott, interview with Kate J. Stockly, July 26, 2019.

18. A brief video at https://www.youtube.com/watch?v=bKjNnSYN_24&feature =youtu.be shows the experience, and the wiring is illustrated at Alan Macy, "Group Physiological Flow," https://alanmacy.com/project/group-physiological-flow/.

19. Siegel, interview with Stockly, July 10, 2019.

20. Ibid.

21. Ibid.

22. Ibid.

23. Privileged communication.

24. Privileged communication.

25. Mark, interview with Stockly.

26. Ibid.

27. Siegel, interview with Stockly, July 10, 2019.

28. Privileged communication.

29. Privileged communication.

30. Aliya A. Tolegenova, Almira M. Kustubayeva, and Gerald Matthews, "Trait Meta-Mood, Gender and EEG Response During Emotion-Regulation," *Personality and Individual Differences* 65 (July 2014): 75–80, https://doi.org/10.1016/j.paid.2014 .01.028; Ian Daly, Asad Malik, Faustina Hwang, Etienne Roesch, James Weaver, Alexis Kirke, Duncan Williams, Eduardo Miranda, and Slawomir J. Nasuto, "Neural Correlates of Emotional Responses to Music: An EEG Study," *Neuroscience Letters* 573 (June 2014): 52–57, https://doi.org/10.1016/j.neulet.2014.05.003; L. I. Aftanas, N. V. Lotova, V. I. Koshkarov, V. P. Makhnev, Y. N. Mordvintsev, and S. A. Popov, "Nonlinear Dynamic Complexity of the Human EEG During Evoked Emotions," *International Journal of Psychophysiology* 28, no. 1 (1998): 63–76, https://doi.org/10.1016/s0167-8760(97)00067-6; Carles Grau, Romuald

Ginhoux, Alejandro Riera, Thanh Lam Nguyen, Hubert Chauvat, Michel Berg, Julià L. Amengual, Alvaro Pascual-Leone, and Giulio Ruffini, "Conscious Brain-to-Brain Communication in Humans Using Non-invasive Technologies," *PLOS One* 9, no. 8 (2014): e105225, https://doi.org/10.1371/journal.pone.0105225.

31. Kirtley E. Thornton, "The qEEG in the Lie Detection Problem: The Localization of Guilt?" in *Forensic Applications of QEEG and Neurotherapy*, ed. James R. Evans (Binghamton, NY: Haworth Medical Press, 2005), 31–43; Lawrence A. Farwell and Emanuel Donchin, "The Truth Will Out: Interrogative Polygraphy ('Lie Detection') with Event-Related Brain Potentials," *Psychophysiology* 28, no. 5 (Sept. 1991): 531–47, https://doi.org/10.1111/j.1469-8986.1991.tb01990.x.

32. Nidhi Subbaraman, "A Gadget to Change Your Mood," *Boston Globe*, February 8, 2015, accessed September 2020, https://www.bostonglobe.com/magazine/2015/02/08/gadget-change-your-mood/hJfjf9Wfgr37p1y7XTUyoO/story.html.

33. Andy Boxall, "Thync Relax Pro Review," *Digital Trends*, August 10, 2017, accessed September 2020, https://www.digitaltrends.com/wearables/thync-relax-pro-review/.

34. Rajesh P. N. Rao, Andrea Stocco, Matthew Bryan, Devapratim Sarma, Tiffany M. Youngquist, Joseph Wu, and Chantel S. Prat, "A Direct Brain-to-Brain Interface in Humans," *PLOS One* 9, no. 11 (2014): e111332, https://doi.org/10.1371/journal.pone.0111332.

35. Grau et al., "Conscious Brain-to-Brain Communication in Humans Using Non-Invasive Technologies."

36. Andrea Stocco, Chantel S. Prat, Darby M. Losey, Jeneva A. Cronin, Joseph Wu, Justin A. Abernethy, and Rajesh P. N. Rao, "Playing 20 Questions with the Mind: Collaborative Problem Solving by Humans Using a Brain-to-Brain Interface," *PLOS One* 10, no. 9 (2015): e0137303, https://doi.org/10.1371/journal.pone.0137303; see also Deborah Bach, "UW Team Links Two Human Brains for Question-and-Answer Experiment," UW News, September 23, 2015, accessed March 2016, http://www.washington.edu/news/2015/09/23/uw-team-links-two-human-brains-for-question-and-answer-experiment/.

37. Stocco et al., "Playing 20 Questions with the Mind."

38. Grau et al., "Conscious Brain-to-Brain Communication in Humans Using Non-Invasive Technologies," abstract.

39. Linxing Jiang, Andrea Stocco, Darby M. Losey, Justin A. Abernethy, Chantel S. Prat, and Rajesh P. N. Rao, "BrainNet: A Multi-Person Brain-to-Brain Interface for Direct Collaboration Between Brains," *Scientific Reports* 9, no. 1 (April 16, 2019), https://doi.org/10.1038/s41598-019-41895-7.

40. Miguel Pais-Vieira, Gabriela Chiuffa, Mikhail Lebedev, Amol Yadav, and Miguel A. L. Nicolelis, "Building an Organic Computing Device with Multiple Interconnected Brains," *Scientific Reports* 5 (July 9, 2015), https://doi.org/10.1038/srep11869.

41. Linxing Jiang et al., "BrainNet."
42. Ibid.

5: VIRTUAL SACRED REALITY

1. D. J. Soto, interview with Kate J. Stockly, May 1, 2018.
2. Lisa Eadicicco, "Microsoft Just Bought a Virtual Reality Company to Challenge Face-book," *Time*, October 3, 2017, http://time.com/4967092/microsoft-altspacevr -virtual-reality/.
3. David R. Glowacki, Mark D. Wonnacott, Rachel Freire, Becca R. Glowacki, Ella M. Gale, James E. Pike, Tiu de Haan, Mike Chatziapostolou, and Oussama Metatla, "Isness: Using Multi-Person VR to Design Peak Mystical-Type Experiences Comparable to Psychedelics," *CHI '20: Proceedings of the 2020 CHI Conference on Human Factors in Computing Systems* (April 2020): 1–14, https://doi.org/10.1145 /3313831.3376649; archived at arXiv, https://arxiv.org/pdf/2002.00940.pdf.
4. Ibid.
5. Glowacki created *Isness*, a video to illustrate some aspects of how the Isness system works: https://vimeo.com/386402891.
6. Glowacki et al., "Isness."
7. Andrew McMillen, "This Vertigo-Inducing Virtual Reality Game Will Scare the Crap Out of You," *IGN Entertainment*, May 27, 2017, http://www.ign.com /articles/2017/05/28/this-vertigo-inducing-virtual-reality-game-will-scare-the -crap-out-of-you.
8. Ibid.
9. Steven Novella, "The Neuroscience of Virtual Reality," *Neurologica Blog*, February 15, 2018, https://theness.com/neurologicablog/index.php/the-neuroscience -of-virtual-reality/.
10. McMillen, "This Vertigo-Inducing Virtual Reality Game Will Scare the Crap Out of You."
11. Kent Bye, "Android Jones on Using VR for Spiritual Transformation & Unlocking Creative Flow," episode 474, *Voices of VR*, podcast, November 14, 2016, http:// voicesofvr.com/474-android-jones-on-using-vr-for-spiritual-transformation -unlocking-creative-flow/.
12. See a video presentation of Samskara at "Samskara—An Experience by Android Jones [DMT Simulation]," https://www.youtube.com/watch?v =UyOKDoBDbW8&feature=emb_logo.
13. Bye, "Android Jones on Using VR for Spiritual Transformation & Unlocking Creative Flow."
14. "Journey Beyond the Mind: Samskara," 360Art, accessed March 25, 2018, http:// 360art.pro/product_samskara.html.

15. Bye, "Android Jones on Using VR for Spiritual Transformation and Unlocking the Creative Flow."

16. Buckley Rue, "Hacking the Droid: An Interview with Android Jones," *Compose Yourself Magazine*, February 19, 2017, http://composeyourselfmagazine.com /2017/02/hacking-droid-interview-android-jones/.

17. Ibid.

18. Bye, "Android Jones on Using VR for Spiritual Transformation and Unlocking the Creative Flow."

19. Jacob Aman, "Exploring the Flow State," interview with Android Jones and Anson Phong, *Future Primitive*, podcast, December 12, 2017, Golden Stupa Media, https://futureprimitive.org/2017/12/exploring-flow-state/.

20. Bye, "Android Jones on Using VR for Spiritual Transformation and Unlocking the Creative Flow."

21. Rue, "Hacking the Droid."

22. Ibid.

23. ASkillz82, comment on Reddit, "Interview with Evan Bluetech, a developer on Android Jones' 'Microdose VR' project, coming soon to Steam / HTC Vive," accessed June 3, 2018, https://www.reddit.com/r/Vive/comments/5rgslj/interview _with_evan_bluetech_a_developer_on/.

24. Sam Lawrence, "[Interview] Bluetech Is a Microdose of Everything Good," February 1, 2017, *Bullett Music*, http://www.bulletmusic.net/features-1/bluetech -interview-2017.

25. Ibid.

26. Aman, "Exploring the Flow State."

27. Ibid.

28. Ibid.

29. Ibid.

30. SoundSelf website, "About," accessed March 2020, https://www.soundself.com /about.

31. Robin Arnott, interview with Kate J. Stockly, July 26, 2019, and July 29, 2019.

32. Arnott, interview with Stockly, August 29, 2019.

33. The Bird of Hermes, "Tibetan Monk Simulator 2020," review on "Mind = Blown: Things People Are Saying About SoundSelf," SoundSelf, accessed November 29, 2020, https://www.soundself.com/testimonials.

34. u/jkobrinart, "A Virtual Reality Trip Report," comment in r/Vive subreddit, https:// www.reddit.com/r/Vive/comments/6j4nmr/a_virtual_reality_trip_report/.

35. Peter Hendricks, quoted in Stephen Cognetta, "We Talked with a Researcher Using Psilocybin to Treat Cocaine Addiction in Alabama," *Psymposia*, April 17, 2018, https://www.psymposia.com/magazine/we-talked-with-a-researcher-using -psilocybin-to-treat-cocaine-addiction-in-alabama/.

36. Alice Chirico, Francesco Ferrise, Lorenzo Cordella, and Andrea Gaggioli, "Designing Awe in Virtual Reality: An Experimental Study," *Frontiers in Psychology* 8 (2018), https://doi.org/10.3389/fpsyg.2017.02351.

37. Alice Chirico, David B. Yaden, Giuseppe Riva, and Andrea Gaggioli, "The Potential of Virtual Reality for the Investigation of Awe," *Frontiers in Psychology* 7 (2016), doi: 10.3389/fpsyg.2016.01766.

38. João Medeiros, "How Scientists Are Manipulating the Mind with VR," *Wired*, July 26, 2017, http://www.wired.co.uk/article/the-secrets-of-consciouness.

39. Ibid.

40. Ibid.

41. Bye, "Android Jones on Using VR for Spiritual Transformation & Unlocking Creative Flow."

42. Arnott, interview with Stockly, July 29, 2019.

43. Arnott, interview with Stockly, July 26, 2019.

44. For example, Limbix VR Library, "Programs for Mental Health, Exposure Therapy, Mindfulness, Pain Management, and More," https://www.limbix.com/vrlibrary. See also, Daniel Freeman, Polly Haselton, Jason Freeman, Bernhard Spanlang, Sameer Kishore, Emily Albery, Megan Denne, Poppy Brown, Mel Slater, and Alecia Nickless, "Automated Psychological Therapy Using Immersive Virtual Reality for Treatment of Fear of Heights: A Single-Blind, Parallel-Group, Randomised Controlled Trial," *The Lancet Psychiatry* 5, no. 8 (2018): 625–32, https://doi.org/10.1016/S2215-0366(18)30226-8; Lynsey Gregg and Nicholas Tarrier, "Virtual Reality in Mental Health: A Review of the Literature," *Social Psychiatry and Psychiatric Epidemiology* 42 (May 2007): 343–54, https://doi.org/10.1007/s00127-007-0173-4.

45. Center for Mind and Culture, "Virtual Reality for Nightmare Disorder," https://mindandculture.org/projects/engaging-virtual-environments/virtual-reality-for-nightmare-disorder/.

46. See, for example, the Virtual Reality Institute of Health and Exercise, https://vrhealth.institute/.

47. Hannah Ewens, "I Tried Out Pornhub's New Budget Virtual Reality Porn," *Vice*, March 24, 2016, https://www.vice.com/en_us/article/qbvaxm/i-reviewed-pornhubs-new-free-interactive-vr-porn; Stacy Liberatore, "'The Next Phase in Adult Entertainment': Pornhub Launches Interactive VR Porn That Works with Phones and Headsets," Mail Online, March 23, 2016, http://www.dailymail.co.uk/sciencetech/article-3507008/The-phase-adult-entertainment-Pornhub-launches-interactive-VR-service-works-phones-headsets.html.

48. Bye, "Android Jones on Using VR for Spiritual Transformation & Unlocking the Creative Flow."

49. Robin Arnott, "Designing a Trance: Meditation and Game Design," Independent Games Summit, Game Developers Conference, 2017, https://www.youtube.com/watch?v=zZ8BFsdbem0.

50. Alex Tisdale, "Gaming in Virtual Reality Could Be the Very Real Death of You," *Vice*, June 8, 2016, https://www.vice.com/en_us/article/4w5g7d/gaming-in -virtual-reality-could-be-the-very-real-death-of-you-911.

51. Craig A. Anderson, Akiko Shibuya, Nobuko Ihori, Edward L. Swing, Brad J. Bushman, Akira Sakamoto, Hannah R. Rothstein, and Muniba Saleem, "Violent Video Game Effects on Aggression, Empathy, and Prosocial Behavior in Eastern and Western Countries: A Meta-Analytic Review," *Psychological Bulletin* 136, no. 2 (March 2010): 151–73, https://doi.org/10.1037/a0018251; Christopher J. Fergu-son, "Evidence for Publication Bias in Video Game Violence Effects Literature: A Meta-Analytic Review," *Aggression and Violent Behavior* 12, no. 4 (July–Aug. 2007): 470–82, https://doi.org/10.1016/j.avb.2007.01.001; Christopher John Ferguson, "The Good, the Bad and the Ugly: A Meta-Analytic Review of Positive and Nega-tive Effects of Violent Video Games," *Psychiatric Quarterly* 78 (Dec. 2007): 309–16, https://doi.org/10.1007/s11126-007-9056-9; Christopher J. Ferguson and John Kilburn, "The Public Health Risks of Media Violence: A Meta-Analytic Review," *Journal of Pediatrics* (2009): 1–5, https://doi.org/10.1016/j.jpeds.2008.11.033.

52. Tisdale, "Gaming in Virtual Reality Could Be the Very Death of You"; see also Will Usher, "VR Gaming Could Cause Death, Says Dev," *CinemaBlend,* August 25, 2014, https://www.cinemablend.com/games/VR-Gaming-Could-Cause-Death -Says-Dev-66923.html.

53. For example, see Huw Oliver, "How Long Before We See Virtual Reality Head-sets in Our Mental Health Wards?" *Vice*, March 25, 2016, https://www.vice.com /en_us/article/3bj33y/virtual-reality-mental-health-treatment-uk.

54. Tobias van Schneider, "The Post Virtual Reality Sadness," *Medium*, Novem-ber 7, 2016, https://medium.com/desk-of-van-schneider/the-post-virtual-reality -sadness-fb4a1ccacae4#.1jpnl38v2.

55. OvertechB, comment on "VR Hangover?" in r/Oculus subreddit, https:// www.reddit.com/r/oculus/comments/4gz9ex/vr_hangover/d2m0whw?utm _source=share&utm_medium=web2x&context=3.

56. Joseph J. LaViola, "A Discussion of Cybersickness in Virtual Environments," *ACM SIGCHI Bulletin* 32, no. 1 (Jan. 2000): https://doi.org/10.1145/333329.333344.

57. Sam Machkovech, "How Side-Mounted LEDs Can Help Fix VR's 'Tunnel Vi-sion' and Nausea Problems," *ARS Technica*, May 9, 2016, https://arstechnica.com /gaming/2016/05/how-side-mounted-leds-can-help-fix-vrs-tunnel-vision-and -nausea-problems/.

58. Van Schneider, "The Post-Virtual Reality Sadness."

59. Bye, "Android Jones on Using VR for Spiritual Transformation & Unlocking the Creative Flow."

60. Rue, "Hacking the Droid."

61. Bye, "Android Jones on Using VR for Spiritual Transformation and Unlocking the Creative Flow."

62. Arnott, interview with Stockly, July 26, 2019.

63. Ibid.

64. Soto, interview with Stockly, May 1, 2018.

65. Ibid.

66. Ibid.

67. Ibid.

68. Ibid.

69. Terence McKenna, "Touched by the Tremendum," talk given at the Reality Club, March 24, 1990, https://www.edge.org/conversation/terence_mckenna-touched -by-the-tremendum-march-27-1990.

6: CLEANSING THE DOORS OF PERCEPTION

1. Ted, interview with Kate J. Stockly, June 22, 2017.

2. Jonathan Ott, "Pharmahuasca: Human Pharmacology of Oral DMT Plus Harmine," *Journal of Psychoactive Drugs* 31, no. 2 (1999): 171–77, https://doi.org /10.1080/02791072.1999.10471741.

3. For a more in-depth look at how neurons communicate with each other and an in-troduction to neuropharmacology, see Eric J. Nestler, Steven E. Hyman, David M. Holtzman, and Robert C. Malenka, *Molecular Neuropharmacology: A Foundation for Clinical Neuroscience*, 3rd ed. (New York: McGraw Hill Education, 2015).

4. Jessica E. Malberg and Katherine R. Bonson, "How MDMA Works in the Brain," in *Ecstasy: The Complete Guide: A Comprehensive Look at the Risks and Benefits of MDMA*, ed. Julie Holland (Rochester, VT: Park Street Press, 2001), 29–38.

5. For example, see Ana Margarida Araújo, Félix Carvalho, Maria de Lourdes Bas-tos, Paula Guedes de Pinho, and Márcia Carvalho, "The Hallucinogenic World of Tryptamines: An Updated Review," *Archives of Toxicology* 89, no. 8 (2015): 1151–73, https://doi.org/10.1007/s00204-015-1513-x; Adam L. Halberstadt, "Re-cent Advances in the Neuropsychopharmacology of Serotonergic Hallucinogens," *Behavioural Brain Research* 277 (Jan. 2015): 99–120, https://doi.org/10.1016/j.bbr .2014.07.016; and James L. Kent, "Psychedelic Pharmacology," in *Psychedelic Infor-mation Theory: Shamanism in the Age of Reason* (Seattle: PIT Press, 2010), 57–66.

6. Paola Zarantonello, Ezio Bettini, Alfredo Paio, Chiara Simoncelli, Silvia Terreni, and Francesco Cardullo, "Novel Analogues of Ketamine and Phencyclidine as NMDA Receptor Antagonists," *Bioorganic & Medicinal Chemistry Letters* 21, no. 7 (April 2011): 2059–63, https://doi.org/10.1016/j.bmcl.2011.02.009; see also Philip Seeman, Hong-Chang Guan, and Hélène Hirbec, "Dopamine D2 High Receptors Stimulated by Phencyclidines, Lysergic Acid Diethylamide, Salvinorin A, and Modaf-inil," *Synapse* 63, no. 8 (Aug. 2009): 698–704, https://doi.org/10.1002/syn.20647.

7. Jordi Riba, Marta Valle, Gloria Urbano, Mercedes Yritia, Adelaide Morte, and Manel J. Barbanoj, "Human Pharmacology of Ayahuasca: Subjective and

Cardiovascular Effects, Monoamine Metabolite Excretion, and Pharmacokinetics," *Journal of Pharmacology and Experimental Therapeutics* 306, no. 1 (2003): 73–83, https://doi.org/10.1124/jpet.103.049882.

8. For example, see Jacqueline Borg, Bengt Andrée, Henrik Soderstrom, and Lars Farde, "The Serotonin System and Spiritual Experiences," *American Journal of Psychiatry* 160, no. 11, (Nov. 2003): 1965–69, https://doi.org/10.1176/appi.ajp .160.11.1965.

9. Albert Hofmann, *LSD: My Problem Child*, trans. by Jonathan Ott (New York: McGraw-Hill, 1980), https://maps.org/images/pdf/books/lsdmyproblemchild.pdf.

10. Ibid.

11. For example, see Walter N. Pahnke, "LSD and Religious Experience," in *LSD, Man, and Society*, ed. Richard C. DeBold and Russell C. Leaf (Middletown, CT: Wesleyan University Press, 1967), 60–85. Chapter available online: http://www .psychedelic-library.org/pahnke3.htm.

12. Maggie, interview with Kate J. Stockly, June 26, 2017.

13. Zendo Project, accessed October 31, 2017, www.zendoproject.org/about/.

14. For an excellent description of how drugs of abuse function in the brain to produce addiction and dependence, see Thomas R. Kosten and Tony P. George, "The Neurobiology of Opioid Dependence: Implications for Treatment," *Science and Practice Perspectives* 1, no. 1 (Aug. 2002): 13–20, https://doi.org/10.1151 /spp021113.

15. Patricia E. Sharp, "Meditation-Induced Bliss Viewed as Release from Conditioned Neural (Thought) Patterns That Block Reward Signals in the Brain Pleasure Center," *Religion, Brain & Behavior* 4, no. 3 (2014): 202–29, https://doi.org /10.1080/2153599X.2013.826717.

16. Saibal Das, Preeti Barnwal, Anand Ramassay, Sumalya Sen, and Somnath Mondal, "Lysergic Acid Diethylamide: A Drug of 'Use'?" *Therapeutic Advances in Psychopharmacology* 6, no. 3 (2016): 214–28, https://doi.org/10.1177/2045125316640440.

17. Erich Studerus, Michael Kometer, Felix Hasler, and Franz X. Vollenweider, "Acute, Subacute and Long-Term Subjective Effects of Psilocybin in Healthy Humans: A Pooled Analysis of Experimental Studies," *Journal of Psychopharmacology* 25, no. 11 (Nov. 2011): 1424–52, https://doi.org/10.1177/0269881110382466.

18. Liesbeth Reneman, Jan Booij, Kora de Bruin, Johannes B. Reitsma, Frederik A. de Wolff, W. Boudewijn Gunning, Gerard J. den Heeten, and Wim van den Brink, "Effects of Dose, Sex, and Long-Term Abstention from Use on Toxic Effects of MDMA (Ecstasy) on Brain Serotonin Neurons," *The Lancet* 358, no. 9296 (2001): 1864–69; https://doi.org/10.1016/S0140-6736(01)06888-X; Felix Müller, Raphael Brändle, Matthias E. Liechti, and Stefan Borgwardt, "Neuroimaging of Chronic MDMA ('Ecstasy') Effects: A Meta-Analysis," *Neuroscience & Biobehavioral Reviews* 96 (Jan. 2019): 10–20, https://doi.org/10.1016/j.neubiorev.2018.11 .004.

19. Danuta Marona-Lewicka, Charles D. Nichols, and David E. Nichols, "An Animal Model of Schizophrenia Based on Chronic LSD Administration: Old Idea, New Results," *Neuropharmacology* 61, no. 3 (Sept. 2011): 503–12, https://doi.org/10.1016/j.neuropharm.2011.02.006.

20. Albert Hofmann quoted in Tom Shroder, *Acid Test: LSD, Ecstasy, and the Power to Heal* (New York: Plume, 2014), 11.

21. William Richards, interview with Kate J. Stockly, September 29, 2016.

22. More specifically, 13 mg of CZ-74 (4-hydroxy-N,N-dimethyltryptamine). William A. Richards, *Sacred Knowledge: Psychedelics and Religious Experience* (New York: Columbia University Press, 2016), 30.

23. Ibid., xix.

24. Ibid.

25. Ibid., xx.

26. Ibid., 30.

27. Richards, interview with Stockly.

28. Ibid.

29. Richards, *Sacred Knowledge*, 167–68.

30. Richards, interview with Stockly.

31. Richards, *Sacred Knowledge*, 28.

32. NYU School of Medicine, "NYU School of Medicine Researchers Seek Religious Leaders for Study" (New York: NYU School of Medicine, 2016), https://maps.org/other-psychedelic-research/211-psilocybin-research/psilocybin-studies-in-progress/6695-nyu-school-of-medicine-researchers-seek-religious-leaders-for-study.

33. Richards, interview with Stockly.

34. Ibid.

35. Ibid.

36. Ibid.

37. Ibid.

38. Ibid.

39. Ibid.

40. Rick Doblin, "From the Desk of Rick Doblin, PhD," *MAPS Bulletin: Research Edition* 26, no. 2 (Summer 2016): 1–2, https://maps.org/news/bulletin/articles/409-bulletin-summer-2016/6297-from-the-desk-of-rick-doblin-summer-2016.

41. William Richards, "The Rebirth of Research with Entheogens: Lessons from the Past and Hypotheses for the Future," *Journal of Transpersonal Psychology* 41, no. 2 (2009): 139–50. See also: R. R. Griffiths, W. A. Richards, M. W. Johnson, U. D. McCann, and R. Jesse, "Mystical-Type Experiences Occasioned by Psilocybin Mediate the Attribution of Personal Meaning and Spiritual Significance 14 Months Later," *Journal of Psychopharmacology* 22, no. 6 (2008): 621–32, https://doi.org/10.1177/0269881108094300.

42. Richards, "The Rebirth of Research with Entheogens," 147.

43. Ibid., 3.

44. Richards, interview with Stockly.

45. Roland R. Griffiths, Matthew W. Johnson, William A. Richards, Brian D. Richards, Una McCann, and Robert Jesse, "Psilocybin Occasioned Mystical-Type Experiences: Immediate and Persisting Dose-Related Effects," *Psychopharmacology* 218, no. 4 (2011): 649–65, https://doi.org/10.1007/s00213-011-2358-5.

46. Carl G. Jung, *Psyche and Symbol: A Selection from the Writing of C. G. Jung*, ed. Violet Staub De Laszlo, trans. by R. F. C. Hull (Princeton, NJ: Princeton University Press, 1991), 340.

47. Richards, *Sacred Knowledge*, 80.

48. Ibid.

49. Ibid.

50. Griffiths et al., "Psilocybin Occasioned Mystical-Type Experiences."

51. Roland R. Griffiths, "The Johns Hopkins Psilocybin Research Project: Overview, Phenomenology, and Therapeutic Applications," Conference Presentation, Horizons: Perspectives on Psychedelics, New York, October 8, 2016.

52. For one example, see Katherine A. MacLean, Matthew W. Johnson, and Roland R. Griffiths, "Mystical Experiences Occasioned by the Hallucinogen Psilocybin Lead to Increases in the Personality Domain of Openness," *Journal of Psychopharmacology* 25, no. 11 (2011): 1453–61, https://doi.org/10.1177/0269881111420188.

53. Griffiths, "The Johns Hopkins Psilocybin Research Project."

54. Ibid.

55. Robert Jesse, "Psychedelics: The Uncertain Paths from Re-emergence to Renaissance," Conference Presentation, Horizons: Perspectives on Psychedelics, New York, October 9, 2016.

56. Richards, interview with Stockly.

57. Current indications point to legalization in 2021. See Allison A. Feduccia, Lisa Jerome, Berra Yazar-Klosinski, Amy Emerson, Michael C. Mithoefer, and Rick Doblin, "Breakthrough for Trauma Treatment: Safety and Efficacy of MDMA-Assisted Psychotherapy Compared to Paroxetine and Sertraline," *Frontiers in Psychiatry* 10 (2019), https://doi.org/10.3389/fpsyt.2019.00650.

58. See for example, Rick Doblin, "The Future of Psychedelic-Assisted Psychotherapy, TED2019, April 2019, https://www.ted.com/talks/rick_doblin_the_future_of_psychedelic_assisted_psychotherapy/transcript.

7: SPIRIT PLANTS AND THEIR HIGH-TECH REPLACEMENTS

1. Matt Toussaint, interview with Kate J. Stockly, December 16, 2016.

2. Ariel Levy, "The Drug of Choice for the Age of Kale," *New Yorker*, September 5,

2016, https://www.newyorker.com/magazine/2016/09/12/the-ayahuasca-boom-in-the-u-s.

3. Ibid. See also Biz Carson, "This Silicon Valley Angel Investor Loves a Drug That Gave Him Hours of Seizures," *Business Insider India*, September 8, 2016, https://www.businessinsider.in/This-Silicon-Valley-angel-investor-loves-a-drug-that-gave-him-hours-of-seizures/articleshow/54201335.cms.

4. Toussaint, interview with Stockly.

5. Barbara Fraser, "How Ayahuasca Tourism Jeopardizes Traditional Medicine," *Atlantic*, August 4, 2017, https://www.theatlantic.com/science/archive/2017/08/the-perils-and-privileges-of-an-amazonian-hallucinogen/535896/; see also Evgenia Fotiou, "On the Uneasiness of Tourism: Considerations on Shamanic Tourism in Western Amazonia," in *Ayahuasca Shamanism in the Amazon and Beyond*, ed. Beatriz Caiuby Labate and Clancy Cavnar (New York: Oxford University Press, 2014).

6. Toussaint, interview with Stockly.

7. Kira Salak, "Hell and Back," first published in *National Geographic Adventure*, anthologized in *The New Age of Adventure: Ten Years of Great Writing*, ed. John Rasmus (Washington, DC: National Geographic Society, 2009); a modified version can be found at http://www.kirasalak.com/Peru.html.

8. Ibid.

9. Ibid.

10. Toussaint, interview with Stockly.

11. Ibid.

12. David Hill, "Peru's Ayahuasca Industry Booms as Westerners Search for Alternative Healing," *Guardian*, June 7, 2016, https://www.theguardian.com/travel/2016/jun/07/peru-ayahuasca-drink-boom-amazon-spirituality-healing.

13. Hill, "Peru's Ayahuasca Industry."

14. Omar Gomez, quoted in Hill, "Peru's Ayahuasca Industry."

15. Toussaint, interview with Stockly.

16. Toussaint, interview with Stockly.

17. Beatriz Caiuby Labate and Gustavo Pacheco, *Opening the Portals of Heaven: Brazilian Ayahuasca Music*, trans. by Matthew Meyer (Berlin: LIT Verlag, 2010), 20.

18. Ibid.

19. Joseph D. Calabrese, "The Therapeutic Use of Peyote in the Native American Church," in *Seeking the Sacred with Psychoactive Substances: Chemical Paths to Spirituality and to God*, vol. 2: *Insights, Arguments, and Controversies*, ed. J. Harold Ellens (Santa Barbara, CA: Praeger, 2014), 57; see also Jan G. Bruhn, Peter De Smet, Hesham R. El-Seedi, and Olof Beck, "Mescaline Use for 5700 Years," *The Lancet* 359 (2002): 1866, https://doi.org/10.1016/S0140-6736(02)08701-9.

20. In addition to a federal law passed in 1994 (American Indian Religious Freedom Act, AIRFA), which protects peyote use for members of federally recognized

Indian tribes (but leaves non-Indian people subject to prosecution), many states have adopted laws granting protections for *any* members of the Native American Church regardless of their heritage, and still other states allow use within "bona fide religious ceremonies" without explicitly requiring them to be members of an organization and without explicitly naming the Native American Church as the site for legal rituals. See Omer C. Stewart, *Peyote Religion: A History* (Norman: University of Oklahoma Press, 1987), 3; for "sacramental medicine," see Calabrese, "The Therapeutic Use of Peyote," 57; John P. Forren, "State and Federal Legal Protections for Peyote Use in the United States," in *Peyote: History, Tradition, Politics, and Conservation*, ed. Beatriz Caiuby Labate and Clancy Cavnar (Santa Barbara, CA: Praeger, 2016), 101.

21. Jay Fikes, "A Brief History of the Native American Church," in *One Nation Under God: The Triumph of the Native American Church*, ed. Huston Smith and Reuben Snake (Santa Fe, NM: Clear Light, 1996). Quoted in Stewart, *Peyote Religion*, 157.

22. Lack of a writing system makes it difficult to know what ancient spiritual meanings were associated with San Pedro ingestion. Nevertheless, anthropologists infer from the content of images of San Pedro an association with certain powerful, mysterious, or mythological animals—"jaguars or deer, mythological beings like fanged-serpents (boas) or jaguars with eye-spots"—or with "propitiation of the ancestors, communion with the realm of the dead, abundant water, and agricultural fertility"; see Bonnie Glass-Coffin, "Shamanism and San Pedro through Time: Some Notes on the Archaeology, History, and Continued Use of an Entheogen in Northern Peru," *Anthropology of Consciousness* 21, no. 1 (March 2010): 58–82, https://doi.org/10.1111/j.1556-3537.2010.01021.x. See also Douglas Sharon, *Shamanism and the Sacred Cactus* (San Diego: San Diego Museum Papers 37, 2000), 6.

23. While San Pedro is not explicitly mentioned in US drug laws in the way that peyote is, its primary psychoactive alkaloid is the same as peyote's: mescaline, a Schedule I substance. Therefore, *owning* a San Pedro cactus (with no intention to ingest mescaline) is a legal gray area, but *ingesting* it is certainly illegal.

24. Beatriz Caiuby Labate, Clancy Cavnar, and Alex K. Gearin, "Introduction: The Shifting Journey of Ayahuasca in Diaspora," in *The World Ayahuasca Diaspora: Reinventions and Controversies*, ed. Beatriz Caiuby Labate, Clancy Cavnar, and Alex K. Gearin, trans. by Matthew Meyer (New York: Routledge, 2017), 1–16.

25. Labate and Pacheco, *Opening the Portals of Heaven*, 52.

26. Centro Espírita Beneficente União do Vegetal in the United States, udvusa.org.

27. Labate and Pacheco, *Opening the Portals of Heaven*, 54–55.

28. John Burnett, "Controversy Brews over Church's Hallucinogenic Tea Ritual," *NPR All Things Considered*, April 23, 2013, https://www.npr.org/2013/04/25/177315132/controversy-brews-over-churchs-hallucinogenic-tea-ritual.

29. Ibid.

30. Ibid., 35.

31. Cefluris. Santo Daime. Normas de Ritual. Cefluris, 1997. Quoted in Labate and Pacheco, 33.

32. Rosa Virgínia Melo, "Between Ecstasy and Reason: A Symbolic Interpretation of UDV Trance," in *The World Ayahuasca Diaspora*, ed. Labate, Cavnar, and Gearin, 44.

33. Ibid., 45.

34. On the new middle class attracted to the various modalities of the ayahuasca diaspora, see also Andrew Dawson, "If Tradition Did Not Exist, It Would Have to Be Invented: Retraditionalization and the World Ayahuasca Diaspora," ibid., 19–37.

35. Beatriz Caiuby Labate and Glauber Loures de Assis, "The Religion of the Forest: Reflections on the International Expansion of a Brazilian Ayahuasca Religion," ibid., 56–76.

36. Ibid., 61.

37. Ibid., 64.

38. Fraser, "How Ayahuasca Tourism Jeopardizes Traditional Medicine," 5. For the list of diet restrictions required by the Rainforest Healing Center, see "Ayahuasca Diet & Prep," Rainforest Healing Center, accessed August 1, 2017, https://rainforesthealingcenter.com/ayahuasca/ayahuasca-diet-and-preparations/.

39. Beatriz Caiuby Labate, "The Internalization of Peruvian Vegetalismo," in *Ayahuasca Shamanism in the Amazon and Beyond*, ed. Labate and Cavnar, 187.

40. Ibid., 186.

41. Ibid.

42. Labate also notes the controversial aspects of cultural appropriation, marginalization, the clear issues having to do with colonialism, and the potential backlashes against traditional communities that arise within the ayahuasca tourism industry. She simply means to say that it's not all one big illegitimate cultural appropriation. The question, she said, is how do we define the lines? Where does something start that is legitimate and where does it end? How do we draw these lines of tradition? How do we say who is entitled and who has the prerogative and who owns what? The entire history of ayahuasca is mixed and complex and hybrid—there has never been a single evolutionary path from a very pure indigenous form to a mix of urban expats. Rather, the colonial influences and mixtures and exchanges of elements from various ethnicities have always been a part of the story of ayahuasca.

43. Glenn H. Shepard Jr., "Foreword: Ayahuasca in the Twenty-First Century: Having It Both Ways," in *The World Ayahuasca Diaspora*, ed. Labate, Cavnar, and Gearin, xv.

44. Beatriz Caiuby Labate, Clancy Cavnar, and Françoise Barbira Freedman, "Notes on the Expansion and Reinvention of Ayahuasca Shamanism," in *Ayahuasca Shamanism in the Amazon and Beyond*, ed. Labate and Cavnar, 3–15.

45. Beatriz Caiuby Labate, interview with Kate J. Stockly, October 6, 2016.

46. For example, see also Bernd Brabec de Mori, "Tracing Hallucinations: Contrib-uting to a Critical Ethnohistory of Ayahuasca Usage in the Peruvian Amazon," in *The Internationalization of Ayahuasca*, ed. Beatriz Caiuby Labate and Henrik Jungaberle (Zürich: LIT Verlag, 2011), 23–48.

47. Jonathan Ott, "Pharmahuasca: Human Pharmacology of Oral DMT Plus Harmine," *Journal of Psychoactive Drugs* 31, no. 2 (1999): 171–77, https://doi.org/10.1080/02791072.1999.10471741.

48. Jonathan Ott, "Applied Psychonautics: Ayahuasca to Pharmahuasca to Ana-huasca," *Journal of Psychonautics,* 2001, https://psychonauticsjournal.tumblr.com/post/2370946009/applied-psychonautics-ayahuasca-to-pharmahuasca.

49. Xavier Francuski, "Pharmahuasca: Can a Chemical Ayahuasca Alternative Compare?" Kahpi: The Ayahuasca Hub, October 14, 2019, http://kahpi.net/pharmahuasca/.

50. J. C. Callaway, D. J. McKenna, C. S. Grob, G. S. Brito, L. P. Raymon, R. E. Po-land, E. N. Andrade, E. O. Andrade, and D. C. Mash, "Pharmacokinetics of *Hoasca* Alkaloids in Healthy Humans," *Journal of Ethnopharmacology* 65, no. 3 (June 1999): 243–56, https://doi.org/10.1016/S0378-8741(98)00168-8.

51. Francuski, "Pharmahuasca."

52. Avery Sapoznikow, Zachary Walsh, Kenneth W. Tupper, Earth Erowid, and Fire Erowid, "The Influence of Context on Ayahuasca Experiences: An Analysis of Experience Reports," *Journal of Psychedelic Studies* 3, no. 3 (Sept. 2019): 288–94, https://doi.org/10.1556/2054.2019.028.

53. Francuski, "Pharmahuasca."

54. Ibid.

55. Sapoznikow et al., "The Influence of Context on Ayahuasca Experiences," 292.

56. Ibid., 292; Piera Talin and Emilia Sanabria, "Ayahuasca's Entwined Efficacy: An Ethnographic Study of Ritual Healing from 'Addiction,'" *International Journal of Drug Policy* 44 (June 2017): 23–30, https://doi.org/10.1016/j.drugpo.2017.02.017; Rafael Faria Sanches, Flávia de Lima Osório, Rafael G. dos Santos, Ligia. R. H. Macedo, João Paulo Maia-de-Oliveira, Lauro Wichert-Ana, Draulio Barros de Araujo, Jordi Riba, José Alexandre S. Crippa, and Jaime E. C. Hallak, "Anti-depressant Effects of a Single Dose of Ayahuasca in Patients with Recurrent Depression: A SPECT Study," *Journal of Clinical Psychopharmacology* 36, no. 1 (Feb. 2016): 77–81, https://doi.org/10.1097/JCP.0000000000000436; Fernanda Palhano-Fontes, Dayanna Barreto, Heloisa Onias, Katia C. Andrad, Morgana M. Novaes, Jessica A. Pessoa, Sergio A. Mota-Rolim, Flávia L. Osório, Rafael Sanches, Rafael G. dos Santos, Luís Fernando Tófoli, Gabriela de Oliveira Silveira, Mauri-cio Yonamine, Jordi Riba, Francisco R. Santos, Antonio A. Silva-Junior, João C. Alchieri, Nicole L. Galvão-Coelho, Bruno Lobão-Soares, Jaime E. C. Hallak, Emerson Arcoverde, João P. Maia-de-Oliveira, and Dráulio B. Araújo, "Rapid

Antidepressant Effects of the Psychedelic Ayahuasca in Treatment-Resistant Depression: A Randomized Placebo-Controlled Trial," *Psychological Medicine* 49, no. 4 (March 2019): 655–63, https://doi.org/10.1017/S0033291718001356.

57. Jonathan Ott, *Pharmacotheon: Entheogenic Drugs, Their Plant Sources and History* (Kennewick, WA: Natural Products, 1993), 18.

58. Calabrese, "The Therapeutic Use of Peyote," 58–59.

59. John H. Halpern, Andrea R. Sherwood, James I. Hudson, Deborah Yurgelun-Todd, and Harrison G. Pope Jr., "Psychological and Cognitive Effects of Long-Term Peyote Use among Native Americans," *Biological Psychiatry* 58, no. 8 (Oct. 2005): 624–31, https://doi.org/10.1016/j.biopsych.2005.06.038.

60. José Carlos Bouso, Fernanda Palhano-Fontes, Antoni Rodríguez-Fornells, Sidarta Ribeiro, Rafael Sanches, José Alexandre S. Crippa, Jaime E. C. Hallak, Draulio B. de Araujo, and Jordi Riba, "Long-Term Use of Psychedelic Drugs Is Associated with Differences in Brain Structure and Personality in Humans," *European Neuropsychopharmacology* 25, no. 4 (April 2015): 483–92, https://doi.org/10.1016/j.euroneuro.2015.01.008.

61. Ibid.

62. Labate, interview with Stockly.

63. For descriptions of the preparation and ceremonial rituals, see Omer C. Stewart, "Peyote Eaters and Their Ceremonies," in *Peyote Religion*, 17–42.

64. On the importance of set, setting, and discipline for Santo Daime ayahuasca rituals, see G. William Barnard, "Entheogens in a Religious Context: The Case of the Santo Daime Religious Tradition," *Zygon* 49, no. 3 (Sept. 2014): 666–84, https://doi.org/10.1111/zygo.12109.

65. "Lamas, Peru: French Tourist Dies from Consuming Ayahuasca Herb," *Latin America Current Events & News*, August 10, 2011, http://latinamericacurrentevents.com/lamas-peru-french-tourist-dies-from-consuming-ayahuasca-herb/11114/. See also Kelly Hearn, "The Dark Side of Ayahuasca," *Men's Journal*, February 15, 2013, https://www.mensjournal.com/features/the-dark-side-of-ayahuasca-20130215/.

66. Lucy Westcott, "'I Really Thought I Was Going to Die': Canadian Man Speaks About Killing at Ayahuasca Retreat," *Newsweek,* January 13, 2016, https://www.newsweek.com/ayahuasca-killing-peru-canada-415293; Jillian Taylor, "Winnipegger Freed after Fatal Stabbing of British Man during Peru Drug Ceremony," *CBC News*, December 18, 2015, https://www.cbc.ca/news/canada/manitoba/winnipegger-freed-after-fatal-stabbing-of-british-man-during-peru-drug-ceremony-1.3371245.

67. Hearn, "The Dark Side of Ayahuasca."

68. Pulse Tours, "Travel Safety," https://www.pulsetours.com/safety/.

69. Barbara Fraser and Sapiens, "How Ayahuasca Tourism Jeopardizes Traditional Medicine," *Atlantic*, August 4, 2017, https://www.theatlantic.com/science

/archive/2017/08/the-perils-and-privileges-of-an-amazonian-hallucinogen
/535896/.

70. Joseph Wickerham, quoted in Max Opray, "Tourist Boom for Ayahuasca a Mixed Blessing for Amazon," *Guardian*, January 24, 2017, https://www.theguardian.com/sustainable-business/2017/jan/24/tourist-boom-peru-ayahuasca-drink-amazon-spirituality-healing.

71. Ibid. See also Hearn, "The Dark Side of Ayahuasca"; "Public Statement to the Ayahuasca Community," Ayahuasca.com, September 28, 2012, http://www.ayahuasca.com/news/public-statement-to-the-ayahuasca-community/.

8: A NEW HORIZON IN SPIRITUAL DIRECTION

1. Devon White, interview with Kate J. Stockly, May 15, 2018.

2. Ibid.

3. Ibid.

4. John Dupuy, "Field: Pushing the Boundaries of Neuro-Enhanced Wellness," Spiritual Technologies 2.0, March 2, 2018, accessed June 8, 2018, https://www.youtube.com/watch?v=3cMzM04yA-c&t=1524s.

5. Leah Prinzivalli, "NYC's Hottest Club Is Selling 'Designer Brains,'" *New Beauty*, April 20, 2018, accessed April 25, 2020, https://www.newbeauty.com/field-brain-optimization/; see also "Ready for Unparalleled Transformation?" Field, accessed June 8, 2018, https://www.experiencethefield.com/retreats.

6. Field, "Start with You," accessed May 31, 2018, https://www.experiencethefield.com/.

7. "What Is Photobiomodulation," VieLight, accessed June 2, 2018, https://vielight.com/photobiomodulation/.

8. Dupuy, "Field: Pushing the Boundaries of Neuro-Enhanced Wellness."

9. White, interview with Stockly.

10. Ibid.

11. Ibid.

12. Ibid.

13. Ibid.

14. Ibid.

15. Ibid.

16. Ibid.

17. James Keegan, SJ, on behalf of the 2005 Coordinating Council of Spiritual Directors International, as quoted on Holding the Sacred, accessed November 2020, http://www.holdingthesacred.com/.

18. Marian Cowan, CSJ, as quoted in "What Is Spiritual Accompaniment or Spiritual Direction?" On the Third Day Renewal and Formation Center, accessed November 2020, https://www.spiritualformation.center/spiritual-direction/.

19. Karin J. Miles, quoted in "Do I Need a Spiritual Companion? Spiritual Companionship across Traditions: Buddhist Spiritual Companionship," Spiritual Directors International, accessed November 2020, https://www.sdicompanions.org/do-i-need-a-spiritual-companion.

20. Laura E. Captari, Joshua N. Hook, William Hoyt, Don E. Davis, Stacey E. McElroy-Heltzel, and Everett L. Worthington Jr., "Integrating Clients' Religion and Spirituality Within Psychotherapy: A Comprehensive Meta-Analysis," *Journal of Clinical Psychology* 74, no. 11 (Sept. 2018): 1938–51, https://doi.org/10.1002/jclp.22681; Thomas G. Plante, "Principles of Incorporating Spirituality into Professional Clinical Practice," *Practice Innovations* 1, no. 4 (2016): 276–81, https://doi.org/10.1037/pri0000030; Craig S. Cashwell and J. Scott Young, eds., *Integrating Spirituality and Religion into Counseling: A Guide to Competent Practice*, 2nd ed. (Alexandria, VA: American Counseling Association, 2011).

21. "Therapy Training," MAPS Public Benefit Corporation, accessed November 2020, https://mapspublicbenefit.com/training/; see also the website for the California Institute of Integral Studies, which has several degree programs that integrate spirituality in a variety of ways: http://www.ciis.edu/.

22. Sara Gael, "Services," Sara Gael: Soul-Centered Counseling, accessed May 11, 2018, http://www.re-membering.com/about.html.

23. White, interview with Stockly.

24. "About," Loving AI, retrieved April 5, 2020, lovingai.org/#about.

25. Ibid.

26. The quotes from this section are from "Not Just a Robot—I Am Sophia," https://www.youtube.com/watch?v=AEpiOrFoNtI.

27. "Meet Sophia, World's First AI Humanoid Robot | Tony Robbins," January 16, 2020, https://www.youtube.com/watch?v=Sq36J9pNaEo.

28. See the Enigmatic Wisdom of Deepak Chopra, http://www.wisdomofchopra.com/, for the quote generator and the *Skeptic Canary* (blog), http://www.skepticcanary.com/, for information about Tom Williamson. For details on the test to see if people could correctly guess whether a quote is authentic Chopra wisdom, see http://www.wisdomofchopra.com/quiz.php.

29. Harold G. Koenig, Elizabeth G. Hooten, Erin Lindsay-Calkins, and Keith G. Meador, "Spirituality in Medical School Curricula: Findings from a National Survey," *International Journal of Psychiatry in Medicine* 40, no. 4 (2010): 391–98, https://doi.org/10.2190/PM.40.4.c.

30. Rina Raphael, "These 10 Market Trends Turned Wellness into a $4.2 Trillion Global Industry," *Fast Company*, October 8, 2018, retrieved April 23, 2020, https://www.fastcompany.com/90247896/these-10-market-trends-turned-wellness-into-a-4–2-trillion-global-industry.

9: IS SPIRIT TECH AUTHENTIC?

1. "Mission," Science & Nonduality, https://www.scienceandnonduality.com/mission.
2. "Nonduality," Science & Nonduality, accessed June 16, 2019, https://www .scienceandnonduality.com/nonduality.
3. Lucia N°03 promotional poster displayed at the Science and Nonduality Conference in San Jose, California, October 18, 2018.
4. Ibid.
5. Ibid.
6. "Federico Faggin, Award Recipient," *IEEE Computer Society*, https://www .computer.org/profiles/federico-faggin.
7. See Vincent's website: https://www.vincehorn.space/.
8. Carole Griggs, https://drcarolegriggs.com, https://drcarolegriggs.com/about -iconscious.
9. Federico Faggin, in "Soul Tech: An Unpanel Discussion with Mikey Siegel," *Science and Nonduality*, October 28, 2018.
10. Ibid.
11. Audience member 1 at "Soul Tech: An Unpanel Discussion with Mikey Siegel," *Science and Nonduality*, October 28, 2018.
12. Audience member 2 at "Soul Tech: An Unpanel Discussion with Mikey Siegel," *Science and Nonduality*, October 28, 2018.
13. Audience member 3 at "Soul Tech: An Unpanel Discussion with Mikey Siegel," *Science and Nonduality*, October 28, 2018.
14. Ibid.
15. Naykid, comment on "Topic: Shakti Helmet?" Astral Pulse forum, January 26, 2011, http://www.astralpulse.com/forums/welcome_to_astral_consciousness/shakti _helmet-t32980.0.html;msg272025.
16. For a classic example of the transcend-the-group-criterion—from 1799—see Friedrich Schleiermacher, *On Religion: Speeches to Its Cultured Despisers*, trans. by John Oman (New York: Harper and Row, 1958).
17. Ancient and contemporary supernaturalist religious traditions, both theistic and nontheistic, and also ancient and contemporary nonsupernaturalist spiritual traditions, affirm the contrast between conventional and spiritual reality. This implies that these two dimensions or levels of reality are interpreted very differently, obviously. But that's actually helpful because it allows the categories of conventional reality and spirituality to work across a variety of worldviews. Given this flexibility, it makes sense to regard the conventional-spiritual contrast as defining the "real thing": spiritual experiences engage us with spiritual reality in and through conventional reality.
18. If you are a Buddhist, you would probably invoke the Noble Eightfold Path as a source of consequential criteria. If you are a Christian, you would probably invoke the Fruit of the Holy Spirit. If you are a humanist, you would probably invoke

criteria related to human well-being and social justice. Interestingly enough, while there are significant variations in consequentialist criteria across traditions, cultures, and eras, there seems to be a fair degree of convergence. For a classic example of consequential criteria based on effects, see Jonathan Edwards, *Religious Affections*, ed. John E. Smith (New Haven, CT: Yale University Press, [1746] 1959). For a more contemporary example, see Patrick McNamara's theory of religious experience as contributing to the formation of an ideal self: Patrick McNamara, *The Neuroscience of Religious Experience* (New York: Cambridge University Press, 2009).

10: IS SPIRIT TECH HEALTHY?

1. Elizabeth Segran, "What Really Happens to Your Brain and Body During a Digital Detox," *Fast Company*, July 30, 2015, accessed June 25, 2019, https://www.fastcompany.com/3049138/what-really-happens-to-your-brain-and-body-during-a-digital-detox.

2. David Jaffee, "Get Your Head Out of Your Apps," *Inside Higher Ed*, May 22, 2015, accessed June 26, 2019, https://www.insidehighered.com/views/2015/05/22/professors-lament-about-students-and-their-cell-phones-essay.

3. Zander Ford, "Mikey Siegel—Consciousness Hacking and Group Flow," *Conscious Founders*, podcast, May 28, 2018, http://consciousfounders.org/podcast/2018/5/28/mikey-seigel.

4. Mark, interview with Kate J. Stockly, July 26, 2019.

5. Ibid.

6. Ibid.

7. Nichol Bradford, "Modern Age Awakening: The Future of Consciousness, Well-Being, and Technology," Mindvalley A-Fest 2017, https://www.youtube.com/watch?v=MThItWtLSBA.

8. Ibid.

9. Garry Kasparov, "Don't Fear Intelligent Machines. Work with Them," TED2017, April 2017, https://www.ted.com/talks/garry_kasparov_don_t_fear_intelligent_machines_work_with_them#t-938870.

10. Jeffery A. Martin, *The Finders* (Jackson, WY: Integration Press, 2019), 6.

11. Ibid., 7.

12. Bradford, "Modern Age Awakening." See also "About A-Fest," *Mind Valley*, https://www.afest.com/?_ga=2.266756493.2084853230.1606272155-1315001874.1606272155.

13. Martin, *The Finders*, 195.

14. The Dalai Lama, as quoted by David Pearce, guest writing on George Dvorsky's blog, "A World Without Suffering?" *Sentient Developments*, May 1, 2009, http://www.sentientdevelopments.com/2009/05/world-without-suffering.html.

See also Dalai Lama, "The Neuroscience of Meditation," Society for Neuroscience 2005, November 12, 2005, https://www.sfn.org/meetings/past-and -future-annual-meetings/abstract-archive/abstract-archive-details?absID =144&absyear=2005; and for an article based on the text of the Dalai Lama's keynote address, see Tenzin Gyatso, "Science at the Crossroads," His Holiness the Fourteenth Dalai Lama of Tibet, https://www.dalailama.com/messages /buddhism/science-at-the-crossroads.

15. Bradford, "Modern Age Awakening."
16. Mikey Siegel, "Visioning Our Awakened Futures," Awakened Futures Summit 2019, https://www.awakenedfutures.org/videos.
17. Mikey Siegel, interview with Kate J. Stockly, July 10, 2019.
18. Ibid.
19. "Meet Sophia, World's First AI Humanoid Robot | Tony Robbins," January 16, 2020, https://www.youtube.com/watch?v=Sq36J9pNaEo.
20. Siegel, interview with Stockly, July 10, 2019.
21. Ibid.
22. Ibid.
23. Monastic Academy, "Will You Answer the Call?: Apprenticeship," Monastic Academy, accessed July 14, 2019, https://www.monasticacademy.com/apprentice/.
24. Monastic Academy, "Vision," Monastic Academy, accessed July 14, 2019, https:// www.monasticacademy.com/vision/.
25. Ibid.
26. Monastic Academy, "The Training: Awakening, Love, Responsibility," Monastic Academy, https://www.monasticacademy.com/the-training/.
27. Ibid.

11: SPIRIT TECH AND THE FUTURE OF SPIRITUALITY

1. Ivan Casselman, Catherine J. Nock, Hans Wohlmuth, Robert P. Weatherby, and Michael Heinrich, "From Local to Global—Fifty Years of Research on *Salvia divinorum*," *Journal of Ethnopharmacology* 151, no. 2 (Feb. 2014): 768–83, https://doi .org/10.1016/j.jep.2013.11.032. One religious group that uses *Salvia divinorum* as a sacrament is the Church of the Divine Sage (http://www.divinesage.org/index.htm).
2. William A. Richards, John C. Rhead, Francesco B. Dileo, Richard Yensen, and Albert A. Kurland, "The Peak Experience Variable in DPT-Assisted Psychotherapy with Cancer Patients," *Journal of Psychedelic Drugs* 9, no. 1 (1977): 1–10, https:// doi.org/10.1080/02791072.1977.10472020; William A. Richards, "Mystical and Archetypal Experiences of Terminal Patients in DPT-Assisted Psychotherapy," *Journal of Religion and Health* 17, no. 2 (April 1978): 117–26, https://doi.org/10 .1007/BF01532413. See also the website for the Temple of the True Inner Light (http://psychede.tripod.com)

3. The Church of the Toad of Light's primary text, "*Bufo alvarius*: The Psyche-delic Toad of the Sonoran Desert" (1983), written by the founder Albert Most, can be found online (https://www.erowid.org/archive/sonoran_desert_toad /almost.htm). For a scientific perspective on the *Bufo alvarius*, see Andrew T. Weil and Wade Davis, "*Bufo alvarius*: A Potent Hallucinogen of Animal Origin," *Journal of Ethnopharmacology* 41, nos. 1–2 (Jan. 1994): 1–8, https://doi.org/10 .1016/0378-8741(94)90051-5; see also Ralph Metzner, *The Toad and the Jaguar: A Field Report of Underground Research on a Visionary Medicine: Bufo Alvarius and 5-Methoxy-Dimethyltryptamine* (Berkeley, CA: Regent Press for Green Earth Foundation, 2013).

4. Thomas K. Brown. "Ibogaine in the Treatment of Substance Dependence," *Current Drug Abuse Reviews* 6, no. 1 (April 2013): 3–16, https://doi.org/10.2174 /15672050113109990001.

5. There are many studies identifying correlations between religiousness and im-proved physical and mental health outcomes; for example, Christopher G. Ellison, David A. Gay, and Thomas A. Glass, "Does Religious Commitment Contribute to Individual Life Satisfaction?" *Social Forces* 68, no. 1 (Sept. 1989): 100–23, https://doi.org/10.1093/sf/68.1.100; Harold G. Koenig, Judith C. Hays, David B. Larson, Linda K. George, Harvey Jay Cohen, Michael E. McCullough, Keith G. Meador, and Dan G. Blazer, "Does Religious Attendance Prolong Survival? A Six-Year Follow-Up Study of 3,968 Older Adults," *Journals of Gerontology: Series A* 54, no. 7 (July 1999): M370–76, https://doi.org/10.1093/gerona/54.7.M370; William R. Miller and Carl E. Thoresen, "Spirituality, Religion, and Health: An Emerging Research Field," *American Psychologist* 58, no. 1 (2003): 24–35, https:// doi.org/10.1037/0003-066X.58.1.24; and Carl E. Thoresen and Alex H. S. Har-ris, "Spirituality and Health: What's the Evidence and What's Needed?" *Annals of Behavioral Medicine* 24, no. 1 (Feb. 2002): 3–13, https://doi.org/10.1207 /S15324796ABM2401_02.

A few studies have found correlations between religiousness and decreased physical and mental health. For example, see Michael King, Peter Speck, and Angela Thomas, "The Effect of Spiritual Beliefs on Outcome from Illness," *Social Science and Medicine* 48, no. 9 (May 1999): 1291–99, https://doi.org/10.1016 /S0277-9536(98)00452-3. Other studies have detected no effect; see Ellen L. Idler and Stanislav V. Kasl, "Religion, Disability, Depression, and the Timing of Death," *American Journal of Sociology* 97, no. 4 (Jan. 1992): 1052–79, https://doi.org/10 .1086/229861. As opposed to Marc A. Musick, John W. Traphagan, Harold G. Koenig, and David B. Larson, "Spirituality in Physical Health and Aging," *Journal of Adult Development* 7, no. 3 (April 2000): 73–86, https://doi.org/10.1023 /A:1009523722920; and William J. Strawbridge, Richard D. Cohen, Sarah J. Shema, and George A. Kaplan, "Frequent Attendance at Religious Services and

Mortality Over 28 Years," *American Journal of Public Health* 87, no. 6 (June 1997): 957–61, https://doi.org/10.2105/AJPH.87.6.957.

6. Ann MacDonald, "Using the Relaxation Response to Reduce Stress," *Harvard Health* (blog), Harvard Health Publishing, November 10, 2010, https://www.health .harvard.edu/blog/using-the-relaxation-response-to-reduce-stress-20101110780; Herbert Benson, *The Relaxation Response* (New York: Morrow, 1975); James W. Anderson, Chunxu Liu, and Richard J. Kryscio, "Blood Pressure Response to Transcendental Meditation: A Meta-Analysis," *American Journal of Hypertension* 21, no. 3 (March 2008): 310–16, https://doi.org/10.1038/ajh.2007.65.

7. Koenig et al., "Does Religious Attendance Prolong Survival?"; Samuel Stroope and Joseph O. Baker, "Whose Moral Community? Religiosity, Secularity, and Self-Rated Health across Communal Religious Contexts," *Journal of Health and Social Behavior* 59, no. 2 (Jan. 2018): 185–99, https://doi.org/10.1177 /0022146518755698.

8. "Shinzen Week-Long Retreat: November Neuro-Mindfulness," Eventbright Description, View Details, https://www.eventbrite.com/e/shinzen-week-long-retreat -november-neuro-mindfulness-tickets-48673088518#.

APPENDIX 1. HOW DID WE GET HERE?

1. See, for example, Colin Wark and John F. Galliher, "Timothy Leary, Richard Alpert (Ram Dass) and the Changing Definition of Psilocybin," *International Journal of Drug Policy* 21, no. 3 (May 2010): 234–39, https://doi.org/10.1016/j.drugpo .2009.08.004.

2. William A. Richards, *Sacred Knowledge: Psychedelics and Religious Experiences* (New York: Columbia University Press, 2016).

3. On the hypothesis that people with high capacities for dissociative and hypnotic states are more vulnerable to suggestion in certain ritual processes and that this vulnerability may, when harnessed in appropriate ritual contexts, confer health benefits, see James McClenon, "The Ritual Healing Theory: Therapeutic Suggestion and the Origin of Religion," in *Where God and Science Meet*, vol. 1, *Evolution, Genes, and the Religious Brain*, ed. Patrick McNamara (Westport, CT: Praeger, 2006), 135–58; and James McClenon, *Wondrous Healing: Shamanism, Human Evolution, and the Origin of Religion* (DeKalb: Northern Illinois University Press, 2001).

4. Ann Pellegrini, "'Signaling through the Flames': Hell House Performance and Structures of Religious Feeling," *American Quarterly* 59, no. 3 (Sept. 2007): 911–35, https://doi.org/10.1353/aq.2007.0067.

5. Kevin McElmurry, "Alone/Together: The Production of Religious Culture in a Church for the Unchurched" (PhD diss., University of Missouri, 2009), https:// doi.org/10.32469/10355/7035.

6. See James K. Wellman Jr., Katie E. Corcoran, and Kate J. Stockly, *High on God: How Megachurches Won the Heart of America* (New York: Oxford University Press, 2020).

7. Kathleen Taylor, *Brainwashing: The Science of Thought Control* (New York: Oxford University Press, 2004).

8. For example, see Fred Travis and Jonathan Shear, "Focused Attention, Open Monitoring and Automatic Self-Transcending: Categories to Organize Meditations from Vedic, Buddhist and Chinese Traditions," *Consciousness and Cognition* 19, no. 4 (Dec. 2010): 1110–18, https://doi.org/10.1016/j.concog.2010.01.007; Jonathan Shear, ed., *The Experience of Meditation: Experts Introduce the Major Traditions* (St. Paul, MN: Paragon House, 2006); and Daniel Goleman, *The Meditative Mind: The Varieties of Meditative Experience* (New York: Jeremy P. Tarcher/Putnam, 1988).

9. Jean L. Kristeller, in *Principles and Practice of Stress Management*, 3rd ed., ed. Paul M. Lehrer, Robert L. Woolfolk, and Wesley E. Sime (New York: Guilford Press, 2007), 393–427.

10. Ibid.; see table on page 398. For an additional example of a research study that demonstrates the importance of the degree of expertise dimension, see Richard Davidson's study of both Tibetan Buddhist monks (expert meditators) and novices, described in Antoine Lutz, Lawrence L. Greischar, Nancy B. Rawlings, Matthieu Ricard, and Richard J. Davidson, "Long-Term Meditators Self-Induce High-Amplitude Gamma Synchrony during Mental Practice," *PNAS* 101, no. 46 (2004): 16369–73, https://doi.org/10.1073/pnas.0407401101.

APPENDIX 2. HOW DO WE KNOW WHAT WE KNOW?

1. Alfred North Whitehead, *Science and the Modern World* (1926; repr., New York: Mentor, 1948), 52.

2. To read more about the ways in which the development of quantitative methods transformed humanity's ways of understanding and engaging with the world, including developments such as Galileo's employment of Brahe's measurements and the history of science and religion in general, see David C. Lindberg and Ronald L. Numbers, eds., *God & Nature: Historical Essays on the Encounter Between Christianity and Science* (Berkeley: University of California Press, 1986). On Galileo and Brahe specifically, see chapter 3: "The Copernicans and the Churches" by Robert S. Westman.

3. Christopher White, "A Measured Faith: Edwin Starbuck, William James, and the Scientific Reform of Religious Experience," *Harvard Theological Review* 101, nos. 3–4 (Oct. 2008): 431–50, https://doi.org/10.1017/S0017816008001946.

4. For more information on Alister Hardy's collection of more than six thousand firsthand narrative accounts of religious experience and the current research

projects surrounding it, see the Alister Hardy Religious Experience Research Centre, University of Wales, http://www.uwtsd.ac.uk/library/alister-hardy-religious-experience-research-centre/.

5. Alister Hardy, *The Spiritual Nature of Man: A Study of Contemporary Religious Experience* (Oxford: Oxford University Press, 1979).

6. Peter C. Hill and Ralph W. Hood Jr., eds., *Measures of Religiosity* (Birmingham, AL: Religious Education Press, 1999).

7. Ralph W. Hood Jr., "Religious Orientation and the Report of Religious Experience," *Journal for the Scientific Study of Religion* 9, no. 4 (Winter 1970): 285–91, https://doi.org/10.2307/1384573; John Rosegrant subsequently updated this questionnaire in 1976: John Rosegrant, "The Impact of Set and Setting on Religious Experience in Nature," *Journal for the Scientific Study of Religion* 15, no. 4 (Winter 1976): 301–10, https://doi.org/10.2307/1385633.

8. Rosegrant, "The Impact of Set and Setting on Religious Experience in Nature."

9. Ralph W. Hood Jr., "The Construction and Preliminary Validation of a Measure of Reported Mystical Experience," *Journal for the Scientific Study of Religion* 14, no. 1 (March 1975): 29–41, https://doi.org/10.2307/1384454.

10. Walter T. Stace, *Mysticism and Philosophy* (Philadelphia: Lippincott, 1960).

11. On several occasions, researchers have used a procedure called *factor analysis* to identify clusters within the thirty-two items used to describe these eight experiential aspects. These clusters are something like dimensions within the M scale. This technique looks for items that tend to push in the same direction for respondents—that is, most people tend to answer high on those items simultaneously. Once the items that push in the same direction have been identified, researchers can examine those items to determine the meaning of the dimensions (also known as factors). The factor-analytic proposals for a dimensional structure within the M scale have varied a bit over the years. See Ralph W. Hood Jr., Ronald J. Morris, and P. J. Watson, "Further Factor Analysis of Hood's Mysticism Scale," *Psychological Reports* 73, no. 3 (1993): 1176–78, https://doi.org/10.2466/pr0.1993.73.3f.1176.

12. Keith J. Edwards, "Sex-Role Behavior and Religious Experience," in *Research in Mental Health and Religious Behavior: An Introduction to Research in the Integration of Christianity and the Behavioral Sciences*, ed. W. J. Donaldson Jr. (Atlanta, GA: Psychological Studies Institute); "Religious Experience Questionnaire," *Dissertation Abstracts International* 36 (1976).

13. Theodore T. Y. Hsieh, "Cognitive Styles and Word versus Spirit Orientation among Christians," *Journal of Psychology and Theology* 9, no. 2 (1981): 175–82, https://doi.org/10.1177/009164718100900207.

14. Richard L. Gorsuch and Craig S. Smith, "Attributions of Responsibility to God: An Interaction of Religious Beliefs and Outcomes," *Journal for the*

Scientific Study of Religion 22, no. 4 (Dec. 1983): 340–52, https://doi.org/10
.2307/1385772.

15. Jared D. Kass, Richard Friedman, Jane Leserman, Patricia C. Zuttermeister, and Herbert Benson, "Health Outcomes and a New Index of Spiritual Experience," *Journal for the Scientific Study of Religion* 30, no. 2 (June 1991): 203–11, https://doi.org/10.2307/1387214.

16. Ronald J. Pekala, *The Phenomenology of Consciousness Inventory* (Thorndale, PA: Psychophenomenological Concepts, 1982).

17. Wesley J. Wildman and Patrick McNamara, "Evaluating Reliance on Narratives in the Psychological Study of Religious Experiences," *International Journal for the Psychology of Religion* 20, no. 4 (Oct. 2010): 223–54, https://doi.org/10.1080 /10508619.2010.507666.

18. Ronald J. Pekala, *Quantifying Consciousness: An Empirical Approach* (New York: Plenum Press, 1991), see especially chapters 5 through 7. See discussion in Wildman and McNamara, ibid., 229.

19. Ronald E. Shor and Emily Carota Orne, *Manual: Harvard Group Scale of Hypnotic Susceptibility, Form A* (Palo Alto, CA: Consulting Psychologists Press, 1962); https://hypnosisandsuggestion.org/assets/files/HGSHSA_Manual.pdf; André M. Weitzenhoffer and Ernest R. Higard, *Stanford Hypnotic Susceptibility Scale: Forms A and B, for Use in Research Investigations in the Field of Hypnotic Phenomena* (Palo Alto, CA: Consulting Psychologists Press, 1959); and André M. Weitzenhoffer and Ernest R. Higard, *Stanford Hypnotic Susceptibility Scale: Form C, to Be Used in Conjunction with Forms A and B in Research Investigations in the Field of Hypnotic Phenomena* (Palo Alto, CA: Consulting Psychologists Press, 1962).

20. Immanuel Kant's trilogy on human reason, comprising his *Critique of Pure Reason* (*Kritik der reinen Vernunft*), 1781; *Critique of Practical Reason* (*Kritik der praktischen Vernunft*), 1788; and *Critique of Judgment* (*Kritik der Urteilskraft*), 1790, remains the root of many scholarly discussions of human reason, whether as a foundation to build upon or a foil to push against in the development of new and different theories of mind.

21. Stefano Sandrone, Marco Bacigaluppi, Marco R. Galloni, Stefano F. Cappa, Andrea Moro, Marco Catani, Massimo Filippi, Martin M. Monti, Daniela Perani, and Gianvito Martino, "Weighing Brain Activity with the Balance: Angelo Mosso's Original Manuscripts Come to Light," *Brain* 137, no. 2 (Feb. 2013): 621–33, https://doi .org/10.1093/brain/awt091. Shortly after the publication of Sandrone et al.'s article, Chris Benderev of *NPR Weekend Edition Sunday* covered the story. The audio and transcript of his summary is available at Chris Benderev, "The Machine That Tried to Scan the Brain—in 1882" *NPR Weekend Edition Sunday*, August 17, 2014, http://www.npr.org/2014/08/17/340906546/the-machine-that-tried-to-scan-the -brain-in-1882.

22. David Millett, "Hans Berger: From Psychic Energy to the EEG," *Perspectives in Biology and Medicine* 44, no. 4 (Feb. 2001): 522–42, https://doi.org/10.1353/pbm.2001.0070. See also Hans Berger, "Uber das Elektroenkephalogramm des Menschen," *Archiv für Psychiatrie und Nervenkrankheiten* (*European Archives of Psychiatry and Clinical Neuroscience*) 87 (Dec. 1929): 527–70, https://doi.org/10.1007/BF01797193.

23. For a comprehensive history and overview of the current state-of-the-art methods and techniques for diagnosing ADHD with qEEG, see "QEEG for Differential Diagnosis of ADHD," Behavioral Neurotherapy Clinic, 2016, http://www.adhd.com.au/QEEG.htm.

24. The most common way to produce an image from decaying radioactive tracers fixed in the brain depends on an effect of subatomic particles known to us from quantum physics. We can't safely use radioactive decay of the alpha type because those types of decay emit helium nuclei, which are heavy enough to damage DNA. So we use radioactive decay of the beta type instead, which is much safer because the particles produced are much smaller. There are two types of beta decay and the key to the type that matters here is the spontaneous transition of an up quark into a down quark, effectively transforming a positively charged proton into an electrically neutral neutron. Through a brief cascade of particle emissions, this type of beta decay emits a positron. Those positrons, being antimatter, interact strongly with nearby electrons after no more than a millimeter or two of travel. The positron and electron annihilate each other into another brief particle cascade. The result is a pair of photons that don't interact much with anything in the human body, so they pass through the brain to be measured by sensors. The fact that the emitted photons always move in precisely opposite directions from one another means that the location of all that subatomic action can be inferred from the places where the particles are detected, and that location will be within a couple of millimeters of the place where the metabolic action we are really interested in took place.

25. Shinji Nishimoto, An T. Vu, Thomas Naselaris, Yuval Benjamini, Bin Yu, and Jack L. Gallant, "Reconstructing Visual Experiences from Brain Activity Evoked by Natural Movies," *Current Biology* 21, no. 19 (Oct. 2011): 1641–46, https://doi.org/10.1016/j.cub.2011.08.031; see also Alexander G. Huth, Tyler Lee, Shinji Nishimoto, Natalia Y. Bilenko, An T. Vu, and Jack L. Gallant, "Decoding the Semantic Content of Natural Movies from Human Brain Activity," *Frontiers in Systems Neuroscience* 10 (Oct. 2016), https://doi.org/10.3389/fnsys.201600081.

26. Michael Persinger, interview with Kate J. Stockly, January 1, 2018.

27. Michael A. Persinger, "Vectorial Cerebral Hemisphericity as Differential Sources for the Sensed Presence, Mystical Experiences and Religious Conversions," *Perceptual and Motor Skills* 76, no. 3 (June 1993): 915–30, https://doi.org/10.2466/pms.1993.76.3.915.

28. C. P. L. Johnson and Michael A. Persinger, "The Sensed Presence May Be Facilitated by Interhemispheric Intercalation: Relative Efficacy of the Mind's Eye, Hemi-Sync Tape, and Bilateral Temporal Magnetic Field Stimulation," *Perceptual and Motor Skills* 79, no. 1 (Aug. 1994): 351–54, https://doi.org/10.2466/pms.1994.79.1.351.

29. Persinger, interview with Stockly.

30. Michael A. Persinger and Faye Healey, "Experimental Facilitation of the Sensed Presence: Possible Intercalation Between the Hemispheres Induced by Complex Magnetic Fields," *Journal of Nervous and Mental Disease* 190, no. 8 (Aug. 2002): 533–41.

31. Kevin S. Saroka and Michael A. Persinger, "Potential Production of Hughlings Jackson's 'Parasitic Consciousness' by Physiologically-Patterned Weak Transcerebral Magnetic Fields: QEEG and Source Localization," *Epilepsy & Behavior* 28, no. 3 (Sept. 2013): 395–407, https://doi.org/10.1016/j.yebeh.2013.05.023.

32. Persinger, interview with Stockly.

33. Todd Murphy, interview with Kate J. Stockly, February 7, 2018.

34. Persinger, interview with Stockly.

35. Ibid.

36. Persinger and Healey, "Experimental Facilitation of the Sensed Presence." See discussion in L. S. St.-Pierre and M. A. Persinger, "Experimental Facilitation of the Sensed Presence Is Predicted by the Specific Patterns of the Applied Magnetic Fields, Not by Suggestibility: Re-analyses of 19 Experiments," *International Journal of Neuroscience* 116, no. 19 (July 2006): 1079–96, https://doi.org/10.1080/00207450600808800.

37. Persinger, interview with Stockly.

38. Leslie A. Ruttan, Michael A. Persinger, and Stanley Koren, "Enhancement of Temporal Lobe–Related Experiences during Brief Exposures to Milligauss Intensity Extremely Low Frequency Magnetic Fields," *Journal of Bioelectricity* 9, no. 1 (1990): 33–54, https://doi.org/10.3109/15368379009027758.

39. Jack Hitt, "This Is Your Brain on God," *Wired*, November 1999, http://www.wired.com/1999/11/persinger/; in 2003, BBC Two's science documentary series *Horizon* produced an episode entitled "God on the Brain," http://www.bbc.co.uk/science/horizon/2003/godonbrain.shtml.

40. Susan Blackmore, "Alien Abduction: The Inside Story," *New Scientist*, November 19, 1994, 29–31, http://www.susanblackmore.co.uk/Articles/alienabduction.html.

41. Susan Blackmore, "Michael Persinger and the God Helmet—Susan Blackmore" Web of Stories—Life Stories of Remarkable People, https://www.youtube.com/watch?v=Zo-achedLMs.

42. Ibid.

43. Don Hill, in *Horizon*, "God on the Brain," aired April 17, 2003, on BBC, transcript at http://www.bbc.co.uk/science/horizon/2003/godonbraintrans.shtml.

44. Persinger, interview with Stockly.

45. M. A. Persinger, W. G. Roll, S. G. Tiller, S. A. Koren, and C. M. Cook, "Remote Viewing with the Artist Ingo Swann: Neuropsychological Profile, Electroencephalographic Correlates, Magnetic Resonance Imaging (MRI), and Possible Mechanisms," *Perceptual and Motor Skills* 94, no. 2 (2002): 927–49, https://doi.org/10.2466/pms.2002.94.3.927; M. A. Persinger, C. M. Cook, and S. C. Tiller, "Enhancement of Images of Possible Memories of Others during Exposure to Circumcerebral Magnetic Fields: Correlations with Ambient Geomagnetic Activity," *Perceptual and Motor Skills* 95, no. 2 (2002): 531–43, https://doi.org/10.2466/pms.2002.95.2.531; see also discussion at Todd Murphy, "Magnetic Stimulation and Psychic Skills—the Evidence," Spirituality and the Brain, accessed March 2018, https://www.god-helmet.com/wp/shiva/shiva_evidence.htm.

46. For information about each of the headsets currently marketed by Shakti Technologies, see https://www.god-helmet.com/.

47. Todd Murphy, "Spirituality & the Brain," accessed November 2020, https://www.god-helmet.com/wp/about_us.htm.

48. Murphy, interview with Stockly.

49. Nick Groff, Facebook post, January 22, 2018, https://www.facebook.com/permalink.php?story_fbid=10155402476447887&id=135879392886.

50. Murphy, interview with Stockly.

51. Ibid.

52. Ibid.

53. Persinger, interview with Stockly.

54. Ibid.

55. Murphy, interview with Stockly.

56. Ibid.

57. Ibid.

58. Pehr Granqvist, interview with Kate J. Stockly, March 7, 2018.

59. Ibid.

60. Ibid.

61. Ibid.

62. Pehr Granqvist, Mats Fredrikson, Patrik Unge, Andrea Hagenfeldt, Sven Valind, Dan Larhammar, and Marcus Larsson, "Sensed Presence and Mystical Experiences Are Predicted by Suggestibility, Not by the Application of Transcranial Weak Complex Magnetic Fields," *Neuroscience Letters* 379, 1 (2005): 1–6, https://doi.org/10.1016/j.neulet.2004.10.057.

63. Granqvist, interview with Stockly.

64. Ibid.

65. Ibid.

66. Ibid.

67. Ibid.

68. Michiel van Elk, "An EEG Study on the Effects of Induced Spiritual Experiences on Somatosensory Processing and Sensory Suppression," *Journal for the Cognitive Science of Religion* 2, no. 2 (2014): 127–57, https://doi.org/10.1558/jcsr.v2i2 .24573.

69. Persinger, interview with Stockly.

70. Granqvist, interview with Stockly.

71. Michael A. Persinger, "Replication of God Helmet Experiment and Many Other of Our Results," *Sacred Neurology* (blog), June 7 2015, Sacred Pathways—Blogs in Neurotheology, Todd Murphy's forum/blog, https://sacredneurology.com /2015/06/07/god-helmet-and-many-other-of-our-results-have-been-replicated-a -blog-by-dr-michael-a-persinger/.

Illustration Credits

Figure 12. Image courtesy of Sergeant Rupert Frere RLC/MOD, OGL v1.0 (http://NationalArchives.gov.uk/doc/open-government-licence/version/1/), via Wikimedia Commons.

Figure 13. Image courtesy of Robin Arnott.

Figure 14. Image courtesy of Jeff Tarrant and The NeuroMeditation Institute.

Figure 15. Image courtesy of Jeff Tarrant and The NeuroMeditation Institute.

Figures 16a and 16b. Images courtesy of Jeff Tarrant and The NeuroMeditation Institute.

Figure 17. Image courtesy of Mikey Siegel.

Figure 18. Image courtesy of Mikey Siegel.

Figure 19. Image courtesy of Pastor D. J. Soto and AltspaceVR.

Figure 20. Image courtesy of Dr. David R. Glowacki; available under Creative Commons License SA 4.0 (https://creativecommons.org/licenses/by-sa/4.0/).

Figure 21. Image courtesy of Robin Arnott.

Figure 22. Image courtesy of Pastor D. J. Soto and AltspaceVR.

Figure 23. Image courtesy of Gerd Altman, Pixabay License, free for commercial use (https://pixabay.com/illustrations/drawing-nerve-cell-neurone-732830/).

Figure 24. Image courtesy of Natalia Romanova; royalty-free stock photo (https://www.123rf.com/photo_61655870_stock-illustration-neural-network-neurons-brain-connections-3d-illustration-.html).

Figure 25. Photo courtesy of Greg Goodman, https://adventuresofagoodman.com.

Figure 26. Image courtesy of Lalo de Almeida.

Figure 27. Matthew W. Johnson, CC BY-SA 3.0, https://creativecommons.org/licenses/by-sa/3.0, via Wikimedia Commons.

Figure 28. Image courtesy of Juan Carlos Huayllapuma/CIFOR, from https://www.flickr.com/photos/cifor/36357131740/.

Figure 29. Image courtesy of ITU Pictures from Geneva, Switzerland, CC BY 2.0 (https://creativecommons.org/licenses/by/2.0), via Wikimedia Commons.

Index

Italic page numbers refer to figures.

acoustic spectrum, 34
addiction, 146
agree-with-us-or-else criterion re spiritual authenticity, 227–28
AI beings, training of, 212. *See also* artificial intelligence
AI Guru (an AI being), 212–13
Allen, John, 17
alpha waves, 48
alternative therapies movement, 178
Altspace VR social platform, 103
Aman, Jacob, 116
Amazon region, 181–83
amulets, 265
anam cara (soul friend), 203
angel dust (PCP), 140
animal experiments, 16–17, 97–98, 292
antidepressants, 140
archetypal visionary domain of consciousness, 159–60
Arizona Meditation Research Interest Group (AMRIG), 18

Arnott, Robin, 83, 116–18, 123, 124–25, 128–29
artificial intelligence (AI), 208–14
  beings, 212
  and chess, 242
  power as goal, 247–48
  risks of, 247–48
Asif, Hasan, 196–99
Asitov, George, 111–12
Asperger's syndrome, 37
Astral Pulse forum, 222–23
atheists, 105, 227–28, 300
athymhormia, 19–22
attention deficit hyperactivity disorder (ADHD), 49–50
authenticity, evaluation of, 216–33
autism spectrum disorder (ASD), 37
autopagnosia, 289
Avadhut, Swami, 111–12
avatars, 103, 105, 259–60, photo insert fig. 19
Awakened Futures Summit, x, 246
Awakened Mind, 59–60

awe, feeling of, 120
Axilum Robotics, 95
ayahuasca, 137, 139, 140, 165–73, 175–87,
    344
  popularity of, 166
  preparation of, 166, 184–85, 188–89
  safety of, 188–90
  setting for use of, 185–86
  synthetic (pharmahuasca), 137
Ayahuasca Safety Association, 190
ayahuasca shamanism, 180–83
ayahuasca tourism industry, 168, 181, 344

Badran, Bashar, 40
bad trips, 141–45
baptism, Christian, 130–32
Barker, Anthony, 37
basal ganglia, 22, 25, *25*
  damage to, 19
Benazzo, Maurizio, 210–11
Berger, Hans, 292
Berger, Peter L., 10
beta waves, 48
Bill (veteran with PTSD), 63–65
biofeedback, 46, 49
biomedicine, scientific vs. spiritual aims,
    68–69
bipolar disorder, diagnosis of, 64
Blackmore, Susan, 300
Blake, William, quoted, 133
Blue Morpho Tours, 167–73, 175
Bluetech, Evan, 114
Bodhi Neurotech, 39
body, and self, 289–90
Bouso, José Carlos, 188
Bradford, Nichol, x, 28, 242, 244–45
  quoted, 234
brain
  blood flow in, 292
  circuitry of neurons in, 138
  damage to, from drugs, 148
  electrical activity in, 292
  and mind, 287–90

physiological effects of meditation, 15
  section drawing of, *25*
  tricking with optical illusions, 107–9
brain maps, 51–52, 202
Brain Net, 98–99
brain nets, 97–99
brain optimization, customized, 197
brain stimulation
  fast results from, 244
  four modalities of, 33
  historical background of, 35–41
  how it works, 42–43
  for inducing emotions, 92
  methods approved for clinical use, 41
  noninvasive, 17, 37
  risks of, 41–42, 207, 245
brain surgery, 37
brain-to-brain communication, 94–100
  dangers and ethics of, 96–97
brain waves, 47–52
  synchrony of, 48
Brain Wellness Center, 42–43, 196
Brainworks, 44, 53
  Transformational Retreats, 73
Brazil, 176
breathing, synchrony of, 84–85
breath work, 272
Brewer, Judson, 25
Briset, Celine Rene Margarite, 190
Bronfman, Jeffrey, 179
Buddhism, 14, 30, 203, 224, 272
Buddhist Geeks, 218
Bufo alvarius, 251
Buzsáki, György, 40
bystander effect, 88
"by your fruits shall you know them,"
    254

caapi vine, 166, 184–85, 191
Cade, Maxwell, 59
California Institute of Integral Studies,
    156, 206
cannabis, 137

cannon, firing one in a telepathic
experiment, 94–95
Carnegie Mellon University, 15
Catholicism, 131, 176, 177, 179, 224, 225
Center for Mind and Culture, 212
Center for Mindful Learning, 248–49
Center for Optimal Living, 155
Chinese herbalists, 164
Chōdrōn, Pema, 57
Chopra, Deepak, 212
churches. *See* religion
Church of the Toad of Light, 251–52
coca ceremony, photo insert fig. 25
Coe, George, 277
cognitive-emotional-behavioral function,
148
collective effervescence, 78–79, 97
collective unconscious, 159
computerized tomography (CT), 291
connectivity in new technology, 240
consciousness, healing domains of, 158–60
consciousness hacking, 22, 41
Consciousness Hacking (a nonprofit), x
consequential criteria, 349
contagious (word), 89
continuity-with-ordinary-experience
criterion re spiritual authenticity,
228–30
coronavirus pandemic, 77, 236–37
Cowan, Marion, 203
creativity, 296
cross-cultural ceremonial settings of
ayahuasca use, 185–86
crowds, energy of, 88–89
Crowley, Aleister, 194
crystals (spiritual), 265
cybersickness, 126

Dalai Lama, 16, 63, 245
dance, 269
Dawkins, Richard, 300
decisions in life, AI-directed, 208
default mode network, 25–26

deindividuation, 88
delta waves, 47
Devlin, Joe, 80
dietary restrictions before ceremonies, 181
dimethyltryptamine (DMT), 139, 166–67,
174
drug packaging of, 183
illegal, 187
dipropyltriptamine (DPT), 251
Discord chat app, 110
dissociative identity disorder, 289
doctor-patient relationship, 240–41
Donatist controversy, 226
doors of perception, xix
dopamine circuits, 138
double-blinding, 305
downregulation, 145–48
Dreyfus, Hubert, xiv
drugs
illegal (Schedule I), 187
legalization of, 148, 162
research studies of, 149–64
drugs of abuse, 145–48
Dupuy, John, 199
Durkheim, Émile, 78

Eastes, Richard, 107
ecological validity, 121
Edwards, Keith, 280
efficiency vs. connectivity in new
technology, 240
ego-self, 24–25
Einstein, Albert, quoted, 13
electrocardiography (ECG), 83
electroencephalography (EEG), 34, 43,
45–52, 98–99, 292
EEG cap, 94–96
readouts, *46, 47*
electromagnetism, 36
brain stimulation by, 33–34
electromineralism, 111
electronic medical records, 240–41
embodiment, 121

E-meditation headsets, 39–40

emotions, qEEG signatures of, 89–91

enlightenment
  elitism in, 226
  fast, for everybody, 245
  neurofeedback as shortcut to, 55–65
  pseudo, due to athymhormia, 20–22
  restricted to those who can spend ten
    thousand hours meditating, 245
  shortcut to, 246
  time and resources devoted to achieving,
    226

enlightenment engineering, 41, 231, 247

entheogens, 137
  as birthright, 162–63
  drugs classified as, 147–48
  history of, 267
  kinds of, 251–52
  microdosing of, 199
  prescribing of, 205–6, 260
  safety of, 149–50

entrainment, 89

equanimity, 24

Erowid Center, 185

Esalen Institute, 59, 81–82

Ethnobotanical Stewardship Council,
  191

evangelicals, 129–31, 269

excitability, 33–34

experience, VR type of, 122–23

"expertise takes effort" criterion re
  spiritual authenticity, 224–26

factor analysis, 355

Faggin, Federico, 218, 219
  quoted, 216

Faraday, Michael, 35

fast food, 234–35

Fehmi, Les, 48

Ferriss, Tim, 166

festivals and raves
  bad trips at, 142–45
  drugs favored at, 174, 183

Field wellness center, 197–202, 204, 205, 215

The Finders (book by Martin), 243–44

focused meditation, 67

food, real vs. fast food, 234–35

Food and Drug Administration (FDA),
  302

Forall, Soryu, 248–49

Fotiou, Evgenia, 167

Francuski, Xavier, 185

Freud, Sigmund, 159

FulldomeLab, 112

functional magnetic resonance imaging
  (fMRI), 294

Fundamental Wellbeing, 243–44

Gael, Sara, 206

gaming, 123–25

gamma waves, 48

Garten, Ariel, 74

Glowacki, David, 106–7

goal states, 276

God, 78, 111, 132, 203, 280
  meeting, 169, 271
  in presence of, 137–38

God helmet, 41, 297, 299–300, 306–10

Gomez, Omar, 171

Gorman, Ingmar, 155

Gorman, Peter, 171

Gorsuch, Richard, 281

Graham, Billy, 224

Granqvist, Pehr, 279, 303–10

Grau, Carles, 95–96

great chain of being, xv

Griffiths, Roland, 161–62

Griggs, Carole, 218, 231

Grof, Stanislav, 164

Groff, Nick, 301

group consensus criterion re spiritual
  authenticity, 227–28

GroupFlow, 81–88, 94, 100, 240, photo
  insert fig. 18

groups, neurofeedback for, 90

guide (in psychedelic therapy), 155

Halpern, John, 187
Hanson Robotics, 209
Hardy, Alister, 278
Hare Krishna, 179
harmine, 183
harmine, harmaline, and
    tetrahydroharmine (THH), 185
Harvard Group Scale of Hypnotic
    Susceptibility, 282
Harvard Medical School, 15
headsets, *26*
    in a church, 256
    E-meditation, 39–40, 42
    market for, 260
health, spirituality as an aspect of, 214–15
heartbeats
    synchrony of, 85–88
    visual display of, with ECG, 83
HeartMath, 217
HeartSync, 80–81, photo insert fig. 17
hell houses, 269–70
Hendricks, Peter, 120
Hensley, Albert, 175
herd morality, 88
Hertz, Heinrich, 35
hierarchy of needs, 243
Hill, Don, 300
Hill, Peter, 279
Hofmann, Albert, 141–42, 150
holy leader criterion re spiritual
    authenticity, 226
Hood, Ralph, 279
Hood Mysticism Scale (M scale), 158
Horn, Vincent, 218
Hsieh, Theodore T. Y., 281
human bodies, in contact with each other,
    synchronization of, 79–89
human circulation balance, 292
human nature, spirituality as part of, 261
Human Operating System (H.OS), 195, 200
human species
    crowd psychology of, 89
    technology's role in history of, 238–40

hypnogogia, 217
hypnotizability, 282

ibogaine, 252
iConscious, 208–9, 218
    Human Development Model, 209
Index of Core Spiritual Experience
    (INSPIRIT), 281
infectious (word), 89
Institute for Learning and Brain Sciences, 94
Internet, 239
Iquitos, Peru, 168, 181
IRCCS Istituto Auxologico Italiano, 120
Irineu Serra, Raimundo, 176–77
Isness, 106–7, photo insert fig. 20

Jaffee, David, 237
Jain, Anshul, 92–93
James, William, 76, 210, 266, 276, 277, 279
Japanese Buddhism, 14
Jesse, Robert, 162
Jesus, 228
Jewish people
    and anti-Semitism, 180
    attracted to UDV and to Buddhism, 179
Jiang, Linxing, 96, 98–99
Johns Hopkins University, 156, 161
Johnston, William (Bill), 15
Jones, Android, 111–16, 122, 124, 127–28
Jung, Carl, 159–60

Kant, Immanuel, 152, 288–90
Kasparov, Garry, 242
Kass, Jared, 281
Keegan, James, 203
ketamine, 140
ketamine treatment clinics, 156–57
koan, Zen, 273
Kojouri, Kamand, quoted, 76
Koren, Stanley, 296, 300, 303
Kōyasan (Mount Kōya), 14
Kristeller, Jean, 273
kundalini, 272

Labate, Beatriz Caiuby, 173, 176, 178–80, 189

Lane, Justin, 212

Lanier, Jared, quoted, 101

laughing gas, 140

leader charisma, 89

Leary, Timothy, 268

Lieberman, Jeff, 41

Lincoln, Abraham, quoted, 251

Llerena Pinedo, Maestro Don Julio, 170

loneliness, 331

Loures de Assis, Glauber, 179

Loving AI, 208, 218, 247

low-intensity magnetic fields with intricate rhythmic variations, 41

LSD, 140, 149–50, 174
   discovery of, 141–42

Lucia Nº03, 217

Maggie (psychologist with Zendo), 143–45

magnetic-resonance images (MRI), 291–92

Magnetic Resonance Imaging (MRI), 22

magnetoencephalography (MEG), 295

Manchanda, Sanjay, 28

Mantashashvili, Aza, 196–99

mantras, 272

MAOIs, 140

Mark and Lynne (GroupFlow participants), 81–83, 86–88, 240–41

Martin, Jeffery A., x, 28, 242–45

Maslow, Abraham, 243

Maxwell, James Clerk, 35

Mazatec shamans, 251

McCarthy, Kate, xiv, xvi

McCraty, Rollin, 79

McElmurry, Kevin, 270

McKenna, Terence, 132

McMillen, Andrew, 108–9

McNamara, Patrick, 124, 282

MDMA (ecstasy), 139, 149, 155–56, 164, 174
   in psychotherapy, 205–6
measuring, 275–76

medicine, Western, conferring legitimacy, 68–69

meditation
   absence of downregulation in, 146
   brain stimulation of, in a Buddhist center, 256–57
   craze of, 56
   dangers of, to psychologically vulnerable people, 72
   effect on brain, 30
   enhancement of, from brain stimulation, 21, 22–27
   forming and having a practice, 14–17
   four types offered by Neuromeditation Institute (focus, mindfulness, open heart, quiet mind), 66
   hard work of, 56, 69
   health effects of, 56
   neurofeedback-guided, 53
   physiological effects of, 15
   prototechnologies for, 272–74
   purpose and effect of, 24, 26

meditation spaces, future developments, 100

megachurches, 270

Melo, Rosa Virgínia, 178

mescaline, 139, 174
   illegal, 187

Mexico, 174

Michelle, Heidi, 44–45, 52–55, 58, 70

Microdose VR, 112–16, 118–20, 132, 259
   on the Internet, 116

Microsoft, 103

Miles, Karin, 203

mindfulness meditation, 67, 273

Mind Mirror, 59–60

mind reading, 89–90

mind-to-mind communication of emotions, 43

mind writing, 89–94

ministry, careers in, 153–54

miscibility of religions, 179–80

mob morality, 88

Modern Mindfulness, 248
Monastic Academy for the Preservation of
    Life on Earth (MAPLE), 249
monastic lifestyle, 249
monks, 224, 249, 276
monoamine oxidase inhibitor (MAOI),
    166
moral injury, 63–64
Mossbridge, Julia, 209–10
Mosso, Angelo, 292
Most, Albert, 251
motivation, loss of (athymhormia), 19–22
mudra gloves, 106
mudra pose, 106
Multidisciplinary Association for
    Psychedelic Study (MAPS), 143–44,
    156, 205–6
Murphy, Todd, 298, 301–3
Muse. *See* The Muse
mushrooms, psychedelic, 134, 137
music, 269
music-dance-painting, 114
mystical domain of consciousness, 158–59
mystical experiences
    healing power of, 150–60
    naturally occurring, 161
mystical left, 179
Mysticism Scale (M scale), 279–80

Narupa project, 106
Native American Church, 175, 187–88, 343
Naykid, 222
Nearness to God Scale, 281
Neo-American Church, 149
neural network, photo insert fig. 24
neurofeedback, 32, 46, 49–50, 53
    noninvasive, 54
    for spiritual insight, 62
    for treating mental disorders, 61, 63–65
neurofeedback-guided meditation, 55–65
    future of, 69–75
    market for, 65–69
    minimal dangers of, 72

speed of, 71
    and traditional meditation techniques,
        differences, 72
NeuroField, 38, 39, 53–54
neuroimaging, 287–95
    functional, 292–95
    structural, 291–92
NeuroMeditation Institute, *45,* 66, 73
NeuroMeditation Style Inventory, 66
neuromodulation, 32
neurons, 138, photo insert fig. 23
neuropsychological test scores, 188
neuropsychopharmacology, 164, 252
neurosurgery, 16–17
neurotherapy, 46
neurotransmitters, 138–39
new age spirituality, 178
New Mind Academy, 60–61
New Mind Center, 60–61
NewMind Neurofeedback Center, 73
New Mind qEEG Analysis and Client
    Management System, 62
New York Consciousness Hacking
    Meetup, 196
Nishimoto, Shinji, 294
nitrous oxide, 140
Nolan, Kyle, 190–91
nonduality, 216
norepinephrine, 93
Novella, Steven, 109
numedelics, 107

Oculus Rift, 102
oneness, 116
open heart meditation, 67
Opray, Max, 191
optical illusions, 107–9
orthodoxy argument re spiritual
    authenticity, 227–28
Ott, Jonathan, 183–84, 187

Pacheco, Gustavo, 173
Pacific Lutheran University, xxi

Pahnke-Richards Mystical Experience
    Questionnaire, 158–59
Pais-Vieira, Miguel, 97
Paititi Institute, photo insert fig. 25
Pascual-Leone, Alvaro, 95
PCP (angel dust), 140
Peck, Tucker, 17
Pekala, Ron, 282
Pentecostals, 102, 269
perennial philosophy, xv, xx
Persinger, Michael, 41, 296–310
Persistent Non-Symbolic Experience
    (PNSE), 243–44
personality changes, 161–62
personal-psychodynamic domain of
    consciousness, 159
Peru, 165–72, 175
Peterson, Eugene H., quoted, 193
peyote, 174, 189, 343
    safety of, 187–88
pharmahuasca, 183–87
    setting for use of, 185–86
Phenomenology of Consciousness
    Inventory (PCI), 282–83
Phenomenology of Consciousness
    Inventory for Religious and Spiritual
    Experiences (PCI-RSE), 283–87
philosophy (study), 152
phosphenes in peripheral vision, a message
    received by, 95
plants. *See* spirit plants
Plato, 153
pornography, 124, 239
positron-emission tomography (PET), 294
posterior cingulate cortex (PCC), 25, *25,* 26
post-traumatic stress disorder (PTSD),
    133, 155–56
    diagnosis of, 63–64
    therapy for, 163
Prat, Chantel, 94
Pratt, James Bissett, 277
presence, 121, 123
Psilocybe subaeruginosa ("shrooms"), 134

psilocybin, 134–35, 139
    legalization of, 136
    in psychotherapy, 161–64
    research on, 150–54
psychedelic drugs
    healing effects of, 157–64
    in human history, 137
    legal prohibition of, 206
    and mystical experiences, 107
    renaissance of, 162
    research on, 268–69
    social disapproval of, 134–37
    virtual reality similar to, 113
Psychedelic Harm Reduction Project, 143
psychedelic mushrooms, 134, 137
psychoactive substances (drugs), long-term
    effects of, 145, 148
psychometric techniques, 277–87
psychonautic settings of ayahuasca use,
    185–86
psychosis, and unreal beliefs, 229
psychosocial prototechnologies, 269–72
psychotherapy
    entheogenes prescribed in, 205–6, 260
    psychedelic-assisted, 157–64, *157,* 205–6
    psychedelic training, 154–57
    secularized, 204
pulsed electromagnetic field (pEMF), 38,
    41, 53
Pulse Tours, 190

quantitative analysis of EEG (qEEG),
    51–52, 89–91, 202, 293
    brain map, 288, photo insert figs. 14,
    15, 16
    typical profiles, 52
quantitative methods, 276
quiet mind meditation, 67
quote generator, 212

radioactive tracers, 293–94, 357
Rainforest Healing Center (Chakra Alegría
    de Amor), 171

Rao, Rajesh, 94
reality, conventional vs. spiritual, 349
real world, 229
Reiki, xxi
relaxation response, 252
religion
  apps relating to, 2
  intersection with
    neuropsychopharmacology, 164
  spirit plants used in, 176–87
  study of, xx
  See also spirituality
religions, traditional
  alienation from, 100
  early forms of neurotechnology in, 204–5
  future of, 100, 255–58, 261
  lists of moral virtues (e.g., Ten
    Commandments), 230–31
  spaces (churches, mosques, etc.), 100
religious (word), 308
Religious Experience Episodes Measure
  (REEM), 279
Religious Experience Questionnaire, 280
religious leaders, 270
Religious Leaders Study, 154
religious practice
  communal, 76, 78, 79, 270
  decline of, supposedly, 9
  diversity of, 3–4
  health effects of, 252
  individual, 76
  involvement in, and length of life, 252
  livestreaming of services, 2
  modern changes in, 10
repetitive TMS (rTMS), 37, 41
retreat centers, 167, 169–73, 175, 192, 197
rhythm (musical), 269
Richards, William A., 150–63, 268–69
Richie's Plank Experience, 107–9
ritalin, 49
rituals
  involving synchrony, 82–88
  shared emotion in, 97, 267

Robbins, Tony, 211, 247
Robinson, Jonathan, 4
Robison, John Elder, 37–38
rosary beads, 265
Rosegrant, John, 279
Roy, James, 44–45, 49, 52–54, 58, 70
Roy, Sarah, 44–45

Sackler Centre for Consciousness Science,
  121
sacraments, authenticity of, even if
  performed by scoundrels, 226–27
Salak, Kira, 169, 227–28
Salvia divinorum, 137, 251
samadhi, 57–58, 272
Samskara, 111–12, 132
samskara (word), 111
Sanguinetti, Jay, 16–19, 22–35, *23,* 42, 205,
  242, 244
San Pedro, 174–75, 343
  safety of, 188
Santo Daime religion, 176–78, 179–80,
  192, photo insert fig. 26
  origin of, 176–77
Sapoznikow, Avery, 185
science
  history of, 276
  understanding of, 13–14
Science and Nonduality (SAND)
  Conference, 209, 216–18
screens, ubiquity of, and lifestyle, 236
Searle, John, xiv
secularization thesis, 9–10
selective serotonin reuptake inhibitors
  (SSRIs), 140
self, 289–90, 296
self-actualization, 243
self-optimization, 195
self-transcendence, 243–44
serotonin system, 138
set and setting, 140, 174, 185–86
Seth, Anil, 121
sex, having, 225

sex industry, 239

Shakti magnetic brain stimulation helmet, 222, 301

shamanic tourism industry, 175
 dangers in, 190–91

shamanism, ceremonies, 175

shamans
 finding one to work with, 169
 knowledge of sacred plants, 268
 training of, 168, 172

Shambhala, 194

Shimbre Shamanic Center, 190

Shingon, 14

Shipibo people, 181, *182*

Shiva Neural Stimulation headset, 301

Short, Edward Baron, 40

Siegel, Mikey, 22, 77–78, 80–88, 217, 231, 235, 237–40, 246–49
 quoted, 1, 6

Silicon Valley
 conferences, 217
 entrepreneurship, 30–31

Simon, Paul, quoted, 165

single photon emission computed tomography (SPECT), 294

smartphones, ubiquity of, and lifestyle, 236

Smith, Craig, 281

Smith, Huston, xiv, xv, 149–50

Society for Neuroscience, 16

SOMA breathwork, photo insert fig. 16

Sonication Enhanced Mindful Awareness (SEMA) Lab, 31–33

Sophia (robot), 209–12, *209,* 247

Soto, D. J., 101–5, 110–11, 122, 124, 129–31, photo insert fig. 19

SoundSelf, 116–20, *117,* 132, 259, photo insert fig. 21

Soutar, Richard, 58, 59, 60–69, 74, 205
 quoted, 44

Souther, Hamilton, 168

spirit plants, 165–92
 guides to use of, 189–90
 legalization of, 192
 popular ones, 174
 research on, 191
 ritual settings for use of, 173–75
 safety of, 187–91, 192

spirit tech
 anxiety about, 221–22
 authenticity of, 216–33, 258
 Brave New World of, ix
 commercial exploitation of, 255
 dangers and safety concerns, 207, 232–33, 255
 defined, ix
 dubious options, not discussed, 252
 future of, 251–61
 history of, 265–74
 innovations in, 11, 77–78
 objections to, 5–12
 potential for human advancement, 241–50, 255
 a research controversy (the God helmet), 296–310
 skepticism about, xxi
 variety of, 193, 206

Spirit Tech (this book), x, xxiii

spiritual (word), 308

spiritual directors, 193–215
 an AI as, 208–14
 dynamic new type of, using spirit tech, 207–8
 entheogen prescribing by, 215
 new role of, as guide and coach, 202–3
 not faith-guided, 194
 as psychotherapists, 203–4
 team approach, 200

spiritual experiences
 authenticity of, judged, xix, 6
 brain mechanisms of, 253–54
 cause of, and authenticity, 220, 222–27, 231–32
 effects/consequences of, and authenticity, 220, 230–31, 232, 254
 evaluating authenticity of, three factors (qualities, effects, and causes), 219–32

human interventions aiding in, 224
quality/contents of, and authenticity,
   220, 227–30, 231
quantifying of, 275–310
skepticism about, 9
spectrum of (pure contemplative, plant-
   induced, tech-induced), 220
spontaneous nature of (supposed), 5–8,
   223–24, 254
supernatural origins, 5–8, 223–24, 253
technology as aid in, 1–12
traditional vs. tech-assisted, 7, 62–63
unreliability of reporting, 1
spirituality
   as aspect of human wellness, 214–15
   postsupernaturalist, postreligious, 204
   study of, 266
   traditional technologies of, xi
   See also religion
Stace, Walter, 279
Stanford Hypnotic Susceptibility Scale,
   282
Starbuck, Edwin, 277
Stocco, Andrea, 94, 98
Stockly, Kate, xx, 161, 172, 176, 216–18,
   242–43
Sufi mystics, 224, 271
suggestibility, 299, 308
supernatural, 6
   spontaneous appearance of, claimed,
      223–24
supernatural beings, belief in, xvii, 8
swami (word), 111
synapses, 138, photo insert fig. 23
synchrony of human bodies, 79–89

Tantra, 225
Tarrant, Jeff, *45,* 66, 68
Taylor, Kathleen, 271
technodelics, 106–7, 111–23
technology
   alienating effects of, 236
   fast-food versions of, 235–36

as a nourishing force, 237–38
   speed of innovation, xxiv, 99
Ted (PTSD patient), 133–36
telepathy, 89–100
Temple of the True Inner Light, 251
Texas, 174
The Muse, 73–74
   headband, 73–74, 260
The Muse 2, device and app, *74, 75*
theology (study), 152
theta waves, 48
Thier, Sascha, 190
Thompson, Silvanius P., 36
Thync, 92–93, *93*
   Relax Pro, 93
Tibetan religion, 63
Tilt Brush, 114, 126
Tisdale, Alex, 125
toads, psychedelic, 251–52
toé, 191
tolerance, 145
Torres Davila, Maestro Alberto, 170
Toussaint, Matt, 165–72
Transcendental Meditation, 252, 272
transcend-the-in-group criterion re
      spiritual authenticity, 228
transcerebral stimulation (TCS), 297
transcranial direct-current stimulation
      (tDCS), 39–40, 41
   headset, 22
transcranial focused ultrasound stimulation
      (tFUS), 21–24, *21, 23,* 27, 29, 32–35,
      41, 244–45, 291
transcranial magnetic stimulation (TMS),
      33, 37–38, 98–99, 297
Transformational Retreats, 44, 55
Transformative Technology Conference, x
Transformative Technology Lab (TTL),
      28–29, 242–44
trigeminal nerve stimulation, 93
true self (Buddha nature), 24
Trungpa Rinpoche, 194
twenty-questions experiment, 96

ultrasound, 34
ultrasound stimulation, 17–19, 253
    experiment with, 22–27
    how it works, 34–35
    safety concerns, 29–35
UNESCO Constitution, x
Unger, Denny, 125
União do Vegetal (UDV), 176, 178–80, 192
    origin of, 177
University of Arizona, 31
University of California, Berkeley, xiv
University of Vermont, 15
urban upper class, 178

van Elk, Michiel, 308
van Houten, Frans, quoted, 234
van Schneider, Tobias, 125–26
Vedas (Hindu), 112, 128
video games, 123–25
    mental health risks of, 125–27
viridis leaves, 166–67
virtual reality (VR), 101–32
    experienced as real, 120–23
    future developments, 124–32, 259
    headsets, 102, *108,* 121
    mental health risks of, 125–27
    modalities of, 68
    "putting virtue into" (Android Jones),
        124, 132
    in a religious setting, 257
    resistance to, 128–32
vocal toning, 117
VR Church, 103–6, 109–11, 129–31, 257,
    photo insert fig. 19
    baptism in, photo insert fig. 22

wandering mind, 26
war on drugs, 268
Watts, Alan, xii
wearable devices, 73–74
Welch, Claude, xiv
wellness centers, 197, 199
Wells, H. G., 43
Western culture, spiritual longing in,
    260–61
White, Christopher, 278
White, Devon, 194–202, 204–5, 208,
    214
White, Julie, 197
Whitehead, Alfred North, 275–76
Wickerham, Joshua, 191
Wildman, Wesley, xiv, 149–50, 221,
    282
Williamson, Tom, 212
Winfrey, Oprah, quoted, 193
Wise, Anna, 59–60
Word-Spirit Orientation Scale, 281

X factor, 89
X-rays, 291

yoga, xxi, 68
Young, Shinzen, 13–15, 18–31, *23, 26,* 40,
    42, 57, 205
    book by, 43
    quoted, 13

zazen, 272
Zen, 273
Zendo, 143–45
    headset, 39–40, *39,* 260